WEBCASTING WORLDWIDE

BUSINESS MODELS OF AN EMERGING GLOBAL MEDIUM

WEBCASTING WORLDWIDE

BUSINESS MODELS OF AN EMERGING GLOBAL MEDIUM

Edited by

Louisa Ha
Bowling Green State University

Richard J. Ganahl III
Bloomsburg University

Routledge
Taylor & Francis Group

NEW YORK AND LONDON

First published 2007 by Lawrence Erlbaum Associates, Inc., Publishers

This edition published 2015 by Routledge
711 Third Avenue, New York, NY 10017, USA
2 Park Square, Milton Park, Abingdon, Oxon OX14 4RN

Routledge is an imprint of the Taylor & Francis Group, an informa business

CIP information for this volume can be obtained
from the Library of Congress

Senior Acquisitions Editor: Linda Bathgate
Senior Editorial Assistant: Karin Wittig-Bates
Cover Design: Kathryn Houghtaling-Lacey

This book was typeset in 10/12 pt. Times Roman, Italic, Bold,
and Bold Italic.

ISBN   978–0–8058–5915–7   (hbk)
ISBN   978–0–8058–5916–4   (pbk)

To

Kit, Cherice, and Anchor Chan

and

Sang-Suk and Irene June Ganahl

Contents

PART V
Webcasting Business Practices and Dynamics in the Arab Region

Table of Contents for the Accompanying CD

Power Point File Presentation for Each Chapter

Screenshots of the Leading Webcasters in Each Chapter

A List of Leading Webcasters in Each Chapter With Hyperlinks

A List of Useful Reference Hyperlinks About Webcasting
Or Media Environment

Additional Tables and Charts in Each Chapter

Authors' Digital Pictures With a Bio, E-Mail Contact,
and Home Page Link

Foreword

The maturation of the internet, expansion of broadband telecommunications capacity, adoption of internet services by large numbers of users worldwide, and advertisers' recognition of its benefits have created a nexus in which commercial opportunities on the web are no longer a potential but a reality. Today, commercial audio streams in the form of internet radio are available in many languages across the globe. Streaming video and internet television channels are increasingly becoming significant parts of content consumption and offering new business opportunities in many regions as well.

The development of the core infrastructure and the large content creation capabilities and content libraries in the United States and European nations initially gave those nations advantages in the development of web services, but heavy investments in telecommunications infrastructures in Asia are shifting much of the advantages to those nations and they are now leaders in the provision of much streaming video.

The internet provided a new avenue into homes and offices that was not dependent upon radio spectrum and subject to less control than previously existed because of national policies, the traditional reliance of distributors on domestic distribution networks, and complicated content licensing arrangements. Contemporary developments of broadband are making richer audio and video content available through larger bandwidth capacities in office, home, and mobile environments, improving infrastructure speed and capabilities to produce a more desirable user experience.

Because webcasting transcends national boundaries it provides opportunities to receive content that was not previously available through domestic distributors. Webcasting enabled American expatriates to watch the White Sox win the baseball World Series in 2005; it permits viewers on Taiwan to watch television programs whose rights have not been purchased by channels for airing on domestic terrestrial television and cable services; it allows audio fans in Kenya and Argentina to listen to a favorite jazz channel from the United Kingdom, and businessmen and women in Australia to tune in online to NHK's Radio Japan English language service.

The service also improves domestic content availability, especially in large nations. Listeners in Montana now have a much wider choice of audio available to them than was offered by limited number of broadcast radio stations that market could financially support a decade ago. Viewers in Malaysia now have the possibility to view far more content than was previously available on the four dominant domestic television channels.

The availability of video on television and motion pictures in cinemas was artificially limited by spectrum and facilities constraints in the past, and even availability at video stores has been restricted by shelf space availability and stocking choices based on return per title. Choices in audio were similarly limited. webcasting overcomes those difficulties by allowing content provides to aggregate narrower audiences and by permitting choice by individual users without those constraints.

This is possible, from the business perspective, because webcasting provides broader opportunities to develop workable business models than those available with traditional broadcasting and cablecasting. The technologies of the internet allow companies to offer both free and paid webcasting. Some services are supported by advertisers or sponsors, whereas others are available by subscriptions or individual payments that can be paid immediately through digital payment systems. Other operators are able to provide the ability to view or listen to the content at no cost because they can cross-subsidize the services through e-commerce of downloads or physical copies should users wish to purchase what they see or hear.

Although the fundamental technologies of webcasting are similar around the world, the patterns of development, the companies involved in webcasting, the content and services provided, and the business models supporting the operations differ and are determined by unique domestic market conditions. Scholars and those who operate webcasting businesses can benefit significantly by learning about the different approaches and potential methods of operation that are found in different parts of the world.

This book contributes to that understanding by presenting the first comprehensive examination of the markets and the emerging business models and practices in webcasting in different parts of the world. It was produced by bringing together distinguished researchers around the globe to employ similar research methods, while applying their unique expertise and intimate knowledge of domestic markets. It thus presents a well-coordinated and cohesive survey of the contemporary state of webcasting globally.

Webcasting, by the very definition of the term, involves the distribution for public or general use over the web. Because its initial use was linked to live videoconferencing and then audio in the form of internet radio, it carries the connotation of streamed content similar to that found in broadcasting. The definition is being transformed, however, because of developments in content downloads such as podcasting, as well as non-live streams of content and other kinds of user-selected downloads selected from packages of content. This changes forces all of us to think more broadly about the place webcasting will have in audience and advertiser media choices in the years to come.

This book explores the phenomenon by focusing on premier webcasters worldwide because their activities are engendering the current technology and business practices of the field. Their operations are evolving rapidly, however, and low barriers to entry make it possible for new firms to appear very swiftly and to offer competing services that may produce different practices in the coming years. Although these leading firms have first-mover advantages, consumers' behavior regarding webcasts has not yet been normalized and habitualized, thus making it easier for entrants to overcome media use patterns and loyalties that exist in more established media and stymie some new entrants there.

It is clear that the consumer environment of webcasting is far different from that of traditional media. What separates it from that of traditional media is that the control over choice of content is in the hands of users and they are not bound to use only the limited number of domestic services available. Choices to view or listen to webcasting, and choices of particular services, are deliberate and specific and not bound by the limitations on traditional broadcasters or cablecasters. This shifts power in communication from the sender to the receiver of the communication and makes them a far more active participant in the process. As a result, webcasters needs to be far more attuned to consumer behavior and pay greater attention to consumer relationship management that many other content providers.

Providers of webcasting services thus face huge competition for audience time, as well as for audience and advertiser payments. The business environment thus requires great efficiency and cost leadership, making it difficulty for them to produce significant amounts of original content. Most thus reuse content produced for other purposes—audio recordings, films, television programs—or content that is consumer generated to reduce production expenses. From the content perspective this emulates the content provision of music broadcasting, syndicated television, and video rental and sales businesses. The relatively fragmented and nationally based webcasting systems that exist today are clearly not the most economically efficient means of providing services. This presents impetuses for large structural change in the webcasting industry as it matures and develops in the years to come.

Webcasting presents an intriguing opportunity to view a new content business emerging and maturing. This book provides an important foundation for understanding that development and the strategies and approaches being taken by the foremost operators in the field today. It is an important waypoint for those who wish to understand the industry today and for those who will study its development in the future.

Robert G. Picard
Editor, *Journal of Media Business Studies*

Supplementary Resources Disclaimer

Additional resources were previously made available for this title on CD. However, as CD has become a less accessible format, all resources have been moved to a more convenient online download option.

You can find these resources available here: www.routledge.com/9780805859157

Please note: Where this title mentions the associated disc, please use the downloadable resources instead.

Industry Insights

Dave Gardy
Chairman and CEO, TV Worldwide
President, International Webcasting Association

Perhaps there is not a more exhilarating experience for an entrepreneur than to be on the ground floor of a fledgling industry at its inception and survive long enough to still be an active participant when the classic "tipping point" of mainstream acceptance occurs. The business of webcasting and streaming media is undergoing just such a transformation and global awakening today. Innovative new webcasting concepts are being spawned just as the crest of this wave is about to hit and the potential for growth is mind-boggling.

Yet there has been no true comprehensive and incisive documentation of the emerging trends and business model evolution in this exciting industry space on an international level...until now. I believe that *Webcasting Worldwide: Business Models of an Emerging Global Medium* is that definitive work and that the book's editors, Louisa Ha and Richard J. Ganahl, through their tireless efforts in producing this manuscript, have made a significant contribution in facilitating mainstream understanding of the burgeoning webcasting sector and the promise it holds. It couldn't have come at a better time.

The current excitement has special meaning to those of us who have been there through the turbulence of webcasting's nascent adoption cycle. When the Internet bubble burst back in 2000, the webcast and streaming media industry was left at the altar...all dressed up, with a plethora of promising applications. It was an industry poised to take off, thanks to its courtship with the telecom sector's broadband-driven high-speed Internet access that would power the delivery of a whole range of interactive media solutions, changing the way we communicated in the workplace, at home and even in-between, thanks to wireless. But the dot-com bomb went off, taking the telecommunications industry with it and as venture investors scrambled to do triage on their evaporating portfolios, the webcasting and streaming media sector came to a standstill...or at least it so appeared. Some analysts wrote webcasting off as an anomaly that would disappear as fast as the

Pets.com sock puppet of Super Bowl commercial fame. In the devastated tech sector, the last place any investor would even think about placing a bet was webcasting and streaming media.

But many in our industry didn't believe we had met our demise. From internet radio to web video, a hard-core cadre of survivors, professionals who believed in the value proposition of streaming media and in their own business models, circled the wagons and hunkered down for the long term, bootstrapping their dreams, depleting their savings and sometimes even mortgaging their homes in the process.

They did it because they believed in their webcasting vision and were determined to follow their convictions. A few others in the press and media side of the industry believed too, as did a small group of token analysts and research firms. Together they stepped up to the challenge before them, never succumbing to the doubts raised by those who questioned whether webcasting and streaming media could ever live up to its full potential. Rather, through innovation and unrelenting determination these industry leaders deployed strategies and created the solutions that would drive webcasting and streaming media as an industry, to meet its full potential. I am honored to have known and worked with many of these individuals and other webcasting professionals who never gave up on our sector.

For streaming media and webcasting, the journey back from the abyss of the internet crash to today's promising economic viability wasn't easy. Many say that a critical juncture was reached with the horrific events of September 11, 2001. While many struggled to deal with the economic aftershocks of this tragic and defining moment in U.S. and world history, business travelers gasped at the prospect of planes being used as missiles. As legions of politicians implored commercial travelers to go on with business as usual, many weighed the risk of air travel to events such as trade shows, seminars, and business conferences. It was here that our industry responded to the challenge with real solutions. Web-conferencing firms, webcasters, streaming media providers, content delivery networks, and eLearning firms stepped up with on-line applications that really worked to fill the need. The business community was surprised to find that a slow but steady adoption of broadband access through corporate LANs, T–1's cable modems, and DSL had taken root out of the bubble-related telecom industry collapse and was beginning to power streaming media, webcasting, and web conferencing applications. Many corporate professionals were quick to adopt this method of meeting online with interactive conferences and business presentations for everything from financial reporting to eLearning. From data logs, webcasters could see the average bandwidth usage per streaming user accelerate quickly as on-line participants upgraded to broadband connections to facilitate new robust multi-media and content delivery applications that were suddenly in demand.

As the demand for streaming media and webcasting solutions grew, our industry gelled as a technology sector. Microsoft, Real, Apple, and Macromedia rose to the occasion with solutions that met the new appetite for online interactive audio and video applications. Media entities such as StreamingMedia.com and its associated conferences and exhibitions helped galvanize and define our industry as demand grew. Statistics and metrics began to appear from Nielsen, Accustream, and Interactive Media Strategies that to this day are validating what everyone in our industry knew about the symbiotic growth of broadband and streaming media.

Today, there are numerous indicators that the webcasting wave has hit worldwide. From exciting new applications driven by the introduction of products such as Apple's video iPod, services such as Google's Video Upload Program, and the surge in internet media-based advertising, live and archived streaming media is everywhere on-line. The country-by-country approach Ha and Ganahl utilized in their book to track this webcasting revolution is extremely revealing and provides a unique perspective on each society's evolving media infrastructure.

Where are we headed over the next year and beyond? I can speak for the internet video side of the business we serve at TV Worldwide. Many feel we may be where cable was in 1979…but without the regulatory hurdles that cable had to overcome. Just as cable successfully targeted "niche" markets to challenge broadcast television's dominance in the 80s, many internet TV providers are leveraging the low cost of internet video distribution, along with its interactivity and content archiving advantages to serve "micro-niche" audiences that can't be economically served by cable, in lucrative sectors worldwide, where a content provider can solidify first-mover brand presence to establish competitive barriers to entry. We call that "thinking vertically…interacting globally." While there are similarities to cable, there are also differences. For instance, we recognize the "lean-in," motivated nature of our internet TV audiences, intent on interacting with highly targeted, specific content for mainly professional purposes, as opposed to the less-engaged "lean-out" audiences associated with the entertainment content of cable and broadcast. Time will only tell how well these comparisons and contrasts with cable hold up as high speed broadband access (ironically often delivered by cable companies) becomes ubiquitous as it continues to power the growth of webcasting and streaming media. Speaking of ubiquity, lets not forget the growing presence of wireless connectivity, another webcasting market accelerator.

I'm confident the future success and growth of webcasting and streaming media will be measured more by the creative content applications and solutions Internet webcasters and streaming media professionals develop, and not the proliferation of the content such as the latest media-hyped, tasteless video that terrorists post on the web to further their agenda. In the end, I believe that webcasting and streaming media content applications will be the catalysts for a new productive boom in the technology sector, worldwide.

Preface

This book is about webcasting, the convergence of the internet with the television and radio media. Its origin came about at the first Convergence Conference in 2002 at the University of South Carolina where the two editors first met. They found a common interest in the changing media environment, especially broadband internet's potential to revolutionize the electronic media. Soon after, the two editors initiated a comparative study of the leading webcasters in two of the most advanced broadband countries in the world—Korea and the United States. The study eventually was presented at the World Media Economics Conference in 2004 at Montreal, Canada, and then subsequently published in the *International Journal on Media Management.*

We found the ACR business model framework that we proposed in the original study held much promise, and we wanted to test its robustness by including more countries with different political, media and cultural environments. At the World Media Economics Conference, we recruited several of this book's current contributors who shared a common interest in the topic. We then sought additional colleagues from other parts of the world with expertise in online media. We then assembled a 13-country team and started a truly cross-national collaborative project that involved content analysis of webcasts and interviews with experts in the field. The results of this study are published in this book's Chapter 2.

Creating the book's vision and establishing a balanced mix of countries was a challenging task. We managed to add several other countries after the original 13-country study and increased its breadth to include the current 17-country/region project. Most of the authors are home-country scholars, and we benefit much from their native insights on webcasting in their countries.

This book focuses on the leading webcasters in leading broadband markets because webcasting's quality is highly dependent on the availability of a broadband internet connection. We acknowledge that it is very hard to find consensus regarding leading webcasters or even leading broadband markets. So much depends on the perspective used to identify the leaders. Yet, by focusing on leading webcasters in leading broadband markets, we can establish how trendsetters are utilizing the webcasting medium. We expect more and more countries are improving their broadband infrastructure, and today's leaders may be overtaken by tomorrow's newcomers.

Certainly, we may not be able to escape anytime soon the problem of the world's digital divide. However, you will soon learn that some countries are more successful than others in utilizing the broadband communication infrastructure to improve their economies and media institutions.

Unlike other collective edited works, this book utilizes a framework shared by all contributors. In addition, to help our readers get the most out of this book, we provide a CD that highlights each chapter in a Power Point format. We encourage its use in your classrooms or other presentation settings. The CD also contains hyperlinks and screenshots that add additional information, research sources, and colorful illustrations of the webcasters' websites. To encourage more contact between the authors and the readers, the CD also provides an interactive biographical page. All these enhancements require many extra efforts from our contributors. But we believe our readers will utilize these features to maximize our book's benefits in their research and teaching endeavors.

We also believe this book will be useful to researchers and students in several fields. International communication researchers will find this book a very handy reference with updated media environment data on a wide variety of countries. It also provides insights about how a country's media background affects the development of its webcasting, a growing medium with global reach. In fact, this book is a grand comparative study of 17 countries/regions and their webcasting development.

Media economics and management researchers will find the business models and the ACR framework useful in their study of media economics, especially where technology plays an important role in the emerging media business models. The various types of traditional media sectors such as radio and television, telecommunications carriers, and native internet media brands are jockeying for leadership in the media content provision business. Thus, media technology researchers will find this book useful to their understanding of how technology is being used to create, assemble, package and disseminate content. The various technologies used in webcasting, the relationship between new and existing media, and the innovative use of technology to create new business opportunities in various countries should be an eye-opening experience!

While this book is written by academics, our disinterest from the media industry should benefit the industry with impartial observations that merge business practices with an academic orientation. Rather than selling this report for thousands of dollars, we hope it provides our industry practitioners with a perspective well beyond the boundaries of their own countries.

This book is divided into six parts. The first part examines the nature of webcasting as an emerging global medium and the ACR framework in explaining the business models of emerging media. The second part examines the webcasting business practices and dynamics in North America. the third part shows how Europe, much influenced by public broadcasting, provides a very different picture from its North American counterparts. The fourth part is an interesting discussion on the diverse development of webcasting practices and dynamics in Asian Pacific countries. The fifth part is an overview of the Arab region, which has a high disparity in broadband development but an intense homogeneity in language and religion. The sixth part is the conclusion and the lessons learned from the study of webcasting's development in the 17 markets and regions discussed in this book.

ACKNOWLEDGMENTS

This book is a collaborative effort of our 26 contributors, their research assistants and staff. We are indebted to many others from the book proposal development process to the final preparation of the book. For example, Oliver Boyd-Barrett, the School of Communication Studies Director at Bowling Green State University, provided useful advice in the preparation of the book's prospectus. He also graciously shared his book editing experiences. Thomas Baldwin of Michigan State University also offered useful advice on book publishing. We also want to thank the industry experts that kindly agreed to provide valuable information and data to the various contributors in this book. They are listed in the respective chapters. The support of the editors and reviewers at LEA is greatly appreciated by the editors. Rather than risk missing anybody, we extend a gigantic global "thanks" to all who made this book possible. You inspired us with your high hopes. We hope we have delivered. We did our very best, and think this book sheds a unique light on the brave new world of webcasting.

Louisa Ha and *Richard J. Ganahl III*

Contributors

Ilhem Allagui, PhD, Université de Montréal, is assistant professor in communication at the American University of Sharjah (United Arab Emirates). She has an interest in advertising as she has been working in an advertising agency in Montréal where she has also worked in the internet industry while contributing to the development of virtual communities. Before she joins the American University of Sharjah, she was lecturer at the Université de Montréal where she has served as well as a graduate research assistant for the research unit *Culture Populaire, Connaissance et Critique* which focuses mainly on Quebec cultural industries.Her research and interests are advertising and the new media in the Arab region. Her dissertation (2006) entitled Le web arabe à succès, une étude empirique d'un espace médiatique émergent (The successful Arab cyberspace. An empirical study of an emergent media space) analyzes the Arabic cyberspace through successful websites and under a political economy approach.. She's an editorial committee member of the electronic journal *Commposite, la revue des jeunes chercheurs et chercheuses en communication/electronic journal of young communication researchers* (www.commposite.org).

Alexandros Arampatzis is a lecturer in Journalism and New Media at Edge Hill University, Ormskirk, Liverpool. He holds a BA in Law (Aristotle University of Thessaloniki), an MA in Journalism Studies (Cardiff University) and an MA in International Journalism (City University, London). He is currently finishing his doctorate on the business models behind news websites, at Westminster University, London. His research and teaching interests center around online journalism, new media, media business models, media ethics and media organizations. Alexandros has worked both as a journalist and producer for the BBC, BBC Online, the Daily Telegraph website (electronictelegraph.co.uk) and a plethora of Greek print, broadcast, and electronic media. He is a working journalist occasionally contributing to Greek and UK publications. He is also the co-author of the forthcoming text, *Journalism Online*.

Piet Bakker studied Political Science at the University of Amsterdam. He worked as a journalist for several newspapers, magazines and radio stations and was a teacher at the School for Journalism in Utrecht. Since 1985 he works at Department of Communications at the University of Amsterdam/Amsterdam School of Communications Research (ASCoR) as an associate professor. He edited and published books and articles on reading habits, media history, local journalism, internet, Dutch media, international news, investigative journalism, the future of the music industry in the internet area, newspaper innovations and free daily newspapers. This last three subjects are the most recent research areas. He teaches mass communication, media economics and journalism at undergraduate and MA-level.

Tiziano Bonini is a doctoral student in Media, Communication and Public Sphere at University of Siena. His research areas are media, immigration, globalization. He is a scholarship researcher in Radio Languages Theory and Technics at Communication Institute of IULM University, Milan. Member of the International Radio Studies Network based in London, and of Xchange Network, international community of indipendent net-casters, based in Riga, Latvia. His articles have appeared on *Media, Culture and Society* magazine, and he has just written a book on the history, the aesthetics and the social uses of Radio and Internet. Among the founders of the first Italian college radio (Radio Facoltà di Frequenza, in Siena), he has experience of community radio and of public radio. He now collaborates with Radio Popolare, a community radio of Milan and with Radio 24, a national all news commercial radio, as an independent producer of radio documentaries and features.

Marylaine Chaussé is a doctoral student in communication at University of Montreal and a *Culture Populaire, Connaissance et Critique* research laboratory member. Since 2003, she has followed the preparation of the World Summit on Information Society, owned by the United Nations. This research terrain helps her having a picture of globalization and localization movements, mainly of governments and civil societies. In this sense, she aims to understand beyond dichotomies, how the globalization is actualizing itself by the recognition of his mechanisms of production. Her thesis deals with political relations on micro and macro levels in order to define globalization in an historical and philosophical perspective. In addition, she has completed a dissertation titled *Television on Internet*.

Mike Friedrichsen, Ph.D, is a Professor of Media Management at University of Flens- burg. He studied Political Economics, Business Administration, Journalism and Political Sciences in Kiel, Mainz and Berlin. He earned his doctorate at Freie Universität Berlin in 1996 at the Institute of Empirical Market and Communication Research. His main research interests are Media Management and Media Economics, Digital Radio and Television, Opinion Research, New Media Technologies and Business Communication. Friedrichsen's emphasis is the transfer between the University and Economy and he leads several Networking Organizations. He published several works among others a standard work on media management for the German market.

Richard J. Ganahl, PhD, is a Professor of Mass Communications at Bloomsburg University, PA. He earned his doctorate at the School of Journalism, University of Missouri, Columbia, MO, where he served as the graduate research assistant for the School's William Stephenson Media Research Center. Dr. Ganahl has been a newspaper publisher and owner, writer, and a radio talk-show host. He has worked as a media consultant for Fortune 500 businesses, national and state political candidates, and non-profit organizations. He recently spent a semester as a Visiting Scholar at Yonsei University in Seoul, South Korea. He has published academic articles and book chapters related to his research interests, which include media convergence, media credibility, webcasting, comparative studies of college student media use and the role of advertising following September 11.

Louisa Ha, PhD, is an Associate Professor in the Department of Telecommunications at Bowling Green State University, U.S.A. She received her doctorate in Mass Media from Michigan State University and M.Phil. from the Chinese University of Hong Kong. Her research interests are Media Management and Economics of Convergence, Media Technologies, International Advertising, and Audience Research. She is the Webmaster and founder of the International Advertising Resource Center web site since 1996 (http://www.bgsu.edu/departments/tcom/faculty/ha/intlad1.html). She has published over 30 refereed scholarly journal articles in journals such as the *Journal of Broadcasting and Electronic Media, Journal of Communication, Journal of Advertising, Journal of Advertising Research* and the *International Journal on Media Management.. Her works also appear in trade publications. She won several research awards including the Advertising Research Foundation's Outstanding Research in Media and Outstanding Reviewer Award of the Journal of Advertising.* Prior to her academic career, she has been Media Manager of Leo Burnett Advertising in China and a Research Director at the Gallup Organization.

Min Hang, Ph.D, is working as a doctoral candidate and researcher in the Media Management and Transformation Center of Jönköping University, Sweden. Hang holds master degree of European Business Administration and Business Law and master degree of Management Science. Hang had been working in the Ministry of Communications of the P.R.C. and Hohai University in China. Her research interests include cross-national management, strategy in the media companies and market differences in the media industries. Hang is the author of several book chapters, journal articles and conference papers on International Media Product Portfolios Management, Media Economics Research, Media and Entrepreneurship, Media Human Resources Management, published in the books and journals including the *Media Product Portfolios*, the *Journal of Modern Communication* and the *Pro-*

ceedings of the European Institute for Advanced Studies in Management. Hang's current dissertation research area is the new media strategy and corporate venturing for emerging media business.

Mónica Herrero is an Associate Professor of Media Management and Assistant Dean for Student Affairs at the School of Communication (University of Navarra, Spain). She holds a MSc in Media Management from the University of Stirling (Scotland). She won the annual Award for her doctoral dissertation in the University of Navarra and she also holds the honorific title of European PhD. She lectures Media Management to undergraduate students, as well as Operations Management in the MSc in Media Management at the University of Navarra. She has been a Visiting Researcher at the University of Westminster (London) and at the University of Glasgow. Her research focuses on television economics, new television products and on the new relationships in the digital era. Her publications include *Programming and Direct Viewer Payment for Television: The Case of Canal Plus Spain* (2003), Eunsa, Pamplona, and "Spain: A Market in Turmoil" in *Digital Terrestrial Television in Europe* (2005), Lawrence Erlbaum, New Jersey.

Kenichi Ishii, PhD, University of Tsukuba, is an associate professor in the Graduate School of Systems and Information Engineering at the University of Tsukuba. His research interests include effects of new communication technologies, advertising, and international cultural influences. He has published on these topics in journals including *Journal of Broadcasting and Electronic Media, Telecommunications Policy, Telematics and Informatics*, and *Gazette*.

Astrid Kurad is an Associate Professor and a doctoral candidate in Media Management at the University of Flensburg. She Studied International Management in Flensburg and Buenos Aires and received her MBA in 2003. She lectures Media Management to undergraduate and graduate students, as well as general Business Administration in the BBA and MBA at the University of Flensburg. Astrid Kurad is the author of several book chapters, journal articles and conference papers on Media Management, Mobile Business and Revenue Management. Her current dissertation research area is the theoretical analysis and application of Revenue Management and Pricing Theory concepts to the media industry.

Alice Y. L. Lee, PhD, is an Associate Professor at the Department of Journalism, Hong Kong Baptist University. She worked for various media organizations (including *Ming Pao Evening News, Hong Kong Economic Times*, Asia Television Limited, information section of the Chinese University of Hong Kong) before she received her doctorate from the University of British Columbia. She has served as the Coordinator of the Broadcast Journalism Concentration at the Department for many years. Her major research interests include media education, new communication technology, and news websites. She teaches courses in critical studies of mass media, TV news reporting, media management, etc. She has published a number of book chapters as well as academic articles in the areas of media education and online journalism both locally and abroad. She is actively involved in promoting media education in Hong Kong. She is now the vice chairperson of the Hong Kong Association of Media Education.

Yu-li Liu is a Commissioner of the National Communications Commission in Taiwan. She is on leave from the professorship of the Department of Radio and TV at National Chengchi University in Taiwan. She served as the former chairperson in 1994– 1996. She has received grants from U.S. Fulbright Foundation and Taiwan's National Science Council for research projects in the areas of Convergence, broadband networks, and interactive TV in Taiwan. Her research interests include digital broadcasting, electronic media law and regulation, new communications technology, telecommunications and media management. Liu has been a reviewer for various journals and funding agencies. She has published more than 20 journal articles and book chapters. Liu earned her master degree in mass communication at Washington State University in 1983 and PhD degree in telecommunications at Indiana University in 1992. She was a Fulbright visiting scholar of the Graduate Telecommunications Program of George Washington University (August 2002– February 2003).

Claude Martin is an economist (Doctorat en sciences économiques, Université d'Aix–Marseille II, 1983), now professor at the Département de communication of Université de Montréal and before at Université Laval in Québec city. He teaches courses on cultural industries, media history and statistics. His research activities bear on culture and communications statistics, development of cultural industries in Québec, recording industry statistics, best-selling books in Québec and television programming. He is now conducting research for the Observatoire de la culture et des communications du Québec and member of Statistics Canada National Advisory Committee on Culture Statistics.

Catherine B. Monsen holds a degree of doctor economiae (Dr. Oecon) from the Norwegian School of Management BI (NSM- BI) in Oslo. She is the director of Centre for Media Economics (www.bi.no/sfm) and associate professor at the Department of Public Governance at NSM-BI. She has published academic articles and book chapters related to her research interests, which include media management, webcasting, regulation, European telecommunications policy, strategy and comparative studies.

Dahong Min is a director of Internet and Digital Department of the Journalism and Communication Institute of the Chinese Academy of Social Sciences (CASS). He is the member of the Internet News Information Service Working Committee and the Internet Policy and Resource Working Committee of the Internet Society of China. He is also the council member of the Beijing Association of Online Media and China Technical News Association. Min is specialized in the Communication

Technology, particularly Internet Communication. His publications include *The Digital Media, The History and Development of the Communication Technology* and *The Internet, Politics, and Democracy*, and his articles are collected in a special CJR column: "Dahong's View." Min had led the launching of the CASS academic research site: MediaResearch.com in 2002, the founding of the premier electronic weekly journal: *e-Media Week* in 2001, and the inauguration of the first Chinese communication and journalism academic site: *China Journalism Review (CJR)* in 1999.

Kyle Nicholas, Ph.D, is an Assistant Professor at Old Dominion University in Norfolk, Virginia. He is the editor of *Open Windows: Remediation Strategies in Global Film Adaptations* (Aalborg Univesrity Press, 2005) and has authored several articles and chapters on contemporary practices in digital media, including telecommunications policy, distance education, participative media and the integration and television and new media.

Morihiro Ogasahara is a doctoral student in the Graduate School of Interdisciplinary Information Studies at the University of Tokyo. After working in NTT for 14 years, he entered the Graduate School mentioned above for academic study in 2003. His research interests include effects of new communication technologies, media credibility, and communications between companies and consumers. He has published on these topics in *Journal of the Japan Society of Information and Communication Research*.

Sora Park is an Assistant Professor of Hanyang University, Seoul, Korea. Her research focuses on the media industries and media markets. She has written widely on the economics of television, newspaper markets and other information industries. She is also interested in media user patterns and economics. She also has experience in consulting for the broadcast and telecommunication industries. She is the co-author of the book, *Children and the Internet Media* (2004). Some recent publications include Competition's effects of programming diversity of different program types in the *International Journal on Media Management* and China's consumption of Korean television dramas: An empirical test of the cultural discount concept in *Korea Journal*.

Asle Rolland holds the magister artium degree in political science from the University of Oslo. He now works as senior adviser at Statistics Norway. Previously he has worked in the media as newspaper journalist and broadcasting researcher, for the media as audience research director in Norwegian and Swiss market research, on the media as media policy analyst for the Norwegian government, at the European Institute for the Media, and at the Center for Media Economics, the Norwegian School of Management BI. As political scientist he has worked mainly in the field of public performance quality measurement. His media research interests are in the fields of media and politics, media management, and media markets.

Charo Sádaba is an Associate Professor of Interactive Marketing and Chair of the Media Management Department at the School of Communication of the University of Navarra (Spain). She coordinates the Advertising and Public Relations Degree at this School. She lectures Interactive Marketing and New Advertising Media for undergraduate students and New Media in the MSc in Corporate Communications at the University of Navarra. She acts as Vice-Chair for the A20 COST Action, a European research network on the Impact of the Internet on the mass media. Her research focuses on the commercial uses of the new interactive media platforms, and on the special relationship between youth and information technologies. During the last years she has published several articles as "Advertising in Digital Television: The Spanish Case" in *The Public* (2002), or "Interactivity and Analogue Commercial Television in Spain," in *TV and Interactivity in Europe* (2004).

Miriam A. Smith is an Associate Professor in Broadcast and Electronic Communication Arts at San Francisco State University where she teaches in the areas of electronic media law, media management and economics and media ethics. Her publications and presentations span the globe. She has published articles on Internet law in the U.S. and China and lectured on international Internet jurisdiction in Russia. Miriam has also lectured on the U.S. television industry in China and taught a media law seminar in Switzerland. In 2004, she received a Fulbright award to study visual culture in Germany.

Clement Y. K. So, PhD, is Director of the School of Journalism and Communication, the Chinese University of Hong Kong. He graduated from the Chinese University of Hong Kong with a BA in Sociology and MPhil in Communication. He received his doctorate from the Annenberg School for Communication, University of Pennsylvania. He once worked as newspaper reporter and editor in Canada and TV audience researcher in Hong Kong. His major research interests include media sociology, citation study, new communication technology, and the Hong Kong press. He has co-authored a book entitled *Global Media Spectacle: News War over Hong Kong* and co-edited several books including *Impact and Issues in New Media: Toward Intelligent Societies*, *TV Program Appreciation Index: Hong Kong Experience*, and *Press and Politics in Hong Kong: Case Studies from 1967 to 1997*. His articles have appeared in *Journal of Communication*, *Human Communication Research*, *Journalism Quarterly*, *Asian Journal of Communication*, *Scientometrics*, *Gazette*, etc.

Niranjala Weerakkody, PhD, Rutgers University, is a Senior Lecturer in Media and Communication at the School of Communication & Creative Arts, in the Faculty of Arts at Deakin University, Geelong, VIC 3217, Australia. She holds a MA in Mass Media & Communication from Temple University, PA, a Postgraduate Diploma in International Affairs (Sri Lanka) and a Bachelor of Science from the University of Sri Jayawardenapura, Sri Lanka. a former national and international award winning TV producer at Rupavahini (the National TV of Sri Lanka), she currently teaches Qualitative and Quantitative Research Methods, Media Effects and Audiences, and Organizational Communication at undergraduate and post-graduate levels. Her other research interests in the of adoption and diffusion of new communication technologies involve Digital TV in Australia and the USA and Biometric devices in everyday life, in Australia, Malaysia, and the USA.

Binyan Yang has joined the Institute of Journalism and Communication, Chinese Academy of Social Science in 2000, after having graduated with a BA in Information Technology and Management from Beijing Normal University. Yang is the main LAN administrator of the Institute as well as webmaster and editor of the Institute's website, www.mediaresearch.cn as well as pursuing her Master studies in the Faculty of Internet and Digital Media Research. Yang's research focus lies in the two fields of "functions and influence of new internet technologies as means of mass communication" and "supervision and regulation of new media." Yang has published articles on the topics of Blog, Wiki, RSS, and Cyberlaw in several professional journals.

WEBCASTING WORLDWIDE

BUSINESS MODELS OF AN EMERGING GLOBAL MEDIUM

PART I

Worldwide Webcasting Overview: A Framework for Analyzing Business Models of Emerging Media

CHAPTER 1

Webcasting as an Emerging Global Medium and a Tripartite Framework to Analyze Emerging Media Business Models

Louisa Ha
Bowling Green State University

Richard Ganahl
Bloomsburg University

WEBCASTING AS AN EMERGING GLOBAL MEDIUM

Since the emergence of the World Wide Web as a mass medium, many scholars and practitioners have established its great potential as a liberating and possibly highly profitable medium that transcends geographic boundaries. The web can display media content in a variety of formats such as texts, graphics, audio, and video. In the broadest sense, webcasting is simply the delivery of content via the web (e.g, Ha, 2004; Miles, 1998), and is synonymous to online publishing. Nevertheless, if we narrow webcasting as the parallel to broadcasting, which is limited to only the delivery of audio and video content, then webcasting should be defined as the delivery of audio and video content via the web. Webcast contents can be delivered live in real-time or on-demand to the consumers. This book employs the narrow definition of webcasting to focus on the audio and video content delivery on the Web. It explores how webcasting may impact the electronic media industry and examines its close relationship with the broadband internet industry.

Unlike text and graphics sites that offer users information only, webcasts enable users to enjoy a sensory-filled, vivid and complete entertainment experience. There are many different applications of webcasting in both the non-profit and the

3

commercial sector. For informational and instructional applications, webcasts can be used for distance learning, training and conferencing within and between organizations. For marketing applications, webcast can be used to promote the media companies, especially radio, television and movie companies with trailers and program highlights, or non-media companies with commercials and other promotional content. For entertainment applications, webcasts can also be used to substitute or complement the content shown in the offline counterparts of electronic media such as television networks, television stations and radio stations. The web becomes an alternative delivery medium for any organization or individual who wants to build an audio or video presence in cyberspace. No license is required. The potential audience is huge—every internet user of the world, which is estimated to be 960 million (Internet World Statistics, 2005). In an age of consolidation of electronic media distribution, the web is the only free marketplace left that allows media entrepreneurs to create their media and reach audiences with virtually no barrier to entry, except in countries that have legal restrictions in providing webcast services such as China.

This book focuses on the consumer market for webcasting because of the social and economic impacts of consumer webcasting on the society at large and the media industry. Business use of webcasting is an area that deserves another book for discussion.

Unlike television or radio broadcasts that must be displayed on a TV set or a radio receiver, webcasts can be displayed on any device equipped with a media player (the software that decodes the audio and video data on the internet). Some common web receiving devices are computers, cellular phones, personal digital assistants, and even the television set. If one is adventurous enough to explore the various movie, video (including animation) and radio services available on the Web, one will be amazed by how many choices are available. But some types of contents are much more common (such as music videos) than others (such as educational videos). Webcast audiences can range from home-country users, overseas expatriates, and the foreign web visitors.

In analyzing the webcasting industry, one must not forget its developments are shaped by the broadband internet industry and the media industry. The broadband industry provides the foundation for webcasting so that the quality of the video and audio shown on the web is comparable to the regular television and radio broadcasts. The streaming technology and file compression technology advancements make it possible to deliver audio video content in large quantity without distortion by saving the bandwidth needed for mass consumption. The traditional electronic media industry is the main content provider to the webcast industry. The two industries have a symbiotic relationship similar to Hollywood Studios and the television industry, which are mutually dependent on each other.

Despite the common use of the term "emerging media" in the academe, there is no clear definition of what constitutes an emerging medium. We suggest that an emerging medium is a message delivery vehicle that is achieving higher utilization among the general population, but has neither universally accepted technical standards for content transmission and display, nor established operation models such as revenue sources and content strategies. "Emerging media" is a transient status of all successful media technology in their nascent stage.

Webcasting is an emerging medium with these characteristics. Incompatible file formats, varying streaming media technologies such as compression and decompression techniques (codecs), different media players for displaying audio and video files, and the variety of plug-in enhancements when using webcasts all characterize the emerging nature of the medium.

This book uses webcasting as an example of emerging media, and examines the various business models used by webcasters in the world's most developed broadband markets in their efforts to survive financially. To avoid limiting the study's application to only one country or culture, it employs a cross-country comparison approach.

The premise of webcasting is to employ the internet as an efficient distribution outlet for audio and video content. The efficiency of the internet as a video delivery platform is advocated by proponents of internet TV (e.g., Noam, Groebel, & Gerbarg, 2004). Digitizing video content capitalizes on the economic properties of media content as a public good. It is becoming easier and demanding much less bandwidth with the advancement of streaming technology (Chang, Lee, & Lee, 2004).

The growth of the webcasting industry is shown in the most recent report released by the Online Publishers Association and comScore Networks. It reveals U.S. consumer spending on entertainment and multimedia sites (excluding game sites) reached $413.5 million in 2004, a 90% increase over the previous year. These sites are now ranked as the second highest online paid content categories, following online dating and relationship services (McGann, 2005). Subscription and stream-based advertising revenue in the United States will reach $864 million in 2005 (Accustream 2004b).

THE LEADING BROADBAND MARKETS AND BROADBAND CONNECTIVITY ACROSS THE WORLD

Few of us understood in 1992 the communications revolution unleashed by Timothy Berners-Lee's World Wide Web. Netscape and Yahoo! were still two years from their launch, Jeff Bezos and Pierre Omidyar were still 3 years from launching Amazon and E-Bay, and Steve Case's AOL reported only 0.5 million subscribers in 1992.

TABLE 1–1
Leading Countries in Internet Usage

	Top 10 in 1999*		Top 10 in 2005**	
Ranking	Countries	I-Users***	Countries	I-Users***
1	USA	110.8	USA	202.888
2	Japan	18.2	China	103.000
3	UK	13.9	Japan	78.050
4	Canada	13.3	Germany	47.127
5	Germany	12.3	India	39.200
6	Australia	6.8	UK	35.807
7	Brazil	6.8	South Korea	31.600
8	China	6.3	Italy	28.610
9	France	5.7	France	25.614
10	South Korea	5.7	Brazil	22.320
Totals		199.8		614.216

*Source: Computer Industry Almanac.
**Source: Internet World Stats.
***Total internet users within country (in millions).

But by 1999, the global popularity of the internet was unmistakable. By then, more than 243 million people worldwide were considered regular internet users. Early on, though, two distinct patterns emerged in the diffusion of internet adoption. First, the bulk of the world's internet usage was narrowly concentrated in just 10 countries. Table 1–1 illustrates that in 1999 the top 10 leading countries in internet usage accounted for more than 82% of the world's total internet users.

Secondly, the West clearly dominated early on in terms of internet adoption and innovation. Table 1–2 illustrates the West's initial leadership. North America, led by the U.S., accounted for 51% of the world's internet users. Europe and Asia were distant followers with 19% and 16% adoption rates respectively.

Fast-forward six years to 2005, and the rate of change in internet usage is truly astounding. Today, nearly one in six of the global village's total 957 million citizens are regular internet users. Almost one billion people surf the web regularly, a number that is 4 times larger than the number of web surfers in 1999!

And where are these global citizen web surfers?

Interestingly, the early patterns of internet diffusion have changed dramatically. First, no longer does North America lead the world in internet use. Today, it ranks third among the world's seven regions in total number of internet use, and its 223 million users account for only 23% of the world's total users. The Asian region leads the world with 327 million, or 34%. Europe is second with 273 million, or 29% of the world's total users.

TABLE 1–2
Comparison of Internet Usage Among Regions

	Internet Use 1999*			Internet Use 2005**		
World Regions	Rank[a]	Users[b]	% of Population[c]	Rank[d]	Users[b]	% of Population
Africa	n/a	n/a	n/a	5	23.867	2.7%
Asia	3	42	16%	1	327.066	9.0%
Europe	2	47	19%	2	273.262	37.4%
Middle East	n/a	n/a	n/a	6	21.422	8.2%
North America	1	124	51%	3	223.779	68.1%
South America	n/a	n/a	n/a	4	70.699	12.9%
Oceana/Australia	n/a	n/a	n/a	7	17.655	52.8%
World		243			957.753	14.9%

[a]Includes only countries listed in top 10. [b]Figures in millions of individuals. [c]The percentage of the country's total population. [d] Includes all countries listed on Internet World Stats.

*Source: Computer Industry Almanac.

**Source: Internet World Stats.

Secondly, the distance between the two regional leaders and North America can only grow larger over time. Table 1–3 documents that Asia's and Europe's leadership in world internet usage are poised to leap well past North America. Today, while nearly 70% of North American uses the internet, only 9% of Asians and 37% of European use the internet. Clearly, if Asia and Europe achieve a level of internet penetration comparable to present day North America, there will be

TABLE 1–3
Internet Usage Among World Regions

World Regions	Population 2005 (est.)	Population as a % World	Internet Users 2005	Internet Penetration
Africa	896,721,874	14.0%	23,867,500	2.7%
Asia	3,622,994,130	56.4%	327,066,713	9.0%
Europe	731,018,523	11.4%	273,262,955	37.4%
Middle East	260,814,179	4.1%	21,422,500	8.2%
North America	328,387,059	5.1%	223,779,183	68.1%
South America	546,723,509	8.5%	70,699,084	12.9%
Oceana/Australia	33,443,448,	0.5%	17,655,737	52.8%
World	6,420,102,722	100%	957,753,672	14.9

Source: Internet World Stats.

TABLE 1–4
Internet Usage Among Research Countries

	Rank by Usage	Population 2005 (est.)	Internet Users 2005	Internet Penetration
Australia	17	20,507,264	13,784,966	67.20%
Canada	12	32,050,369	20,450,000	63.80%
China	2	1,282,198,289	103,000,000	7.90%
Denmark*	E24	5,411,596	3,762,500	69.50%
Germany	4	82,726,188	47,127,725	57.00%
Greece*	E18	11,212,468	3,800,000	33.90%
Hong Kong	E20	6,898,686	4,878,713	70.70%
Italy*	8	58,608,565	28,870,000	49.30%
Japan	3	128,137,485	78,050,000	60.90%
Netherlands	18	16,322,583	10,806,328	66.20%
Norway*	E25	4,606,363	3,140,000	68.20%
South Korea	7	49,929,293	32,570,000	65.20%
Spain	13	43,435,136	15,565,138	35.80%
Taiwan	16	22,794,795	13,800,000	60.50%
UK	6	59,889,407	35,807,929	59.80%
USA	1	296,208,476	202,888,307	68.50%

*These countries are not ranked overall by Internet World Statistics so ranks are estimated.
Source: Internet World Statistics (2005).

three billion more Asian and European web surfers than North American surfers at current population levels!

While the likelihood of a change this dramatic is distant, the current patterns of diffusion strongly suggest exciting adjustments in regional contributions to the makeup of the world's internet population.

Table 1–4 demonstrates that the countries studied in this book are far along the internet's diffusion curve. All but three have achieved penetration levels exceeding 50%. Understandably, China may lag for some time simply because of its huge population despite its current rapid rate of growth. Greece and Spain present unique examples of cultural, political and economic influences that are discussed in their respective chapters. It is also important to note that the studied countries all rank among the world's top 30 countries in terms of internet usage, and account for 65% of the world's total users.

The level of broadband adoption achieved by the majority of this book's countries is also noteworthy. High levels of high speed, large bandwidth connections characterize most of the countries, and 7 of the world's top 10 broadband leaders are among the book's countries. All rank in the world's top 30 countries on the basis of broadband utilization (OECD, 2005).

TABLE 1-5
Broadband Subscription Rate of Countries Covered in This Book

| Country | *Broadband Subscribers / 100 HH Among Study* | | | | | |
	DSL	CATV	Other	Total	World Rank	Total Number
Australia	8.5	2.4	0.1	10.9	17	2,183,300
Canada	9.4	9.7	0.1	19.2	6	6,142,662
China*	n/a	n/a	n/a	n/a	n/a	
Denmark	13.2	6.1	2.4	21.8	3	1,176,637
Germany	9.9	0.3	0.1	10.2	18	8,439,732
Greece	0.8	0.0	0.0	0.8	30	93,287
Hong Kong**				20.9	e4	
Italy	9.4	0.0	0.6	10.0	19	5,783,319
Japan	11.0	2.4	3.0	16.4	11	20,953,090
Netherlands	13.6	8.9	0.0	22.5	2	3,642,315
Norway	14.8	2.5	0.9	18.2	9	8,369,060
South Korea	13.9	8.9	2.7	25.5	1	12,260,969
Spain	7.0	2.2	0.1	9.3	21	3,949,234
Taiwan**				16.3	e11	
UK	9.7	3.8	0.0	13.5	13	8,095,000
USA	5.5	8.0	1.1	14.5	12	42,645,815

*China is not included in rankings by OECD.
**Hong Kong and Taiwan are not members of OECD. Their rankings are based on ITU's estimate of total household penetration.
Sources: Organization for Economic Co-operation and Development (OECD) and International Telecommunication Union (ITU).

Table 1-5 also notes that DSL is the leading platform for broadband delivery in 14 of the 16 countries studied. Only two countries, Canada and the U.S., have more cable broadband subscribers than DSL subscribers because of their well-developed cable industry. Overall, the OECD concludes that DSL accounts for 61% of global broadband deliveries, cable modems 32% and 7% utilize other technologies including broadband through fiber optics, LAN, satellite, or fixed wireless.

The adoption of broadband is also contingent upon the price of broadband services. The recent Ovum report (2005) shows that Japan offers the lowest cost broadband services among 11 leading broadband countries as per the price index calculated by Ovum (Table 1-6). Italy and Germany have the highest broadband subscription price for their consumers.

TABLE 1–6
Broadband Price Index Comparison

Rank	Country	Price Index Quarter 1, 2005
1	Japan	0.98
2	France	0.94
3	Canada	0.77
4	United Kingdom	0.72
5	Ireland	0.67
6	Sweden	0.63
7	Australia	0.63
8	United States	0.62
9	South Korea	0.53
10	Italy	0.50
11	Germany	0.41

Note.   Only 11 countries are selected for comparison in the Ovum Report. The price index is calculated as the price of the top 5 retail ISPs, weighted by the market share. 1.0 is the lowest cost and 0 is the highest cost with more than $800 year.

Source: Ovum (2005). *International broadband market comparisons: Update June 2005.* A report for the Department of Trade and Industry. United Kingdom.

ONLINE MEDIA BUSINESS MODELS REVIEW

Viable business models are essential to support the development of any emerging medium. There are many studies that examine the adoption of new media by consumers primarily based on Rogers' (1995) diffusion of innovation paradigm. Let's not forget that the consumer's perception of the medium is influenced by the medium's business models and its dissemination of content to consumers. Hence, the medium's business models can be decisive to the acceptance of the medium. Currently there is a lack of theories that explain how emerging media choose business models, and the models' influence on the available content of the emerging medium.

Many consulting companies, such as McKinsey & Company (2002) and Accustream (2004a), offer proprietary research on their forecasts and analyses of online media business models. Their focus is on profitability rather than the larger impact of various webcasting business models on the society. The academe's strong interest in online media business models is demonstrated in a 2004 special issue of the *International Journal on Media Management* dedicated to business models of traditional media and the internet. It received 45 manuscript-length submissions.

The various online media business model theories discussed in published research address two major issues: Whether consumers are willing to pay for the online media content/services (e.g., Chyi, 2005), and whether the online presence of offline media will cannibalize their offline media's revenue (e.g., Fetscherin and Knolmayer, 2004). Table 1–7 is a summary of the previous research on online media business models.

Picard (2002) defines media business models as an architecture that accounts for "the resources of production and distribution technologies, content creation or acquisition, and recovery of costs for creating, assembling, and presenting the content" (p. 26). Business models are modes of practices, and are different from strategies which are the means to attain the business goal. Despite the strong interest of both commercial and academic entities in online media business models, the discussion of online business models is inconsistent and includes no common components for comparison. Among the studies of online media business models, Picard (2002) and Chan-Olmsted and Ha (2003) both argue for an evolutionary development of business models. Picard (2002) describes the development of online media business models as the evolution from the earliest videotext model to the current portal model. Chan-Olmsted and Ha (2003) assert there is a learning curve that media companies must go through. When existing media have developed their knowledge about the web and are able to generate web revenue by meeting consumer needs, then they will be able to sustain a profit-making business model. Nevertheless, their online media business models are either for terrestrial media such as television stations or online media only. These studies are not able to explain the various types of webcasters that exist on the web that may or may not have offline media counterparts.

Other studies on media business models illustrate the issue of cannibalization by showing the influence of basic economic factors such as ownership on online media business models. For example, in Arampatzis's (2004) study of the web sites of British and Greek media organizations, public broadcasters are more likely to experiment with new features than commercial broadcasters. Kolo and Vogt (2004) argue that online media can exist independent of their offline media because there is little overlap between audiences. The media executives' fear of the "free-rider" internet culture supports Fetscherin and Knolmayer's (2004) proposal that the risk of cannibalization depends on the proportion of online free content and the degree of content overlap between online and offline media.

Studies that equate media business models as simply revenue sources focus on the audiences' willingness to pay for content. For example, Mings and White (2000) propose four business models based on revenue sources: (1) advertising, (2) e-commerce (transactional), (3) subscription, (4) bundled (partnership). Chyi (2005) concludes that the subscription business model will not work in Hong Kong because most consumers are not willing to pay for the content. Bartussek (2003) contends that consumers will be willing to pay for content if media can provide content that is exclusive, user-friendly and customized, with other additional benefits to the existing media content service. The revenue sources of online media will differ greatly from offline media.

TABLE 1–7
Online Media Business Model Theories

Study	Empirical Method and Country	Theoretical Propositions
Arampatzis (2004)	Interviews/Case studies. Greece, United Kingdom.	Without worrying about the bottom line, public service media are more innovative than commercial media in offering online media services. Other than innovativeness not much difference in business models between old media and online media.
Bartussek (2003)	Anecdotal examples.	Online media need to adopt a different business model from parent offline media. Consumers' willingness to pay for online media content is based on exclusivity, added benefits and user-friendliness of the online content.
Chan-Olmsted & Ha (2003)	Surveys. U.S. Broadcast TV Stations.	Development of Internet competency over time and evolution of business models from (1) online competency development, (2) enhancement of the value of online products, and (3) generation of online revenue.
Fetschein & Knolmeyer (2004)	Surveys. European and U.S. newspapers and magazines with both offline and online versions.	Risk of cannibalization is determined by the percentage of free digital content and the percentage of content that both offline and online media overlap. The higher the percentage, the higher the risk.
Ha & Ganahl (2004)	Content analysis. United States, South Korea.	Clicks-and-bricks and pure-play media adopt either a content aggregator or a branded content business model with different transmission methods, content strategies and revenue sources and these elements influence one another. More transmission methods leads to more revenue sources and content strategies are different between clicks-and-bricks and pure-play media.
Kolo & Vogt (2004)	Secondary Analysis. Germany.	Online media have their own distinct users. They are destination sites relatively independent of their offline media counterparts. Their business models should be different from the offline media counterpart.
Mings & White (2000)	Analysis from industry press. U.S. online newspapers.	Proposed 4 online media business models based on revenue sources: (1) Advertising, (2) Transactional, (3) Subscription, and (4) Bundled (partnership).
Picard (2002)	Anecdotal examples.	Online media content services business models evolve over time, with the best model adopted by most providers at the time. Four abandoned models are the videotext model, the paid Internet model, the free Web model and the Internet/Web ad push model. The current model is a portal model and the emerging model is a digital portal model.

The number of markets or settings where empirical data or anecdotal examples can support the theories limits the current discussion of online media models. The models may not be applicable to other countries without a rigorous cross-national testing of the theories (Livingstone, 2003). Researchers have employed the multi-country approach to test the universality and robustness of a theory such as cultural fit of advertising appeals (Zanpour et al., 1994) or advertising as a mirror of society (Albers-Miller & Gelb, 1996). This book attempts to fill this void in media economics and emerging media with a cross-national analysis of webcasting business models.

This book defines webcasting business models as the patterns of operation that an organization offer its customers audio and/or video services on the Web, utilizing one or a combination of file transmission methods, content strategies and revenue sources for the purpose of achieving its business goal and sustaining the organization's survival. This definition applies to both for-profit webcasters and non-profit webcasters.

A TRIPARTITE FRAMEWORK TO ANALYZE EMERGING MEDIA BUSINESS MODELS: ACR

Ha and Ganahl (2004) offer a tripartite model to analyze webcasting business models for cross-national comparison, which can be applicable to all emerging media. They apply the model in their study of webcasting in South Korea and the United States and identify the differences and similarities in the two countries on each component of the business model framework. The tripartite model posits that all business models of emerging media consist of three components. The first component is the accessibility of the medium, which includes technical requirements for transmission, location and display of media content. The second component is the content strategies employed by the medium. The third component is the revenue source of the medium. In addition, whether the webcaster has an offline media counterpart can affect the selection of content strategies (see Figure 1–1). This book adopts this framework with some slight modifications to accommodate different markets of the world. Webcasters are categorized into three types: (1) click-and-bricks, (2) pure-plays, and (3) Internet Service Providers, based on the nature of the business. Clicks-and-bricks are webcasters that already have an offline media presence such as a movie company, television network or radio station such as ESPN.com, or webcasters that have an established non-media related organization such as a government unit (Edcity.org.hk) or a religious organization (breakthrough.org.hk). Pure-plays are webcasters that only have online presence and have no offline media/organizational counterparts such as Digitally Imported (www.di.fm). They do not offer their own internet access service to their users. Internet Service Providers are

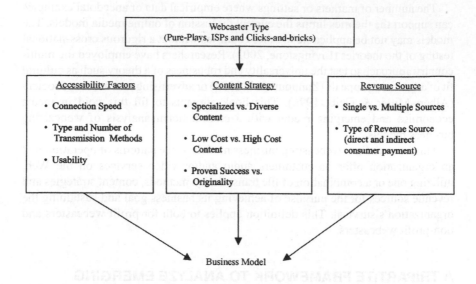

FIGURE 1–1   The ACR Emerging Media Business Model Framework, adapted from Ha and
Ganahl (2004).

those that offer internet access service to their subscribers and also provide their
own webcast content services either on the portal page or as additional services
such as America Online (AOL).

We now rename the framework as the ACR Emerging Media Business Model
Framework using the acronym of the three components of emerging media busi-
ness models: Accessibility (A), Content Strategies, (C) and Revenue Sources
(R).

Accessibility

Whether a medium is accessible to the audience largely influences its adoption
and usage. For example, in analyzing the economics of interactive television,
Pagani (1999) stresses the importance of understanding the technical factors in
shaping the economic models of the new technology. Currently, the access to
and applications of the web are not standardized. First, webcasting of video and
audio files requires high bandwidth from the provider and the broadband internet
connection from the user. The speed of the internet connection can determine the
quality of the user's webcast experience. If the internet connection is slow, such
as a dial-up connection, the transmission of video and audio files becomes gar-

bled and incomprehensible. There is a wide range of internet connection speeds available to consumers in different markets. The full enjoyment of webcast is highly dependent on whether the user has a broadband connection: The higher the speed, the better the quality of the content display. Many studies of internet use show that broadband internet users are much more likely to consume webcasts than narrowband users (Cho, Byun, & Sung, 2003; Rao, 2001).

One of the accessibility factors in webcasting is the multimedia file transmission methods webcasters adopt: (1) live streaming, (2) on-demand, and (3) push. Each method provides a different format for a consumer to use the content service. Live streaming most closely resembles the traditional terrestrial broadcast. There is a fixed show schedule that users must follow in order to view or listen to the content. Downloading on demand allows the user to download the media file to the user's hard drive, so the user can store it and open it for later use. It is similar to a videocassette or DVD that is owned by the consumer. Streaming on demand utilizes the file compression technology to display the file during transmission. The files are stored on the webcaster's server. Users can retrieve at any moment the content on demand, however the streaming does not constitute ownership because content was never saved on the users' computer. Push is a technology that automatically delivers the content to the user's internet reception devices through common computer applications such as screensavers or e-mail programs. In push, users do not need to take the initiative in locating and consuming the content. They are given the content passively. The program update of Microsoft Windows is a common example of the use of the push method. There is a revival of the push method by the technology of Real Simple Syndication (RSS) in which a user can request automatic feeding of video and other content from a content service provider to the users's computer with a RSS newsreader or aggregator software.

While peer-to-peer file sharing of audio and video content is another technology growing in popularity, because its content transmission is not under the webcaster's control, it does not constitute a media service that assembles content to its users. Ultimately, the webcaster's choice of transmission method determines how and when consumers can enjoy the webcast content.

In addition to transmission method differences, there are other usability issues in webcasting. Usability refers to the ease for users to navigate a web site. First, web site designs vary in usability. Some webcasts with complex and confusing designs are very difficult to navigate. Because of the self-paced navigation design of the Web, the user must know where to locate the materials he or she wants to open. If one is confused and gets frustrated, one may leave the webcast. Second, the compatibility of media players is another issue. Whether the user can view or listen to the webcast depends on the compatibility of media players used by the webcaster and the user. For example, if the webcaster uses the Windows Media Player file format and the user only has a Quicktime player, the user cannot open the webcast. To be a regular user of webcasting, consumers need to install several media players to play the webcast in different formats. In addition, some webcasts require additional software such as Macromedia Flash in order to view the page and the webcast. A U.S. study by Ha and Chan-Olmsted (2002) reveals over half of the internet users did not download additional software to view specific features of a web site.

For webcasting to be successful in capturing the largest audience as possible, it must be highly usable. To be highly usable, the webcast should accommodate different internet connection speeds and provide both live streaming and on-de-mand services to consumers. Also, it must be organized with an easy-to-navigate design and a search engine for fast location of materials. It should display a de-scription of the content with file size and length, and accommodate multiple player platforms requiring minimal or no additional software to display the ma-jority of the materials.

Content Strategies

The content strategies used by media organizations are based on a continuum of the scope of the offering, the acquisition cost and the track record of the content. Media organizations can choose between a diversified offering of multiple gen-res and a narrow focus of a certain genre. Usually a more diversified offering can attract more users than a narrow focus offering. But a narrow focus is easier to build media brand recognition and audience loyalty. There are also huge dif-ferences in acquisition costs among the different types of programs. Concerts, live sports games and blockbuster movies are very expensive because of the high license fees. Usually these programs are found in premium cable channels where users pay extra for the content and they are seen by audiences as more valuable than other types of content (Herrero, 2004). Game shows and music videos be-long to the low cost genres as they cost less to produce and the latter are even supplied to the media for free by record labels. A high cost content strategy must be accompanied by an effective compensation system to sustain the service that may involve multiple revenue sources or a premium price for the user. A low-cost content strategy can offer the audience free programs and is more sus-tainable on a continuing basis. Finally, in selecting programs, the media organi-zation can choose to stay with programs with track records such as top-rated television series and box office hits. Or, the media organization may want to em-phasize originality by showing first-run programs on the medium.

In their study of South Korean and American leading webcasters, Ha and Ganahl (2004) demonstrate that webcaster types (clicks-and-bricks and pure-plays) have different content strategies because of their respective competitive advantages. Clicks-and-bricks such as TV networks or radio stations have the advantage of brand recognition and the ownership of media content. They are likely to simulcast their content or repurpose previously aired content. Pure-play webcasters can freely select content sources from a variety of competing content providers. They can also provide original content to create uniqueness without the worry of jeopardizing the offline media's image.

Revenue Sources

There are six common revenue sources for webcasters: (1) advertising/sponsorship, (2) e-commerce, (3) content syndication, (4) corporate or government funding, (5) subscription, and (6) pay-per use/view/download. The first four revenue sources all assume that the audience will not pay for the content, or the payment will be so minimal that it cannot provide sufficient revenue. The advertising/sponsorship mode assumes that audiences will not mind viewing advertising as long as they do not need to pay for the content. Even if they pay, the amount they are willing to spend may be too little to support the online media. The audience for the content is large enough to attract advertisers at a cost-efficient level.

The e-commerce revenue mode also assumes that audiences will not pay for the content. Instead of relying on advertisers for revenue, the e-commerce mode uses the revenue generated from selling merchandise on the site to make a profit. The free content is the bait; the business transactions are the ends.

The content syndication mode uses the web site as the showcase of content that can be readily transferable or adapted to other sites. The assumption of the syndication mode is that consumers will not pay for the content. But there are many sites that need the content and do not have the facilities or expertise to produce it. The profit comes from syndicating the content to other sites. Corporate funding or government funding are found in sites that see webcasting as a public service or a means to promote the company, not as a profit generation center.

The subscription mode and the pay-per-use mode, on the other hand, assume audiences are willing to pay for the webcast content. The subscription mode is the most commonly used business model for payment because it avoids the trouble of charging consumers every time they use the content, and it encourages consumers to use the content without worrying about additional payments. The content is bundled as a package so that all is available to the subscribers. The pay-per-use mode is particularly viable if individual content items are so attractive to the audience that it will pay to own a copy (download) or view it on demand. A few attractive items may be able to generate sufficient revenue for the webcaster. However, there must be a substantial number of people willing to pay for each item if the price is to remain competitive and affordable.

These revenue sources are not mutually exclusive. Webcasters can choose one source or a combination of sources that are appropriate. Webcasters that appeal to a broad audience can choose revenue sources that do not need an audience to pay directly for the content to survive. Webcasters that appeal to a niche audience may have fewer choices because the audience size may not be large enough to attract advertisers or sponsors. Despite the hype about online advertising customized by web site content, the harsh reality of online advertising still follows the golden rule of cost-efficiency (Ha, 2003). Online advertising dollars are concentrated on those sites with the highest traffic. Indeed, the top 20 most visited sites receive 80 percent of the online advertising revenue (Pastore, 2001). Specialized sites with small audiences have little advertising.

Additionally, webcasting's technical characteristic of different transmission methods can determine the type of revenue sources and diversity of revenue sources of the webcaster. For example, the on-demand streaming method facilitates subscription and pay-per-view revenue sources because it provides users flexibility and the convenience of using the content whenever they want. Also the choice of content is not limited to scheduled programming.

Content Aggregators and Branded Content: Two Business Models of Webcasters

Based on the ACR framework, Ha and Ganahl (2004) propose a parsimonious taxonomy of content aggregator and branded content as the two general business models for webcasting in their study of webcasting business models in the United States and South Korea. The content aggregator model refers to the operation of the webcaster as an entertainment or information portal that works like a cable system operator. The webcaster assembles content from a wide variety of competing content suppliers. The branded content model refers to the operation of the webcaster as a media brand with unique image and content. Its business success is based on specialized content or a well-known media brand. The content can be original or repurposed (i.e., shown before in another medium), however, content from another media brand is not available. Content aggregators provide much more content variety than the branded content business model. They need to make site navigation and content location easy to prevent the user from being lost and confused amid the huge amount of available content from various sources. In contrast, users of branded content webcasts are generally familiar with the webcasters' content and probably need less help on the navigation.

Pertinent Issues in Webcasting

The cost of digital content and copyright protection laws are currently the bigger issues to webcasters, especially for web radio that broadcast music on the internet for their listeners. The U.S. Congress enacted the Digital Performance Right in Sound Recordings Act of 1995. This act only applies to digital audio retransmission and requires webcasters to obtain a performance license from the owners of the sound recording rights. The Small Webcaster Settlement Act (HR5469) was introduced and passed in the U.S. Congress in 2002 to help small webcasters. The bill offers a lower royalty rate to small commercial webcasters by only charging 8% of the gross revenue or 5% of the webcasters' expense for the royalty fee for the retroactive period before December 2002. Now webcasters with less than $50,000 in gross revenue will pay a minimum annual fee of $2,000. Still many web radio stations have been shut down to protest the copyright fees and avoid being fined.

Because of the ease to duplicate in identical quality as the original and to retrieve and store digital content on the Web, webcasters have to protect their own copyright for original content. The Digital Millennium Copyright Act (DMCA), written in 1998 under the treaties by the United Nation's agency World Intellectual Property Organization, provides for a simplified but statutory licensing system for digital performance of sound recordings on the internet and via satellite. Its provisions include a programming restriction called the "Sound Recording Performance Complement." (SRPC). The restriction includes no more than three songs from a particular album, no more than four songs by a particular artist and no more than three consecutively in a three-hour period and no advance song or artist playlist announcement may be published. Despite the international agreement on digital copyright protection, news of copyright infringements is always a daily staple in the online world with many amateur and illegal services coming into the field.

There are other regulatory issues pertinent to webcasting especially when more and more webcast content creators are amateurs. These issues include extension of the right of publicity online (state laws prohibiting the unauthorized taking of an individual's name, likeness, voice or other elements and using them for commercial purposes), invasion of privacy by the internet's ability to collect data and customize information, libels in bulletin boards and chat rooms and freedom of speech on the internet and censorship issues. The U.S. Supreme Court ruled the Communication Decency Act of 1996 unconstitutional. Its ruling has established that the internet enjoy the same First Amendment rights as other print media even though it may publish audio and video content.

Audblogs, Video Blogs, Video Search Engines

Weblogs (or blogs) are online chronicles of a writer's ideas and opinions on certain subjects posted on the web in descending chronological order (Beach, 2003). With the increased affordability of digital video cameras and audio devices such as i-pods, more and more amateurs are entering the webcasting business as videobloggers or audbloggers. They post video clips and audio clips on their blogs. Although most of the videoblogs (vlogs) and audblogs are non-commercial in nature and are mainly commentaries of individuals, the growing audience of some of these videoblogs may create new business models by aggregating the videoblogs using RSS. Yahoo! reportedly was working with several organizations providing videoblogging services such as Ourmedia and Creative Commons to provide RSS service to users. Users can choose the types of videos they want to see and have them sent automatically to their computers. Advertising can be seen and DVDs may be sold on these RSS services (Green, 2004). The online industry is actively exploring the advertising revenue potential of blogs. For example, for a cost of 25 million, AOL recently acquired Weblog Inc., a blog advertising network that reported $1 million in advertising revenue with 10 blogs sold out in advertising space (Brown, 2006).

The development of video search engines such as SingingFish.com and by major search engines such as Google Video Search and Yahoo Video Search have alleviated some of the problems associated with the location of webcasters. But after locating a webcaster, the navigation and design of one webcaster can differ greatly from another. It becomes another learning process to the user. Similar to the user's reliance on a specific search engine such as Google and Yahoo, webcasting users will gradually learn to be selective and focus on a few webcasts that can fulfill their entertainment and informational needs. Webcasters that are part of an established media's online service, a portal site service, or an internet service provider can enjoy a larger audience base through heavy cross-media promotion and by eliminating the users' need to search for webcast services as the default home page of the users. Independent webcasters need to use various publicity measures and other tactics to reach out to the web users. Hence, the video search services will serve as the future gatekeepers, and will provide viewing guides for the webcasting businesses. With the world's increasing penetration of broadband internet connection, webcasting is bound to grow. Will webcasting be another cable or satellite TV service that rules the entertainment world this decade? The business models of current and future leading webcasters may be the key to this question.

OVERVIEW OF THE BOOK

After conceptualizing webcasting as an emerging global medium, and introducing the ACR framework in this chapter, we provide an application of the ACR framework in a 13 country comparison in Chapter 2. In that study, business models of 220 leading webcasters were examined from 13 Asian, European, and North American countries with a high number of broadband users. These countries are Australia, China, Canada, Germany, Greece, Hong Kong, Japan, the Netherlands, South Korea, Spain, Taiwan, the United Kingdom, and the United States. The study shows the limitation of the webcast medium's globalness and the robustness of the ACR framework in analyzing business models across countries. The largely domestic nature of webcasters and their content demonstrates the strong preferences for local content within home country boundaries.

Chapter 3 begins the emphasis on individual countries and their webcast business models. Each country chapter describes the media market environment and internet usage in the country. Then it will introduce the webcast audience research in that country (if available) and analyze the business practices of leading webcasters. The business models of the leading webcasters are analyzed with the ACR framework. The international influence on the webcast content is also examined. Each chapter concludes with an outlook of the webcast industry and other pertinent issues of webcasting in that country.

We begin our individual country profiles with two large North American countries that are leaders in broadband usage: The United States and Canada. Despite their close proximity, the two countries differ substantially in media traditions. In Chapter 3, Ha shows that the U.S. has a very strong commercialized media tradition, and its webcasting industry continues this legacy through the domination of large commercial webcasters that are mostly publicly traded companies. In a way though, the long history of internet development and a well-developed media industry hinder broadband adoption and limit webcast content to mainstream media. Leading webcasters generally adopt a short format and seldom provide full-length and blockbuster materials. The big four content aggregators (America Online, Yahoo, RealNetworks and Microsoft) have a large lead over other branded content webcasters both in terms of revenue and audience traffic.

Canada is a country with a strong public broadcast tradition and a bilingual country with English and French as official languages. Nevertheless, media are not bilingual and they are either in English or in French only. In Chapter 4, Martin, Allagui and Chaussé show that the leading Canadian webcasters are often part of a media conglomerate or as an added value service of internet service providers. The unregulated webcast industry makes it difficult for the Canadian government to enforce its cultural diversity policy because how much market and cultural forces can create diversity in webcast is questionable.

Chapters 5 through 12 are profiles of the business dynamics of webcasting in Europe. We begin with Europe's largest internet user, the United Kingdom. The British government's commitment to establishing a strong digital infrastructure has created a favorable business environment for webcasting. Arampatzis believes the U.K. will realize the largest promise of webcasting growth in Europe. The British webcasting industry is one of the most internationalized, as competition includes both foreign and domestic webcasters. The public broadcaster British Broadcasting Corporation (BBC) extends its longstanding leadership in broadcasting to webcasting. Interestingly, public broadcast leadership is also reflected in almost all other European countries where public broadcast dominates electronic media. Hence, clicks-and-bricks are most commonly found among leading European webcasters.

Chapter 6 presents an interesting case of the Netherlands' innovative webcast offerings by public webcasters. The country has the highest broadband penetration in Europe and may take over the leadership of South Korea by the end of 2005 (Ovum, 2005). Because Dutch public broadcasters have huge libraries of materials, they have no problem in offering full content on their webcasts. Webcasting is just part of the mission of public broadcasting. Bakker also addresses the important role played by ISPs, adult content, and business-to-business webcasting in generating profits in the Dutch market.

The German public broadcast tradition as presented in Chapter 7 raises the interesting question of license issues. Download services is treated as media services but live-streaming is treated as broadcasting subject to state laws and requires a broadcast license. As in other European countries, the most dominant webcaster is the German public broadcaster Deutsche Welle. Yet, as the authors Friedrichsen, Smith, and Kurad point out, if webcasting is considered broadcasting, then everyone with a computer may be charged the licence fee and subject to state laws. Webcasts of public broadcasters must base their revenue sources on licence fees by law.

Southern Europe generally lags behind the rest of Europe in broadband adoption. In Chapter 8, Herrero and Sádaba discuss how multi-media conglomerates dominate the Spanish webcasting industry, and that webcasting is not well received in Spain. The low availability of broadband, the unpopularity of e-commerce, and the lack of Spain's pay-for-content culture are attributed to the lackluster webcasting industry in Spain. Yet in contrast to Spain, Italy is the fastest growing broadband market in Europe with free DSL connections despite its humble beginning. Webcasting, in particular web radio, flourishes as portals rich with new contents and community tools. In Chapter 9, Bonini illustrates the Italian consumer's strong interest in on-demand for video content the and live streaming for radio content.

In Chapter 10, Arampatzis discusses why Greece, with one of Europe's lowest broadband penetration market, has a small webcast industry. Because of the lack of bandwidth, most leading Greek webcasters are primarily web radio stations that have simply extended platforms of existing radio or TV stations. Cable News Network (CNN) is the only foreign webcaster that captures a spot on Greece's leading webcaster roster. He also notes a huge potential for the webcasting industry by serving the large number of Greek expatriates who reside overseas and seek Greek media content.

Chapters 11 and 12 present two Scandinavian countries with high broadband penetration rates. Their strong public broadcasting traditions are reflected in the domination of domestic public broadcast media as leading webcasters in the market. Rolland and Monsen illustrate in Chapter 11 how webcasting is challenging the authority of the Norwegian government in the control of electronic media. It also shows how webcasting is threatening the legitimacy of licence fees as a source of revenue, and the importance of web audience research in the development of the webcast industry.

Denmark is a case of a high broadband penetration with a concentrated ownership of webcasting by the public broadcaster. Nicholas shows in Chapter 12 that the small size market of Denmark facilitates the concentration of the webcasting industry. Basically, through abundant government support and resources, the Danish Broadcasting Corporation dominates the webcasting industry with its DR NetRadio, and DR1 and DR2 with video news and archive videos. Microsoft achieves a monopoly as the only compatible web browser for the two largest webcasters, DR and TV2 video streams. Nicholas doubts the competitiveness of webcast to traditional broadcast because of the superior quality of public broadcast radio and television in Denmark and other cultural factors.

Chapters 13 through 16 demonstrate the rapid development of broadband in the Asian countries. First, we present in Chapter 13 the largest broadband market in Asia, China. The tight government control of the media industries continues in the webcasting industry. A licence is required to provide webcast services. Many government-owned media organizations are jockeying for a leading position in the new medium by offering their webcast services. Interestingly, the participants are not limited to the TV and radio stations, but also newspapers, news agencies, ISPs, and other media companies. Despite the licence requirement, there are many illegal Chinese webcasters that are accessible to web users. The rapid development of web technologies such as internet television and blogging are fueling the development of the industry. Hang, Min, and Yang offer a glimpse of the webcast consumption pattern through a national internet-delivered survey of web users.

Chapter 14 demonstrates that non-profit media can shine in the webcast world even within a highly commercialized media environment. Hong Kong, although now returned to China, maintains its own capitalist system, legal and political structure, and has a high degree of autonomy. It deserves separate attention because of its almost city-state status, and its highly developed broadband market. It has the world's most affordable broadband service and as in other small markets, clicks-and-bricks are the leading webcasters. The highly competitive broadband service also facilitates the ISP to serve as a leading webcaster. Four out of 10 leading webcasters are non-commercial organizations. In a small market like Hong Kong, Lee, and So argue that the future of webcasting is largely determined by the utilization of webcasting as an effective media platform for non-profit organizations.

Chapter 15 shows that Taiwan webcasters are very versatile in developing their businesses. As Liu observes, the webcasting industry is largely dominated by two leading domestic webcasters—hiChannel and Webs-TV. Both are pure-plays that have no off-line counterpart. The multiple strategic alliances that Webs-TV has developed with various portal sites make it omnipresent to web users. Hence, even though by itself Webs-TV does not generate much traffic, redirected traffic from various entertainment sections of newspapers sites and other portal sites make it the most frequently used webcaster. HiChannel, a content aggregator owned by Taiwan's largest telephone company, is the webcast service for the popular ADSL service provider, HiNet. Clicks-and-bricks are not aggressive webcasters because they see webcasting as only a supportive service to their regular on-air broadcast.

South Korea enjoys the world's highest broadband penetration rate. It appears that webcasting should have a prosperous future in South Korea. Park describes in Chapter 16 the decline of traditional broadcast media, and the high hopes the broadcast media has on webcast as the next big medium. All major broadcast networks launch internet video on-demand services and the market is growing for such services. Although the majority of webcasters provide domestic content, those that provide foreign content primarily feature U.S. films. Yet, many industry specialists are uncertain if the development of webcasting can continue with the competition of alternative media services.

Japan is the world's third largest broadband user and is very advanced in communication technology through fiber to the home. Ishii and Ogasahara explain in Chapter 17 that webcasting services on the PC-based internet are still in the early stages of development despite relatively advanced broadband technologies. In contrast, the webcasting business on the mobile internet is much more successful. They attribute the difference to three factors: (1) copyright protection, (2) payment system, and (3) competition structure. First, copyright protection is easier to obtain on the mobile phone. Second, mobile phone carriers offer a more convenient payment system for customers. Third, the competition structure in the mobile internet is a win-win situation for content providers and the carriers. In the PC market, some obstacles, including the difficulty in rights clearance, the technological disadvantages, and the closed media market structure, have impeded the growth of webcasters. The chapter also discusses future directions of the webcasting business based on the four typologies of webcasters in Japan.

In Chapter 18, Weerakkody illustrates how webcasting in Australia currently experiences low adoption and diffusion because of technical constraints of internet transmission speeds, bandwidth, and lack of incentives for commercial media to embrace it. It examines Australia's media industry structures, its internet and broadband usage, and the challenges of providing broadband access to its vast and sparsely populated rural and remote regions. An analysis of the leading webcasters show that the most active webcasters are those funded by the Federal Government who do not need to worry about making profit on webcasting.

Chapter 19 demonstrates the pan-regional market potential of the Arab world. Allagui and Martin discuss the wide disparity in broadband use and infrastructure within the Arab region. Yet, the common cultural interests, language, and religion in the Arab region tie the consumers together. The strictly censored broadcast media in the Arabic countries also creates room for webcasting to become an alternative choice for media consumers. Al-Jazeera is able to capitalize on this need and extend its satellite TV news leadership to its webcasting efforts.

In the concluding chapter, we discuss some patterns that emerged from this analysis of webcasting business practices among 17 countries. First we propose that five factors: (1) geography, (2) political structure, (3) media market tradition and environment, (4) technology infrastructure, and (5) cultural background affect the development of the webcasting industry within a market. Next we discuss the dynamics of webcasting's revenue sources and explore the possible paths of the webcasting industry future. We also offer some suggestions regarding the direction of future research on webcasting.

Since webcasting is such a fast-changing field that facts and statistics reported in the book can rapidly become outdated, we created a weblog at http://webcastingworldwide.blogspot.com/ to provide updates for the book. The blogs will be written by the editors and authors. Readers of this book are recommended to bookmark it and contribute comments to them. I hope you will find it useful in your future research on webcasting.

REFERENCES

Accustream. (2004a). *iBroadcast stream report*. September 16, *4*(3).

Accustream. (2004b). *Accustream Research: Streaming advertising and subscription revenue forecast at $625 million in 2004*. Retrieved November 12, 2004, from http://www.accustreamresearch.com/news/june–12–04.html

Albers-Miller, N. D., & Gelb, B. (1996) Business advertising appeals as mirror of cultural dimensions: A study of eleven countries, *Journal of Advertising, 25*(4), 57–70.

Arampatzis, A. (2004). Online business models in Greece and the United Kingdom: A case of specialist versus generic and public versus privately owned online news media. *International Journal on Media Management, 6*(1&2), 88–101.

Bartussek, J. (2003). From newspaper to news filter. In A. Vizjak & M. Ringlstetter (Eds.), *Media management: Leveraging content for profitable growth* (pp. 43–52). New York: Springer-Verlag.

Beach, A. (2003). Vlogging: Video weblogs. *WebReference Update*: March 6, 2003. Retrieved July 6, 2005 from http://www.Webreference.co/new/030306.html

Brown, E. (2006). Revenge of the dotcom poster boy. *Wired*, January, 116–118.

Chan-Olmsted, S., & Ha, L. (2003). Internet business models for broadcasters: How television stations perceive and integrate the internet. *Journal of Broadcasting and Electronic Media, 47*(4), 597–617.

Chang, B., Lee, S., & Lee, Y. (2004). Devising video distribution strategies via the internet: Focusing on economic properties of video products. *International Journal on Media Management*, 6(1&2), 36–45.

Cho, S., Byun, J., & Sung, M. (2003). Impact of the high-speed internet on user behaviors. Case study in Korea. *Internet Research: Electronic Networking Applications and Policy 13*, 49–60.

Chyi, H. I. (2005). Willingness to pay for online news: An empirical study on the viability of the subscription model. *Journal of Media Economics,18*(2), 131–43.

Fetscherin, M., & Knolmayer, G. (2004). Business models for content delivery: An empirical analysis of the newspaper and the magazine industry. *International Journal on Media Management*, 6(1&2), 4–11.

Green, H. (2004). Let a million videos bloom online. *Business Week*, December 29. Retrieved July 6, 2005 from http://www.businessweek.com/bwdaily/dnflash/dec2004/nf20041229_0845_db016.htm

Ha, L. (2003). Crossing offline and online media: A comparison of online advertising on TV web sites and online portals. *Journal of Interactive Advertising*. Retrieved April 10, 2005, from http://www.jiad.org/vol3/no2/ha/index.htm

Ha, L. (2004). Webcasting. In Hossein Bidgoli (Ed.), *Internet encyclopedia* (pp. 674–686). New York: John Wiley & Sons.

Ha, L., & Chan-Olmsted, S. (2002). Enhanced TV as brand extension: The economics and pragmatics of enhanced TV to cable TV network viewership. *A Magness Institute Research Report*. Retrieved April 30, 2005 from http://www.bgsu.edu/departments/tcom/faculty/ha/magness.pdf

Ha, L., & Ganahl, R. (2004). Webcasting business models of click-and-bricks and pure-play media: A comparative study of leading webcasters in South Korea and the United States. *International Journal on Media Management*, 6(1&2), 75–88.

Herrero, M. (2003). *Programming and direct viewer payment for television: The case of Canal Plus Spain*. Media markets monograph, University of Navarre. Pamplona, Spain.

Internet World Statistics. (2005). Retrieved October 29, 2005, from http://www.internetworldstats.com/

Kolo, C., & Vogt, P. (2004). Traditional media and their internet spin-offs: An exploratory study on key levers for online success and the impact of offline reach. *International Journal on Media Management*, 6(1&2), 23–35

Livingstone, S. (2003). on the challenges of cross-national comparative media research. *European Journal of Communication, 18*(4), 477–500.

McKinsey & Company (2002). Can broadband save online media? *McKinsey Quarterly*, June 2002. Retrieved March 13, 2005 from http://news.com.com/2009–1023–934441.html.

McGann, R. (2005). Entertainment leads content spending growth. *ClickZ Statistics*. Retrieved March 11, 2005 from http://www.clickz.com/stats/sectors/entertainment/article.php/ 3489161

Miles, P. (1998). *Internet world guide to webcasting: The complete guide to broadcasting on the web*. New York: Wiley.

Mings, M. S., & White, B. P. (2000). Profiting form online news: The search for viable business models. In B. Kahin & R. H. Varian (Eds.), *Internet publishing and beyond: The economics of digital information and intellectual property* (pp. 62–97). Cambridge, MA: MIT Press.

Noam, E., Groebel, J., & Gerbarg, D. (Eds.). (2004). *Internet television*. Mahwah, NJ: Erlbaum.

Ovum (2005). *International broadband market comparisons: Update June 2005. A report for the Department of Trade and Industry, United Kingdom*. Retrieved November 9, 2005 from http://www.dti.gov.uk/industries/telecoms/pdf/International_Broadband_Report_Q12005.pdf

Pagani, M. (1999). Interactive television: A model of analysis of business economics dynamics. *Proceeding of the Sixth Research Symposium on Emerging Electronic Markets* (pp. 5–30). Muenster, Germany, September 19–21.

Pastore, M. (2001, December 19). It's diversify or die for online media firms. *Cyberatlas*. Retrieved August 7, 2002, from http:///cyberatlas.internet.com/markets/advertising/article/0,,5641_ 943041,00.html

Picard, R. G. (2002). *The economics and financing of media companies*. New York: Fordham University Press.

Rao, B. (2001). Broadband innovation and the customer experience imperative. *International Journal of Media Management, 3*(11), 56–65.

Rogers, E. (1995). *Diffusion of innovations*. (4th ed.). New York, NY: Free Press.

Zanpour, F., Campos, V., Catalano, J., Chang, C., Cho, Y. C., Hoobyar, R., Jiang, S., Lin, M., Madrid, S., Scheideler, H., & Osborn, S. T. (1994). Global reach and local touch: Achieving cultural fitness in TV advertising. *Journal of Advertising Research, 5,* 35–63.

CHAPTER 2

Application of the ACR Framework in a 13-country Study of Leading Webcasters

Louisa Ha
Bowling Green State University

Chapter 1 provides an overview of the Accessibility-Content-Revenue (ACR) Framework to analyze the business models of emerging media. The essence of the framework is that the media market environment will determine what kind of webcaster types will be available. Different webcaster types will have different accessibility to audience through their transmission methods, usability features and other technical standards. They will also employ different content strategies. Content strategies and accessibility will in turn affect the diversity and type of revenue sources in webcasters' business models.

To test the robustness of the ACR Framework and examine the globalness of the webcast medium, a study was conducted to examine the business model practices of leading webcasters in 13 Asian, European, and North American countries that have a high number of broadband users. These countries are Australia, China, Canada, Germany, Greece, Hong Kong, Japan, the Netherlands, South Korea, Spain, Taiwan, the United Kingdom, and the United States. It is limited to leading webcasters because a random sample of webcasters may yield many hobbyists that do not have sustainable business goals at this nascent stage of the webcast industry's development. Also, leading webcasters serve as trend-setters and role-models for other industry newcomers. They represent the mainstream webcast industry and have much more impact on society than small webcasters.

IDENTIFICATION OF THE LEADING WEBCASTERS

The study employed the method of content analysis to identify the business models of leading webcasters. First we identified the leading webcasters in each country. It is impossible to achieve complete equivalence among the countries in sampling because the webcast industry development and web audience measurement research vary widely across countries. Hence, the authors use the informant method and interviewed the countries' experts in the webcast industry to select leading webcasters in each country. These sources include webcast association officers, editors of magazines on internet and streaming media, and authoritative web audience measurement research reports available in the various countries. Because of market size (population) differences, we allocated a larger sample (20) for Australia, China, Canada, Germany, Japan, South Korea, Taiwan, the United Kingdom, and the United States, and a smaller sample size (10) for the remaining countries. Thus, the sample consists of 220 leading webcasters.

Leading webcasters are defined in this study as the most popular web site services offering *publicly accessible* prepared audio or video contents for free or with payment. Webcasters can be categorized as one of the three types: Terrestrial clicks-and-bricks, pure-plays, and ISPs. Clicks-and bricks are terrestrial broadcasters that already have an offline TV or radio station/network and an additional service online, or established organizations with an online presence. An example of clicks-and-bricks is ESPN.com, which ESPN is a cable network and also operates a webcast service under the same name. Pure-plays are organizations that provide audio and or video services online with no other counterpart offline. An example of pure-plays is RealNetworks. Webcasters can also be internet service providers that offer their own audio and video content services in their internet service (ISPs) such as America Online (AOL).

There was no quota for each type of webcaster. The only criterion of selection is the perceived popularity of the webcasters based on the informants' knowledge or audience traffic measurements based on web audience research companies. The only exception is Comcast.net, a cable internet service provider in the United States, which ranked 10th in the Accustream's (2004) *iBroadcast* report in total video streams served. It was excluded in the study because its service is not accessible to all consumers. Only those residing in the Comcast service area have access to the service.

MEASUREMENTS

The coding scheme is based on Ha and Ganahl's (2004) study and adds other items including webcaster ownership and content origin. Categories were modified based on the input of native country collaborators to accommodate the idiosyncrasies of different markets. All research project participants used the same coding sheet except in countries where English fluency is low. In those countries, such as Japan, the instrument was translated by native co-researchers. All codes and definitions of the categories were given to the coders. For any uncertainty about the categories, a common explanation was given to all the co-researchers of the study at the same time to minimize discrepancies. Below is a description how each component of the ACR framework was measured in the study and how the coders determined the business model of the webcaster.

Accessibility

The accessibility of the webcast is measured by the type of file transmission method, file format used by the webcasters as shown on the website, and presence of usability features such as file size description, search engine, accommodation of different internet connection speeds and different media players, and the requirement of additional software to display the media content apart from media players. Please refer to the ACR Framework in Chapter 1 for further description of these accessibility features and their significance in the study of emerging media.

Content Strategies

According to the ACR framework, there are several types of content strategies used by media organizations. First is whether they have a variety or generalized content strategy that carry many different types of genres of programs, or a specialized content strategy that focuses on one or two types of program genres. Second is originality of the content. Programs can be classified as repurposed if they have been shown in other media outlets prior to the webcast. Programs that are produced exclusively or are first run on the web are original programs. If a webcast shows the program on the web at the same time as the showing of the program in other media outlets, then it is considered as simulcast. Third is the number of channels available in the webcast. A channel is an area with designated content of one genre in the webcast. The more channels a webcaster has, the more choices it offers to consumers.

The cost of content also makes a big difference in the content selected for the webcast. High cost content is usually content produced by large media companies with high production value such as blockbuster movies. Full-length content is also different from short video clips or highlights that are usually considered as cheap fare and less valuable by consumers. Another important content feature in webcasting is the presence of participatory features using interactive web applications such as voting, rating, opinion polls, online chats and messages boards.

Revenue Sources

Because the study includes both profit and non-profit webcasters, revenue sources are broadly defined as incomes that the webcaster can use to sustain or operate the webcast service. Revenue of a webcast can come directly from consumers such as pay-per-view or subscription of the webcast service. Revenue sources may also come from corporate funding or subsidy from the webcaster's parent company/offline counterpart. Syndication is the charging of other media or businesses for the use of the webcast content. E-commerce and advertising are revenues sources that do not charge consumers directly for the webcast service. In e-commerce, webcasters earn commissions or split the revenue with the product manufacturers from sales generated from the e-commerce of products sold on the website. In advertising, webcasters earn revenue from advertisers by offering advertising space and audience to advertisers. There are many other possible ways for a webcaster to generate revenue such as donation request, tip-jar, and other non-webcast related income such as consulting or software programming. In analyzing revenue strategies of webcasters, one should take into consideration that webcasters can choose a single revenue source or multiple revenue sources. The nature of the revenue sources can also vary from profit generation from the webcast content itself, or simply getting sufficient financial resources to run the operation such as government subsidy and corporate funding. The webcast operation may not be a profit center in itself.

Business Models: Content Aggregators and Branded Content

According to the ACR framework, webcasters generally adopt either a content aggregator model or a branded content business model. The content aggregator model works like a cable system operator with which the webcaster basically does not own any proprietary content. It only assembles and packages other suppliers' content. Many of these suppliers are networks or studios that are competing offline. The branded content model is characterized by proprietary content and a single media brand being featured on the webcast without any competitive media brand presence. Branded content webcasters can syndicate their content to other content aggregators. Hence in the analysis, when a webcast service offers a clear proprietary media brand and features only content aggregators that are syndicating its content and does not display content of other competitive media brands, it was coded as a branded content. A webcast service that carries many different channels or packages from a variety of sources without its own source was coded as content aggregator.

Coding

The coders were all native researchers of the country of study. They used high speed internet connection in their country to code the sites. Coding was conducted during the first two months of 2005. To assess coder-reliability, 20% of the sample

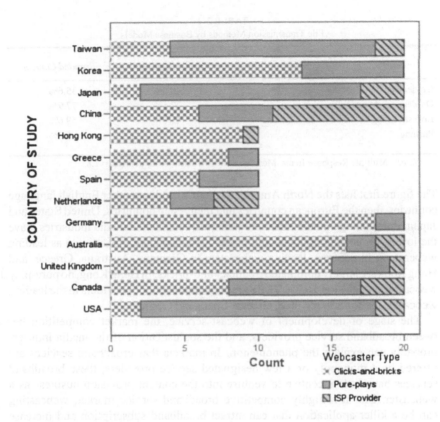

FIGURE 2–1   Profile of leading webcasters in this study.

were double-coded by another native coder. Perreault and Leigh's (1989) intercoder reliability coefficient (Ir) was used to compute the coder reliability and the overall reliability of all items is 0.91. For key variables such as webcaster type and ownership origin of webcaster, the reliability coefficient is 0.94. The reliability coefficient of business model is 0.82.

PROFILE OF WEBCASTER TYPES IN 13 COUNTRIES

All three types of webcasters—clicks-and-bricks, pure-plays, and ISPs, are present in the leading webcasters sample of the study. As shown in Figure 2–1, there is quite a different distribution of webcaster types among the countries' leading webcasters.

TABLE 2–1
File Transmission Methods by Business Models

	Content Aggregator	Branded Content
On-demand downloading	48.6%	35.6%
On-demand streaming	77.5%	77.9%
Live streaming	45.0%	59.6%
Pushing	8.1%	6.7%

Note: Multiple Response Items. Mean number of transmission methods = 1.8.

The figure first lists the North American countries and two other English language countries, then the European countries and then Asian countries. United States and Japan, the two large media exporters with well-established media industries, have the lowest proportion of clicks-and-bricks (or established institutions) as leading webcasters. In contrast, leading webcasters in Germany, Australia, Greece, and Hong Kong are largely dominated by clicks-and-bricks. In Hong Kong, no pure-play webcaster is on the top 10 list. There are no internet service providers in the leading webcaster list for South Korea, Greece, Spain and Germany.

The stage of development of webcast service, the market competition between broadband service providers, and the sophistication of the media industry probably can explain the phenomenon. In markets that broadband services are offered by a monopoly or a few designated service providers, these broadband services have little incentive to venture into the content provision business as a webcaster. But in a highly competitive broadband service market, webcasting can be a killer application that can attract broadband subscription and increase the loyalty of subscribers. ISPs can play an important role in providing the services. The bundling of the broadband internet connection service and webcast content services place them in an advantageous position in the webcast market.

ACCESSIBILITY OF LEADING WEBCASTERS

Leading webcasters in this study mostly employ multiple transmission methods. As shown in Table 2–1, on-demand streaming is the most commonly used file transmission method (78%), followed by live streaming (52%), and on-demand downloading (42%). Push is rarely used by webcasters (7%). The most common media player is Windows Media Player (58%), followed by RealPlayer (29%) and Apple Quicktime Player (7%). File formats clearly follow the media player preference. Windows Media Player-compatible formats ASF, WMA, WMV, WM, ASX, WAX, WVX, WMX, and WPL are the most commonly found file formats

TABLE 2–2
Usability and Technical Capability

	Content Aggregators $N = 111$	Branded Content $N = 109$
Presence of search engine and directories*	78.4%	63.8%
Text description of content with estimated file size	36.9%	36.2%
Have connection speed choice	44.1%	45.7%
No need to use additional software	67.6%	63.8%
Average number of media players accommodated	1.49	1.33
Presence of participatory content (such as video ratings, chat rooms)	60.4%	65.7%

*$p < 0.01$

(44%), followed by RealPlayer-compatible formats of RA, RAM, and RM (21%), WMP (15%), and MP3 (12%). (See Table 2–2.)

The ACR framework predicts higher usability among content aggregators than branded content. If usability is measured by the presence of search engines or directories that facilitate users' navigation and location of content, then content aggregators are indeed more user-friendly because 78% of content aggregators have search engines, while only 63% of branded content have search engines or directories. However, if usability is measured by other dimensions such as provisions of file size and description to users, the elimination of additional software installation to display the content, the availability of connection speed choices, the accommodation of multiple media players, and the presence of participatory content, then there is no significant difference in usability between content aggregators and branded content webcasters. Almost 70% of both business model users do not require their users to install additional software to display their content. Slightly less than one half of the leading webcasters accommodate users' different internet connection speeds. Most of the webcasters try to accommodate more than one media player. On average, they supported 1.4 media players.

CONTENT STRATEGIES OF LEADING WEBCASTERS

Ha and Ganahl (2004)'s taxonomy of content aggregators and branded content is applied to all webcasters in the sample. There are 111 content aggregators and 109 branded content business model users. The ACR framework predicts that clicks-and-bricks webcasters are more likely to adopt the branded content model. Table 2–3 demonstrates this prediction is supported as almost three quarters of the branded content model users are clicks-and-bricks webcasters. Pure-play webcasters and ISP webcasters are more likely to use the content aggregator

TABLE 2–3
Business Models by Type of Webcasters

	Content Aggregator $N = 111$	Branded Content $N = 109$
Clicks-and-Bricks	29.7%	72.4%
Pure-Plays	50.5%	23.8%
ISPs	19.8%	3.8%

Note. $\chi^2 = 41.9$; $df = 4$; $p < 0.01$.

model. Almost 70% of the content aggregator model users are either pure-plays or ISPs ($\chi^2 = 41.9$; $df = 4$; $p < 0.01$).

The ACR framework also predicts the difference in content strategies among different webcaster types. Clicks-and-bricks are expected to carry more high cost content and to be more focused in content genres than pure-play and ISP webcasters. They are also expected to be more likely to simulcast or repurpose their content than pure-play and ISP webcasters. Table 2–4 show mixed support for this prediction. More clicks-and-bricks (56%) do carry high cost content than pure-plays and ISPs (45%), but the difference is not statistically significant. All leading webcasters have similar strategies of providing a wide variety of program genres to the audience. Clicks-and-bricks score even higher in the number of program genres (mean = 7.8 genres) than pure-play and ISPs (mean = 6.2 genres). However, in terms of the number of channels, pure-play/ISP webcasters (mean = 16 channels) far outpaced clicks-and-bricks (mean = 6 channels). Overall, repurposed content is the primary source of content of all webcasters. Contrary to the ACR framework's prediction, clicks-and-bricks have a higher percentage of original content (23%) than pure-plays and ISPs (21%), but they have lower percentage of repurposed content (40%) than pure-plays and ISPs (50%). But consistent with the ACR framework, clicks-and-bricks have a significantly higher percentage of simulcast content (24%) than pure-plays and ISPs (15%).

The content features of the webcasters also illustrate the participatory culture of webcasting. More than 60% of all leading webcasters have some sort of participatory content features such as chat rooms, message boards, video ratings, and polls, etc. Many sites also encourage members to submit their own videos to be viewed by other site members.

Revenue Sources and Transmission Methods

Among the revenue sources, advertising is the most common among leading webcasters. As shown in Table 2–5, almost 70% of all leading webcasters have advertising as a revenue source. But it is not as dominant (90%+) as reported in

TABLE 2–4
Content Strategies by Webcaster Type

Source of Content	Clicks-and-Bricks N = 111	Pureplays/ISPs N = 109
Original	23.6%	21.5%
Repurpose*	40.3%	50.2%
Simulcast*	24.0%	15.4%
High cost content**	56.0%	45.0%
Average number of program genres*	7.8	6.2
Average number of channels*	5.6	15.6

*$p < 0.05$.
**Full-length movies, popular TV shows, sports, news.

other previous online media business model studies such as Ha and Ganahl (2004). E-commerce seems to be quite important as a revenue source for webcasters. Almost 40% of all leading webcasters support e-commerce on their sites. The products sold on the site are either media-related such as music or program download and the sale of the videos, or commercial products (both are present in 75% of all e-commerce sites). Subscription is the third most popular revenue source used by one third of the leading webcasters in the study.

The ACR framework also postulates a positive relationship between the number of transmission methods and the number of revenue sources. A bivariate regression of the number of transmission method on the number of revenue sources shows a significant positive relationship between the two ($r = 0.18$, $p < 0.01$). The ACR framework's prediction that more transmission methods will facilitate more diversification of revenue sources is supported. But it should be noted that the coefficient is not very high, indicating that there are other factors that influence the number of revenue sources of a webcaster such as the mission of the webcast (e.g., a public broadcast service), the role of the webcast in the media corporate business, and the expertise of the webcaster. Nevertheless, media companies that contemplate the creation of several revenue streams must consider increasing the accessibility of their service through a variety of transmission methods.

Globalness of the Webcast Medium

No webcaster achieves a leading position in more than six countries in this study. Only four webcasters are identified as leading transnational webcasters that rank as the top 10 of 20 webcasters in more than one country. These four are all U.S.-based webcasters. It should be noted that all transnational webcasters have their web sites' localized versions listed as the host countries' leading webcasters, not the U.S. version of their sites. Yahoo is the most transnational webcaster, rank-

TABLE 2–5
Revenue Sources by Business Model

	Content Aggregator N = 111	Branded Content N = 109	Total N = 220
Advertising	67.6%	72.4%	69.9%
E-commerce	40.5%	38.1%	39.4%
Subscription	37.8%	28.6%	33.3%
Pay-per-view	25.2%	14.3%	19.9%
Content syndication	12.6%	22.9%	17.6%
Tip-jar/Voluntary contributions	1.8%	3.8%	2.8%
Other (e.g., government/corporate funding)	12.6%	25.7%	19.0%

Note: Multiple Response Items. Mean number of revenue sources = 2.0

ing as the leading webcaster in six countries (United States, Canada, United Kingdom, Australia, Japan, and Taiwan).[1] Another most transnational webcaster is Microsoft Network (MSN). It is also ranked as the leading webcaster in also six countries (United States, United Kingdom, Germany, Japan, Taiwan and a joint venture in Australia, NINEMSN). America Online captures leading spots in only three English-language countries including the United States, Canada, and the United Kingdom. Real Networks ranks as a leading webcaster in both the United States and Japan.

Even though some transnational webcasters rank as leading webcasters in a foreign country, the majority of leading webcasters are still domestically owned webcasters. The data shows the domination of domestically owned webcasters and domestically produced content is consistent with the cultural discount theory.

Cultural discount is a media economic theory that posits the preference of local consumers for local media content (Hoskins & Mirus, 1988). Such cultural discount creates a barrier to foreign media's market entry. Only when the foreign media provides a much superior content that has no domestic media substitute will the foreign media earn a stronghold in the foreign market. In particular, if the domestic market is strong and big such as the United States, cultural discount acts an important market entry barrier to foreign media. Also domestically owned webcasters know the market demand better and should be able to offer more appealing content to the consumers. Therefore, in this cross-national study, even though the web can reach across the globe without much barrier, we expect that domestically owned webcasters and domestic content are likely to dominate

---

[1] Yahoo! just launched its webcast service in Hong Kong in December, 2005.

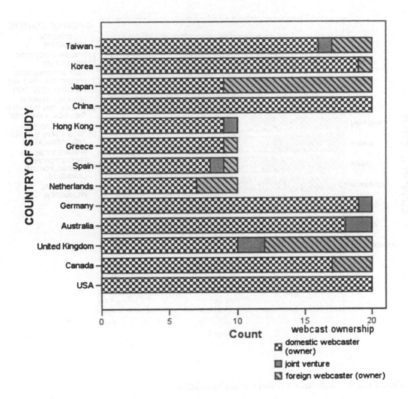

FIGURE 2–2   Webcast ownership origin by country.

among leading webcasters. Indeed, 82% of all leading webcasters are domestic webcasters. Almost 80 percent of all leading webcasters carry either solely or mostly domestically produced content.

Figure 2–2 shows the distribution by country of the country of origin of the webcaster owner. The cultural discount effect is most pronounced in large markets such as the United States and China where none of the leading webcasters are foreign webcasters or joint ventures with foreign webcasters. Australia and Germany, two other large markets, have no pure foreign webcasters on their leading webcaster rosters. Japan and the United Kingdom, both island countries, are the only two countries with almost half of their leading webcasters coming from foreign countries. But as noted earlier, the foreign webcasters in Japan have all localized their content to meet the needs of the Japanese consumers. In particular, many popular foreign webcasters in Japan offer adult Japanese made content that is not allowed on Japanese television. In the United Kingdom, all the

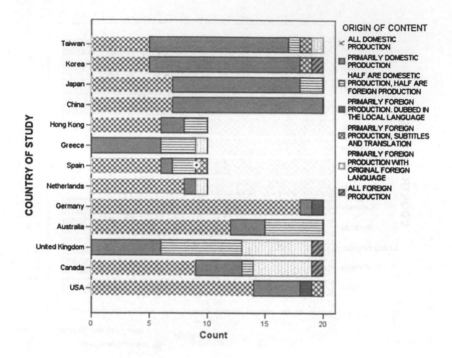

FIGURE 2–3   Webcaster's content origin by country.

leading foreign webcasters are major U.S. webcasters such as AOL, MSN, and Yahoo!.

Figure 2–3 compares the 13 countries' webcast content origins. Most webcast content originates in the native country. The pattern of content origin mirrors the pattern shown in the country comparison of webcaster origin. Webcast content in China is either primarily or only domestic content. Leading webcasters in Germany and Japan also employ primarily or purely domestic content. The United Kingdom is the only country that no leading webcaster uses solely domestically produced content. But still a majority of the British leading webcasters' content is still domestically produced content.

The business models of webcasters are compared by country in Figure 2–4. In general, the distribution between content aggregator models and branded content models is quite different among countries. The content aggregator model is the most prevalent among Japan's and Taiwan's leading webcasters. The branded

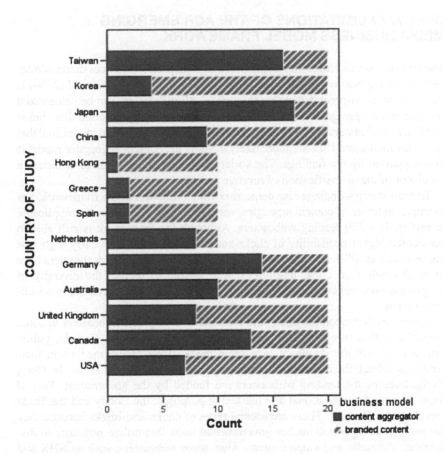

FIGURE 2-4   Webcast business models by country.

content model is the most dominant in Hong Kong, Greece, Spain, and South Korea. Such distribution difference can be mostly attributed to the nature of the webcaster. As mentioned earlier, bricks-and-clicks webcasters often employ the branded content model. Hong Kong, Greece, Spain, and South Korea are all countries that are dominated by bricks-and-clicks and almost no ISPs (except for Hong Kong which has a single ISP webcaster). Hence the business model is most likely to be branded content.

USES AND LIMITATIONS OF THE ACR EMERGING MEDIA BUSINESS MODEL FRAMEWORK

The findings of this 13 country-comparison of webcasters' practices demonstrates the webcasting business model framework proposed by Ha and Ganahl (2004) is quite robust in different market environments. All webcasters can be categorized by the content aggregator or branded content model. Their prediction that clicks-and-bricks webcasters are more likely to adopt the branded content model, and that pure-play media and ISPs are more likely to adopt the content aggregator model is also supported by the findings. The variety of transmission methods is indeed a facilitator of the diversification of revenue sources.

But this study's findings also demonstrate the limitation of the framework. For example, in terms of content strategies, some of its predictions are not applicable to this study's 220 leading webcasters. Although the framework is still able to predict the higher probability of clicks-and-bricks webcasters to carry high cost content such as full-length movies and sports, and that pure-play webcasters have more channels than clicks-and-bricks, it is unable to predict the diversity of program genres and similar proportion of original content between the two web-caster types.

One possible reason for this is the presence of non-profit webcasters in some countries within this study. In many European countries and Canada, public broadcast is still the dominant ownership mode of electronic media and their webcasts reflect their non-profit and diverse programming mission. In Hong Kong, three of the leading webcasters are funded by the government. Two of them webcast for educational and marketing purposes: the Edcity and the Trade Development Council. These are special types of clicks-and-bricks because they are not media organizations but governmental units that utilize webcasts to dis-seminate the audio and video content. Also, some webcasters, such as NHK and Anime Express in Japan, view their webcasts as a tool for self-promotion, a cus-tomer service, or an intelligence gateway of audience's feedback and informa-tion as discussed by Chan-Olmsted and Ha (2003). These webcasters may not directly apply a profit generation mode when devising their content strategies. Their decisions regarding content offerings are not based on bottom line consid-erations. Another possible explanation is that the increasing intensity of compe-tition for audience forces more clicks-and-bricks webcasters to diversify their webcast program genres to compete with pure-play media. For example, in the United States, the declining audience share of clicks-and-bricks webcasters has been documented by Accustream's (2003) streaming traffic report. The report shows that broadcast and cable TV brands used to capture 86% of the streams served by the top 10 sites in 2001, but their share fell to 5 percent in October 2003.

In general, all leading webcasters in this study offer a large selection of content to its web users through multiple program genres that are packaged into a variety of channels or playlists available on-demand. But identifying these many webcasters and locating the specific content is a challenge to consumers. Most leading webcasters address this problem with search engines and directories. Still one third of them do not provide site search tools.

There is a clear trend in the diversification of revenue sources by leading webcasters in this study. Webcasters are still searching for different ways to make their sites financially viable. Most webcasters use two or more revenue sources. Indirect consumer payment revenue sources such as advertising and electronic commerce are still the most popular choice. This reflects the webcasters' acknowledgement of the consumers' unwillingness to pay for webcast content. Revenue sources that are directly linked to media content such as subscription and pay-per-view are still moderately used. It is particularly interesting to note that apart from government or corporate funding, there are also many creative ways that webcasters generate revenue such as consulting and web hosting services. In light of the variety of revenue sources and the multiple revenue sources used by webcasters, business models based solely on revenue source type are inadequate to account for the complex revenue scheme of webcasters.

The presence of participatory content in most of the webcast services constitutes a distinct feature of the webcast medium, making it superior to the traditional broadcast medium. The encouragement of video submission such as iFilm and AOL makes the webcast medium an amateur producers' paradise, and will foster a new generation of producers with alternative and diversified viewpoints and style. Such participatory content or user-generated content can be the primary content of a leading webcaster such as Stupidvideos.com. It is a low-cost content strategy that can be highly profitable if it is the type of content that people like to share and contribute.

The difference in popularity of the branded content model and the content *aggregator* model across countries indicates that one model is more accepted than the other in different countries. Due to different broadband penetration levels, media production industry maturations, and technology gaps among webcasters, the development of the webcast industry varies greatly among the countries under this study. These are areas to be further explored as determinants of business models. Future research on business models of other emerging media such as digital video recorders and interactive television can apply the framework proposed by Ha and Ganahl (2004) with slight modification based on specific items such as specific content strategies. The emphasis of the interplay among the transmission method/technical standards (accessibility), content strategies, and revenue sources as components of emerging media business models will facilitate the tracking of the development of business models of emerging media.

Finally, this study also demonstrates the limitation of webcasting as a global medium. Despite the ease to achieve a global reach and the lack of license constraints or ownership requirements in most countries, webcasting is still primarily a domestic medium dominated by domestically owned webcasters offering domestically produced content. The study not only reaffirms the cultural discount theory, it also indicates that the "global" audience of a webcaster may concentrate among the peripheral groups of different countries, and not in the countries' mainstream.

Khiabany (2003) recognizes the economic forces in the internet and suggests that social relations among nation states and within nation states can determine how "globalized" the internet medium can become. Transnational media giants continue to expand their markets internationally in their localized webcast services. The only countervailing force is the local media giants in the host country. Search engines influence the ability of the consumers to locate webcast services. When sites are not placed in the top 10 or 20 listing, they are simply out of the picture.

Government regulation is another factor that will affect the globalness of webcasters in some countries. For example, in China, to set up online video and audio business, webcasters must obtain official approval from the governmental authorities, and only domestic webcasters are allowed access to the webcasting business. Hence future research that attempts to examine the globalness of the web medium in countries with ownership regulation must take both the cultural discount and the absence or presence of government regulations into consideration to better explain the country origins of media content and ownership.

ACKNOWLEDGMENTS

This chapter is a modification of a conference paper presented at the Communication Technology and Policy Division, Association for Education in Journalism and Mass Communication Annual Convention, San Antonio, Texas, August 10–12, 2005. The research team members of the project are Louisa Ha, Bowling Green State University; Richard Ganahl, Bloomsburg University; Alex Arampatzis, Edge Hill University College, United Kingdom; Ilhem Allagui, University of Montreal, Canada; Piet Bakker, University of Amsterdam, The Netherlands; Marylaine Chausse, University of Montreal, Canada; Baoguo Cui, Tsinghua University, China; Petar Djekic, University of Cologne, Germany; Mónica Herrero, University of Navarre, Spain; Kenichi Ishii, University of Tsukuba, Japan; Alice Lee, Hong Kong Baptist University; Yu-Li Liu, National Chengchi University, Taiwan; Claudia Loebbecke, University of Cologne, Germany; Claude Martin, University of Montreal, Canada; Hang Min, Jonkoping University, Sweden; Sora K. Park, Kwangwoon University, South Korea; Charo

Sádaba, University of Navarre, Spain; Clement So, Chinese University of Hong Kong; and Niranjala D. Weerakkody, Deakin University, Australia.

REFERENCES

Accustream. (2003). *Accustream research report shows declining market share for broadcast and cable TV networks as stand alone brands in streaming media.* Retrieved November 12, 2004 from http://www.Webcasters.org/news/20040219.htm

Chan-Olmsted, S., & Ha, L. (2003). Internet business models for broadcasters: How television stations perceive and integrate the internet. *Journal of Broadcasting and Electronic Media, 47*(4), 597–617.

Ha, L., & Ganahl, R. (2004). Webcasting business models of click-and-bricks and pure-play media: A comparative study of leading webcasters in South Korea and the United States. *International Journal on Media Management, 6*(1&2), 75–88.

Hoskins, C., & Mirus, R. (1988). Reasons for the U.S. dominance of the international trade in television programs. *Media, Culture & Society, 10*(4), 499–504.

Khiabany, G. (2003). Globalization and the internet: Myths and realities. *Trends in Communication, 11*(2), 137–153.

Perreault, W. D., Jr., & Leigh, L. E. (1989). Reliability of nominal data based on qualitative judgments. *Journal of Marketing Research, 26*(May) 135–148.

PART II

Webcasting Business Practices and Dynamics Across North America

CHAPTER 3

The United States: The Largest Broadband Market in the World

Louisa Ha
Bowling Green State University

WEBCASTING MARKET ENVIRONMENT

Media Industry Structure

The webcast industry in the United States grew from a very well developed media industry. The country is the largest exporter of electronic media in the world. A total of 150 countries show U.S. films and 125 countries broadcast U.S. television programs, generating $31 billion in export income (*Hollywood Reporter*, 2002; Motion Picture Association of America, 2005). The success of the U.S. media export industry is supported by its position as the largest domestic media market in the world. The media industry generated $689.8 billion in 2004, according to merchant bank Veronis Suhler Stevenson (2005).

The United States also leads in information communication technology (Albarran & Chan-Olmsted, 1998). Information communication technology (ICT) producing industries contributed 13% to real gross domestic product (GDP) growth in the United States in 2004, although they comprised just 4.2% of current-dollar GDP (U.S. Bureau of Economic Analysis, 2005).

The U.S. media industry is highly commercialized and primarily relies on advertising as the principal source of revenue. The total advertising spending in 2004 is $231 billion according to Kagan Media Research. Recently, pay television and radio services increased in importance with the rise of cable and satellite services. Indeed, 91 percent of TV households use multi-channel video services such as cable and direct broadcast satellite (National Association of Cable Television, 2005).

The electronic media industry is primarily based on a network-affiliate structure or chain ownership. Nationally, there are eight broadcast TV networks (including one non-profit PBS network), 390 national cable networks, two national

49

direct-to-home broadcast satellite television services (DirecTV and Dish Network), and two satellite national radio services (XM Radio and Sirius Radio). Locally, it hosts 8,875 cable systems, 1733 broadcast TV stations (most are either broadcast network affiliates or owned by broadcast TV networks), and 13,476 radio stations (about 7% are non-commercial radio stations). Fox is the largest TV station group with 35 stations and $2.3 billion in revenue in 2003. Clear Channel is the largest radio station group with 1,200 commercial radio stations (*Broadcasting and Cable Yearbook*, 2005). Already 1,491 local broadcast TV stations in 211 markets were broadcast in digital as of April 2005 (National Association of Broadcasters, 2005). A total of 900 feature-length films were produced in the United States in 2003, and there are about 36,000 movie screens (Motion Picture Association of America, 2005).

The webcasting industry in the United States is taking shape as there are at least three trade associations representing the industry's interest. The three industry associations are the International Webcasting Association (http://www.webcasters.org), the Digital Media Association (http://www.DiMA.org) and the Webcasters Alliance (http://www.webcasteralliance.com/). According to the 2003 estimates of Webcaster Alliance, there are about 25,000 webcasters in the United States, of which 10,000 are small commercial webcasters (Narancic, 2003).

Internet and Broadband Usage

As the country of origin, or the inventor of the internet, the U.S. has a population of 159 million internet users. According to 2004 Quarter 4 *World Broadband Statistics Report* released by Point Topics, Ltd., the country has the highest number of broadband lines in the world with 3.4 million broadband lines. The broadband industry in the U.S. is slightly dominated by cable service providers servicing 60% of broadband users (*ScreenPlays*, 2005). Cable modem users totaled 21 million by December 2004. But broadband service via DSL is growing at a much faster pace than cable broadband services (51% vs. 22% growth). According to the May 2005 survey of the Pew Internet & American Life Project, broadband users have grown to 33% of the U.S. households in 2005 (Horrigan, 2005). Nationally, almost 66 million internet users connect to the internet via broadband from home. According to the *April 2005 Bandwidth Report*, broadband's share in internet connection in the U.S. should exceed 70% by January of 2006 (Website Optimization, 2005). In some of the top markets such as San Diego and Phoenix, the percent of broadband connections within the local market is close to 70% (Nielsen/Netratings; *Internet Retailer,* 2004).

The latest Arbitron/Edison Media Research's study on internet and multimedia shows 81% of Americans have internet access (Rose & Lenski, 2005). About 20 million people listened to a web radio station or watched a video on the web in the past month in January 2005. The main reasons cited for listening to web radio were to get audio not available elsewhere, and to have full control of the music played by the station.

Broadband service providers are an important force in pushing the development of the webcast industry because attractive content is the key reason for users to subscribe to broadband. Since webcasts require high bandwidth to provide good quality audio and video, broadband service providers use webcast content to attract broadband subscribers.

The three largest cable companies (Comcast, Time Warner, and Cox) all offer portal services with webcasts to attract subscribers. Comcast works with a content aggregating and managing company to provide its proprietary webcast service to subscribers. Time Warner Cable utilizes its sister company America Online (AOL) as its portal. Its high-speed broadband connection Roadrunner service will offer AOL's broadband content services. Cox partners with its cable program suppliers such as Oxygen and America Movie Classics by linking subscribers to the network's video highlights. Meanwhile, the top three telephone companies that provide DSL services (SBC Communications, Verizon, and Bellsouth) all partner with online content service providers. SBC and Verizon have agreements with Yahoo! that utilize it as their DSL broadband subscribers' home page. Verizon also offers subscribers a link to MSN, another leading webcaster, in its broadband services (*ScreenPlays*, 2005).

Webcast Consumption

Consumer webcasting has become an industry of considerable size in the United States. Accustream forecasts (2004a) that webcasting subscription and advertising revenue will reach $864 million by 2005. Broadband users often use their high-speed connection to download video and music and watch or listen to webcasts. In 2001, broadcast and cable television networks were the leaders in webcasting, serving 86% of the video streams on the internet. But their domination in audience share quickly eroded to only 5 percent by 2003, excluding their services available on other sites such as RealNetworks (Accustream, 2004b). Music videos constitute the largest content viewing category in webcasting with an audience share of 34% at 5.6 billions streams in the first half of 2004. News videos and sports constitutes 19% and 16% respectively in webcast audience share (Accustream, 2004c).

Audience Research on Webcasting

In the U.S. there are four research firms that provide regular audience measurement for webcasters based on two different approaches. The first approach obtains data from a meter installed on a panel user's computer. The second approach obtains data from the webcaster's media server. The most well-known among the web audience measurement services is Nielsen's NetRatings. It reports the percentage of active internet users that use internet from home. NetRatings uses a panel of 40,000 to 50,000 people with installed software meters on their computers. These meters detect connection speeds. Each month they do an enumeration study to call a number of people to calibrate the panel by adjusting weightings to match the population at large. Because its reports focuses on unique users of all web sites including text-and-graphic only sites and non-media sites, rather than video or audio streams actually used by audiences, it is not used to identify the leading webcasters in this book chapter.

The second source of ratings is comScore Arbitron's online radio ratings service. The joint venture of comScore Media Metrix and Arbitron is a strategic alliance between a web audience measurement company with the radio ratings giant in the U.S. The rating is based on approximately 250,000 U.S. participants within the comScore consumer panel. Using proprietary technology, comScore passively and continuously captures the online behavior of its panelists, including online radio listening behavior. Currently it only reports audience ratings for its four webcaster subscribers: AOL, Yahoo, MSN and Live365. Hence it is far from representative of the whole webcast industry.

Webcast Metrics uses actual listener data gathered directly from webcasters' media servers to report actual usage. It limits its measurement to web Radio stations only. It attempts to replace Measurecast, a similar service bought out by Arbitron but discontinued in April 2004. Accustream, a research consulting firm specializing in streaming media, issues a monthly report called *iBroadcast Stream Report*. It tracks online audio and video streaming from the webcaster's server by site, network, aggregator, channel, and service. Its research also includes in-depth audience, market share, broadband, and narrowband streaming media consumption patterns, and total streams served.

To identify the leading webcasters in the U.S. for this book chapter, the author first consulted industry experts including Peggy Miles, the executive editor of *Digital Media* Magazine, President, Intevox communications, and Vice-Chair of the International Webcasting Association; Dave Gardy, current president of the International webcasting Association; Paul Palumbo, research director and founder of Accustream; and Kurt Hanson, the editor of *Radio on the Internet Newsletter*. While none of them can produce an authoritative list of leading webcasters, they all feel comfortable using either Accustream's or Ando Media's *Webcast Metrics* audience research reports. Based on these experts' recommendation, the author uses Ando Media's *Webcast Metrics's* top 10 rankings to select the leading radio webcasters, and Accustream's top 10 video sites in total number of streams as the sources for the leading webcasters. Accustream's radio ranking was not used because it reports by internet radio networks, not individual stations.

OWNERSHIP AND BUSINESS PERFORMANCE OF LEADING WEBCASTERS

Leading Video Webcasters

Among the 20 leading radio and video webcasters, only seven have parent companies that are publicly listed in the stock market. All other webcasters are privately owned and provide no business revenue data. Tables 3–1 and 3–2 summarize the profile of the 20 leading webcasters. Three of the top 10 video webcasters are owned by the computer software giant Microsoft: MSNBC, MSNVideo, and Windows Media. The other four publicly-listed webcasters are AOL, Yahoo, RealNetworks, and ESPN (owned by Disney/ABC). Well-funded and with deep-pockets, these seven publicly traded webcasters are the most popular webcasters. All of them provide both video services and radio or music services as well. The top ranked AOL is part of the Time Warner/AOL conglomerate. Until recently, AOL provided its own content services without Time Warner's content. It earned $1 billion in advertising revenue in 2004 in addition to revenue from its dial-up internet connection and broadband content services (Oser, 2005). It offers 12 TV channels on TV AOL, and 200 Radio Channels on Radio@AOL. In addition, there are premium contents such as live concerts on its AOL Broadband.

Yahoo! is considered the most successful portal in the U.S. with online advertising support. Its U.S. revenue in the first quarter of 2005 was $819 million with a vast majority of revenue coming from advertising. To boost partnership with the film and television industries, Yahoo formed an entertainment group headed by former ABC TV network executive Lloyd Braun (Shields, 2005). Its webcast service, Yahoo! Launchcast, offers 283 radio stations and thousands of music videos. Users can customize their selection by genres and artists. They are asked to rate songs and music videos that are webcast on the site. The basic Yahoo Launch service is free. But if users want to find more specialized genres and commercial-free internet radio stations such as children's radio station, then users must subscribe to Launchcast plus for $2.99 a month. To avoid abuse by heavy users, Yahoo! set a limit of 800 songs that users can stream for free. Free videos are also accompanied with pop-up commercials at the beginning.

Leading webcaster RealNetworks's first quarter revenue in 2005 was $76.6 million, representing a 27% growth over the previous year. RealNetworks reported it has more than one million subscribers to its premium subscription music services, including its Rhapsody service and commercial-free internet radio services. RealNetworks also partners with Comcast, who provides RealNetwork's music services to its broadband subscribers. Under the agreement, the subscription download feature will be added to Real's existing Rhapsody

TABLE 3–1
Top 10 Video Webcasters Profile

Webcaster	Parent Company	Type	Streams (in 000s)	Unique Users (in 000s)	Revenue ('04)	Ownership	Business Model
1. America Online	AOL/TimeWarner	ISP	292,000	9,200	8.7 billion	Public	CA
2. Yahoo Launch	Yahoo!	PP	250,000	10,792*	3.6 billion	Public	CA
3. RealNetworks	RealNetworks	PP	146,000	1,450	267.0 million	Public	CA
4. MSN Video	Microsoft	PP	43,705	5,203	892.0 million	Public	CA
5. ESPN	Disney	CB	34,865	15,159*	n/a	Public	BC
6. Stupidvideos	Stupid Videos	PP	25,600	1,957	n/a	Private	BC
7. MSNBC	Microsoft/NBC	CB	24,309	20,601	n/a	Public	CA
8. Windows Media	Microsoft	PP	17,712	24,263	n/a	Public	CA
9. iFilm**	iFilm	PP	17,619	1,741	n/a	Private	CA
10. AtomFilm	AtomShockwave	PP	3,000	448	n/a	Private	BC

Note. ISP: Internet Service Provider; PP: Pure-Play; CB: Click-and-Brick; CA: Content Aggregator; BC: Branded Content.

*Unique User Number based on Nielsen Netratings.

**Data in this table dates from when iFilm was a private company (prior to October 20005).

Source: Rankings based on Accustream's *iBroadcast Stream Report, IV*, for the month of June 2004.

TABLE 3–2
Top 10 U.S. Audio Webcasters Profile

Webcaster	Parent Company	Type	Audience (AQH)*	Revenue	Ownership	Business Model
Digitally Imported—di.fm0	Digitally Imported	PP	18,481	n/a	Private	BC
AccuRadio.com	AccuRadio	PP	10,033	n/a	Private	BC
RadioIO.com	RadioIO	PP	5,119	n/a	Private	BC
EnergyRadio.fm	Energy Radio	PP	2,317	n/a	Private	BC
BoomerRadio.com	Boomer Radio	PP	2,215	n/a	Private	BC
Beethoven.com	Martin Broadcasting, LLC	PP	1,758	n/a	Private	BC
3WK.com	3WK	PP	1,295	n/a	Private	BC
90sFM.net	Big R Multimedia, LLC	PP	1,224	n/a	Private	BC
WolfFM.com	Wolf FM	PP	1,196	n/a	Private	BC
80sFM.com	Big R Multimedia, LLC	PP	894	n/a	Private	BC

Note. AQH: The average number of persons who listened to a station for a minimum of five minutes within a reported day part (This number is the average of the number of listeners recorded every fifteen minutes for each station monitored by the Webcast Metrics heartbeat, or it is the number derived from the total time spentlistening data obtained by Webcast Metrics directly from station server log data); ISP: Internet Service Provider; PP: Pure-Play; CB: Click-and-Brick; CA: Content Aggregator; BC: Branded Content.

Source: Ranking based on Ando Media's *Webcast Metrics Report*, November 2004.

streaming music service. For $14.95 per month, customers are able to download songs and transfer them to compatible MP3 music players. Those songs remain available to customers while they maintain their subscriptions.

As a unit of Microsoft, MSN's focus is more technological than content. Jupiter Research's analyst Joe Wilcox points out that "Microsoft's portal strategy is really about selling Microsoft technology," and "Microsoft leverages its own technology to deliver a content and service. MSN Video produces content related to ads, but at the same time the content showcases the technology because it's Microsoft technology" (Oser, 2005).

On the MSN Video site, consumers get free access to all of its content. They can create their own play list from content in the news, business, technology, sports, entertainment, house, and home within MSN Video categories. They are also obligated to watch one ad for every two content clips. There is no way to click out of the ad if they want to see the content. Essentially, MSNBC's webcast is part of MSN video. MSN portal has content agreements with Fox Sports, MSNBC, CNBC, and Discovery Networks to provide content. Ads provide a large portion of MSN's revenue. For the second fiscal quarter of 2005, for instance, ad revenue grew 17%, or $49 million on a total MSN revenue of $588 million. In March 2005, MSN boosted its branded-entertainment capabilities by renaming its custom-publishing division as the branded-entertainment experiences team. It doubled the unit's staff, increased its budget and announced that it would focus more on entertainment content (Oser, 2005).

Windows Media is the default link for Microsoft Windows computer users. It has five video channels and 11 radio channels. It carries BBC radio news and all types of music. Videos on Windows Media are primarily movie trailers and music videos. It positions itself more as a portal or media guide to webcast content around the world than an original or branded content service provider.

ESPN.com is one of the few clicks-and-bricks leading webcasters that also has a strong offline media counterpart-the ESPN cable network. Its web site has departmentalized news by sports and users can customize their content by using "My ESPN." It is the only leading webcaster that charges per use, or by game such as College Basketball. ESPN Motion provides users with crystal-clear instant-on video right inside the ESPN.com front page without streaming. Every time new ESPN Motion video is published out to ESPN's servers, the ESPN Motion component on the user's computer will automatically go out and fetch the newest video and store it in a temporary location on the user's hard drive. When a new video has been downloaded and is ready to view, the ESPN Motion video will start playing automatically whenever the ESPN front page is opened or the E icon is clicked on the user's task bar. According to the online media marketing and advertising magazine *OMMA*, EPSN Motion already has 1.5 million registered users (Smith, 2005).

Among the various independent leading private video webcasters, iFILM offers channels of movie trailers, short films, TV clips such as Superbowl commercials, video-game trailers, music videos, action sports, and the Viral Videos collection which is contributed by its members. According to iFILM.com, it delivers more than 30 million streams per month. Users can choose the free low-speed ad-supported iFilm service, or iFilm plus, which is commercial free with high speed streaming. Users of the free service will see primarily movie trailers and many pop-up ads, which are mainly movie promotions, rather than watching original movie content. Through its distribution partners, including RealNetworks, WindowsMedia, MovieWeb, Rotten Tomatoes, Starpulse and AskMen, the iFilmNetwork reaches more than 20 million visitors per month. The company is based in Hollywood, California. In October 2005, iFilm was acquired by Viacom International, Inc., and is now part of the MTV Networks.

AtomFilm is an online video service for original short-form. It offers on-demand viewing of a diverse and distinguished catalog of more than 1,000 shorts in every genre. The company is based in San Francisco, California. Its AtomFilms To Go section offers users high-quality downloads in a format that can be used in portable devices such as PSP, iPod, and laptops. It has seven genre channels and a spotlight channel. Each channel has 7 to 8 categories with 20 plus videos in each category.

Stupidvideos.com, based in Oceanside, California, has the lowest professional program quality among all leading video webcasters. Yet it sells on the single concept of stupid videos that are contributed by its members. Ads dominate the web pages, and the selection of videos is very limited. Membership cost is only $0.99 per month. As a member, users can enjoy higher quality videos and download the videos of their choice and create video postcards using the videos. The videos are also commercial free.

Leading Internet Radio Stations (Audio Webcasters)

Including AOL@Radio, Yahoo Launchcast, and MSN Radio, Accustream (2003) estimates that the top 10 internet radio sites and networks captures almost 85% of the total market. In general, the web radio market is very fragmented outside the big 10. The top 10 internet radio stations are all pure-plays that have no offline counterparts.

Digitally Imported is a multi-channel internet radio service specializing in electronic dance music genres. It fills a global niche for this type of music. All of its channels are offered in two streaming formats: MP3 and Windows Media. While it is the top commercial internet radio station, its financial condition is not good according to the station. On its web site, it states that the station's employees are all volunteers and its bandwidth is donated by companies and fans.

AccuRadio is a multichannel internet radio station specifically designed to showcase the potential of internet radio for adults with sophisticated musical tastes. The station's web site claims to reach over 1,000,000 listeners per month (as many as a large New York City radio station), with an audience of over 12,000 simultaneous listeners on weekdays during business hours. It is the only U.S. based leading internet radio station that offers more than one language in its webcast. Its Chinese version caters to the audiences in China. Its strong international orientation is reflected in its featuring of foreign record labels and artists. AccuRadio is also a perfect example of how online media can partner with the music recording industry. It explicitly helps record companies and recording artists sell records by: (1) giving exposure and airplay to numerous genres of music and hundreds of artists that virtually never receive broadcast radio airplay; (2) constantly displaying the title, artist and album name while the song is playing; (3) displaying the CD covers of the last three songs played, with each cover linking to the appropriate Amazon (the largest e-tailer) web page for purchase; and (4) selling almost $40,000 worth of CDs per month through its Amazon links. By streaming the music at only 32 kbps (not a quality level comparable to CDs), it encourages sampling of the music online and CD ownership. It also reports using e-mail marketing to its 850,000-person mailing list for various record labels.

RadioIO is an internet-only radio from St. Augustine, Florida. It offers multiple music genres for free and for members-only in multiple formats and multiple bandwidths, including MP3. Its package service ranges from AM quality (Silver), FM quality (Gold) to CD quality (Platinum) with a monthly fee of $2.99 to $9.99. Its free version contains many banner ads and paid text links. Users must turn off their ad blocker to listen to the free streams that are filled with advertisements. It is a highly commercialized radio station with very little information on file size or the artists.

EnergyRadio is also an internet-only network featuring eight channels: 80s and 90s, dance, club, jazz, smooth jazz, energy X, chillout lounge, and Bombaybeat.fm. The station offers short video clips in its Funnies section, in addition to its professional quality radio programs. It posts audience statistics on its site and emphasizes entertainment news and events in cities. It is also highly commercialized with many advertisements on its home page.

Boomer Radio was launched to bring baby boomers, now in their 50s and 60s, the best music from the past, as well as a variety of program channels that appeal to their current lifestyles because terrestrial radio stations are focusing on younger audiences and ignoring this largest and most affluent consumer group. More than 20 musical genres are offered. Its future plans include the addition of news, talk and sports programming. The station offers a wide song selection and information on the music and file size. Yet it is in preliminary stages of development as it is still searching for investors through its web site.

Beethoven.com is an internet radio station owned and operated by Marlin Broadcasting, LLC, which is a private terrestrial radio company. The internet radio offers 24/7 contemporary classical music programming hosted by on-air personalities. It contains typical radio station content such as live requests, listener contests and specialty shows. In addition, it provides detailed information on the current and past playlists. The station also provides cultural information, classical music news and shopping tailored to the style and taste of the classical music lover.

3WK is a privately-held internet radio company based in St. Louis, Missouri. It claims to be an underground radio station focusing on rock and indies. It is a pure radio station without other information non-related to its webcast. It features two radio channels: Underground radio and Classic Underground. In addition to low quality free streams, it provides a high quality 128K streams and free song downloads for $10 a month. The station also requests donations and it sells station-related merchandise.

Wolf FM is located in Nashville, Tennessee. It webcasts the "hottest mix" of 70s, 80s, and current hits. The internet radio station was founded and is programmed and managed by Steve Wolf, an experienced broadcaster. Wolf is blind and runs and manages Wolf FM using sophisticated voice-enabled software for operating a computer. It offers free low definition radio, and high definition radio for $5 a month. The station focuses on songs. Although it has a static web camera displaying the studio, it does not add much value to the station.

80s FM and 90s FM both are owned by the internet radio group, Big R Multimedia Company, which is headquartered in Mill Creek, Washington. The company currently owns 11 internet radio domains, of which six are in operation including 80s FM, 80s Metal FM, 90s FM, Grundge FM, Jazz FM and the Edge FM. It plans to launch an online Country FM station and Top 40 FM station in 2005. Rick White, the founder and president, started the Big R Multimedia in November 2003 with one internet radio station (the Edge FM). His initial intent was to create a radio station where great "unsigned bands" could be aired on par with the "signed bands" (personal communication, April 25, 2005). This concept had never been tried by any terrestrial stations. This unique type of programming was a huge success. He decided to create other stations with similar concepts that focus on programming neglected by the local radio stations.

WEBCASTING BUSINESS MODELS

Among the top 20 webcasters identified in this chapter, 16 are pure-play native internet media brands that have no offline media counterparts. Two are internet Service Providers (AOL and MSN) and two are clicks and bricks (ESPN and MSNBC). All of the leading webcasters are based in the United States and fully-owned by U.S. companies/individuals. Inheriting the commercial media tradition in the United States, all leading webcasters are commercial webcasters even though few report making profits. Branded content is the most common business model used by U.S. leading webcasters. Thirteen of the 20 leading webcasters have their own branded content that is distinct to their media brand. However, the seven content aggregators in the leading webcasters roster are all high profile, large webcasters. All except one is publicly listed, well-funded and reportedly making profits. The following is an analysis of the three components of the business models of the 20 leading webcasters: accessibility, content strategies, and revenue sources based on Ha and Ganahl's (2004) online media business model framework.

Accessibility

Among the 20 leading U.S. webcasters examined in the study, a majority of the webcasters (65%) use only one transmission method. About a third employ two transmission methods. Only one uses three transmission methods. Live streaming is the most popular transmission method used by radio webcasters. About 55% use on-demand streaming method, 10% use on-demand downloading. In addition to the video or audio shown on their websites, many webcasters have additional features that take advantage of the interactivity of the internet. For example, 40% of the webcasts have chat room or message boards, 30% have interactive games, 55% have other participatory features such as video or playlist rating or opinion polls.

We can measure usability of the webcasters from several aspects. First is the internet connection speed accommodation. About one half of the webcasters offer more than one choice of internet connection speed to consumers. Only two of the leading webcasters offer three or more choices of internet connection speed. Second is the media player. Most of the webcasters (65%) offer webcasts that can be played only on one media player. Windows Media Player is used by 85% of the webcasters. RealPlayer is used by 40% of the leading webcasters. Apple Quicktime Player is used only by three of the leading webcasters. Third is the requirement of additional software installation. A majority of the webcasters (70%) do not require any additional software to view or listen to the webcast apart from the media player. Fourth is the text description of program content and file size information. Only one half of the leading webcasters provide such information on their sites. Fifth is the presence of search engine or directory to facilitate users to locate the content. Sixty percent of the leading webcasters provide such service. Those that do not provide such services offer live streaming on a fixed schedule and users can only listen in real time to the webcast.

TABLE 3–3
Media Content Sources

	Top 10 Video Webcasters	Top 10 Radio Webcasters	Total
Original	26%	0%	13%
Repurpsoed	52%	0%	26%
Simulcast	15%	100%	57%
Unknown	7%	0%	4%

Content Strategies

Very few U.S. leading webcasters have original content that is not shown by other media. On average, 25% of the webcasters' content is original, and 52% of their content is repurposed and shown previously somewhere else. All radio webcasters simulcast their content by showing their programs live on a schedule. (See Table 3–3.)

TABLE 3–4
Program Genres of Leading Webcasters

Video

Blockbuster movies	1 (5%)
TV commercials	1 (8.3%)
TV programs (entertainment)	1 (4.2%)
Education/instruction	1 (8.3%)
Trailers/highlights	8 (40%)
Business (business news/speech/conference)	4 (20%)
News clips/interviews (non-business)	4 (20%)
Music videos	6 (30%)
Documentaries	2 (10%)
Cartoons/animation	3 (15%)
Sports	4 (20%)
Pornography (adult content)	2 (10%)
Other	4 (20%)

Audio

Music	15 (75%)
News	4 (20%)
Talk/Speech/Interview	1 (5%)
Sports	2 (10%)
Other	1 (5%)

In terms of content strategies, three quarters of the leading webcasters chose a specialized content strategy by providing only one or two program genres. The conservation of bandwidth is evident as most offer only short clips or live streaming. The median number of channels offered by each webcaster is 7.5 ranging from a single channel to 283 channels. Among the two that do not have any channels, they offer 830 and 1100 video clips respectively. Those that have multiple channels usually show one program at a time if they use live streaming. All the internet radio webcasters broadcast content live, and no radio webcaster offers any other transmission method. Generally, video webcasters have a higher variety of transmission methods than radio webcasters, and offer both original content and repurposed content, and even simulcast programs live. (See Table 3–4.)

Revenue Sources

Few webcasters rely on a single revenue source. On average, leading webcasters have two revenue sources. Only 30% of them have one revenue source. Ten percent of the sites have four revenue sources. Hence, webcasters are trying to experiment with different revenue sources.

Advertising is still the most popular revenue source for U.S. webcasters. Among the free webcasts, 90% have advertising. E-commerce is the second most popular revenue source with 60% offering e-commerce on their sites. Subscription is moderately used by 35% of the webcasters. Only one webcaster has pay-per-view as a revenue source and one webcaster uses content syndication. Even though all are commercial webcasters, two seek listeners' donations. One webcaster has consulting as an additional revenue source.

Among those eight webcasters that charge by subscription or pay per view, all package their services in varying tiers. RealNetworks offers a monthly pass for its subscribers. Subscription are usually charged monthly, except one that uses a quarterly subscription fee. The monthly subscription fee ranges from $1 to $24.95. Credit card is the most common accepted form of payment used. Paypal, the online payment service, is adopted by five smaller webcasters. Usually the webcaster directly collects the payment from the users instead of going through the ISP service providers. Webcasters generally respond to consumers' concern about privacy online. Only three of the 20 leading webcasters collect information about the users during registration. Only the user's name and address are collected, and not demographic or psychographic information.

Among 12 leading webcasters who offer e-commerce opportunities, two-thirds of them offered products that are media-related such as videos, DVDs, and CD albums purchase or download, a quarter offer licensed merchandise, and only three offer commercial products with no relation to media content or entertainment.

INTERNATIONAL INFLUENCE

The cultural discount phenomenon is most pronounced in the United States. As Doyle (2002) explains, the U.S. is a large domestic market that enjoys all the advantages its market size provides for the benefit of exports. In the webcast industry, the U.S. also relies primarily on domestically produced content. Nearly all of the webcasters (90%) have only domestically produced, or primarily domestically produced, content. The two webcasters that have some foreign content primarily import from the United Kingdom, another English-speaking country. The occasional presence of other countries can be found only on the classical internet music station Beethoven.com, and webcasters featuring movie trailers such as ATOM film or iFilm. But none of the foreign countries constitute a major presence in any of the leading webcasters. Hence the influence of other countries on webcasts in the U.S. is almost negligible. In essence, mainstream webcast programming is designed primarily for domestic consumption.

OUTLOOK OF THE WEBCAST INDUSTRY

Broadband service providers will increasingly play an important role in the development of webcasting because it is one of the "killer" applications that will encourage people to subscribe to broadband. There is also a clear trend of traditional media providing content to the webcasters. But a reciprocal trend is also emerging where more original content is developed by the webcaster. The proven success of webispodes demonstrates that content can migrate to traditional media such as AOL's licensed Princess Natasha webipsodes to the Cartoon Network (Davis, 2005). Competition between clicks-and-bricks and pure-play webcasters is intensifying. Already most of the click-and-bricks have lost their earlier leadership in webcast consumption. Clear Channel, the leading radio station group owning 1,200 stations in the U.S., discovered it lags behind in the internet radio, and hopes to boost its advertising sales in both offline and online radio by offering original online video programming for 200 of its stations' web sites (Reuters, 2005). Currently, webcast is mostly an alternative medium for consumers who look for things they miss on-air and that are not available on air, or to be in more control of their media consumption (Rose & Lenski, 2005). But as young people spend more time online than other media, and are equipped with the convenience of broadband, webcasting can build a solid audience base that can attract advertising or obtain sufficient subscription revenue.

There are still different views on the business viability of consumer webcasting. Webcasting industry insiders show optimism in the growth of the industry. Paul Palumbo, founder and research director at Accustream Research, believes that the U.S. webcast industry is growing by leaps and bounds, and that broadband is driving users' consumption of webcasting (personal communication, November 30, 2004). Content is distributed at a higher bit rate with the increasing broadband usage, and webcasters are finding new ways to make money on the streams. His company forecasts the U.S. webcast industry (including streaming download media) to reach $2 billion by 2006 (Accustream, 2005).

Dave Gardy, president of TV Worldwide and the current president of the International Webcasting Association also concurs that the webcasting industry is booming and is driven by the growth in broadband penetration (personal communication, January 6, 2005). Apart from mass webcasting, he believes in "aimcasting" at niche markets such as the maritime TV (www.maritimeTV.com) for the maritime industry, or his own company TV Worldwide that serves special industry sections, and in using the webcast technology to serve the disabled such as Internet TV for Assistive Technology (www.at508.com). He also believes that an important trend is emerging in the webcast industry that combines webcasts and web conferencing that allow up to 1,000 people to watch 10 people talk to each other in a webcast.

Peggy Miles, Vice-Chair of the International Webcasting Association and a webcast consultant (personal communication, December 1, 2004), notes that there is increased growth in all sectors of webcasting after the settlement on royalty fees by the Small Webcasters Settlement Bill. She asserts that integration of technologies will change the webcasting landscape with more and more outlets for webcasting services. For example, the integration of cellular phone technology and voice over internet Protocol (VOIP), increased connections with interactive TV, and TV, and other internet networks.

Integration with games and toys is another trend that webcasters can utilize. Integration with interactive programming guides or electronic programming guide (IPG/EPG) opens up the access of webcast to the TV audiences. Another development is the increasing webcast portability as a result of transporting the webcast to any screen in the house with new technologies. Children are increasingly using the technology on portable devices such as portable media centers and other non-PC static location devices.

In addition, the industry is testing and refining different advertising models. Advertisers are increasing their investment on the web. Advertising spaces in major news webcasts such as ABC, CNN, and MSNBC are often sold out. Other technological developments such as advanced tracking will increase accountability to the advertisers. Production Software and DAM, MAM, and content management systems are increasingly user-friendly and can facilitate the offering of webcast services. Webcast is also seen as useful for educational and health care institutions. Finally, the location of webcast services and content is easier to find with video search services offered by the large search engines such as Google and Yahoo! and specialized audio video search services such as Singing Fish.

To Kurt Hanson, Editor of *Radio and the Internet Newsletter* and Founder/CEO of AccuRadio, internet radio listenership is growing tremendously because bandwidth prices continue to drop and advertising revenues continue to increase (personal communication, December 31, 2004). Advertisers are starting to experiment with the medium. Ronning-Lipset Radio and Net Radio Sales are advertising representatives for many internet radio stations. Webcasters are seeing a variety of revenue streams. Terrestrial radio stations are again streaming on the web, after a cutback several years ago. "My impression is that most terrestrial broadcast groups are NOT making significant internet-only efforts (where the vast majority of the consumer interest is)," said Hanson regarding the traditional media's fear of cannibalization by webcasting. "As wireless broadband internet access becomes ubiquitous (3G networks, WiFi, WiMax, etc.) and more consumer devices (cell phones, PDAs, MP3 players), I believe the audience for internet radio will continue to grow—in fact, at an increasing rate, continuing to stay ahead of, and perhaps eventually supplant, satellite radio."

Hanson's optimistic view of internet radio is echoed by another webcast entrepreneur, Rick White of Big R Multimedia (personal communication, April 26, 2005). As he sees it, the terrestrial radio station counterparts such as Clear Channel and Infinity Broadcasting are also spending millions of dollars to catch up with internet Radio. In his opinion, local radio stations have seen a huge decrease in listeners during the last year. In order to regain the listeners and the advertising, the entry of terrestrial radio into internet broadcasting seems to be inevitable, and their presence will stimulate another round of competition. Pure-play internet-only radio stations and content aggregators must find their own niche to continue their stronghold in consumer webcasting.

Although the U.S. lags behind 10 other countries in terms of broadband penetration, it has a huge potential for growth in webcasting. First, it has the largest number of broadband lines and fiber optic in place that can provide broadband services. Second, the development of WiMax wireless communication will allow the national provision of broadband services to 98% of the population at a low cost of $3 billion (Lacy, 2005).

Increasing partnerships between webcasters and terrestrial broadcasters is evident. Yahoo! is stepping up its entertainment content with the appointment of a Hollywood veteran as its content chief, and the hosting of reality shows with video footage from behind the scenes such as *The Apprentice* (Kopytoff, 2004). America Online, in its new version to be launched this summer, will partner with XM satellite radio service to strengthen the radio offerings to its premium service subscribers with XM satellite radio that offers AOL content reciprocally (Online Reporter, 2005).

Among the harshest critics of webcasting's future are the owners of big electronic media. Many media executives are afraid of webcasting's cannibalization of audience and advertising revenue from their stations or networks. They see webcasting as giving money away to audiences rather than providing monetary returns to the stations. Many networks still view their text-and-graphics only web sites or their webcasts as tools of self-promotion rather than true media content services (Ha, 2003). Yet they must also face the reality that U.S. teenagers and young adults spend more hours on the internet than watching TV (16.7 hours vs. 13.5 hours) according to a study in 2003 (Greenspan, 2003). In order to keep the younger audience, traditional media cannot neglect the web. Forrester Research (Bernoff, 2005) predicts that web videos are going to be the most common web media experience of consumers and take over the role of text in the medium.

The leading webcasters examined in this chapter are all trying to educate consumers that high quality media content is not free. To receive ad-free content, one must pay for the premium service through subscription, membership or pay-per-view. Some webcasters are also pushing the limits of the technology by introducing high definition, DVD quality video or CD quality radio content. Such cutting edge services come at a higher price that consumers may or may not accept. At the moment, all leading webcasters are concerned with saving the bandwidth and webcast only short video clips instead full-length materials. When broadband becomes ubiquitous, content strategies of webcasters will move toward materials that users want most or that are either not available on air or available only on demand. The general lack of international content and the domestic market orientation among leading U.S. webcasters indicate that these webcasters believe that American users still prefer content from their own country, rather than unfamiliar foreign materials. It is now up to webcasters to develop innovative programming concepts. Webcasters must be able to offer something that is different or better than traditional media. The market probably cannot have too many large content aggregators because consumers will only focus on a few large ones such as Yahoo! for one-stop services. Consumers will seek for alternative branded content to satisfy their needs and interests. The success of the business model used by StupidVideos that creates a unique brand of "stupid" content based on the low cost contribution of its members may be an example for small webcasters to follow if they want to compete with the big portals and established media companies.

This chapter has no mention about non-profit webcasters in the United States. There are plenty of non-profit webcasters out there. But their use is not as common as commercial webcasters, and none make it to the top of the top 20 list. Yet the non-profit use of webcasting in the United States is growing. For example, the International Webcasters Association, based in the United States with members primarily from the United States, displays links of 54 video and audio webcasters in providing emergency information through live streaming in their home page (http://www.webcasters.org). Whether non-profit webcasters will become one of the leading webcasters in the United States remains to be seen. It is quite unlikely to happen in the near future because both the federal and most state governments show little enthusiasm in and promotion of using webcasting for public service purposes and few non-profit organizations have as many resources as commercial organizations to compete in providing state-of-the-art webcast services to the general public.

REFERENCES

Accustream. (2003). *Streaming video market growth and analysis 2003*. Retrieved November 12, 2004 at http://www.accustreamresearch.com/products/streamngmedia2003.html

Accustream. (2004a). *Streaming advertising and subscription: A complete market analysis 2003–2005*. Retrieved November 12, 2004 at http://www.accustreamresearch.com/news/june12–04.html

Accustream. (2004b) *Broadcast and cable TV network brands inside streaming media: A market share analysis: 2001–2003*. Retrieved November 12, 2004 at http://www.accustreamresearch.com/products/broadcastnetwork.html

Accustream. (2004c). *Accustream report: streaming video viewing share topped by music at 33% in '04, news and sports follow.* Retrieved November 12, 2004 at http://www.accustreamresearch.com/news/nov09–04.html

Accustream. (2005). *Streaming subscription an download media percent up by 109% in '05 to 1.4 billion.* Retrieved November 1, 2005 from http://www.accustreamresearch.com/news/ oct-19-05.html

Albarran, A., & Chan-Olmsted S. (1998). *Global media economics*. Ames: Iowa State University Press.

Bernoff, J. (2005) the *real potential of internet video*. September 13. Forrester Research.

Broadcasting and Cable Yearbook. (2005). New Providence, NJ : R.R. Bowker.

Davis, W. (2005) AOL licenses "Natasha" to Cartoon Network. *Online Media Daily*. Retrieved March 30, 2005 from http://publications.mediapost.com/index.cfm?useaction = Articles.san&ts = 28533 &Nid = 12722&p = 204370

Doyle, G. (2002). *Understanding media economics*. London, Sage.

Greenspan, R. (2003). The kids are alright with spending. *Cyberatlas*, September 9.

Ha, L. (2003). Crossing offline and online media: A comparison of online advertising on TV web sites and online portals. *Journal of Interactive Advertising*. Retrieved from http://jiad.org

Ha, L., & Ganahl, R. (2004). Webcasting business models of click-and-bricks and pure-play Media: A comparative study of leading webcasters in South Korea and the United States. *International Journal on Media Management, 6*(1&2), 75–88.

Hollywood Reporter. (2002). Major haul: $31 bil in 2001: MPAA members' global feature income up $1.3 bil. June 18, 373(46), 1–2.

Horrigan, J. B. (2005). *Broadband adoption at home in the United States: Growing but slowing*. Paper presented to the 33rd Annual Telecommunications Policy Research Conference, September 24, 2005, Washington, D.C. Retrieved October 28, 2005 from http://www.pewinternet.org/pdfs/PIP_Broadband.TPRC_Sept05.pdf

Internet Retailer. (2004). The broadening reach of broadband. October, p.72.

Kopytoff, V. (2004, November 8). Yahoo looking at new arena: Delivery of online entertainment may be portal's future. *San Francisco Chronicle*.

Lacy, S. (2005). America: Still the high-speed laggard. *Business Week,* April 6. Retrieved April 15 from http://www.businessweek.com/technology/content/apr2005/tc2005046_3472_tc206.htm

Motion Picture Association of America. (2005). *About MPA, MPAA.* Retrieved April 28, 2005 from http://www.mpaa.org/about/index.htm

Narancic, P. J. (2003). Web*caster Alliance's Letter to RIAA*. Retrieved October 28, 2005 from http://www.webcasteralliance.com/modules/news/article.php?item_id = 93

National Association of Broadcasters. (2005). *DTV stations in operation*. Retrieved April 20, 2005 from http://www.nab.org/Newsroom/issues/digitaltv/DTVStations.asp

National Association of Cable Television. (2005). *Industry overview*. Retrieved April 20, 2005 from http://www.ncta.com/Docs/PageContent.cfm?pageID = 86

Online Reporter. (2005). AOL, XM team on net radio services. April 16, p.9

Oser, K. (2005). Video in Demand: With broadband at the tipping point, Yahoo, MSN and AOL have to figure out what consumers want and how to deliver. *Advertising Age*, April 2004, 76(14), p.S1–6.

Reuters. (2005, March 24). Clear Channel overhauls its net strategy.

Rose, B. & Lenski, J. (2005) *Internet and multimedia 2005: The on demand media consumer.* Retrieved April 24, 2005 at http://www.arbitron.com/downloads/IM2005Study.pdf

ScreenPlays. (2005). *Competitive pressures drive SPs to push the limits in broadband.* March/April, 26–28.

Shields, M. (April 25, 2005). Yahoo Double Profits. *Mediaweek,* April 25. Retrieved April 25, 2005 at http://www.mediaweek.com/mw/news/recent_display.jsp?vnu_content_id = 1000893681

Smith, S. (2005). ESPN.com.: Cross-platform synergy in a fan and advertiser-friendly package. *OMMA magazine*, February, p.30.

U.S. Bureau of Economic Analysis. (2005). *News release: Gross domestic product by industry, 2004.* Retrieved April 2005 from http://www.bea.gov/bea/newsrel/gdpindnewsrelease.htm

Veronis Suhler Stevenson. (2005). *Media industry segments*. Retrieved April 25, 2005 from http://www.veronissuhler.com/mediasegments/segments_home.html

Web Site Optimization. (2005). *April 2005 bandwidth report*. Retrieved April 25, 2005 from http://Websiteoptimization.com/bw/0504/

CHAPTER 4

Webcasting in Canada: The Imbedded Media

Claude Martin, Ilhem Allagui, and Marylaine Chaussé
University of Montreal

Canadian webcasting has been developing in a quite favorable context. Internet penetration is high and spending on cultural products or telecommunication services is strong enough to have sustained the development of all forms of media, including Canadian ownership of organizations of every caliber.

CONTEXT

The population of Canada is now around 32 million people spread over 9,984,670 square kilometers (3,855,000 square miles—more than the area of the U.S.). Spending on cultural goods and services in 2003 accounts for 2.3% of total consumer spending or around $640 U.S. yearly for every Canadian resident (Hill Strategies Research, Inc., 2005). One should note here that cultural goods include what would be considered in the U.S. as "entertainment" but does not include spending for internet. The main items in this amount are home entertainment services and equipment (cable or satellite services, electronics, etc.) and reading material. If internet services were added, they would come near cable or satellite services for amount spent. Nevertheless one can see that financial resources are available in the population for the funding of webcasting.

The Canadian population is concentrated in 3 of the 10 provinces, two of which are in Central Canada: Ontario with 38.4% of the Canadian population, followed by Québec with 23.8%. British Columbia, on the Pacific coast, has 13.2% of the Canadian population. Most of the population lives in the southern part of the country near the U.S.. Very long, and generally unpopulated distances separate the main cities as well as separating the Atlantic coast from the Pacific. When Canada was put together in its actual political form in 1867, railways were given huge resources in the hope of uniting provinces east and west. At the time, spontaneous trade had been developing north and south with the U.S.. Thus communication and transportation remain fundamental to Canada with railways at the beginning of the country and later, telecommunications. The same can be said about media. Canadians have easy access to American media, especially radio and television, because they are so near the border. Since the majority of Canadians speak English, it becomes clear that U.S. influence can be very strong, but less so in Québec.

Canada is a bilingual country, but this does not mean that all citizens use two languages. French-speakers are concentrated in Québec and around 82% of Quebecers are French-speakers in everyday life. Although many Canadians were born outside of Canada, use of languages other than French or English is very fragmented. Some cities do have important language or ethnic minorities. Vancouver has a thriving Chinese community while the population of Toronto displays a very wide diversity of ethnic origins. Nevertheless, French and English are the two official languages of Canada. Most media are either in French or English. Bilingual media are a rarity. A small segment of the media are available in other languages. One can find newspapers, radio and television stations producing in many languages in Canada, but their audience share is small. It is worth noting here that most radio and television stations have their license tied to either French or English and that this can imply very specific linguistic content. For example, on French radio, 65% of songs broadcast in the popular music format must be French.

As in many countries, the most important media industries are television and newspaper. In the very early stages of their historical development, Canadian media lagged behind the pace set by American and European newspaper and book industries. But newspapers flourished in the 19th century. The pace accelerated at the turn of the 20th century as the advertising-backed popular press occupied the field. Soon after, radio took off. At that time the press and radio were mostly in the hands of private Canadian capital.

Canadian media did not grow solely under the influence of market forces. When radio became popular, a debate over the influence of U.S. stations led to the founding in 1936 of the Canadian Broadcasting Corporation (CBC). The winning side coined the slogan "The state or the States." The idea was that without state intervention, Canadian media would quickly come into American hands. So one aspect of state intervention is the existence of public organizations in the media. The most important is the CBC, now active in radio, television, and internet, as well as webcasting. We will speak about the CBC a little later.

Nowadays the Canadian government still acts as a very active watchdog and supporter of the cultural (including "entertainment") and telecommunication industries. This is also true of the Québec government as the Canadian constitution gives jurisdiction over cultural matters, including official language and education, to the provinces. Both Canadian and Québec governments own a television station (the CBC and Télé-Québec). The most important provisions of Canadian cultural policy are those regulating media ownership. In broadcasting and, for now, telecommunications, organizations must be Canadian owned. In all other cultural industries, foreign ownership is allowed but Canadian ownership is supported and even enforced through other means such as provisions governing the fiscal treatment of advertising spending. The authority regulating radio, television, cable, and satellite (the CRTC) defines levels of Canadian, linguistic and even genre content depending on the type of media. Very roughly, 50% of what is broadcast must be Canadian, and French stations or networks must use the French language. Cable and satellite operators must balance the availability of Canadian and foreign channels. On the other hand, a vast array of subsidies is available for the production of Canadian content, especially for film and television, including provisions for internet. Before going further, it should be noted that Canada is nevertheless very open to cultural products from elsewhere. What is meant is that there are enough laws and regulations to generate critics from south of the border.

The Canadian government, in an effort to designate the enormous number of media and artistic or cultural organizations, very often uses the concept of cultural industries (with no reference to its Marxist origins). Webcasting can be framed as a branch of the cultural industries. In previous work, we defined cultural industries as the domains of human activity where the work of cultural creators (artists, journalists, etc.) is transformed into cultural products in an industrial environment (Martin, 1992). Cultural products can be defined as symbolic goods or services that express attitudes, opinions, ideas, values or artistic creativity and offer information, entertainment and aesthetic emotions. This includes the mass media (book publishing, newspapers and magazines, publishing, broadcasting, film and sound recording production), the performing arts, festivals, museums, and the part of the internet devoted to the (industrially organized) dissemination of symbolic goods. Excluded here is telecommunications itself. Framing webcasting in this way implies inquiries into the way "the making and circulating of products—that is, texts—...have an influence on our understanding of the world." (Hesmondhalgh, 2002). With regard to webcasting, we are not yet at this stage. We are still trying to define the economic characteristics of a nascent activity.

Let's return to media history. Many branches of the Canadian cultural industries became prosperous in the 1950s and 1960s. This was supported by the strong economy that emerged following the Second World War. Television first appeared in 1952 in the hands of the CBC and was quickly taken up by private stations in 1961. Book, record and film production also developed to a world-class level.

Television is now mostly received through multi-channel cable and satellite systems, although the main networks are available on air for free. Stations available only through cable or satellite are mostly so-called "specialized" channels, but as a group their market share is growing. Cable systems and telephone operators are both internet providers. Bell Canada (a subsidiary of BCE), the largest telephone operator, is also in television distribution, having invested in satellite television. Cable operators are now promoting internet Protocol (IP) telephone over coaxial cable in direct competition with incumbent telephone companies. Both industries also own television stations and, often, radio stations. The industrial core of electronic media is thus heavily invested in both traditional broadcasting as well as in the internet.

Many financial links integrate these electronic media organizations and newspapers (as well as other cultural industries) forming media conglomerates. Newspapers are also very interested in the internet, generally owning well-developed web sites of their own. Classified advertising is well suited for internet. So the Canadian media scene is characterized by a limited number of giant Canadian owned private organizations with interests in most type of media. Bell Canada Enterprises (BCE) is one of them. During the monopoly era it was limited to telephone only, but has recently expanded into television (CTV) and newspaper (*The Globe & Mail,* a quality national daily), forming Bell Globemedia. Quebecor is the giant in Québec. It started first with popular newspapers (*Le Journal de Montréal*) and printing and then became one of the largest printers in the world. It then moved into cable (Vidéotron) and television (TVA), extended into book publishing, record production, and distribution, then into the internet through cable. Also noteworthy is CanWest Global Communication originating in Western Canada, unlike Bell and Quebecor that both come from Central Canada. CanWest owns a television network (Global) and a major newspaper chain and is also active in radio. We will see these organizations later when looking at webcasters.

Canadian cultural industries are clearly divided between English and French language organizations or divisions of organizations, although many other types of segmentation can be seen. Although this is in no way accepted by every Canadian, one might say that Canada is formed of two nations (many would argue more than two if aboriginal nations are counted, but for our purposes, two will be sufficient to explain webcasting structure). This is important, as it introduces another factor in the development of cultural industries, which is the drive to sustain a French-speaking society in North America. Historically, this has implied the existence of French language media. French media have generally been more successful than English media at getting a strong market share for their products or services within their own linguistic market. The concept of cultural discount (Hoskins, McFadyen, & Finn, 1997) can apply here. Cultural discount lessens the value of cultural goods consumed in societies different from their origin because audiences can find it difficult to identify with their values or other characteristics. One could say that the cultural discount between French Canada and the U.S. is higher than that between English Canada (Ontario, B.C., etc.) and the U.S., thus creating a protective barrier for Québec industries. However, another more dynamic view would be that

Québec, the French-speaking province, succeeded in creating a working cultural model at an industrial level. Unfortunately, this argument cannot be extended to the web or to webcasting without specific examination as it is well documented that internet development and use has lagged somewhat in Québec relative to Ontario and other western provinces.

INTERNET IN CANADA

Internet in Canada is different in at least one important aspect from other cultural or telecommunication industries. We have seen that Canadian cultural industries have developed under quite strict regulation by government. But the Canadian government broadcasting regulatory arm has clearly let the internet escape outside of its rules...for the time being.

We saw that the Canadian geography has been an important factor in the development of its telecommunication network. Telegraph and telephones were operating in Canada immediately after their invention. Later, Canada was at the vanguard in the use of microwave networks and telecommunications satellites. This is also true of broadcasting, cable networks and telecommunication satellites. Electronic mail and WWW were also working in Canada as soon as the technology was available. But then, geography can also hinder internet development in rural and remote locations. Broadband access is difficult in many such areas although provincial and federal governments are active in trying to change the situation.

In December 2004, 76% of Canadians had access to the internet and 63% were connected from their home (CRTC, 2005). This figure varies according to many situations: As to income, access is limited to 50% in the lower bracket but rises to 97% in the higher brackets. Access also varies with location. According to the ComQuest data (CRTC, 2005), access is lower in Québec and in the eastern provinces, higher in Ontario (in the center of Canada) and even higher in the western provinces, Alberta and British Columbia. Using a different methodology, Ipsos-Reid estimates that Ontario and British Columbia are equal and leading in Canada for the highest level of internet access (Ipsos-Reid, 2004).

Home access to broadband internet has gone up swiftly from 30% of homes with internet in 2001 to 77% in 2005. Different sources conclude that the share of total online population using broadband is higher in Canada than in the U.S.: 53.6% vs. 33.8% in 2003 (ComScore Networks, 2003) and lately 77% vs. 57% in 2005 (WebsiteOptimization, 2005). Wide access to high quality telephone lines and broadband coaxial cable plus relatively low subscription fees could explain part of this difference.

Home broadband access is almost equally carried over telephone wires and coaxial cable, the latter having been first developed for the distribution of television and radio signals. A small number of homes are connected through micro-

TABLE 4–1
Internet Connectivity Service Revenues by Market Participant Group

	Revenues (in millions, $ Canadian)	% of Total	CAGR 1999–2003
Incumbent telephone company	1,270.5	41.6	39.7
Cable	1,108.2	36.3	66.2
No network competitors	675.2	22.1	22.6
Total	1,657.4	100.0	40.8

Note.   CAGR= Cumulative Annual Growth Rate
Source: Canadian Radio-television and Telecommunication Commission, *Status of Competition in Canadian Telecommunications Markets. Deployment/Accessibility of Advanced Telecommunications Infrastructure and Services,* 2004.

wave relays. As a result, telephone and cable operators have become the dominant internet providers (see Table 4–1), although smaller companies do sell internet access. In 2003, telephone companies led with 42% of internet connectivity revenues, but cable was not far behind with 36% (see Table 4–2). Other providers, operating usually over telephone lines, take up the remaining 22%. The four largest organizations occupy 54% of the market. The list of the largest operators is a mix of telcos (Bell—independent from U.S. Bell; Telus—associated with U.S. Verizon) and cable operators (Shaw, Rogers, Vidéotron—a part of Quebecor).

TABLE 4–2
Largest ISP in Canada

Company	Dial-up Subscribers (000)			High-speed Subscribers (000)			Total (000)		
Year	2002	2003	2004	2002	2003	2004	2002	2003	2004
Bell	1,031	911	743	909	1,287	1,808	1,940	2,198	2,551
Telus*	432	352	282	326	469	690	758	821	972
Shaw	—	—	—	758	881	1,069	758	881	1069
Rogers	—	—	—	541	755	937	541	755	937
Quebecor	—	—	—	265	379	476	265	379	476
Look	96	83	51	3	3	10	99	86	61
Sprint	85	66	60	—	—	—	85	66	60
Cogeco	—	—	—	154	196	262	154	196	262

Note.   — = number unavailable and not calculated in total.
*Only company associated with U.S. entity in this list.
Source: CRTC, 2005.

TABLE 4–3
Share of Canadians Connected at Least Once a Month to Internet Selected
Activities

Activities	Most of the Time				Some of the Time			
	2001	2002	2003	2004	2001	2002	2003	2004
Download or listen to music	13	13	16	9	22	19	24	17
Watch video	2	1	4	3	17	14	18	16
Listen to radio	4	3	4	4	12	11	12	14

Source: CRTC. 2005.

Users with broadband access do report activities that can be associated with webcasting: listening or downloading music (46% of users), watching videos (27%), listening to radio (30%) and, at a lower rate, downloading films (7%) and watching television (5%) (see Table 4–3).

LISTING AND LOOKING AT LEADING WEBCASTERS

In response to advertiser's needs, audience measurement is generally well developed in Canada, employing methods similar to those used in the U.S. n the broadcasting industries, the market is split between Nielsen, the international corporation, and the Bureau of Broadcast Measurement (BBM), a Canadian cooperative. They recently announced the merging of their television rating services done with "people meters." U.S. affiliated ComScore Media Metrix is the dominant firm in web audience measurement. Although ComScore is a source for lists of web sites classified by their traffic, there is no data on webcasting volume or audience, a sign that this is not yet an industry on its own.

This makes it impossible to have a list of leading webcasters in order of their audience size. However, knowing the importance of the web sites of which they are a part or even the importance of the organizations of which they are a part, it is possible to create a list of leading webcasters (see Table 4–4), if not the list of the leading webcasters, By this we mean that the 20 webcasters in the table are probably not the top 20 webcasters according to traffic, but that they would be part of a longer list anyway. Our search was facilitated by the fact that a member of our team had already done research on internet television (Chaussé, 2001) We can also thank members of the multimedia industry and one of our colleagues from Vancouver for their help in the identification of webcasters (see Acknowledgments).

TABLE 4-4
Leading Webcasters in Canada (listed alphabetically)

Webcaster	URL	First Languages	Ownership	Site Type*	Business Model**	Genre Type
AOL	http://www.aol.ca	English and French	Subsidiary of US stock listed co.	ISP	CA	Portal
Audiogram	http://www.audiogram.com	French	Private	CB	BC	Music
Canada.com	http://www.canada.com/national	English	Division of stock listed co.	PP	CA	Broadcaster
Canoë Digital—La Fréquence web	http://cd.canoe.com/	French and English	Division of stock listed co.	PP	CA	Portal
CBC (Canadian Broadcasting Corp.)	http://www.cbc.ca	English	Government agency	CB	CB	Broadcaster
CNW (Canada NewsWire)	http://www.cnw.ca	English and French	Private	CB	BC	Public relations
CTV	http://www.ctv.ca/	English	Subsidiary of stock listed co.	CB	BC	TV broadcaster
GlobeTrotter	http://www.globetrotter.net/gt	French	Division of stock listed co.	ISP	CA	Portal
Horse Player Interactive	http://www.horseplayerinteractive.com	English	Not-for-profit organization	CB	BC	Betting
Iceberg Radio	http://www.icebergradio.com/	English	Division of stock listed co.	PP	BC	Radio broadcaster
Jump TV	http://www.jumptv.com/	English	Private	PP	CA	TV
Lynx Internet Radio Network	http://www.lynxradionetwork.com	English	Private	PP	BC	Radio
Media on Tap	http://www.mediaontap.com	English	Private	PP	CA	Webcaster
NFB/ONF (National Film Board)	http://onf.ca	English and French	Government agency	CB	BC	Film
Occupation double	http://www.occupationdouble.com	French	Division of stock listed co.	CB	BC	TV show
Radio énergie	http://www.radioenergie.com	French	Division of stock listed co.	CB	BC	Radio broadcaster

Radio-Canada (SRC)	http://www.radio-canada.ca/	French	CB	Government agency	BC	Broadcaster
Star Académie	http://www.staracademie.ca/acc	French	CB	Division of stock listed co.	BC	TV show
Sympatico	http://sympatico.msn.ca	English and French	ISP	Division of stock listed co.	CA	Portal
Yahoo	http://www.ca.yahoo.com	English and French	PP	Subsidiary of US stock listed co.	CA	Search & portal

*Site type: Internet Service Provider, Clicks and Bricks, and Pure-Player.
**Business Model: Content Aggregator; Branded Content.

Our study used the content analysis methodology developed in the seminal study of webcasting at the origin of this book (Ha & Ganahl, 2004). Access to web sites was generally easy, but it should be noted that some parts of some sites could not be examined because of restricted access. Internet providers tend to give their clients special access. Some parts of some sites are restricted to paying customers. But one can generally obtain an idea of what is hidden.

Our list of leading webcasters is in alphabetical order since we are unable to put it in order of production (volume or output) or of demand (audience time spent or reach) because the data does not exist for Canada. As our aim is to discuss the economic model of webcasting in Canada, it is a "rationalized" sample partially aimed at including different types of webcasters. By "rationalized" we mean that we chose to include certain types of webcasters (public broadcasters, ISP, radios, horse racing, etc.) in order to get a richer representation of the field. Again, if our aim is to understand the economics of webcasting, a pure "in the order of demand" list may be poorer than a sample built including a factor for diversity. Nevertheless, our list includes only webcasters known to be successful and showing high output. Our sample also needs to be distinguished from a random sample. It can give us information on business practices, but does not measure the importance of different types of practices in all webcasting activities.

WHO'S WHO

For someone who already knows the Canadian media scene, most of the sites on this list are familiar because they are associated with or part of internet providers or of one of the media conglomerate. A few are new names or players active only in the internet. Also striking is the presence of state organizations. Finally, we see a few stand-alone sites. We will use this structure to lead us into a detailed analysis of the leading webcasters.

We can look first at the Canadian Broadcasting Corporation (CBC) and Société Radio-Canada (SRC) duo. They are both parts of the same legal entity, Canada's public radio and television broadcaster, but they are not the same because CBC/Radio-Canada's English and French operations are almost completely separated, with their respective headquarters in Toronto and Montréal, although there is a common head-office in Ottawa. Radio-canada.ca claims to be the most visited French media web site in Canada (that is a site owned by a media). This claim is acceptable because the SRC has access to all available media data in Canada and is reliable source for any information; furthermore www.alexa.com puts radio-canada.ca site at the 47th rank among the sites of the world in French. The site started in 1995 and began full webcasting of its radio in 1996. In 1999, live images of the radio studio were webcast during the morning program. In 2001, a strictly web radio program began and a music store for new styles of popular music was made available at no cost. Today, radio-canada.ca contains 350,000 pages of content including 4,000 hours of audio and video clips, many of which are of historical importance. Its two radio stations are fully webcasted and bandeapart.fm webcasts audio and video content about new musical genres, including live concerts. On the whole, this site is considered highly innovative. The federal government finances CBC/Radio-Canada, but its television networks also sell advertising time. There is no advertising on the web sites at the time of writing, but it is expected that there will be soon. There is a section devoted to the selling of CBC/Radio-Canada's own products.

The National Film Board / Office National du Film (NFB/ONF) is also a federal government agency. Originating as an organization to promote the war effort during World War II, it is now a film production organization well recognized for the quality of its products. Its web site is rich and diversified. Education and social inquiries are very visible objectives of the site. A data bank gives information about every NFB production. Hundreds of films, clips, and games are available on line with provision for feedbacks. Access is free. There is no advertising, except for the NFB's own products of which there are a very large selection. The home page automatically gives incomers a complex presentation of the site.

These three sites are themselves members of a larger family, the sites of media organizations which can be divided into sub-categories: television, radio, or media conglomerates, recording companies, and lately, specific television programs. The two CBC/Radio-Canada sites fit all these categories. Conglomerates, all television network or stations or groups of stations have elaborate web sites. So do major radio networks. Specific sites for television programs are typical for so-called reality tv shows. Almost every organization of the cultural industries or institutions has a web site.

CTV is the leading commercial television broadcaster (English language) in Canada. It is a subsidiary of Bell Globemedia itself own by BCE, the leading telecommunication organization in Canada and, more specifically, the leading internet provider in Canada (over telephone lines). The web site is mostly a companion for the television network and its local stations. Audio and video content is linked to its programs, including access to content not shown on television and stories from the morning show. The CTV Newsnet Live Stream is available for a subscription fee of $5.21 U.S. ($6.95 Canadian) per month ($3.71 U.S. for low speed). Advertising is highly visible throughout the site.

Horse Player Interactive (HPI) is also linked to television channels, but to a very specific genre, horse racing. It is a division of Woodbine Entertainment, formerly the Ontario Jockey Club. Clients must register to get access to live horse races. The site shows a selection of the company's five television channels. Bets can be placed on-site or by phone. There is no advertising on the site aside from HPI's own promotions.

JumpTV was created in 1999 with the idea of retransmitting on web television stations around the world including U.S. stations to be retransmitted in Canada only. But this initial plan did not fully take into account the complex problem of retransmission rights. A Canadian law passed in 2003 defined the rules of the game and made it clear that retransmission fees must be paid. Now, JumpTV offers 26 international stations like Jaya TV (India), Deutsche Welle (Germany) and the well-known Al Jazeera. Each stations costs $9.95 (high speed) or $5.95 (low). There is no advertising on the site.

Canada.com is the web division of CanWest Global, a multimedia conglomerate with interests in television (Global), newspapers and radio. The site is rich in content from newspapers, including classified advertising. Video from Global News is available freely. Live audio streaming is available for two radio stations, one of which only after registration. Webcams show traffic in many Canadian cities. Advertising is evident as well as links to commercial operations.

IcebergRadio.com is a division of Standard Broadcasting, Canada's largest radio group also active in television. IcebergRadio is the biggest radio portal in Canada with 250 channels covering almost every genre. It is an internet-only operation. It is possible to listen for free for 30 minutes, but past that point, registration is necessary. Registration is also free, but demographic information is asked for advertising purposes. Legal downloading of music is available with the Puretracks system. Advertising is visible but limited.

Radioénergie.com is a portal for a French radio network and its local stations. It is part of the Astral Media organization, also very active in television over cable and satellite. An automatic audio segment greets you as soon as a person logs on the site. There is full live streaming from the 10 local stations of the network. One can contact the stations in many ways. A section of the site is for listener feedback on a selection of musical pieces. Advertising is highly visible.

Occupation double and *Star académie* are web sites dedicated to two reality shows of the TVA private television network, a division of Quebecor, Québec's largest multimedia company. TVA heads the ratings in French television. Both programs were big successes in the ratings. *Star académie* is a music show like *American Idol* where participants try to be the winner remaining after all the other are eliminated. It also produced very successful musical CDs. Their secret was labeled as a clear effect of convergence, i.e., most parts of the conglomerate (television stations, internet including webcasting, newspapers and magazines, record productions and sales, etc.) were put to work to push for the many products of *Star académie*. In *Occupation double* the participants live in a closed apartment and vote to impeach their colleagues from forming the winning couple. The sites continue to operate even though the original programs were running in 2004. But new seasons are running or coming. The names of these programs were the most requested names on the search engine *La toile du Québec* while they were on the air. The sites now contain clips from the programs. Access to webcam records of *Star académie* is limited to clients of Vidéotron high speed internet service. Vidéotron is the subsidiary of Quebecor competing head to head with Bell Canada for broadband services, so limited access is not so limited. For *Occupation double,* users must pay a small fee for full access. Both sites contain links to other Quebecor sites. Advertising content is low, but this can be explained by the fact that our observation took place off-season.

Audiogram is the leading recording company in Québec. The Québec music market is different from that of English-speaking provinces in Canada. It has a strong basis in local production and the market share for local products remains much higher in Québec. The Audiogram site dates back to 1995. One can find artist biographies as well as audio and video clips. As soon as one logs on, one of the six streaming channels starts playing any of the 1303 available tracks. Information is given on coming events or shows and tickets can be purchased on the site.

Canoë Digital—La Fréquence web is a part of Canoë, the French language portal of Quebecor owner of Vidéotron. Its English language sister is Canoe. Canoë Digital is dedicated to the promotion and sale of music. Quebecor also owns the largest record distributor in Québec, Select, as well as the largest chain of retail record stores, Archambault. Archambault also sells records and music files over the internet. The site, after registration, contains a virtual jukebox that can be tailored to suit its listener's tastes. Shows broadcast by TVA television are also available. Unknown artists can upload demos to the site and compete for the demo of the month award. Twenty demos are available on the web site but the number of artists who participate each month is unknown. Finally, Archambault music (and book) store is only one click away.

The next site, indirectly related to the media, is a one of a kind in Canada: Canada NewsWire (CNW) a subsidiary of CNW Telbec. It is not a site intended for the general public but it is an important institution in the financial community. It is also an interesting case as to its business model. It is mainly a service for the public relations departments of organizations. Through its services, organizations can distribute professional texts or any type of document, including live webcasting of press conferences for instance. Audio and video is used extensively. Clients who want to reach the media and the public pay for CNW services. This is aimed primarily at journalists, but the general public can access the site. Archives of past events are kept for 90 days and a calendar of coming events is maintained. The site is quite stark and there is no advertising.

Turn now to the portals of the large internet access providers. They were already discussed earlier in a limited sense, as they are part of the larger telecommunication or media concerns. The most important is Sympatico, the bilingual portal of Bell Canada's internet division. Web surfers who are not connected through Sympatico also visit the site. It often appears on top of most lists of sites by traffic in Canada. It is a very complex site with a complete array of services and hundreds of links to other sites. Webcasting is highly visible, especially about cultural products (popular music of the day, film on screen in town, etc.). Audio and video content is plentiful. So are advertisements as well as cultural products for sale, including legal downloading of music files. Site content is mainly Canadian, but recently, Bell entered in an agreement with Microsoft, thus in- creasing its U.S. content. This would mean more music, information, games from sources associ- ated with Microsoft like Trans World Entertainment known for music and video content.

Similarily, GlobeTrotter is the portal of the Québec division of Telus, the sec- ond largest Canadian telecommunication company based on revenue. Globe-Trot- ter is quite different from MyTelus, the English language portal of Telus. This stems from the history of the company. Its Québec operation was locally owned in the beginning. Telus, in contrast to Bell, is not part of a multimedia conglomerate and so does not have access to news or entertainment from sister organizations. The site gets news and entertainment from sources like Radio-Canada or Canadian Press. Audio and video content is available on demand in the entertainment section of the site. Legal downloading of music is available. A part of the GlobeTrotter site, SlacheMusique offers 10 channels of streaming music for those using Telus high speed internet access. Some advertising is seen on the site and links to com- mercial operations are easy to find.

The next two sites are the extensions of U.S. organizations whose operations cover many countries. AOL Canada is a subsidiary of the giant Time Warner. It is an internet service provider that reaches its customers through telephone company networks (called "competitors" in Table 4–1). The site is bilingual. It offers the usual array of portal services including 140 radio stations, music downloading, webcasting of concerts, etc. In video, one can see documentaries, past television programs, promotional items and 1.5 million titles of video-clips, mainly from Time Warner. Many links lead to the sale of goods and services. Advertising is present but not plentiful.

Yahoo! Canada is the extension of the well-known search engine and portal. It comes in a Canadian venue. Its French language version is different from the English one. Audio and video content is freely available. Registered customers cans access a great number of radio channels including channels tailored for Canadians. In contrast with its U.S. cousin, this service is free in Canada. Ad- vertising and sale of products are always visible.

Lynx Internet Radio Network or crikfm.com is a webradio based in Calgary of- fering four channels loosely defined by genres (rock, disco, retro, and variety). Each is available freely without registration. The site asks for a donation from its listeners using credit cards or Paypal. Some promotional objects are for sale. Ad- vertising is scarce on the site.

Media on Tap is independent from the large Canadian media organizations. It is part of a larger site, Dowco, offering interactive services to businesses. Media- ontap.com harbors many types of sites. One can find sporting events and other types of entertainment, news, and education. Examples of this are Teletoon (cartoon), *Canadian Idol* (the television program), or CTV Newsnet Live Stream. Each of these is a site in itself and is available without cost *or* for a fee.

OVERVIEW

The 20 sites we visited offer a very wide assortment of content. Aesthetics and technical aspects are on a par with the best and, specifically, the technical quality of the webcasting is very good. The constitution of our sample does not allow for any conclusion on the proportion of different types of webcasters in Canada, but it is interesting to cite some numbers. In our list, half of the webcasters (10 of 20) could be labeled clicks and bricks. Many are established broadcasters like the CBC or CTV. Also a little less than half of our list (7 of 20) could be labeled pure-play, most being specialized in radio-type webcasting like Icebergradio or Lynxradio. Beside these types, we see internet services providers whose huge portals offer webcasting among other services, e.g. Sympatico. Note that only two of our leading webcasters are not Canadian (we are excluding here the joint venture Sympatico/Microsoft because the portal remains in the hands of BCE). Note also, state corporations are major webcasters in Canada (CBC, NFB). None of the commercial webcasters is by itself listed on a stock exchange, but many are part of large organizations that are, like BCE and Quebecor, both public companies. Commercial webcasters often act as a publicity arm for an organization, but they also often seek their own revenues, selling advertising space, goods and services or limiting access to customers paying a fee. Eleven of our 20 webcasters could be labeled as offering a branded content. The others are content aggregators, the most important being Sympatico, Yahoo! and AOL.

Using the Ha and Ganahl (2004) model, we can describe our webcasters along the dimensions of access, content strategy and sources of revenues.

Only six of the 20 allow for the tailoring of their output to the speed of the incomer. Content can be accessed using different methods (streaming, on demand, push, etc.). Three out of four offer transmission by more than one method. More than half (12 of 20) use direct streaming or streaming on demand, while about half use downloading on demand. Mush less in use is the push technology. Direct streaming transmission is of good technical quality. Players in use are the well-known Windows Media Player (19 of 20), RealMedia (10 of 20) and, less in use, Quicktime, while 8 of 20 supply content usable without special software. File formats follow these lines: WMP for most, six are use either RM, MP3, AVI, or MOV. Many sites do facilitate navigation by offering descriptions of audio and video files (10 of 20) or a search engine (9 of 20). A majority also offers interaction in the forms of chat or forums, but games, surveys or voting pages are much less frequent.

TABLE 4–5
Number of Leading Webcasters According to Type of Content

Share of the content which is...	Original Content	Reruns	Simultaneous Webcast
100%	1	3	1
From 50 to 99%	3	3	4
From 1 to 49%	5	10	4
0%	11	4	11

One of the major questions about content is the balance between repurposing and new material. A little more than half of our sites (11 of 20) do not show original content (Table 4–5) and only one is 100% original. Reruns of Canadian TV shows are very frequent but only 6 are over 50% of their content on this count. Simulcast is not the general rule except for a few sites while only one is 100% simulcast. Most of the sites (18 of 20) have video content and genres palette is quite widespread (Table 4–6). News is a sort of staple of webcasting (9 of 20) but other genres are almost as popular: musical video clips (8 of 20) or music videos (7 of 20), business videos (7 of 20), and cartoons (6 of 20). Most of those videos are Canadian productions and seven or our webcasters are 100% Canadian as to videos while five supply mostly U.S. video content (notably AOL and Yahoo!), on the whole, international and Canadian content tend to follow traditional media. More

TABLE 4–6
Number of Sites Exhibiting Selected Genres Among the Leading Webcasters Sites

Genre	N
News, interview	9
Video clip	8
Business	7
Music video	7
Cartoon	6
Sport	5
Documentary	4
TV serial	4
Talk show	3
Comedy	2
Education	2
Entertainment show	2
Religion	2
Drama	1

TABLE 4–7
Advertising Revenue by Media (selected media, Canada)

Media	Revenue in 2003 (in millions, $ Canadian)	Percentage of Total	5 Years Increase (%)
Television	2,840	26.4	23
Radio	1,187	11.0	28
Daily newspapers (i.e., classified)	1,697	15.8	6
Consumer magazines	610	5.7	35
Outdoor and transit	289	2.7	32
Internet	156	1.4	624
Yellow pages	1,121	10.4	20
Direct mail	1,598	14.8	28
Other print	1,263	11.7	16
Total	10,761	100.0	22

Note: Total not calculated.
Source: Canadian Media Directors' Council, n.d..

Canadian content can be seen on the French language sites and on the public sites like the CBC. Commercial English Canadian sites are more prone to offer foreign and rather American content. On the audio side, around half of our webcasters offer music (11 of 20), news (7 of 20) or interviews (11 of 20). One on five has audio-based sports. Musical ringtones for cellular phones are almost unheard of.

Seven our list relies on only one source of revenue. Advertising is often seen (13 of 20) and the sale of goods and services is also popular (9 of 20). Subscription fees are seen on only four sites. To this we must add that the CBC and NFB get revenues from the federal government and that many sites are marketing tools for larger concerns and that they do not have to show a profit at the end of the year. Internet advertising is growing in Canada, but there is no agreed upon definition of what should be included in it, so estimates can be far apart. An advertising industry source (Canadian Media Directors' Council, n.d.) set internet advertising revenues in Canada at $133 million U.S. ($156 million Canadian) in 2003, which means 1.4% of the total in Table 4–7, but the source excludes some media like community newspapers and trade magazines in its total. A document from Industry Canada puts the share at 2% in 2004 (Industry Canada, 2004). The Interactive Advertising Bureau of Canada, using "a comprehensive survey" estimates advertising revenues at $288 millions U.S. ($337 million Canadian) in 2003 and $253 millions U.S. ($295 millions Canadian) in 2004 (IAB Canada, 2004). On the other hand, buying over the internet is also growing, but still under 1% of consumer spending

(Statistics Canada, 2005). It should be noted that cultural products are among those most widely sold on the internet (books, records, etc.).

CONCLUSION AND PERSPECTIVES

Although webcasting is a well-established technology in Canada, it cannot be seen as an industry in and of itself. Our list of leading webcasters reveals a variety of organizations and concerns. Moreover, it is telling to note that webcasters do not have a united public voice in the form of an association. Webcasting is then mainly one of the outputs of organizations operating in a wide number of industries, even though some webcast-only entities do exist, as we have seen. Leading webcasters in Canada are often, but not always, part of a media conglomerate. Canadian webcasters are mostly mirroring the traditional media. Outside the list of web-casters we have studied, one can see many small and dynamic organizations. But when one looks at the top of the list, one finds the well-known players. Webcast sites tend to be integrated in the media portfolio of multimedia organizations or can also be value-added for clients of internet providers. These organizations have now accepted webcasting as a tool of the trade although the development remains prudent, if not slow.

Traditional media are not on the point of letting internet take their place. Television distribution is changing to offer even more channels, on-demand content and high definition. Both telcos and cables are heavily investing in these new services while at the same time promoting faster internet. The internet is making a dent in television and radio ratings, but listening to music on the internet still represents only a very small fraction of total listening. In 2004, a mere 0.2% of radio listening was done through the internet (CRTC, 2005). Podcasting may add some percentage to that. But again, the traditional Canadian institutions and commercial entities plus a few new players are ready to offer Canadians this recent technology. Our hypothesis holds that webcasting technology is not disruptive enough to alter the general equilibrium of Canadian cultural industries because what is called webcast is quite similar to what is now broadcasting i.e. music, news, sports and reports. That is why we call it an "imbedded" media, a media working inside, almost hidden in the structure of traditional media.

Two other major problems now confront webcasting in Canada. The first is also a world wide issue. Laws will have to be tailored to allow for copyright management of a type practical for internet diffusion. This is not only a problem for webcasting, but also for any use of the internet to disseminate content. One important aspect of this is the use of internet content in education.

The second question is typically Canadian and even Québécois. But, it is also a concern that has arisen around the word. What is the effect of communication technologies on societies? How threatened are societies or nations by the development of media that are able to stretch around the world without regard for frontiers? Is it an uneven contest between the big nations (with their large webcasters) and small ones? Should or can there be rules? Recently, the issue has been reformulated at UNESCO as the defense of cultural diversity, long the kingpin of Canadian cultural policy. A project for an international treaty on the trade of cultural products is under development. On the other hand, voices can be heard in Canada that questions the unregulated status of internet content. If cultural and market forces are strong enough to give Canadians and Québécois a strong sense of place when they are on the receiving end of webcasting, it will be easier for everyone. If not, many will look to conventional media with the intention of making the new one more effective. In other words, a new technology must also provide answers to old questions even as it raises new ones.

ACKNOWLEDGMENTS

Ilhem Allagui and Marylaine Chaussé were responsible for data collection and analysis for this chapter. Claude Martin wrote the final draft. We are grateful for the kind help received from Marie-Claude Ducas, editor of *Infopresse* (http://www. infopresse.com/), the site and magazine of communication and advertising in Québec; Hugh Dobbie, owner of Interactive Netscanning Systems Inc. (http://www.insinc.com/); Catherine Warren (http://www.cathwarren.com/frameset_ft. htm), president of FanTrust Entertainment Strategies; and our colleague Richard Smith (http://www.sfu.ca/communication/people/faculty/smith_r. html) at Simon Fraser University. They all helped our understanding of the webcast market in Canada and in our selection of the leading webcasters. We also have specials thanks for Reynolds Kanary at the Département des langues, Collège Édouard-Montpetit (http://www.collegeem.qc.ca/cemdept/anglais/default5.htm) for his kind help with the English language.

REFERENCES

Canadian Media Directors' Council. (n.d.). *Media Digest 04/05*. Supplement to *Marketing Magazine*. Toronto.
Chaussé, M. (2001). L'émergence de la télévision sur internet. (The beginnings of television over internet). Unpublished doctoral dissertation, Université de Montréal.
ComScore Networks. (2003). *Canada Trumps U.S. in Broadband Use, ComScore Media Metrix Canada Reports*. Retrieved August 5, 2005, from http://www.comscore.com/press/release.asp?press = 403
CRTC (Canadian Radio-television and Telecommunications Commission). (2005). *Broadcasting Policy Monitoring Report 2005* (p.118). Retrieved August 9, 2005, from http://www.crtc.gc.ca/ eng/publications/reports.htm#monitoring

Ha, L., & Ganahl, R. (2004). Webcasting business models of click-and-bricks and pure-play media: A comparative study of leading webcasters in South Korea and the United States. *International Journal on Media Management,* 6(1&2), 75–88.

Hesmondhalgh, D. (2002). *The cultural industries.* London: Sage.

Hill Strategies Research, Inc. (2005). *Consumer spending on culture in Canada, the provinces and 15 metropolitan areas in 2003.* Report funded by the Canada Council for the Arts, the Department of Canadian Heritage, and the Ontario Arts Council.

Hoskins, C., McFadyen, S., & Finn, A. (1997). *Global television and film: An introduction to the economics of the business.* Oxford, England: Oxford University Press.

IAB Canada. (2004). *Canadian interactive marketplace grows 68% in two years.* Retrieved August 9, 2005, from http://www.iabcanada.com/newsletters/041102.shtml

Industry Canada (2004), *Advertising services.* Retrieved August 9, 2005 from http://strategis.ic.gc.ca/epic/internet/inimr-ri.nsf/en/gr117002e.html

Ipsos-Reid (2004). The *Canadian Inter@ctive Reid Report. Fact Guide.* Retrieved August 9, 2005, from http://www.ipsos.ca/pdf/CIFG.pdf

Martin, C. (1992). Les industries culturelles québécoises, situation économique ou "Tout le monde se plaint, mais s'ils se plaignent, c'est qu'ils vivent encore" [Economics of cultural industries in Québec: Crying is living]. In R. De La Garde. & D. Saint-Jacques (Eds.), *Les pratiques culturelles de grande consommation. Le marché francophone* [Mass consumption of French language cultural products {in Québec}]. Québec: Nuit Blanche Éditeur.

Statistics Canada. (2005). Electronic commerce and technology. *The Daily.* Retrieved August 9, 2005 from http://www.statcan.ca/Daily/English/050420/d050420b.htm

WebsiteOptimization. (2005), U.S.–Canadian Broadband Penetration Gap at 20 Points. Retrieved September 29, 2005 from http://www.websiteoptimization.com/bw/0506/

PART III

Webcasting Business Practices and Dynamics Across Europe

CHAPTER 5

United Kingdom: Webcasting's Biggest Promise in Europe

Alexandros Arampatzis
Edge Hill University, United Kingdom

WEBCASTING MARKET ENVIRONMENT

Overview

It is common place that the UK media industry is one of the strongest in the world and perhaps the one at the forefront in Europe. Newspapers present a remarkable variety that caters for every need and taste, boast high circulation and readership rates, and play a significant role in the formation of public opinion. They are commercially-centered and constitute strong and viable businesses in a press market that is largely concentrated. In terms of broadcasting, the dominant position in the field is occupied by the country's PBS (Public Service Broadcaster), the BBC, which is clearly the most established and highly-respected broadcaster in Europe and thus sets the standards for the rest of the UK's audiovisual industry.

Within this highly competitive and developed media market environment, webcasting is a sector with a slow but steady growth, largely supported by the UK's audiovisual media which saw a business opportunity in casting their video and audio content through the web and exploited their audiovisual content development expertise to transit this type of content through the web. Nevertheless, it is beyond any doubt that webcasting is still in a formation stage, an industry in pursuit of viable business models that will elevate it into the status of a significant player in the media UK media arena.

MEDIA INDUSTRY STRUCTURE

Press

The UK press market is one of the largest globally, with more than 1,000 newspapers and more than 10,000 magazines distributed in the country. It is clearly beyond the purposes of this study to examine this enormous and ever-growing industry in detail. One of the major characteristics of the written press in the UK is the existence of a large national newspaper sector divided into 14 daily and 15 Sunday titles. Newspapers in Britain are traditionally divided into "quality," "mid-market," and "popular" ones, a stratification that until recently was reflected on the titles' actual size, with broadsheets representing the quality press and tabloid-sized publications being linked with the popular, high-selling publications. Yet, this schematic division is of little importance today due to the growing trend (imposed by commercial imperatives and usability purposes) by the quality papers to get published in small tabloid-sized format.

The strength of the press industry in the UK, which, as a mature market presents some relative stability, stems from the high readership percentages which reach 60% for national daily papers, and about 70% for national Sunday publications (Audit Bureau of Circulations, 2005). Overall, the UK's national press reaches a mass audience with 94 million copies sold each week and national titles which attract 38 million readers each week (The Guardian, 2004). Viewed within the wider European context, readership and circulation statistics in the UK are largely aligned with those observed in other western central-European countries (such as Austria and Germany). These figures are considerably higher that those registered by southern European countries (Greece, Italy, Spain and Portugal), which, traditionally, achieve poor press readership and circulation figures (roughly, around 35–40% of southern Europeans read a daily publication), but lower when compared to the countries of the Scandinavian peninsula (indicatively, readership figures of daily newspapers in Norway reach almost 85% of the total population) (Eurostat, 2005).

The total sales of national daily newspapers are nearly 14 million, and of national Sundays nearly 15 million, and although these figures may appear to be high, in fact they are well below peaks reached in the late 1950s, ever since national newspaper reading continues to be in decline (Audit Bureau of Circulations, 2005). Table 5–1 shows that popular and mid-market publications have been particularly hit by this decline in circulation, whereas the quality press managed to stay largely unaffected by this downwards trend. Moreover, these figures also include "freesheet" titles that bear no price, are supported by advertising and whose popularity has risen spectacularly during the past decade.

The concentration of ownership in the UK press market is in par with that monitored in other European countries (Sparks, 1995, 1999; European Federation

TABLE 5–1
Newspaper Readership Figures

	1998	2005	Change
Number of people who read a national newspaper each week	39,000,000	37,500,000	–1,500,000
Number of people who read a popular newspaper each week	26,000,000	24,000,000	–2,000,000
Number of people who read a mid-market newspaper each week	15,000,000	13,000,000	–2,000,000
Number of people who read a quality newspaper each week	12,000,000	12,000,000	stable

Source: Joint Industry Committee for Regional Press Research, 2005.

of Journalists, 2004). The UK press is distinctive in that the big-circulation national newspapers dominate the press scene, yet regional and local newspapers are not an insignificant entity.

The UK magazine sector is large and has been growing consistently over the past decade. There are between 8,800 and 10,000 titles (estimates vary). About 6,000 are "business and professional" titles, and the rest are "consumer" magazines. Although there are almost 1,000 magazine publishers, as with the newspaper industry, effectively ownership is concentrated in relatively few hands (Emap and IPC are the publishers of the dominant periodicals).

Given the press' strong penetration in UK's social and business life as well as the strong presence of the UK leading newspapers in the internet (see below), one would expect newspaper and magazine web sites to constitute a key player in the development of webcasting services in the UK. Yet, none of UK's leading webcasters represents the online presence of a print medium. "This is largely because print media don't have either the infrastructure nor the know-how to work with video and audio. They do online what they are good at doing offline too, which is working with words," says Richard Clark, the editor of *Web User Magazine*.

AUDIOVISUAL MEDIA

Television

If there is an overarching philosophy that encompasses the overall structure and function of British broadcasting, then this is identified in the notion of "public service," according to which broadcasting is a service of information, education, and entertainment for everyone in the community who wants it free from the direct influences of both government and commerce. This shaped the programming and the corporate mission not only of the largest UK broadcaster, the BBC, but also to a large degree of its commercial rivals, which started emerging after the end of the domestic television monopoly of BBC in 1955. It was the 1974 Television Act that brought commercial television into being but , although funded by advertising, the UK's first commercial channel (ITV—Independent Television) was obliged to offer a range and balance of programming, a fact that moderated competition with the already existing BBC channel. "From 1995, monopoly in broadcasting was replaced not so much by full-blooded competition as by duopoly—by two broadcasters serving broadly similar objectives," Crisell (1999, p. 62) observes.

This public service broadcasting ethos that has informed British broadcasting is widely attributed to the first General Director of the BBC, the emblematic John Reith, and was determined, or at least inspired, by technology and the scarcity of the wavebands (Briggs, 1961; Crisell, 1999).

Today, the BBC, dubbed "Auntie" to signify people's fondness of its service as well as its role as the voice of Britain abroad, runs eight interactive TV channels, of which two are national terrestrial television channels (with national and regional sub-divisions) free to access, five national radio stations, cable and digital TV channels, and more than 40 local radio stations. Additionally, the Corporation has global enterprises in both television and radio as well as a broadcast monitoring service, and Europe's most visited web site (The Guardian Media Guide, 2003).

Although predominantly a public service organization, which raises revenue from a the so-called "license fee" and not advertising, the BBC also operates commercially in many domains both inside and outside the UK. The "license fee" annual cost (set by the government) is currently £126.50 (approximately $160.00), it is being paid by every UK household with a color television set (citizens over 75 are not obliged to pay for this fee), and those who avoid payment are identified and prosecuted. The license fee works as a form of direct annual taxation and gives access only to BBC's two analogue terrestrial TV channels, BBC-1 and BBC-2, which pride themselves for providing programming "free of adverts and independent of advertisers, shareholders or political interests" (BBC web site, 2005).

BBC's digital channels (BBC-3, BBC-4, CBBC, Cbeebies, BBC News24 and BBC Parliament) are also financed through the license fee but are made available only to users who wish to bye the set-top box (costing approximately £40 [$60]) that will digitize the signal and will allow them free access to these. BBC's commercial operations (such as BBC Training, beeb.net and bbcamericashop. com) constitute separate divisions and companies which operate at arm's length from the BBC.

Indicative of the BBC's magnitude is the fact that it employs 23,000 people and received, in the financial year 2003–2004, close to £3 billion via the license fee

(BBC web site, 2005). Today, the Corporation claims to reach more than 94% of UK's population. In 2004 BBC-1 (26.8%) and BBC-2 (11%) combined for nearly a 40% share of the total TV audience. BBC Radio had 52% of the radio audience at the beginning of 2004.[1]

Nevertheless, the UK also has a large, and expanding, commercial audio-visual sector, on which, as explained above, public service duties were imposed by the piece of governmental legislation that brought it into being, the 1954 Television Act. The main competition to BBC television comes from Independent Television (ITV), whose two major shareholders, Carlton and Granada recently (1994) merged into one company. Fifteen regionally based franchisees provide both local and national (network) services. ITV's share of the television audience in 2003–2004 was just a little under 30% (The Guardian Media Guide, 2003). Although funded by advertising, ITV was obliged to offer a range and balance of programming, thus subscribing at least partly to public service broadcasting causes.

Channel 4 is a hybrid public service, minority interest service which also raises revenue through advertising sales, and reaped an audience share of just over 10% in the period 2003–2004.

The interesting aspect behind the development and the operation of Channel 4 is that instead of making programs itself, it is commissioning them to independent producers, thus constituting a pure broadcaster rather than a program maker. In response to this, a large independent production industry numbering about 1,500 firms emerged in the UK. Since the 1990s both the BBC and ITV have been required to buy 25% of their programming from independent producers.

Indicative of the sector's blooming presence is the fact that in 2004 the BBC commissioned over 170 companies in television, most of them with revenues under £6 million ($7.8 million).

Finally, the more commercially-oriented TV terrestrial free-to-air channel began broadcasting in the UK in April 1997. Channel 5 ("Five") is partly owned by Pearson and the German broadcaster RTL, it covers about 80% of the country, and in 2003 registered a 6.4% share of the audience (The Guardian Media Guide, 2003).

In terms of the specific characteristics of the programming itself, what appears to differentiate BBC-1's provision from that of BBC-2 is the latter's stronger reliance on factual and current affairs programming, whereas BBC-1 appears to be stronger on news, sports, drama, and entertainment programs, which clearly accounts for its larger popularity. on the other hand, ITV's programming is strongly aligned with that of BBC-1, only that it places less emphasis on news and more on drama and sport. Channel 4 is weak on sport and religion programs but strong on general factual, entertainment, and drama, whereas "Five" seems to rely

---

[1] Figures taken from http://www.bbc.co.uk

heavily on films and drama while placing little importance on current affairs and sport.

The UK cable and satellite TV market, which started its development in the mid 80s, when, glimpsing the informatic potential of fiber optic wires, the government conceived the idea of a national cable infrastructure that could be entertainment-led and privately funded (Negrine, 1985), was worth £3.8 billion (circa $4.5 billion) in 2004 (Ofcom, 2005a). The market has grown by 59.6% since 2000 on the back of strong growth in subscriber numbers and a constant push by the platform operators to raise the average revenue per subscribing unit (ARPU). The market segments into four sectors: digital terrestrial TV (named Freeview, this is free to access after the purchase of a set-top box), analogue cable, digital cable, paid-for satellite, and free satellite. From the non-terrestrial services, only the digital cable and paid-for satellite are assumed to have a long-term future in the UK.

Overall, 15 million UK households now receive multichannel (cable, digital satellite, and terrestrial) TV services, a figure that corresponds to a slightly more than 50% of total UK households. The UK market is dominated by the satellite platform and one key player, BskyB (owned by Rupert Murdoch's News International), which is both the leading platform operator and a leading content provider, with more than 7 million registered households and a 60% share of the UK digital and multichannel households. BskyB offers in excess of 260 channels.

As of September 2004, there was a total of 3.5 million cable television subscribers, a service dominated by two companies; NTL (which is owned by the U.S.-based International CableTel and currently controls around 57% of the UK cable TV subscribers) and the UK-based Telewest.

Finally, Freeview, the UK's free-to-air terrestrial digital service, currently reaches around 2 million UK households, assuming a share of almost 15% of the UK multichannel market.

As a result of the rapid growth of digital multichannel services, the market share of the main terrestrial TV channels as a whole and the number of people watching them each week ("reach") has fallen over the period, as viewers increasingly take advantage of the wider choice available on digital services. Most of the decline has been on BBC-1 and ITV-1, whereas losses for BBC-2, ITV-1 and Channel 4 are moderate (Ofcom, 2005b).

Radio

The presence and the importance of BBC in UK's radio scene is equally pivotal as that of TV. The BBC also operates regional radio for Scotland, Wales and Northern Ireland, and, although commercial radio arrived an astonishing 70 years after the launch of the first BBC service and as a result of the 1990 broadcasting Act

TABLE 5–2
The Broadcasting Scenery

Type of Station	Analogue MW (AM)	Analogue FM (VHF)	Total Analogue*	DAB Digital Radio	Total Analogue and DAB*
Local commercial	59	213	272	159	289
UK-wide commercial	2	1	3	8	8
BBC UK-wide networks	1	4	5	11	11
BBC local and nationals	36	46	46	32	46
Total	98	264	326	210	354

*Excludes double-counting of stations simulcasting on more than one platform or waveband.
Source: Ofcom, 2004.

(Crisell, 1994), today there are several regional commercial radio stations based in major cities outside London (see Table 5–2).

Almost 300 local commercial radio licenses have been granted. Nineteen radio stations broadcast using satellite and 15 through cable. As a whole, commercial radio has expanded rapidly since 1996. The average UK listener has 15 stations to choose from 24 in London (Commercial Radio Companies' Association., 2005).

Concurrent with patterns observed in other media, ownership concentration is prevalent in radio too. The commercial scene is dominated by three major players—Emap, Chrysallis, and GWR Media—raising concerns with regards to channels' programming homogenization and free competition. The largest seven companies account for around two-thirds of all listening to commercial radio

Radio is the most popular day-time medium in the UK, reaching 92% of the population. BBC national services reach more than twice as many people as the national commercial stations, and have 40% of the radio audience, compared to only 8% of the three national commercial stations (Classic FM, Virgin radio, and Talk Sports).

Regulatory Framework

The election of a Labor Party Government in 1997 and its re-election in 2001 resulted in no significant change in media policy from that pursued by the Conservatives for the previous 18 years. And this is because the centerpiece of government media policy in Britain lies in the fostering of the development of large media conglomerates, whose clout in the market will stimulate competition domestically and will secure the capacity of British media to compete internationally. Over the past decade, increasing attention has been placed on Rupert Murdoch's News International (owner of *The Times, The Sunday Times, The Sun,* the *News of the World,* BskyB and others), the Pearson Group, (publishers of *The Financial Times* and *The Economist*), The Daily Mail General Trust (which controls the largest share of UK's regional press), and Emap (a firm with a stronghold on the magazine market and a large share in the UK radio market) (ZenithMedia, 2003). The market in the UK is seen as the main mechanism for ensuring pluralism in output through the exploitation of niches and segments.

Over the past decade tighter controls were implemented onto BBC's operating expenses that eventually lead (and still do) to cuts in public funding and a subsequent corporate restructuring, reductions in staff, greater managerialism, and new commercial ventures.

Contrary to what applies to the press, broadcasting in the UK is still highly regulated thus providing the basis for broadcast media accountability. In 2003 a set of previously distinct and separate regulatory bodies (the Broadcasting Standards Commission, the Independent Television Commission [ITC], and the Radio Authority) were replaced by an overarching authority, the super-regulator Ofcom.

Ofcom assumed its powers under the Communications Act 2003 on December 29, 2003 and has become the regulator for the UK communications industries with responsibilities across television, radio, telecommunications, and wireless communications services. According to its mission statement, Ofcom exists to further the interests of citizen-consumers as communications industries enter the digital age. In essence, and as far as broadcasting is concerned, the codes of practice of all three statutory bodies mentioned above have been transferred to Ofcom

As a super-regulator, Ofcom has assumed a great deal of power and a wide range of supervisory control in key industries. So far, it has restrained its role in producing a rich set of comprehensive volumes of consultation documents (such as those regarding the current stage and the future of digital TV and radio).

Moreover, as a public corporation, the BBC is ultimately responsible to Parliament through its 12 publicly appointed governors. Many of its plans have to be approved by Government Ministers. on a more day-to-day basis, the BBC's *Producer Guidelines* act like a code of practice and the Corporation has a Program Complaints Unit available to the general public (Bromley, 2001).

Attempts to introduce statutory regulation of the press in the late 1980s and early 1990s were unsuccessful. Instead, the newspaper and magazine sectors adopted a self-regulatory regime operated through the Press Complaints Commission (PCC). It has a code of practice, hears complaints and publishes its findings.

For the most part, the UK media are regulated more by general law. In total, it is estimated, more than 140 pieces of legislation have specific relevance to the media, and litigation remains a favored method (at least among those who can afford it) of bringing the media to account (Garnham, 1998).

Arguably, the UK has embraced media digitization with a remarkable zest. This clearly prepared the ground for the adoption and further development of webcasting, since digital technologies, and in particular the fostering of broadband, are pivotal in the growth of this medium. Therefore, UK's regulatory framework, with its undisputed focus on new technologies and digitization, enabled the formation of a significant webcasting sector. This was developed due to the efforts of broadcasting media, which, having the relevant expertise in hand, saw a business and editorial opportunity in casting their, already largely digitized content, through the web.

The question today is whether this imminent development of digitization will give the *coup de grace* to the old broadcasting establishment, since as many as ten television channels can occupy the frequency space presently occupied by a single analogue service (Crisell, 1999).

Responding to this set of challenges and in an attempt to satisfy the government's demands and to protect its position as a major international television organization, the BBC has positioned digitization on top of its priorities.

According to an Ofcom's (2005c) recent assessment of the market impact of the BBC's new digital TV and radio services, it appears that on the positive side, the BBC's new services have contributed to digital uptake, in both television and radio, although the scale of the contribution shall not be overstated.

It was publicly admitted that the BBC's new services have not taken as much audience share as it was expected at launch. BBC-3 has an audience share of 0.6%, BBC-4 takes up 0.3%, CBBC occupies 0.4% of audience share while Cbeebies attracts 1.2% of audience share. These poor percentages are clearly an area of concern for the Corporation's future plans and developments in the digital arena.

Internet Penetration and Broadband Usage

The UK has undisputedly embraced a strong digital, new media and online policy. The ranking of the country in all major internet penetration and broadband usage lists is among the highest in Europe. According to the latest statistics (Internet World Stats, 2005) the UK has close to 35.5 million internet users which gives a penetration rate of 59%. In 2004 the number of UK internet users with broadband connection climbed to 4 million according to statistics by Ofcom (May 2004), out of which 2.5 million are DSL connections and 1.5 million cable modem connections. 15% of homes have broadband while DSL services are available to 84% of UK homes and businesses and cable modem services are available to 45% of UK homes and businesses.

In Summer 2005 high-speed internet connections outpaced dial-up access for the first time as some 8.1 million households—or nearly 30%—had signed up for broadband services by June 2005, more than double the number just 18 months before, according to figures released by the industry regulator, the Office of Communications (Ofcom). This compares with some 7.5 million homes that have slower dial-up connections (The Guardian, 2005).

According to the latest market research survey (June 2005) commissioned by Ofcom, 59% of UK adults have internet access at home, of which:

- 62% connect to the internet using broadband;
- 30% connect to the internet using narrowband;
- 28% connect using a narrowband unmetered service;
- 27% connect using a narrowband metered service;
- 1% connect using ISDN service; and
- 11% are unsure what type of narrowband connection they have.

In its second annual review of the communications market, Ofcom predicted that virtually all British homes (99.6%) would have access to a broadband connection by the end of this year. By 2010, it suggested that more people could be watching television over the internet than via analogue sets (The Guardian, 2005).

A further strong indication of the UK's acceleration into the digital age is also the fact that close to 70% of UK businesses have their own web site, a figure which is moving steadily upwards year after year (Internet World Stats, 2005).

All the major print and broadcast UK media have established an online presence, and some occupy a leading position in Europe wide charts which measure their usage and popularity. The first UK print publication to launch a web site was *the Electronic Telegraph* which started in 1994 and was followed by the *Guardian* and *Observer*. About 85% of local newspapers have web sites, and approximately 80% of local radio stations have an online presence too (The Guardian Media Guide, 2003).

Beyond any doubt, the leading position among UK media web sites belongs to the BBC. BBC Online claimed to have 4.9 million users, and registered more than 100 million page impressions in 1999, 60% of which were at the News site. By March 2004, the BBC was claiming 1.5 billion page impressions and 45 million unique users. The country's quality publications also achieve high popularity on the web. In April 2005 *Guardian Unlimited* registered nearly 115 million page impressions claiming to have more than 10 million unique users, which, given that the hard copy circulation is less than half a million, raises significantly the medium's readership. During the same period, the *Electronic Telegraph* recorded 38.5 million page impressions and almost 3.9 million unique users when last measured; *The Times* achieved 41 million page impressions and registered 4,6 million unique users, while in the tabloid/popular front the web site of *The Sun* registered more than 125 million page impressions and close to 4.5 million unique users (ABCE, 2005).

The more popular media (tabloid newspapers and the ITV companies) were slower to go online; but in 1999–2000 there was a sudden spurt of interest—and new investment often ran into £100 million, stimulated by a large increase in online shopping. The dotcom crisis of 2000 resulted in many of these ventures being curtailed or abandoned (Bromley, 2001).

WEBCASTING BUSINESS MODELS

Accessibility

The size of the UK market meant that for the purposes of a content analysis a reasonably big sample of 20 webcasters had to be selected and analyzed. Unfortunately, due to the nascent stage of the industry, there are not as yet independent, widely accepted measurements identifying the leading webcasters in the UK and separating them from those with moderate or very little understanding of the business of webcasting. Many webcasters with a strong presence in the UK market were bidding for a place in the list of the leading 20, but after consultation with a group of informants[2] and a close study of the lists of media web site popularity which are frequently compiled by research firms (such as Nielsen/NetRatings), a choice of the 20 leading UK webcasters was made.

The final list comprises mainly of clicks-and-bricks, i.e., the web versions of traditional broadcasters that operate TV or radio stations offline. Seven of the webcasters selected (35%) are pure-plays, in the sense that they constitute a stand alone, non ISP provider webcasting service, while one entry in the list was made by an ISP provider (AOL). These webcasters are not necessarily owned by UK companies. In fact, a closer analysis reveals that only 50% of the sample analyzed are UK-owned with the rest operating as joint ventures between a domestic and a foreign company or merely as foreign webcasters. (See Table 5–3.)

The advanced position of the UK in the internet market and its well established technological infrastructure is clearly demonstrated in the types of content that are webcast: Freed by the constraints imposed by slow and problematic transmission speeds, UK webcasters, irrespective of their nature as pure-plays or clicks-and-bricks, offer webcast users video files almost equally as much as audio, text, graphics, and animation.

---

[2]The informants panel consists of the following: (1) Richard Clark, editor, web User Magazine (editor@web-user.co.uk); (2) Andy Flint, Head of Client services, ABC Electronic (andy-flint@abce.org.uk); (3) Alex While, Director of AOP and Head of PPAi (alex.white@aop.org.uk); (4) Lee Salter, Lecturer in Journalism and Media Studies, School of Cultural Studies, University of West England (Lee.salter@uwe.ac.uk); (5) Ruxandra Trandafoiu, lecturer in Media and Journalism, Edge Hill University College, Livepool, Ormskirk (trandar@edgehill.ac.uk).

TABLE 5–3
Program Genres of Leading Webcasters

	Units	Percentage
Video		
Blockbuster movies	4	20
TV commercials	6	30
TV programs (entertainment)	11	55
Education/instruction	6	30
Trailers/highlights	15	75
Business (business news / speech / conference)	10	50
News clips/interviews (non-business)	14	70
Music videos	12	60
Documentaries	4	20
Cartoons/animation	7	35
Sports 4	12	60
Pornography (adult content)	1	5
Other	1	5
Audio		
Music	16	80
News	16	80
Talk/Speech/Interview	15	75
Sports	11	55
Other	4	20

More importantly, the provision of video files does not only encompass the relatively small sized music videos and trailers, but extends to the inclusion of large video files such as those of TV programs and TV series, as more than half of the leading UK webcasters studied have uploaded TV programs and series onto their web sites, thus reaffirming the definition of webcasting as "the broadcasting of video and audio content on the web" (Ha & Ganahl, 2004). The use of broadband technologies allows consumers to enjoy video and audio content in a quality similar to television and radio, and the leading UK webcasters seem to successfully capitalize on the high penetration of broadband in the country. Business news (50%), generic news clips (70%), talk shows and sports (60%—yet rarely in the form of a live transmission of a football match, for example) are also positioned high in UK webcasters' most favored content. on the other hand, religious and pornographic materials (5%) as well as documentaries and blockbuster movies have a very weak presence, with only 20% of the webcasters studied carrying such kind of content.

As far as the provision of audio content is concerned, predictably enough music, news, and talk shows top the list of preferred programming with more than two thirds of the webcasters analyzed opting to provide these genres in their content mix, followed by sports (55%). (See Table 5–4).

In terms of the preferred methods through which this content is transmitted, it is important to emphasize that the sites examined present users with a rich set of transmission options in a obvious attempt to better meet their needs and likes. Emphasis is given both on on-demand streaming (all except one [95%] offer on-demand streaming, giving users the chance to access and use the content at their convenience) and live streaming which is made available by 85% of the top 20 UK webcasters. Third in the transmission methods list is on-demand downloading, a transmission method employed by half of the UK webcasters studied and clearly favored by pure-plays primarily and disfavored by others, probably due to reasons connected with the protection of copyright infringement. Through on-demand downloads, content copyright is scarcely protected, as the downloaded file sits on the users' hard drive and can be used, repurposed, and distributed in various ways.

In light of this, pure-plays tend to offer a richer selection of channels on their webcast. In some case, such as the radio portal Live 365, the offering exceeds over 200 channels. on average, each channel carried around 25 clips/shows.

Content Strategies

A substantial percentage (in most cases reaches 50%) of the content carried by the UK leading webcasters originates from abroad. Out of the 20 webcasters examined, only 6 (30%) produce primarily domestic content whereas the presence of foreign content in the rest varies but in many cases occupies the majority share. Even the BBC, whose content is almost exclusively domestically produced (and this includes BBC staff who are based outside the UK), carries stories, video, and audio from foreign news agencies and also commissions on a yearly basis at least 25% of its output to independent producers who also may be based outside the UK.

Apart from AOL, a foreign-based ISP, dominant position in UK's webcasters have MSN and Yahoo!, two primarily e-mail access services with a dominant position in the content field too, especially webcasting. Also iFilms, MP3 and Live 365 are foreign operated pure-plays webcasters that strike a high popularity with UK users as they work as one-stop-shops for those interested in receiving video and/or audio content through the web. The rest of the foreign webcasters with a leading position in the UK market (CNN, Rolling Stone, Bloomberg), are internationally renown brands, whose offline presence almost "guarantees" a leading online positioning too. Finally, OneWorld is a U.S.-based non-governmental organization, aiming at developing a strong civil society network online which supports "people's media to help build a more just world." OneWorld has a strong presence in the UK due to its high popularity with media -savvy people (who are very likely to be strong webcast users).

TABLE 5–4
Top 20 UK Webcasters

Sitename	URL	Parent Company	Type	Unique Users	Revenue (04)	Ownership	Business Model
BBC	www.bbc.co.uk	BBC	CB	50,000,000	n/a	PSB	BC
AOL	www.aol.com	AOL/Time Warner	ISP	9,200,000	8.7 billion	Public	CA
Channel4	www.channel4.com	Channel 4 Group	CB	2,000,000	n/a	PBS	BC
Ananova	www.ananova.com	Orange	PP	3,500,000	n/a	Public	CA
MSN	www.msn.co.uk	Microsoft	PP	45,000,000	n/a	Public	CA
Yahoo	www.yahoo.co.uk	Yahoo!	PP	10,792,000	3.6 billion	Public	CA
iFilms	www.ifilm.com	iFilm	PP	1,741,000	n/a	Private	CA
MTV	www.mtv.com	MTV Networks	CB	1,950,000	n/a	Public	BC
CapitalFM	www.capitalfm.co.uk	Gcap Media	CB	7,504,500	n/a	Public	BC
MP3	wwww.mp3.com	CNET Networks	PP	1,030,000	n/a	Public	CA
OneWorld	www.oneworld.net	One World	PP	2,000,000	n/a	Trustee	BC
Virgin	www.virgin.com	Virgin	CB	2,500,000	n/a	Public	CA
Reuters	www.reuters.co.uk	Reuters	CB	20,000,000	n/a	Public	BC
BskyB	www.sky.com	News International	CB	8,101,000		Public	BC
CNN	www.cnn.com	Time Warner	CB	23,000,000	n/a	Public	BC
Jazz FM	www.jazzfm.co.uk	Guardian Media Group	CB	n/a	n/a	Public	BC
Rolling Stone	www.rollingstone.com	Rolling Stone	CB	n/a	n/a	Private	BC
Bloomberg	www.bloomberg.com	Bloomberg	CB	3,238,000	n/a	Public	BC
Live365	www.live365.com	Live 365	PP	8,700,000	n/a	Private	CA
XFM	www.xfm.co.uk	Gcap Media	CB	235,000,00	n/a	Public	BC

TABLE 5–5
Media Content Sources

Content Sources	Percentage
Original	20.50%
Repurposed	35.75%
Simulcast	32.25%
Unknown	5.25%

The important presence of foreign-generated content in UK's leading webcasters list is indicative of the dynamism of the UK market and of course reflects the strength of the English language in opening up the market to an international marketplace (see Table 5–5).

This is reasonable and perhaps expected in a globalized and ultra competitive media market, and in a country where the use of English makes it very receptive to foreign media products and cultural influence. Thus webcasting programs which are strongly positioned in the UK market tend to come from English speaking countries (primarily the United States but also other Asian English-speaking countries) alongside countries which simply produce video and audio products in English, irrespective of the actual language of origin (such as Scandinaviation and other EU countries). Similarly, countries with strong audiovisual exports and an established cultural influence in the world scene, such as France and Japan, have put their feet in the UK webcasting market. CNN, MTV, MP3, Rolling Stone, Bloomberg and iFilms are the leading UK webcasters whose majority content (be it in an audio or video format, of news or entertainment nature) originates outside the UK, primarily from the country at the leading end of audiovisual production and exports, the U.S..

As far as the source of the webcast content is concerned, simulcast and repurposed content take the lion's share. Original content is not produced to a large degree (see Table 5–6). More specifically, a comparative analysis of all leading 20 UK webcasters shows that almost 36% of their content is simulcast and 32% is repurposed. Original content occupies only 21% of the total provision while close to 5% of content comes from other sources. Ha and Ganahl (2004) argue that clicks-and-bricks webcasters, with their advantage of possessing readily available content from their offline counterparts, are much more likely than pure-play webcasters to use repurposed content or simulcast, whereas, to compete with clicks-and-bricks, pure-plays are more likely to offer original content. Indeed, this is evident in the analysis of the leading UK webcasters, whereby the web-only ones (such as Ananova for instance, which webcasts 80% of original content) tend to rely more heavily on original content to make their provision more appealing to the average user.

Table 5–6
Program Genres of Leading Webcasters

Video	Units	Percentage
Blockbuster movies	4	20%
TV commercials	6	30%
TV programs (entertainment)	11	55%
Education/instruction	6	30%
Trailers/highlights	15	75%
Business (business news/speech/conference)	10	50%
News clips/interviews (non-business)	14	70%
Music videos	12	60%
Documentaries	4	20%
Cartoons/animation	7	35%
Sports 4	12	60%
Pornography (adult content)	1	5%
Other	1	5%
Audio		
Music	16	80%
News	16	80%
Talk/Speech/Interview	15	75%
Sports	11	55%
Other	4	20%

Only 6 of the 20 leading UK webcasters analyzed (a mere 20%) required users to register in order to access the webcasting content, but no significant pattern emerged as to whether this is linked to their nature as pure-plays or clicks-and-bricks. The webcasters who did not opt for registration clearly weighted the advantages of acquiring some data about your users (very useful in creating more targeted advertising campaigns) against the disadvantage of discouraging them to browse the site's content and chose to save users from the trouble of registering.

Nevertheless, when registration is required, webcasters typically asked for identity, contact, and other demographic information (such as gender, income, occupation, etc.) but rarely extended the users' data collection to billing and psychographic information (such as shopping preference and life-style questions).

The majority of the UK leading webcasters (12 out of 20, i.e., 60%) chose the branded content business model as opposed to that of the content aggregator. This is reasonable since most of the top 20 UK webcasters are clicks-and-bricks and not online-only, and therefore they already rely on ready-made content and do not want to carry the media content of offline and online competitors (Ha & Ganahl, 2004). They tend to build their business success on specialized content usually in the form of a mix between original and repurposed or simulcast programs and they are much less varied in their use of revenue generation and transmission methods, compared to their content aggregator rivals.

Windows Media Player was the preferred media player to display the site content on 15 of the webcasters examined (75%), but it is closely followed by RealPlayer which is offered by 60% of the leading UK webcasters as an alternative option and not as a standalone. Four leading UK webcasters (a percentage of 20%) developed their own proprietary media player whereas Quicktime was given as an option only by 15% of the webcasters examined. When additional software was required to view the site content, in 70% of the cases the software was Flash.

The area where UK leading webcasters fair high involves the provision of features which aim at enhancing users' online experience by streamlining web site navigation and making content description explicit and content location easy and efficient. In light of this, 19 out of the 20 webcasters studied (95%) incorporate search engines and content directories on the home pages of their sites whereas the description of the content and the size of the audio and/or video files posted is made available in many cases (around 60% of the webcasting sample) and in sufficient depth. However, eight of the UK leading webcasters (40%) offered no file size and playing time information on their sites, thus potentially off-putting users who otherwise may had clicked to view audio and/or video programs.

Revenue Sources

Advertising is clearly the prime revenue source for the leading UK webcasters, although signs of an attempt to enrich and widen the revenue sources available are evident. All but two of the sites examined (90%) employ advertisements as the main means of recovering their operating costs, and largely post them on their home pages in the format of banner advertisements.[3] The number of advertisements vary, from a minimum of 1 to a maximum of 5, a factor probably linked to the popularity of the site and the skills of its selling team. E-commerce comes a distant second, however with a growing dynamism since it is utilized by 11 of the 20 (55%) webcasters analyzed.

Similarly, subscription, the revenue source that demonstrates the adoption of a business model which reflects the confidence of the producer on the value of the content produced (Arampatzis, 2004) is clearly emerging as a viable revenue generation option in some cases, since 25% of the leading UK webcasters have placed some of their content behind a subscription wall. Clearly, these are the ones which possess the strongest brand names and, interestingly enough, none of these five webcasters is a pure-play one. Finally, nine of the webcasters studied (45%) syndicate their content to interested third parties but very few (10%) incorporate the pay-per-use option on their sites.

In their research, Ha and Ganahl (2004) found that the transmission method seems to have an impact on the variety of revenue sources being used, with webcasters using live streaming having a much more limited choice of revenue sources than those using on-demand or both streaming and on-demand. This certainly holds true in the exploration of the UK leading webcasters as well, since those generating revenue through pay-per-use and subscription schemes transmitted all or part of their content on-demand as well. However, it seems that by no means can we give an axiomatic value to this conclusion, on the basis of this study alone. This is because, as outlined above, all 95% of the leading UK webcasters transmit their content via on-demand streaming but not all employ pay-per-use or subscription schemes to charge for it. The answer to this ostensible paradox lies in the fact that some of this on-demand content is simply given away for free, possibly anticipating the users' reluctance to pay and in an attempt to keep site traffic high to attract advertising.

Those who actually charge for content, do so by either charging by tiers (basic, premium, etc.) or they charge a monthly or annual subscription fee, which on average is around 10 dollars a month. In terms of pay-per-use schemes, the cost is on average $0.005 per streamed or downloaded item. Popular methods of payment include credit cards (which are very popular and widely used in the UK), Paypal or other online payment services, as well as transfers from bank accounts. Debit card payments are currently of little use.

Webcasters involved in e-commerce typically sell media and entertainment-related products through their sites, such as CDs, DVDs, and they often charge fees for downloading third party content and so on. Almost half of them sell licensed merchandise of TV programs and shows, capitalizing on the added-value created by the success stories of many such brands. Others would also charge for added value services such as e-mail accounts with large space capacity (e.g., Yahoo! and MSN).

Overall, no difference is identified in the choice of revenue source between pure-play and clicks-and-bricks leading UK webcasters, a finding which is in line with Ren and Chan-Olmsted's (2003) research. However, the nature of the webcaster impacts on the source of the content posted on their sites with pure-plays placing larger emphasis on offering original content as opposed to clicks-and-bricks. Indicatively, Ananova carries 80% of original content and MP3 45%. Yahoo!, MSN and Live365, also make sure that some of their content provision includes original offering so that they can compete with the repository of offline content of their bricks-and-clicks rivals.

---

[3]Of the sites which do not employ advertising, the first is the BBC, a public service broadcaster who is not permitted to carry advertising; the second is OneWorld, a non-governmental organization.

CONCLUSION

The UK leading webcasting market cleverly exploits the capabilities offered by the strong broadband technology penetration in the country, to expand, develop and formulate the anyhow inchoate industry of webcasting. The governmental commitment in establishing a strong digital infrastructure creates a favorable business environment which, in many respects, brings British webcasting at the forefront of the developments in this industry and at a central position in the EU webcasting scene.

Employing an open and outgoing approach, British webcasting presents a strongly pronounced international outlook and appears to actively examine and participate in all the industry's pivotal issues, from the selection and packaging of content to deciding transmission methods, revenue streams and the business models that work best.

The leading UK webcasters are remarkably experimental in their usage of revenue streams, exploiting to a large degree all the currently available means of generating revenue, even though emphasis is given to advertising and subscription. More importantly, a varied approach in the revenue sources is linked with a varied approach in transmission methods, although paradoxically pure-plays are less keen in launching subscription schemes, possibly due to their perceived lack of brand awareness from online users (who may be more familiar with webcasters that operate an offline counterpart).

Moreover, clicks-and-bricks tend to rely more heavily on their repository of content from their offline counterparts which they either repurpose or simulcast, whereas pure-play webcasters are seeking to produce more original content.

Overall, the UK webcasting market is so important to the industry of webcasting that constitutes one of the few markets worldwide that drives and shapes future developments. Due to technological advances, linked mainly with the high and ever-growing penetration of broadband technologies, political determination to support and actively promote new technologies linked with the internet and digitization as well as a set of cultural advantages such as the use of English language and a strong and vibrant media and broadcasting, in particular, market, the UK webcasting market experiences a high level of activity. The key question in terms of the industry's future prospects lies in "the overall internet business capacity to identify viable business models in which it can rely, invest and exploit so that strong and reliable revenue sources can be generated. This very factor will consolidate the industry and will impact hugely on the pace of its future development," says Lee Salter, a lecturer in Journalism and New Media at the University of West England and one of the informants of this piece of work.

Together with Germany and the Nordic countries, UK leads the top end of an industry in Europe, whereby the gap between those at the top and those at the bottom is ever-widening. Beyond any doubt, those interested in observing the developments in all fields of webcasting (transmission methods, revenue streams, business models, cultural influences, content origination and so on) had better channel their attention to the UK, for the years to come.

REFERENCES

Arampatzis, A. (2004). Online business models in Greece and the United Kingdom: A case of specialist versus generic and public versus privately-owned online news media. *International Journal of Media Management.* 6 (1&2),

Audit Bureau of Circulations. (2005). [Various articles] Retrieved March 22, 2005 from: www.abc.org.uk

Briggs, A. (1961). *The History of broadcasting in the United Kingdom* (Vol. 1: The Birth of Broadcasting). London: Oxford University Press.

British Broadcasting Corporation (BBC). (2005a). *About the BBC.* Retrieved March 27, 2005 from: http://www.bbc.co.uk/info/licencefee/

British Broadcasting Corporation (BBC). (2005b). *Response by the Board of Governors of the BBC to the Secretary of State's review of the BBC.co.uk,* Conducted by Philip Graf. Retrieved July 16, 2005 from http://www.bbc.co.uk/info/policies/pdf/bbc_graf.pdf

Bromley, M. (2001). *The British media landscape.* Retrieved March 24, 2005 from: http://www.ejc.nl/jr/emland/uk.html

Commercial Radio Companies' Association. (2005). *CRCA: The trade body for UK commercial radio.* Retrieved March 25, 2005 from: http://www.crca.co.uk

Crisell, A. (1994). *Understanding radio* (2nd ed.). London: Routledge.

Crisell, A. (1999). Broadcasting: Television and radio. In J. Stokes. & A. Reading (Eds.), *The media in Britain: Current debates and developments.* Palgrave: New York

European Federation of Journalists. (2004). European media ownership: Threats on the landscape. Brussels: EFJ.

Eurostat. (2005). *EU press circulation.* Retrieved July 22, 2005 from: http://epp.eurostat.cec.eu.int/portal/page?_pageid=1996,45323734&_dad=portal&_schema=PORTAL&screen=welcomeref&open=/&product=Yearlies_new_industry&depth=2

Garnham, N. (1998). Media policy. In Briggs, A. & Cobley, P., the media: An introduction. Harlow: Addison-Wesley Longman.

Guardian, The. (2004). *UK newspaper market.* Retrieved July 12, 2005 from http://adinfo-guardian.co.uk/non-uk-advertisers/pdf/uknewspapermkt.pdf

Guardian, The. (2005). *Television took 30 years to reach a mass audience—bbroadband has taken three.* Retrieved July 18, 2005 from : http://www.guardian.co.uk/business/story/0,,1528079,00.html

Guardian Media Guide, The. (2003). (Ed) by Peak, S. Guardian Books.

Ha, L., & Ganahl, R. (2004). Webcasting business models of clicks-and-bricks and pure-play media: A comparative study of leading webcasters in South Korea and the United States. *International Journal on Media Management,* 6(1&2), 75–88.

Internet World Stats. (2005). *European internet usage and population statistics.* Retrieved April 1, 2005 from: http://www.internetworldstats.com/europa.htm

Negrine, R. (1985 ed.). *Cable television and the future of broadcasting.* London and Sydney: Croom Helm.

Office of Communications (Ofcom). (2004). *About Ofcom.* Retrieved March 29, 2005 from http://www.ofcom.org.uk/about_ofcom/

Office of Communications (Ofcom). (2005a). The *Communication market 2005.* Retrieved July 12, 2005 from: http://www.ofcom.org.uk/research/cm/overview05/

Office of Communications (Ofcom). (2005b). *Overview of current provision and recent trends.* Retrieved July 12, 2005 from: http://www.ofcom.org.uk/consult/condocs/psb/psb/volume2/ overview/?a = 87101

Office of Communications (Ofcom). (2005c). *Assessment of the market impact of the BBC's new digital TV and radio services.* Retrieved July 12, 2005 from: http://www.culture.gov.uk/NR/ rdonlyres/4BC09004-FF13–47AA-BF90-BC857A22F23F/0/OfcomAssessmentoftheMarket ImpactoftheBBCsNewDigitalTVandRadioServices.pdf

Ren, W., & Chan-Olmsted, S. (2003, July). Radio business on the World Wide web. : An examination of the streaming clicks-and-bricks and internet-based radio stations in the United States. Paper presented in the Association for Education in Journalism and Mass Communication Annual Convention, Kansas City, Missouri.

Sparks, C. (1995). Concentration and market entry in the UK national daily press. *European Journal of Communication, 10*(2),

Sparks, C. (1999). The Press. In Stokes, J. & Reading, A. (1999). The *media in Britain: Current debates and developments.* Palgrave: New York

ZenithMedia. (2003). *Top fifty European media companies.* London: Zenithopmedia.

CHAPTER 6

The Netherlands: Webcasters in a Public Broadcasting Environment

Piet Bakker
University of Amsterdam

In line with the famous Marshall McLuhan saying that *the content of a new medium is always an old medium* (1964), the content of the first web sites featuring video and audio was often quite similar to the traditional audio and video channels and carriers: radio, television, film, and VCR. Traditional audiovisual media firms like record companies, film studios, and broadcasters used the internet to show and promote their products online. Because of this logic the traditional media landscape of any country very much influenced the content and business models of the internet video and audio providers, the webcasters.

In this chapter the Dutch webcasters are discussed mostly in terms of their relation to the traditional broadcasting system, which explains at least partly their current strong position. Apart from that, other models like that of commercial broadcasters, B2B webcasters, ISPs, and adult content providers are discussed. Also some popular web sites that contain audio and video, but not as a major feature, are analyzed. Because the traditional Dutch media landscape very much explains why webcasting looks the way it does in the Netherlands, we will start this chapter with short description of the Dutch media landscape and its history.

THE DUTCH MEDIA LANDSCAPE

Broadcasting in the Netherlands is traditionally (from 1930 on) public broadcasting. Until 1967 there also was no advertising on radio or television. Until 1989 public broadcasters (private membership organizations, churches, minority organizations, educational broadcasters, regional and local broadcasters, and a national coordinating body) had a joint monopoly. These organizations share three

TV channels and five radio stations; they don't own their own station or channel. This system was quite different from most other European countries where public broadcasting usually meant "national" broadcasting with a strong grip of government on internal broadcasting policy, content, and personnel. In the Netherlands, most important broadcast organizations are linked to political parties, churches, and social movements. The ties with these organizations were strengthened by the fact that all traditional organizations had their own program guide, almost every Dutch household was—and still is—subscribing to such a guide. Public broadcasters have a joint monopoly on program information so it is impossible for a non-broadcaster to publish a weekly television guide. Because of this strong membership feeling, there has always been a great deal of public support for public broadcasters.

In 2005 every Dutch household can receive five national radio stations (four FM, one AM—terrestrial and on cable), at least one regional channel and often more than one local station (all FM and cable); apart from that, there are at least a dozen commercial channels, all of them available through cable while many of them also have a terrestrial FM frequency. Average listening time is more than three hours every day (Bakker & Scholten, 2005, p. 100). The market share of public radio in 2004 was 44%.

Since 1989 several commercial broadcasters have launched Dutch television channels, first RTL (Bertelsmann) and a few years later SBS (Scandinavian Broadcasting System). These two companies are still the most important commercial television-broadcasters in the Netherlands. RTL had a market share of 26% in 2004 with three channels; the SBS-group also owned three channels with a combined market share of 20% (Bakker & Scholten, 2005, pp. 70, 141). In August 2005 a fourth major player entered the market, John de Mol with his Talpa Holding bought the television-rights for the Dutch national soccer competition for the next three seasons, starting in August 2005, while this company also controls telecom operator Versatel, which acquired the rights to webcast live soccer matches over the internet, mobile phones and pay-television. Talpa also launched a new edition (the 5th in the Netherlands) of the famous Big Brother format. By this move Talpa did challenge the fundamentals of Dutch public broadcasting (in which soccer always played a major role) and introduced wide-scale internet-distribution of live soccer matches.

In 2005 the average Dutch household can choose from 10 different general Dutch television-channels, a regional and sometimes a local channel, three different Dutch music channels, two Belgian Dutch language channels and almost half a dozen international channels with Dutch subtitles. Apart from that, there are several foreign language channels (German, English, French, Italian, Spanish and Turkish) available on almost every cable network—English and German can be understood by a large proportion of the population, the other stations are aimed at native speakers of these languages. Television-viewing time grew from 124 minutes in 1988 (just before the introduction of commercial television) to 192 minutes in 2004. Competition on the television market is high and still rising—a market share of a single channel between 10 and 20% is considered as quite high while market shares of 5% or less are quite common.

This means that there is an abundant offer of national Dutch content on both broadcast television and radio for almost everybody (less than 5% of the Dutch population does not have a television connected to cable or a satellite dish). Because of the amount of popular content available on regular channels, services like pay television, digital television and even satellite television are not used by many households. Pay-television channel Canal+ has never been very successful in the Netherlands, even when it still had the rights to broadcast live soccer matches (the company does not reveal the amount of subscribers). The cable market in the Netherlands is quite concentrated; three operators—UPC, Casema and Essent—control 85% of the market. Although they are doing quite well financially (they have a virtual monopoly in their own areas) because of cable subscriptions and broadband internet connections, the introduction of digital TV services seems to be more difficult. Some cable operators in the Netherlands have even begun in 2005 to give away free digital set-up boxes—without increasing the subscription price—to convince the public of the merits of this new possibility. Only 10% of the Dutch households have a satellite dish (Bakker & Scholten, 2005, p. 124); many of these households originally come from Mediterranean countries such as Turkey and Morocco and use it to watch television from their homeland. Experiments with digital radio (digital audio broadcasts—DAB), which started halfway the nineties were ended in 2000 because the public interest in this new medium was considered to be minimal. In 2003 Dutch national broadcaster NOS again started with digital radio but again interest is not overwhelming, not only because consumers need new radio receivers or not enough content is available, but also because Dutch cable radio already offers 30 or more different radio channels (Bakker & Scholten, 2005).

The Netherlands is also still a newspaper reading country; in 60% of the Dutch households a daily newspaper is available, with nearly 90% of these acquired by subscription. But nevertheless newspaper readership and circulation are dropping in the Netherlands as it is in most western countries (World Press Trends, 2005). Apart from 3.9 million paid newspapers each day, almost 800,000 free newspapers are distributed on a daily basis, and magazine reading is also quite high in the Netherlands (Bakker & Scholten, 2005).

FROM BROADCAST TO WEBCAST

Although almost every broadcaster and many other parties participated in webcasting from the beginning, the burst of the internet bubble in 2000 and the recession of 2001 resulted in downsizing many of these operations, public broadcasters being the exceptions: They invested where others pulled out. This resulted in an advantage for public broadcasters on the web—but also in complaints by other (commercial) parties about unfair competition.

Public broadcasters, however, don't broadcast for profit—they claim broadcasting and also webcasting is part of their mission and obligation. This does not mean that other sorts of webcasters are absent from the scene; commercial broadcasters, ISPs, other news media and several other parties are also active as webcasters, but they have to compete with webcasters who not only have a very different business model but who are also in an advantageous position. Comparing webcasters in the Netherlands is therefore not easy, also because public broadcasters don't see themselves as businesses. Dutch law even forbids public broadcasters to make a profit on their operations. But according to the size of the operations and the money involved, many public broadcasters might qualify as businesses.

WEBCAST HISTORY

Although it was technically possible from the beginning of the internet to send any kind of digital content to other users, the introduction of the graphic interface of the World Wide Web with browsers like Mosaic (1993), Netscape (1994), and internet Explorer (1995) (Browser Timelines, 2005) made it possible to view video and listen to sounds. However, files were often huge, which made it next to impossible to download any of them with a normal dial-up telephone connection. Furthermore, most PCs did not have the capacity to play or store these files. Only at the end of the nineties were networks and hardware getting ready for audio and video; crucial was the development of compression techniques (MP3, RealAudio, QuickTime, Windows Media), the introduction of "flat rate" and broadband internet connections (cable and ADSL) and the availability of multi-media computers with sound capacities and video cards, speakers and hard disks big enough to store audio and video files (Bakker, 2005).

In the Netherlands, the first high bandwidth connections were introduced in 1997 (cable) and 1998 (ADSL) (Couzy, 1998). Dutch national telecom operator PTT Telecom experimented together with national broadcaster NOB and the university network Surfnet with webcasts: music videos, educational programs, and news. This meant national broadcasters had an advantage over other parties in developing content, transmission techniques, and interfaces. Cable operators also offered high bandwidth connections, but did not develop their own content.

This advantage of public broadcasters was amplified by the fact that by the time broadband connections were widely available and more households had computers that could play and store audio and video, the economic situation worsened (GDP growth in all OECD (Organization for Economic Cooperation and Development) countries was 3.3% in 1999 and 3.9% in 2000; and dropped to 1.1% in 2001 in 1.6% in 2002) (OECD, 2005, p. 30). The so-called "internet bubble" burst in 2000 and a year later the post-9/11 economic crisis affected businesses and consumers all over the world. New emerging industries and entrepreneurs had much more difficulties to develop successful "business" models than traditional broadcasters who could use their existing businesses to fall back upon.

BROADCASTING AND WEBCASTING IN EUROPE

In European countries where public broadcasters were still enjoying a substantial market share, these broadcasters could put their mark on webcasting. Although commercial broadcasting is available and popular in all European countries, their position is not as strong as for instance in the USA or some Asian countries. European commercial broadcasters developed later in time, were often not allowed to use the terrestrial network and had to compete with subsidized national broadcasters. In 1980 only Luxembourg had a commercial television-system; in 1990 there were still no commercial broadcasters in Denmark, Norway, Portugal, Sweden, Austria, Ireland, and Switzerland—the last three countries still had no commercial broadcaster in 1997. Public and commercial broadcasters compete also for advertising money because most public broadcasters are financed by license fees or taxes and carry advertising (Siune & Hultén, 1998). Subsidies, government support and advertising income were used to invest in a risky medium like the internet.

Webcasting Research

We will try to explain in this chapter why webcasting in countries that traditionally have been dominated by public broadcasting looks as it does. Arampatzis (2004) already raised the issue of the different behavior of public and commercial broadcasters. On basis of interviews in the UK and Greece it was concluded that public broadcasters were more innovative when webcasting was concerned. In fact, this finding is somewhat counter-intuitive because commercial parties have a reputation of fast moving and exploring new formats whereas public broadcasters are often seen as more traditional. It could be agued that the advantage of public broadcasters in terms of available resources and experience could be a possible explanation for the perceived "innovative behavior."

The difference between countries dominated by public broadcasting was also raised in a study on webcasting in 13 countries (Ha, Ganahl, Arampatazis et al., 2005) which concluded that a possible reason for the diverse findings

"... is the presence of non-profit webcasters in some countries within this study. In many European countries and Canada, public broadcast is still the dominant ownership mode of electronic media and their webcasts reflect their non-profit and diverse programming mission. ...These webcasters may not directly apply a profit generation mode when devising their content strategies. Their decisions regarding content offerings are not based solely on bottom line considerations." (p. 20–21)

The different behavior of commercial and public broadcasters (and webcasters) is hard to detect from other studies. In the study mentioned above it is offered as a possible explanation for differences found, but in other studies on webcasting business models, public broadcasters are not even taken into account, perhaps because they are not seen as real "businesses." Chan-Olmsted and Ha (2003) conducted a survey on US commercial television executives, excluding low power and public stations because of their different funding structures. This might be a good approach for the USA but these findings may not apply to other parts of the world where commercial broadcasting is not the dominant format. Ha and Ganahl (2004) studied 48 leading webcasters in the US and South Korea; they included commercial broadcasters like Bloomberg, CNN, and CBS, but no public broadcasters. Kolo and Vogt (2004) studied "traditional media and internet spin-offs" in Germany and included five commercial broadcasters (apart from newspapers and magazines) but no public broadcaster.

Although we will limit our cases to the Netherlands, we assume that findings may also be applied to other European countries with similar conditions: the German-speaking countries Austria, Switzerland and Germany; Belgium; Scandinavia; the UK, and Ireland. In all these countries public broadcasting has been dominant while internet access and broadband connections are relatively high. In Southern and Eastern Europe broadband penetration is lower (World Broadband Statistics: Q4 2004, 2005; Commission Staff Working Paper, 2004). The development of public and commercial television in the Southern part of Europe, however, is more or less in line with what happened in the Northern part with the advance of commercial broadcasters in the eighties. In eastern Europe television developed quite differently.

The Dominance of Public Broadcasters

In the traditional audiovisual media environment, public broadcasters had the "natural" monopoly, frequencies were scarce and access limited. This, of course, all changed with internet: access for everybody who could afford a PC and an internet connection and no scarcity in possible channels. How did public broadcasters manage to keep a substantial market share in such an open market? The explanation for the dominant position of the public broadcaster is threefold.

First they often have the necessary resources to finance the costly operation of setting up a webcast organization. As stated above, many public broadcasters are financed by license fees or taxes and advertising (Siune & Hultén, 1998). Because broadcasters see webcasting often as a way to build audience relations (Chan-Olmsted & Ha, 2003), the budget is party directed to the internet, which is seen as an integral part of their media portfolio. This practice of using broadcasting money for internet activities has led some countries to complaints about unfair competition of public broadcasters on the internet. The BBC spent £132 million ($233 million) in 1998–2000 on the internet. In 2001 the BBC proposed also to spend $195 million on online education, which raised numerous objections from educational publishers. In July 2005 the BBC made classical music labels complain because the public broadcaster made all Beethoven symphonies available as a free download on the BBC web site (Barnes, 2005). Dutch broadcaster NOS announced in 2001 that they would spend between € 10 million and € 15 million ($12 to $18 million) a year on their portal site www.omroep.nl until 2005 (Houtman, 2001). A year later another € 20 million ($24 million) was allocated for internet activities of the combined Dutch public broadcasters, this also led to objections about unfair competition (Kabel, 2002).

Second, public broadcasters often see it as their mission and obligation to use every possible channel to broadcast their products. The argument is that the internet is just another means of reaching the public and that taxpayers money was used to produce the content that can now made available again without too many costs (Kabel, 2002).

A third reason is that public broadcasters usually own the copyright of their own broadcasts, whereas in other models (i.e., content aggregators) copyright must be obtained from third parties. When ADSL was introduced in the Netherlands, apart from technical problems (lack of standardization, quality of signals), copyright was the most pressing problem; broadcasting of music videos, for instance, was a costly operation because of copyright issues (Couzy, 1998). Ha (2004) came to the same conclusions: The cost of digital content and copyright issues were still the larger issues for webcasters (see also Ha & Ganahl, 2004). Public broadcasters in Europe traditionally broadcast much original content: news, domestic soap operas, children programs, sports, culture, live music, educational programs, television documentaries, etc. European public broadcasters often have an obligation to produce and broadcast a certain percentage of domestic content. Commercial broadcasters rely more on foreign products like movies, American and European television series, reality television, and on domestically produced game shows and entertainment products that are not always suitable for re-broadcasts. However, when commercial broadcasters develop their own material they often rely heavily on webcasting for extra income. RTL Netherlands for instance build webcasting facilities for popular formats like Big Brother and daily soap opera Goede Tijden Slechte Tijden (Good Times Bad Times). The extra income, however, seems to come nowadays more from phone and sms-services than from the webcast. The web site (with webcasting) is extending the brand of the program, and makes it possible to access it at any time rather than one or two hours each day. Income is mostly generated (see below) by asking people to vote by sms, or to get newsflashes on their favorite program or character. (Telecom companies are also profiting from this model.)

Other Webcasters: ISPS, Adult Content, B2B, Marketing

The dominance of public broadcasters, however, only partly explains the way the internet is used for audio and video in the Netherlands and other European countries. For other parties, reasons like easy access to users (ISPs), existing strong brands (newspapers or magazines), or highly valued material that cannot be obtained elsewhere (adult content, business information) explain why they went into webcasting. But, making money with webcasts might not be the only or not even the most important reason for webcasting; marketing of other products or strengthening the relation with customers might just be as important for webcasters (Chan-Olmsted & Ha, 2003).

Apart from the dominant public broadcast model, four other business models will be discussed. The first is the B2B model. Quite successful in the Netherlands, these businesses work for newspaper web sites, private companies, non-profit organizations, universities and schools, ISPs, etc. They also work for web sites that do not have the facilities to make their own webcasts. Video-content is either self-produced or bought from third parties—sometimes they act as a reseller of content from local or regional broadcasters. The result is that the same webcasts often can be seen on several different web sites.

The second is the adult content provider. Although it is not clear at first sight where adult content providers are located (a "whois" search on the internet can often clarify that), they can be accessed through national web sites. ISPs often use adult content to sell their internet service (although they tend to do that without too much publicity as peddling pornography can be frowned upon). Adult content is one of the main drivers behind the advance of broadband. A survey conducted by British ISP Homecall revealed that 23% of the people interviewed were getting broadband for the adult content, the most mentioned reason (Orlowski, 2004). These web sites always have been very innovative in getting revenues; they solved problems of anonymity and micro payments long before other parties.

The third related business model is that of the ISP. To promote broadband, they are more or less forced to show as much broadband features as possible: music downloads, adult content, news and sports clips, movie trailers, ring tones, etc. The last model is that of web sites that mainly use video and audio as a marketing/promotion tool. Making money with video or audio is not the main objective but

TABLE 6-1

20 Most Visited Sites in the Netherlands 2000–2004

	2004	2003	2002	2001	2000
1.	startpagina.nl	msn.nl	pagina.nl	startpagina.nl	startpagina.nl
2.	msn.nl	pagina.nl	msn.nl	ilse.nl	ilse.nl
3.	google.nl	google.nl	startpagina.nl	msn.nl	omroep.nl
4.	detelefoongids.nl	startpagina.nl	ilse.nl	omroep.nl	altavista.nl
5.	ilse.nl	Ilse.nl	detelefoongids.nl	detelefoongids.nl	msn.nl
6.	marktplaats.nl	detelefoongids.nl	google.nl	tiscali.nl	planet.nl
7.	postbank.nl	marktplaats.nl	omroep.nl	postbank.nl	webwereld.nl
8.	Anwb.nl	startkabel.nl	telegraaf.nl	rabobank.nl	vindex.nl
9.	startkabel.nl	planet.nl*	planet.nl	nl.altavista.com	teletekst.nos.nl
10.	msn.com	rtl.nl*	kpn.nl	ns.nl	ns.nl
11.	nl.bol.com	rabobank.nl	clubs.nl	lycos.nl	telegraaf.nl
12.	rabobank.nl	omroep.nl*	rabobank.nl	telegraaf.nl	worldonline.nl
13.	schoolbank.nl	kpn.nl	postbank.nl	clubs.nl	happypoint.com
14.	planet.nl*	ebay.nl	nu.nl	planet.nl	aex.nl
15.	rtl.nl*	anwb.nl	kaartenhuis.nl	kaartenhuis.nl	lycos.nl
16.	kpn.nl	Telegraaf.nl*	ns.nl	kpn.com	veronica.nl
17.	telegraaf.nl*	Postbank.nl	hetnet.nl	pagina.nl	rabobank.nl
18.	wehkamp.nl	wehkamp.nl	lycos.nl	ebay.nl	nl.bol.com
19.	ns.nl	lycos.nl	tiscali.nl	anwb.nl	postbank.nl
20.	ebay.nl	ns.nl	wehkamp.nl	nl.bol.com.nl	anwb.nl

*Sites with webcasting features—2003 and 2004 only.
Source: Multiscope.nl..

121

dressing up the web site with these features can lead to more visits, more income from advertisers and more e-commerce. Apart from these four formats, the Fabchannel webcast will be discussed, this web site with live concerts was often mentioned by experts interviewed but does not easily fit into any category. Because it more or less uses the business model of the public broadcaster, it is discussed in that section.

METHOD

To identify the leading Dutch webcasters, Multiscope (www.multiscope.nl), the most used index for site traffic of the Dutch internet, was used. Every year Multiscope publishes the most visited sites in the Netherlands. (See Table 6–1.)

From Netratings, another company involved in tracking site traffic, full data from the last quarter 2003 was used while also the last available top 10 (June 2004) was consulted. In addition, e-mail interviews with 14 experts in webcasting were conducted. These experts included webcaster executives, an editor of an ICT-magazine, ICT and webstreaming consultants, a news site operator, public and commercial broadcaster executives, academic internet researchers, and the manager of an academic internet service provider. The data gathering was originally done for a research on webcasting in 13 countries (Ha, Ganahl, Arampatzis et al., 2005). For this research 10 sites were selected—mostly the most popular sites with some sites that were mentioned often because of their innovative character. For the case studies presented here, these 10 sites plus others often mentioned are selected. The new additions include B2B-operaters, often mentioned by the experts (but outside the scope of the original study) and web sites with adult content, also often mentioned—but the experts interviewed did not provide us with specific web sites.

Public Broadcasters

Omroep.nl (portal.omroep.nl) is a classic portal, the starting point for almost everything public broadcasters in the Netherlands have to offer, which explains the popularity of the site. News is a central element, with links to recent broadcasts and an archive of news items (radio and television). Apart from that, the site contains links to every regional broadcaster with video or audio. Also there are themes (science, sports, history, movies, music etc.), a search function, links to live streams of broadcasts (webradio and webTV) and weblogs, and to "uitzendinggemist.nl" (see below). The strength of the site probably has to do with the completeness of the offerings, and the fact that it is very up-to-date as well as its high usability. The site is not a webcast site per se. But webcast possibilities are

FIGURE 6–1 Homepage of *Uitzending Gemist*.
Note.   Programs can be found in five different ways: by their name (title), the day (dag) of the broadcast, the channel (net/zender), the broadcaster (omroep) or theme (rubriek). Below that (left), new programs, yesterday's programs (middle) and the most popular programs (right, below) can be accessed immediately. The web site also contains an Electronic Program Guide (right, middle).

built smoothly into it. There is no advertising on the main page and only very little on further pages.

The site www.uitzendinggemist.nl ("missed broadcast") is part of the portal of the national public broadcast site (although it is marketed with its own URL). The main function and also the main reason for its popularity is that it contains the full content of almost everything the three public networks and some regional networks have produced in the last months or sometimes even the last years. Navigation is easy, full broadcasts can be found by date, name, network, theme, or broadcaster. Broadcasts from the day before and the most popular searches are displayed on the main site that has only very few advertisements. Webcasts can be played either in a new browser window (with RealPlayer or Windows Media plug-in) or with an external player. Webcasts can be seen with a modem connection (43 kbps) or in broadband (109 kbps).

The music webcast site of the Dutch broadcaster VPRO (3voor12.vpro.nl) was mentioned by many interviewees as one of the most innovative operations in the webcasting environment. In contrast to many other webcast sites, it contains mainly audio and only a limited amount of video, although it carries two webTV channels: music video clips and concerts. At all times it is possible to listen to eight different webradio channels, hundreds of songs, and watch video clips (in different genres: alternative, dance, hip hop, roots, punk, metal, world, etc.), concerts, and DJ-sets. Non-mainstream music is the most important content on the site; there is hardly any advertising and only little e-commerce (t-shirts, DVDs, books). The site also has many other features: local music agendas, news items, artist's information etc. Copyright problems have also arisen in the development of the site; some major labels did not want their music on the site or demanded too much money—which partly explains the emphasis on non-mainstream music. WebTV is available in five formats: narrow band (max. 60 kbps), broadband (max. 500 kbps)—both as Windows Media and RealPlayer—and First Mile (max. 5000 kbps). Audio is available as Windows Media, RealPlayer, Shoutcast and First Mile. On demand songs are played as 96.5 kbps streams, music video clips as 500.5 kbps streams (broadband).

Fabchannell (www.fabchannel.com) started webcasting in 2000. The web site contains more than 400 concerts recorded in De Melkweg and Paradiso (the two most popular concert venues in Amsterdam). These concerts can be viewed in full (up to two hours) with a modem connection (56 kbps) or a broadband connection of 500 kbps max. The concerts are mainly performed by non-mainstream artists with independent labels contracts which solves most of the copyright problems, although concerts by more established artists like Solomon Burke, John Cale, Living Colour, De La Soul, and the Fun Lovin' Criminals are also available. Some live concerts (streaming) can be viewed on Fabchannel; the July 2005 concert by UK ska-band Madness was viewed by 1000 people live in De Melkweg, and by 5000 fans through the live webcast. In the week after the concert 10,000 viewers watched the on demand concert. The reason for the substantial viewing of the live streams and the on-demand webcasts is the fact that these are announced on the artists' web sites, which usually are accessed by fans all over the world—35% of the visitors are from the Netherlands, 25% from the USA. During the webcast, fans can also chat with each other. Viewing is completely free; Fabchannel is sponsored by Paradiso and by the Dutch Minister of Culture. Some extra income is generated when artists use the original footage of the webcast for a live DVD (Pot, 2005).

Commercial Broadcasters

Since 1989 commercial broadcasting has been possible in the Netherlands. The RTL group (with three television channels and two radio stations) and SBS (with three television channels) were the major players in 2004; they had a combined television market share of 46%. Until the autumn of 2005 when new commercial broadcaster Talpa entered the Dutch television market, only RTL did webcasts on a regular basis, but not as abundantly as the public broadcasters. The broadcaster has mainly trailers and "the making of..." clips of their own productions online; also the site has information on movies with the possibility to play clips and buy the movie online. The duration of these webcasts is seldom more than a few minutes. The daytime business news program of one of the RTL-channels is available as an online streaming webcast (with 233 kbps and 796 kbps connection)—first a commercial message that cannot skipped, has to be watched. RTL also links to adult content provided by Midhold (see below). Both RTL radio stations can be listened to online. RTL has used some of their products, specially their Big Brother format and their daily soap program Goede Tijden Slechte Tijden (Good Times Bad Times) for paid webcasts, paying customers or "members" could see exclusive content (not shown on television or previews). Advertising is much more used on the webcast sites of the commercial broadcasters than on public broadcasters web sites.

In the autumn of 2005 Big Brother was broadcast for the fifth time in the Netherlands. The broadcaster was Talpa, the new commercial channel by the only Dutch media tycoon John de Mol. When De Mol was still CEO of production company EndeMol (before it was sold to Spanish telecom operator Telefonica) his company first launched the format. Big Brother has changed from a partly "premium paid" model to a model based on advertising and phone-related income. People can vote, get news, buy ringtones by phone or register for services so they get e-mails with advertisements. Prices start at €0.80 ($0.96) for a simple message.

B2B

In the research on leading webcasters in 13 countries (Ha, Ganahl, Arampatazis et al., 2005) the focus was on webcasting for the consumer market. When the interviews for this research were conducted in the Netherlands, more than half of the people interviewed mentioned that the most successful webcasters in terms of revenues were probably the B2B webcasters and adult content providers (see below for this last category). Three companies were specifically mentioned: DutchView, Jet-stream, and FTV. These webcasters operate somewhat outside the visible field of webcast researchers and the general public, but they are nevertheless important enough to mention. They not only provide other consumer webcasters with content, but also work for businesses and non-profit organizations that use webcasts as an in-company medium or as an educational tool.

DutchView (formerly part of the public broadcasting organization) calls itself a "more camera-business for image and sound," and works for television, radio, and internet. Their webcasting business is focused on businesses that want to communicate with their staff (in-company), client relations (B2B), or with the general public (B2C). Music webcasts on the Heineken Music Hall web site (www.heineken-music-hall.nl) is one example of B2C production. For one of the leading banks in the Netherlands, DutchView, produced the televised webcast of the presentation of the annual results (www.dutchview.nl). Jet-stream is specialized in webcasts and works for broadcasters, telecom operators, governmental organizations, universities, schools, and private businesses. FTV (slogan: Television on your PC—www.ftv.nl) specializes in news webcasts, which it sells to other webcasters like newspapers, magazines, broadcasters, ISPs, and online news services that don't have the facilities to make their own webcasts. Also they operate as a reseller of video content from local or regional broadcasters.

ISPs

Internet Service Providers and cable operators have invested millions of Euros in broadband access. On almost every ISP's homepage are examples of streaming and downloading audio and video. Common features are news items with short video clips, sports, paid music downloads, movie trailers, web radio channels, ring tones, games and an adult section. Although some parts contain paid content (music, adult content and ring tones), marketing seems to be the main reason because the homepage serves mostly as a portal for these paid services—but of course they also receive revenues from third party services. Seven ISPs are in the top 20 of the most visited Dutch web sites of the last three years (www.lycos.nl, hetnet.nl, planet.nl, tiscali.nl, chello.nl, athome.nl, and wannadoo.nl) and all carry audio and video. Every ISP links to or has its own adult section (see also below). Web sites of ISPs in fact all look very similar because all carry more or less the same services.

Adult Content Providers

There are obviously many sites with adult content but for some reason these sites seldom turn up on official rankings of most visited web sites. Reasons may be various for this omission. In surveys, people are probably not eager to admit that they visit sites with adult content while the sites themselves often do not participate in joint operations of tracking web site visits. Another reason might be the very unclear structure of these web sites, surfing to a web site with adult content (or even leaving it) results often in being redirected to another site (many times with leaving the original web site open) while automatic pop-ups and pop-unders make it even more difficult to know were you are surfing at the moment. It is not unusual to start on one page and have more than ten pages open after a few clicks. In many occasions leaving web sites with adult content can only be achieved by quitting the browser altogether.

It is also no secret that the possibility of accessing adult content (pictures, videos and live streams) is one of the main reasons for people to get a broadband connection (see Orlowski, 2004). An often neglected feature of the peer-to-peer networks like Freenet (Kazaa interface) and Gnutella (Limewire) is the availability of adult content movies that are placed there either by other users or by webcasters who use these networks as a marketing tool. Downloading and viewing these movies often results in opening the web site of the adult content provider with more (paid) content. Movie clips ending with .asf (active server files) and .wmv (windows media video) are notorious for this feature; the user in fact only downloads a small file and is connected to a server from which the rest of the movie is streamed. Sometimes full movie clips (in avi, mpg, mpeg, mov, or windows media format) can be downloaded without connecting to a web site, but in those cases the clip ends with a web site URL were more movies can be downloaded (Bakker, 2005).

Almost every expert interviewed, mentioned adult content webcasters as a successful business model, as well in terms of visits as in terms of revenues. There is, however, little known about these revenues. A recent report by internet research firm Visiongain, "Mobile Adult Content 2005–2009," states that the total world adult content market in 2004 is worth €22.1 billion ($26.6 billion), including also DVD, publishing, and television. The biggest growth is expected to be in the new mobile 3G networks which is about to rise to €710 million ($860 million) by the end of 2005 (Vecchiatto, 2005).

While most experts interviewed mentioned adult content web sites, specific URLs were not given or non-existent. That specific URLs are not remembered can be the result of the nature of the web site, clicking on almost any link opens another site, while the pop-ups make it impossible to trace where you've been (another explanation is that people interviewed did not want to admit their knowledge of these URLs). To shed some light on the nature of these sites, two Dutch adult content providers with different business models described below: midhold.nl and askjolene.com.

The first company (midhold.nl) is located in The Hague and does not carry adult content on its homepage but acts as content provider for ISPs like Planet, Versatel, Wannadoo, Athome, Chello, Hetnet, and Lycos. Also commercial broadcaster RTL, the Amsterdam local television station AT5, and the web site of the biggest newspaper in the Netherlands, De Telegraaf, are provided with adult content from Midhold (De Telegraaf only shows a banner for these services after midnight.) Its services contain streaming and on-demand video, pictures, live webcams, chats etc. Midhold mainly acts as a content provider for other parties and also handles technical web site solutions and billings for these sites. The most obvious reason is that that these brands don't want to be associated with adult content although they are quite happy to earn money from this services. The only (visible) connection is the link to the adult service. The most common way of paying for adult content in the Netherlands is with 0906 phone numbers. When someone clicks on the desired content, a page opens with a 0906 phone number to call, when the phone connection is made, the user is provided with a secret four digit number which can be entered on the web site; as long as the phone line is open, the user has

FIGURE 6–2 Screenshot of access site for adult content.

access to the adult content. The phone connection will cost the user between 80 Eurocent and 1 Euro ($0.96 to $1.20) per minute (see Figure 6–2).

The advantage for the user is of course that this keeps his visits more or less secret. It is also possible to connect to the web site with a modem. Pictures of the movies are presented on the site (only accessible after confirming that you are over 18). In some instances free short movie trailers are presented.

Askjolene.com is located in the city of Eindhoven and is an adult portal for pictures and movies. It offers a choice between 25 different categories with comics, models and celebrities being the most innocent. Clicking on one of the categories takes the user first to a page with several search results and pictures. Clicking on one of these search results or picture links takes the user to another (third party) site with some free and more paid content. As most of these sites are non-Dutch (mostly U.S.-based), payment (membership) for the paid content has to be made by credit card or check. Askjolene itself makes money only by referring to these web sites.

MARKETING/PROMOTION

The last category of webcasters consists of web sites (mostly of traditional news media) that carry audio and video clips just to make the site more attractive to users. This mostly concerns short video clips with news items. Watching these videos is free to the user. Webcasting is in fact not very central in their business model nor is it prominently featured on their web site. Revenues from these web sites come from advertising and e-commerce while they also serve as a marketing tool for the traditional medium. The two biggest paid newspapers in the Netherlands, De Telegraaf and De Volkskrant, both carry some video news. De Telegraaf has a video clip page with approximately 30 short clips; some of them begin with a short commercial that cannot be skipped. All videos on the web site of De Telegraaf are from third parties, mostly from B2B webcaster FTV. De Volkskrant moved in the beginning of 2005 to a more elaborated model, the same news videos as on De Telegraaf web site are shown (also by FTV) but some of the videos on the web site are specially made for the paper by their own journalists, have a higher quality (and need therefore more bandwidth) and are longer (several minutes). In the newspaper itself pictures of these videos are displayed with a special logo to draw attention to the web site. Nu.nl, the most popular web-only news site in the Netherlands uses only the short FTV-video clips with advertisements.

CONCLUSION

There are some good reasons for the dominant position of public broadcasters. The financial possibilities of public broadcasters (sponsored by license fees or tax money and income from advertisers) and the absence of the copyright problem (rights of domestic productions are owned by the broadcasters themselves) seem to play a major role in the leading role of the public broadcasters. Also the reliable reputation of the public broadcaster with strong brands like the daily news program and other popular formats are an advantage. The vpro-music site is no doubt one of the most extensive and innovative music sites around, by streaming content and relying heavily on material from non-mainstream artists and small labels, copyright problems are reduced to a minimum. Without government support these sites would not have been possible, independent income from advertising or e-commerce seems to be minimal. Fabchannel uses more or less the same business model. Commercial broadcasters have a tough job competing with this content; their strategy is much more focused on exploiting a few successful formats. Websites that offer audio and video as extras to make the site more attractive profit indirectly from the webcast and can be regarded as operators with a business model that webcasts play a minor role in it.

The only operators who seem to make real money from webcasts on a regular basis are ISPs, B2B-operators and adult content providers. The webcasts are far more central in their business model, with the adult content providers probably as the best example of a "real" webcaster. The typical adult content operator has a business model based on webcasting, and can also be regarded as a "pure-play" webcaster with mostly webcasting original content. But also within this category different models can be found like the examples mentioned above: A portal format where income is generated by referring to other "pure-play" webcasters (askjone.com). The other webcaster mentioned above (Midhold) acted as a pure-play operator on the one hand but also as a B2B intermediary for other companies.

This means that webcasting in the Netherlands, and probably in some other similar countries, is more or less dominated by parties that offer content for free. This makes it for entrepreneurs rather difficult to develop their own business models: Who is going to pay for content that is given away by others for free.

The future of webcasting can, however, also develop in a very different direction. In the beginning of 2005 the new commercial Dutch broadcaster Talpa (owned by Dutch media tycoon John de Mol, former CEO of the Endemol production company) bought the rights on the Dutch soccer competition for the next three years. In addition to that, Telecom operator Versatel (of which John de Mol was the most important shareholder) bought the rights for digital broadcasts of live soccer matches over telephone lines and through pay television. Versatel is offering so-called triple play: telephone, internet, and television over high bandwidth (2 mbps) ADSL-phone lines. Other companies like Tiscali and Chello (owned by UPC) are also experimenting with this model. To view television with this new technology, people need a new setup box for the television. To market the new technique and to create a critical mass setup boxes were are given away for free in the introduction phase. With this Internet Protocol Television development the distinction between webcasting and broadcasting will be very difficult to make.

The most pressing problem with this model—apart from getting a substantial amount of subscribers—is bandwidth. In the first two months of the experiment (August and September 2005) only half of the subscribers could actually watch the soccer matches the subscribed to—and even when it was possible, the quality was inferior to that of a regular television program, it seemed to be almost impossible to offer the promised quality. For regular webcasters bandwidth and transmission problems don't seem to play a major role anymore.

Another form of convergence is watching the regular television channels on your computer. Most modern PCs and laptops can be equipped with a television-tuner card, which makes television-viewing possible. In 2004 already 5% of the Dutch households reported that they could watch television on their computer screen (*Televisie rapport 2004*, 2004, p. 4). Another survey revealed that 6.6% of the people interviewed indeed watched television on their computer; this was most popular in households with children (8.8%), and with people with daytime jobs (8.4%) and households with high incomes (8.1%) (Van de Wal & Kalfs, 2004, p. 13).

Copyright still can be considered as a major challenge for webcasters; with small market shares and relative few people watching, a strict copyright regime can be almost prohibitive. Standardization (another problem identified in the beginning of the webcast history) is almost completely lacking, although this does not seem to be a major problem right now—many web sites use embedded players that should work with most modern browsers while there is also often the choice between different players and bandwidths. The strategy seems to be to offer many choices so there is little chance that people will not be able to view of listen to the content.

REFERENCES

Arampatzis, A. (2004). Online business models in Greece and the United Kingdom: A case of specialist versus generic and public versus privately owned online news media. *International Journal on Media Management, 6*(1&2), 88–101.

Bakker, P. (2005). File-sharing—fight, ignore or compete; paid download services vs. P2P-networks. *Telematics and Informatics 22*, 41–55.

Bakker, P. & Scholten, O. (2005). *Communicatiekaart van Nederland; Overzicht van media en communicatie* (5e druk herziene druk) [Map of Communication in the Netherlands; overview of media and communication]. Alphen aan den Rijn: Kluwer.

Barnes, A. (2005, July 10) Downloading trouble at the BBC. *The Independent*. Retrieved September 8, 2005, from http://news.independent.co.uk/media/article298067.ece

Browser Timelines. (2005). Retrieved November 4, 2005, from www.blooberry. com/indexdot/ history/browsers.htm

Chan-Olmsted, S., & Ha, L. (2003). Internet business models for broadcasters: how television stations perceive and integrate the internet. *Journal of Broadcasting and Electronic Media, 47*(4), 597–617.

Commission staff working paper; Annex to the European Electronic Communications Regulation and Markets 2004 (10th report). (2004). Brussels: European Commission.

Couzy, M. (1998, January 30) Grootmachten werken samen aan ADSL [Major players work together on ADSL]. *Computable, 30*, p. 1.

Ha, L. (2004). Webcasting. In Hossein Bidgoli (Ed.), *Internet encyclopedia* (pp. 674–686). New York: John Wiley & Sons.

Ha, L., & Ganahl, R. (2004). Webcasting business models of click-and-bricks and pure-play media: A comparative study of leading webcasters in South Korea and the United States. *The International Journal on Media Management, 6* (1&2), 75–88.

Ha, L., Ganahl, R., Arampatzis, A., Allagui, I., Bakker, P., Chausse, M., Cui, B., Djekic, P., Herrero, M., Ishii, K., Lee, A., Liu, Y. L., Loebbecke, C., Martin, C., Min, H., Park, S. K., Sadaba, C., So, C., & Weerakkody, N. D. (2005). *Emerging media business models worldwide: A study of leading webcasters in 13 countries*. Paper accepted by the Communication Technology and Policy Division, Association for Education in Journalism and Mass Communication Annual Convention, San Antonio, TX, August 10–12.

Houtman, J. (2001, August 10). BBC bekritiseerd vanwege reclame [BBC critized because of advertising]. *Emerce*. Retrieved September 8, 2005, from www.emerce.nl/nieuws.jsp?id = 44575

Kabel, J. (2002). Publieke omroep op het web: oneerlijke overheidsconcurrentie? [Public broadcasters on the web: unfair competition?] *JAVI*. September 2002, 61–62.

Kolo, C. & Vogt, P. (2004). Traditional media and their internet spin-offs: An exploratory study on key levers for online success and the impact of offline reach. *International Journal on Media Management, 6*(1&2), 23–35.

McLuhan, M. (1964). *Understanding media: The extensions of men*. New York: McGraw-Hill.

OECD (Organization for Economic Cooperation and Development). (2005). *OECD Factbook 2005*. Paris: Author.

Orlowski, A. (2004, December 8). One in four Brits on net for porn. *The Register.* Retrieved December 10, 2004, from www.theregister.co.uk/2004/12/08/brit_net_filth/

Pot, M. (2005, July 28). We waren de eersten, er was niets vergelijkbaars [We were first, there was nothing like it]. *De Volkskrant,* p. 7.

Siune, K. & Hultén, O. (1998). Does public broadcasting has a future. In D. McQuail & K. Siune (Eds.). *Media Policy; Convergence, Concentration and Commerce* (pp. 23–37). London: Sage.

Televisie rapport 2004 [Television Report 2004]. (2004). Amstelveen: Spot.

Van de Wal, A. & Kalfs, N.(2004). *TV in Nederland 2004; Ontwikkelingen in TV bezit en TV gebruik .* [TV in the Netherlands 2004; developments in TV ownership and TV use]. Amstelveen: Stichting Kijkonderzoek.

World Broadband Statistics: Q4 2004. (2005). London: Point Topic Ltd.

World Press Trends.(2005). Paris: World Association of Newspapers.

CHAPTER 7

Germany: Poised for Dynamic Growth

Mike Friedrichsen and Astrid Kurad
University of Flensburg, Germany

Miriam A. Smith
San Francisco State University

The internet is a rapidly growing medium in Germany. More and more people are going online and taking advantage of the wide variety of opportunities offered by internet providers.

Facilitated by faster access, as well as innovative hardware and software, internet offerings are multiplying. In addition to text-only pages, many multimedia websites complete with imbedded audio and video content are now available in German.

Despite the fact that several approaches to profitably market webcasting have failed in the past, this business sector is now attracting attention. Driving this new interest in webcasting are the promises of better technologies, mobile systems, and a very large customer base.

Premium offerings in sports and music as well as niche products are the anticipated content areas for webcasters.

This chapter discusses the development of and future prospects for broadband webcasting (or web TV) in Germany. The first consideration is the key factors influencing broadband webcasting in Germany. Next, is an environmental analysis of the industry using Porter's (1979) five forces framework. The chapter ends with a case study: An examination of Deutsche Welle's strengths and weaknesses.

WEBCASTING DEFINED

Webcasting does not have a unified definition in the German media literature. Goldhammer and Zerdick (1999) equate *webcasting* with *cybercasting* in referring to the transmission of audio and/or video data as a broadcast or in a broadcast-like

133

style over the World Wide Web. They further differentiate between *webcasting*, on one hand, and the transmission of news reports, *newscasting* or *datacasting*, on the other hand.

For the purposes of this chapter, *webcasting* is the transmission of television and radio programs via the internet, as defined by Goldhammer and Zerdick (1999) and Ha (2004). The focus of this analysis is broadband webcasting, i.e., the transmission of video content. The term "webcasting" in this chapter is synonymous with "internet TV" or "web TV."

FINANCING ONLINE MEDIA

Webcasters have a variety of business approaches to choose from. These strategies, individually or in some combination with one another, should lead to economic success. The right mix of business models multiplies the chance for a business to offer a financially rewarding product line of online services. Potential revenue streams include: advertising; subscriptions; e-commerce; and, data commerce.

Out of all these revenue sources, advertising occupies the most important role. Building scope and scale seems to be a determinative factor, as with many offline businesses (Goldhammer & Zerdick, 1999).

One drawback with subscription-based services is that German internet users are not accustomed to paying for online services. As a result, only a few subscription providers will ultimately be financially successful. In general, providers of special information, such as stock market quotes, or niche topics, as well as providers of high-level entertainment have the greatest chance to refinance through subscriptions (Goldhammer & Zerdick, 1999).

German law makes the provision of certain types of information extremely problematic. While in the United States, the selling of personal information has become a well-established business model, Germany's data protection laws and regulations are far more restrictive. Consequently, this popular U.S. online business concept is of little interest in Germany.

In general, webcast offerings have not been profitable on their own and are still supported by revenue from other sources. Since 2000, German law has required that public broadcasting internet sites to be free of commercials and fund themselves entirely from the broadcast fees (Goldhammer & Zerdick, 1999).

Private online providers need only partially support themselves with online revenue. Income from marketing or even public relations cross-finances their online activities. Goldhammer and Zerdick (1999) have observed that this financial climate has resulted online offers being driven not by program content objectives, but instead by commercial objectives.

POLITICAL, ECONOMIC, SOCIAL, AND TECHNOLOGICAL (PEST) ANALYSIS

Political and Legal Factors

The legal environment of the webcasting sector is predicated by the nature of online communication. It is often impossible to determine whether a transmission is an individual or a mass communication.

The legal framework for webcasting in Germany is governed by the following laws and agreements:

- the Broadcasting Agreement of the Federal States, also "Broadcasting Agreement" (*Rundfunkstaatsvertrag*);
- the Telecommunications Act (*Telekommunikationsgesetz*);
- the Information and Communication Services Act (*Informations- und Kommunikationsdienste-Gesetz*);
- the Inter-State Agreement on Media Services (*Mediendienste-Staatsvertrag*); and,
- the Copyright Law (*Urheberrechtsgesetz*).

The federal and state governments share jurisdiction over the online sector. The federal government sets rules regarding communication services (teleservices) directed towards individuals, while state governments regulate mass media services. However, there are always major difficulties in classifying communication services.

Telecommunications law regulates the technical aspects of "sending, transmitting and receiving signals by means of telecommunications systems" (Telecommunications Act, §3 No. 22). All commercial telecommunication providers must register with the Regulatory Authority (*Regulierungsbehörde für Post und Telekommunikation*, [RegTP]) (Telecommunications Act, §6).

While the Telecommunications Act is more concerned with the technical providers of telecommunication services than with the content providers, both the Information and Communication Services Act and the Inter-State Agreement on Media Services regulate content providers.

The Information and Communication Services Act was designed to create a legal framework for the online sector. Article 1 is known as the Teleservices Act (*Teledienstegesetz*). It's focus is "to establish uniform economic conditions for the various applications of electronic information and communication services" (Teleservices Act, §1). Teleservices are not subject to licensing or registration requirements (Teleservices Act, §4).

The Teleservices Act defines teleservices as: "all electronic information and communication services which are designed for the individual use of combinable data such as characters, images or sounds and are based on transmission by means of telecommunication (teleservices)" (Teleservices Act, §2). Examples of teleservices include: telebanking, telegames and services that provide traffic, weather or stock exchange data (Teleservices Act, §2). The individual end-use of these services is key as broadcasting and services intended to influence public opinion are excluded from the Act (Teleservices Act, §2).

The Inter-State Agreement on Media Services differentiates between distribution and on-demand services. Section 2 of that law defines distribution services as services which are directed to the public, such as the transmission of television text or radio text. On-demand services are individually retrievable. Foremost among these on-demand services are those which only transfer data. Like the teleservices, these distribution and on-demand services are free of any licensing or registration requirements. However, they are required to label the content and identify those responsible for the service (Inter-State Agreement on Media Services [*Mediendienste-Staatsvertrag*]).

The chronic challenge is to determine when an internet service is a teleservice, one that relates to individual communication, and when it is a media service, one that is directed to mass communication (Dreiseitl, 2004).

From a legal perspective, the inquiry focuses on how the online service is used. Notwithstanding that focus, attempts to differentiate between media services and teleservices on the basis of technical, content or functional characteristics are not always clear (Goldhammer & Zerdick, 1999).

Broadcasting is defined in Section 2 of the Broadcasting Agreement as:

> ...the provision and transmission for the general public of presentations of all kinds of speech, sound and picture, using electrical oscillations without junction lines or along or by means of a conductor. The definition includes presentations transmitted in encoded form or can be received for a special payment, as well as broadcast video-text. (Broadcasting Agreement, §2)

In contrast to media services, broadcasting includes a performance element. The import of the performance element is the effect it may have on shaping individual and public opinion. This potential impact of broadcasting is due to its wide dissemination, its relevance and its power of suggestion.

If an online media service is determined to have an impact on the formation of public opinion, it may be classified as a broadcaster and required, in accordance with Section III, Article 20 of the Broadcasting Agreement, to obtain a broadcast license. In most cases where internet content is identical to a traditional broadcast transmission, the suggestive power associated with moving pictures is absent due to the lower technical quality of the internet transmission (Goldhammer & Zerdick, 1999).

The decision whether an online service (whether a teleservice, media service, distribution or on-demand service) may be classified as a broadcast is strongly subject to the political will and falls to the state broadcast regulators (*Landes-medienanstalten*). In cases of doubt, the service could be classified as a broadcast service which would bring with it registration and licensing obligations (Dreiseitl, 2004).

Much tension exists between copyright law and online broadcasting. Copyright law is charged with the task of protecting cultural creations such as pictures, music and film in order to secure the creator's rights to exploit the work and to profit thereby.

The problem stems from the internet's ability to make content globally accessible. This conflict has been exacerbated by development of audio compression techniques such as the MP3 format (Goldhammer& Zerdick, 1999). An example of the collision of copyright and internet are the difficulties encountered in attempts to develop a European internet on-demand music business. The first hurdle is the competing national rights of exploitation. Another hurdle is the high cost of using copyright-protected content in a website, even content intended exclusively for use within the confines of one country (Dreiseitl, 2004).

In order to better protect a creator's rights of exploitation, German copyright law has adopted the World Intellectual Property Organization's (WIPO) copyright provisions. The international WIPO copyright treaty grants the right of exploitation exclusively to the authors of the internet creations for products and thereby simplifies international copyright law (Goldhammer & Zerdick, 1999).

Performance rights societies such as GEMA *(Gesellschaft für musikalische Aufführungs- und mechanische Vervielfältigungsrechte)* or GVL (*Gesellschaft Zur Verwertung Von Leistungsschutzrechten*) collect royalties for music performances on behalf the music's authors and performers. The use of music pieces or clips in online broadcasts may be considered to be governed by Section 20 of the German Copyright Law, which controls the right of broadcasting (specifically transmissions over satellite and cable). Such classification increases the tariffs imposed by the performing rights societies (Goldhammer & Zerdick, 1999).

If in addition to one-to-one internet transmissions, other online content is offered, such as an On-Demand service, GEMA has a separate schedule of graduated tariffs (Goldhammer & Zerdick, 1999). For example, a private use of a music-on-demand service has a remuneration basis of 15% or at least 0.25 euros for a work up to five minutes in length (Dreiseitl, 2004).

GEMA has established graduated tariffs for various online categories including, for example: the non-commercial homepage for a university or political party;

homepages for businesses and product presentations; online shopping sites; live transmissions; and, sound archives (Goldhammer & Zerdick, 1999).

Economic Factors

Germany is presently in a period of slow, unstable economic growth. In contrast to constantly rising exports, domestic demand has stagnated for some years. Buzz words such as "consumer calm" and "thriftiness is cool" (*geiz ist geil*) define the retail trade. This slow economic growth coupled with constantly rising unemployment have resulted in investment conservatism by Germans. Significant changes in the next few years are not expected.

The entertainment and media industries are very dependent on national economic health. Much of the change in the media industry is due to higher advertising revenues. Advertising, as an investment with the goal of increasing sales, brings higher returns in times of an expanding economy than in times of economic stagnation or recession. Firms affected by adverse economic conditions tend to reduce advertising expenditures. This decline was very apparent in Germany between 2001 and 2004 when expenditures for advertising fell by 23% overall (PricewaterhouseCoopers [PwC], 2005). Also, consumer expenditures on entertainment and media are related to overall economic cycles as these expenditures are made from discretionary income.

The restrained economic development in Germany over the last five years is one reason why the market for entertainment and media grew more slowly in Germany than the market average for Western Europe. This situation is expected to continue for the next five years. One predicted exception to this flat growth is the World Cup™ soccer tournament which may produce a one-time bump in 2006 (PwC, 2005).

Overall, the German media market will grow more slowly in the coming years than the Western European market average. Germany's 24.9% European market share in 1999 is expected to shrink to 20.9% by 2008 (PwC, 2005). Total expenditures for entertainment and media in Germany in 2003 were approximately 57.1 billion euros with negligible growth in expenditures between 2002 and 2003 (PwC, 2005).

The internet sector posted the highest growth in both 2002 and 2003 with a 22.1% increase and a 22.8% increase, respectively, reaching total expenditures of 5.469 million euros in 2003. Greater penetration of the internet and increasing broadband subscriptions account for this growth (PwC, 2005).

The television industry also outpaced the entertainment and media industry average by reporting growth rates of 3.5% and 2.2% in 2002 and 2003, respectively. Television expenditures for 2002 totaled 13.904 million euros with total expenditures of 14.206 millions euros in 2004. Higher revenues from subscription television compensated for the recession in advertising income, (PwC, 2005).

In the coming years, Pricewaterhouse Coopers has predicted a strong growth of 15.7% for the internet reaching 11.311 million euros in total expenditures in 2008. The television industry is expected to expand at a slower pace, 4.9% annually, hitting 18.027 million euros in 2008. The strength of internet growth in contrast to other entertainment and media markets is grounded in the assumption that broadband will continue to make strong gains (PwC, 2005).

Likewise, expenditures in the German Download market are expected to show strong growth. 2005 should show an increase of 137% with 484 million euros changing hands (Bundesverband für Informations-wirtschaft, Telekommunikation und neue Medien [Federal Association for Information Technology, Telecommunication and New Media] [Bitkom], 2005). The Download market includes online music, games, video, text and pictures. Online videos accounted for more than one third of total expenditures with sales of 187 million euros. This is not the only activity to benefit from the increase in broadband connections. In two years the Download market should cross the billion euro border (Bitkom, 2005). The developing Download market demonstrates that the internet has potential beyond the "free" offers as more people move to high quality and multimedia "pay" offers.

Expenditures for advertising decreased in Germany by 6.1% between 2002 and 2003. In Western Europe, the average decrease amounted to only 0.5%. Excluding Germany, advertising expenditures in Western Europe actually rose by 0.8% (PwC, 2005).

One exception to the overall decline in German advertising expenditures was for internet advertising, though 2003 growth was smaller than experienced in 2002. Internet advertising grew by only 8.4% in 2003 while 2002 saw a 22.7% jump. Notably, all other media segments in both 2002 and 2003 suffered declines.

The television industry reported small downturns in advertising receipts in 2001–2003, though, the next few years should see single-digit increases. Advertising revenues in 2006 will benefit from World Cup™ Germany (PwC, 2005).

Internet advertising revenues are expected to remain strong with double-digit growth forecast each year for an average annual growth of 18.1%. The internet will be the driving force to expansion of this sector of the advertising market (PwC, 2005).

Consumer expenditures for entertainment and media show a small upward trend over the past years spurred by dramatic growth in internet expenditures, which climbed 23.5% in 2003. Without the internet, a different picture would emerge. Television revenues from consumer spending rose 4.5% in 2003 due to growth in rising television subscriptions (PwC, 2005).

It is anticipated that internet expenditures will continue their double-digit growth, averaging 15.5% annually. Consumer expenditures on television will also grow, but at a much smaller average annual pace, 4.5% (PwC, 2005).

Socio-economic Factors

In 2004, 95% of all businesses with a least 10 employees and 60% of all households with at least one person under the age of 75 had an internet connection (*Statistisches Bundesamt* [Federal Statistical Office], 2005). This penetration was ahead of the Western European average of 90% for comparable businesses and 47% for similar households having internet access. Germany also outpaced the Western European average of 43% internet use by 16–74 year-olds. In Germany 50% of all people between the ages of 16 and 74 use the internet (*Statistisches Bundesamt* [Federal Statistical Office], 2005).

Between 2002 and 2004, households with internet access jumped from 46% to 60%—an increase of more than one-third! During the same period, internet access in Western Europe grew only about one-fifth. Increased internet access by businesses and households naturally led to increased online activity (*Statistisches Bundesamt* [Federal Statistical Office], 2005). Weekly internet usage among 16 to 74 year-olds in Germany rose from 44% in 2003 to 50% in 2004. Again, Germany has been ahead of the EU—15 average which showed an increase from 38% to 43% of weekly internet use between 2003 and 2004 (*Statistisches Bundesamt* [Federal Statistical Office], 2005). Since 2002 when the German telecommunications market was opened to competition, competitors such as AOL Germany, 1&1, Freenet and Acor have joined the incumbent, T-Online, in offering DSL and other internet connections.

Estimates of broadband penetration vary from a low of 8.1% by Deutsche Bank in September 2005 (ZDNet Research, 2005) to a more wide-spread estimation in the 13–18% range. Forrester Research calculated a 13% penetration by the end of 2004 (ZDNet.de, 2005); HeavyReading.com reported 15.9% penetration in March 2005 (HeavyReading.com, 2005) with Mercer Consulting placing it at 16% in March and 18% in July (Mercer Management Consulting, 2005a, 2005b). In other countries, the most important technology for broadband distribution is cable, however, cable is virtually non-existent in Germany with over 90% of broadband connections being DSL (ZDNet Research, 2005).

The availability of more broadband systems, including cable modems, wireless broadband and fiber optics, by 2006 will spur growth in the broadband market. Forecasts call for 1.9 million cable households in Germany by 2008. While DSL subscriptions are also expected to rise to 14.6 million, their share of the broadband market will fall to 81% (PwC, 2005). This spectacular growth in the broadband market will cause a dramatic decrease in the narrowband market (PwC, 2005).

More men than women were active online in 2004. 63% of German men logged on compared to 53% of all women. Age does seems to make a difference in bridging the online gender gap. For those under the age of 25, internet usage is almost identical with 87% of men and 85% of women going online. However, among the over 54 set, twice as many men use the internet (30%) as women (15%) (*Statistisches Bundesamt* [Federal Statistical Office], 2005).

In the first quarter of 2004, 47% of all internet users went online almost everyday for either business or personal reasons. One-third (32%) of all internet users logged on but once a week. Daily users are more heavily male (54% male, 39% female) while weekly users are more likely female (37% female, 28% male). As to time spent online in 2004, 36% were online for one hour or less per week while 22% of all users spent 5 to 20 hours online (*Statistisches Bundesamt* [Federal Statistical Office], 2005).

Almost nine out of ten internet users, (82% or 38 million), in 2004 went online to search for information or to use an online service. Only 13% used the internet to access radio and/or television stations. Yet, this is double the 7% who sought radio and/or television from the internet in 2002 (*Statistisches Bundesamt* [Federal Statistical Office], 2005)

This leap from 7% to 14% suggests that webcasting is poised for a period of major growth in the coming years.

Technological Factors

The second quarter of 2005 saw world-wide broadband connections at 176.3 million, rising by almost 24.3 million since the end of 2004—a growth of about 16% (Point Topic, Ltd., 2005). Germany claimed 7.8 million DSL connections and 78,000 cable modem connections, placing it seventh behind the US, China, Japan, South Korea, France and the UK. In 2004, Germany placed fifth ahead of France and the UK (Point Topic, Ltd., 2005). Still Germany's broadband growth in the first two quarters of 2005 was 16.42% (Point Topic, Ltd., 2005).

The continuing growth in broadband makes it obvious that webcasters will receive increasing competition from the fixed-networks, such as Deutsche Telekom, and online giants, such as AOL, who bring to the market a "Triple Play" strategy offering internet, telephone and television (Mercer Management Consulting, 2005b).

Germany, with broadband penetration of only 18% (compared to 45% in the Netherlands), belongs to the tail lights in Western Europe. It won't be until the year 2010, according to the Mercer study, that Germany will occupy a place in the upper center zone with 44% penetration (Mercer Management Consulting, 2005b, ¶7).

Deutsche Telekom still controls the broadband market in Germany with a market share of approximately 83%. The introduction of the resale offers in 2004 has opened up the market. "The advantage of reselling is that the resellers have more flexibility in pricing and can, for example, price both the DSL tariffs and DSL connections more favorably than the [Deutsche] Telekom" (Teltarif.de, 2005, ¶3).

In the long-term, the costs of broadband should drop significantly, even those services providing super-fast connection speeds of up to 6-Mbits/s. In Hamburg, for instance, the share of households with broadband connection rose within a short time to 35% once Telecom Italia subsidiary HanseNet arrived with its own fiber optic network and offers of broadband internet, telephone and video services (Mercer Management Consulting, 2005a).

Since 1995, the number of online users in Germany has jumped from 2 million to 28.8 million users in 2004. By early summer of 2004, 55.3% of approximately 64.4 million Germans over the age of 14 used the internet at least occasionally (Gerhards & Mende, 2005). This high penetration of interactive media in Germany indicates an existing knowledge base for the adoption of web TV and other types of two-way media.

It appears that online-media is becoming more like television over time. In principle, the convergence of online media and television could go in two different ways. The oft-repeated saying is "broadcast goes online—online goes broadcast." One variation of web TV is to install a card that allows one to receive television on a computer. The second variation is internet on television where a special set-top box allows a television set to display internet content (Zimmer, 2000).

The extremely different technical standards for television and computers create display quality problems. The industry's response to this dilemma has been to focus on the development of interactive possibilities for television (Zimmer, 2000). Technical standards for interactive television must be developed, in particular a standard for high-speed upload as well as standards for imbedded interactive applications are needed (Zimmer, 2000).

The development of a broadband infrastructure in Germany, compared with other countries, is at a low level. One cause is the monopolistic control of Deutsche Telekom, which until now saw little economic incentive to upgrade its high-speed network.

There are several options to transmit large data sets to households: telephone lines, broadband (ADSL), satellite and wireless. Another possibility is the use of electric power lines or powerline technology. The "data transfer over power lines is accomplished by feeding the data via a radio relay or cable into a substation, which serves hundreds of households with power, where the electrical current carries the data to the homes" (Zimmer, 2000). With this powerline technology, it is theoretically possible to reach every household in Germany and transmit data at rates of 2–10 Mbit/s. However, there are several reasons why powerline technology is not optimal in the long term. The main reason is that the power lines lack insulation, making them vulnerable to interference from electro-magnetic waves. Another reason is that the question of frequencies for the data has yet to be clarified (Zimmer, 2000).

Point-to-point radio telecommunication is yet another possibility. This system uses an antenna and radio modem and was developed to connect large housing complexes. It could connect an entire village as it is suitable for up to 3,000 households within a 20 mile radius. It can bridge the so-called "last mile" of telephone line to the household which has so far been monopolized by Deutsche Telekom. Unfortunately, the high cost of this technology, also called Wireless Local Loop (WLL), suggests it will only be available to business customers. It is capable of transferring about 2 Mbit/s (Zimmer, 2000).

The DVB-T technology is the digital standard for data transmission. This technology must to be supplemented with another internet connection to enable interactivity. While DVB-T technology is sufficient for current applications, its lack of an upload capability makes it unsuitable for web TV.

Satellites represent a good possibility to transmit large data sets and to transmit data using the Internet Protocol (IP). "A transponder of the ASTRA-Satellite family 1 on 19.2 degrees East offers, for example, a capacity of 38 Mbit/s" (Zimmer, 2000, p. 3). The problem is that parallel downloads must share the same bandwidth, which means that when 100 users download the same data, each of them has only 380 Kbit/s available, although this is still much faster than ISDN with 64 Kbit/s.

The ideal long term solution is to outfit all households with high-speed internet connections thereby allowing the development of webcasting and the improvement of the German broadband network. A more economical, as well as efficient, alternative is to upgrade and expand the bi-filament copper wire (or twisted pair) telephone network for ADSL transmissions. This upgrade would be accomplished on the supplier side by adding converters at local distribution points and, on the recipient side, by providing ADSL modems which would reconvert the signal (Zimmer, 2000).

INDUSTRY ANALYSIS USING PORTER'S FIVE FORCES

The Bargaining Power of Customers

It is safe to assume that the customer side of the webcasting market exhibits the same openly (polypolistic) competitive structure as found in the internet market (Sjurts, 2002). The continuous growth in the number of internet users who want web TV content supports the assumption. The expansion of the broadband network will facilitate better deployment of web TV which will fuel additional demand for the content (PwC, 2005). The bargaining power of customers at present is small.

As with structure of the online advertising industry, the webcasting advertising market is oligopolistic—the highest volume agencies control more than 50% of the market. Internet advertisers are very sensitive to cost, seeking the lowest CPM's (cost per thousand) and advertising rates. Even the slightest change in costs can result in a major shift by advertisers to a better offer. The online advertising industry is, therefore, transient. The bargaining power of customers may likewise be classified as transient (Sjurts, 2002).

The Bargaining Power of Suppliers

The supplier market in webcasting is made up of of multi-media agencies, which offer software programs and broadcasting content and of content providers and producers. The high number of multi-media agencies creates a competitive market structure. Moreover, software is constantly getting easier to use making the services of these agencies unnecessary. This situation results in intense competition and similar product offerings by agencies, each of whom has little market power.

Despite this market structure, there is a great threat to the survival of these suppliers as capital outlays needed to establish a webcasting channel are relatively small and it is therefore easier to create a closed value chain than in other media. For traditional broadcast stations who simultaneously stream their content, there exists a small threat from content suppliers as the broadcaster is able to make multiple uses of its content.

The Threat of New Entrants

The threat of new entrants is determined by barriers to entry. The structural barriers to entry depend on economies of scale. Already-established web TV providers benefit from the "first-copy-cost" effect which give them cost advantages over the new providers. The established web TV providers also have a competitive advantage over new entrants in advertising revenues. As reach increases, the CPM decreases which is manifest in spiraling advertising banner coverage.

Internet TV providers don't have duplication or distribution costs for their content; just monthly web storage costs. Music video providers must also pay performance royalties. However, compared to the cost of content in other media, the costs for internet content offerings are small (Sjurts, 2002).

The strategic barriers to entry depend on access to internet-ready content. As soon as an established provider creates its own internet content, or acquires syndicated content, it has a competitive advantage.

Institutional barriers to entry exist only for those providers that the *Landesmedienanstalt* has ruled to have influence over public opinion. These "influential" providers must obtain a license.

Entering the webcasting market seems particularly attractive to web-hosting companies. For example, Media Asset Management is thinking about forward integration and may offer online music in the future (Philip Schlueter, telephone interview).

In sum, only moderate barriers to entry exist for the online market.

The Threat of Substitute Products

The traditional media products of the broadcast and print industries, as well as mobile communication services, compete with the online industry and likewise with webcasting. The television market is near mature reaching about 70% of the population. However, the German television industry is becoming a companion medium as the viewing time is continuously rising (Sjurts, 2002).

General cyclical weakening of market conditions in Germany led to a 19% drop in demand in the advertising market to 3.8 million euros between 2000 and 2003. However, the television advertising market is expected to recover thanks to adoption of digital technology and the related increase in transmission capacity, as well as overall improvement in general economic conditions.

PricewaterhouseCoopers forecasts that television advertising will exhibit an average annual growth of 5.4% through 2008 when it will reach 4.9 million euros compared to 4.709 million euros in 2000 (PwC, 2005).

The saturation of the viewer market and the slowly recovering advertising market strengthen the view that the threat by television is moderate.

The threat by print media is low due its dissimilarity with web TV. The threat by newspapers is relevant only to web TV providers who offer news. Newspaper circulations are falling. Press runs for all newspaper categories will decline, falling to 110,000 by 2008. Due to falling sales and competition from the internet, newspaper advertising revenue will shrink to approximately 4.7 million euros by 2008 (PwC, 2005).

The magazine market is expected to increase by 2008 to a circulation of 525 million compared with 510 million magazines sold in 2000. This increase reflects a predicted annual growth 0.9% since 2003. The overall boost in circulation is due to the rising number of titles. While the average magazine lost circulation in the last years, which is to be expected in a mature market, increased circulation and new titles should provide the anticipated 3.4% annual growth through 2008. Nonetheless, expenditures for consumer magazine advertising will not, in 2008, reach the 2000 level (PwC, 2005).

The threat by radio is, like print, moderate due to product dissimilarity. The audience was expanding until 2000 but has been slumping ever since. Between 2000 and 2003, radio advertising revenue sank. Despite those down years, prognoses are for radio advertising to rise an average of 3.4% each year through 2008. Total receipts in 2008 would reach 683 million euros, which for the first time would exceed 2001 levels (PwC, 2005).

The Intensity of Competitive Rivalry

The webcasting sector is characterized by highly differentiated providers. This leads to low overall provider rivalry. Growth in the recipient and internet advertising markets, coupled with a lack of saturation leads to only moderate competitive rivalry among the established providers (Sjurts, 2002).

Capital outlays by providers to establish a webcasting service are small compared to to other media industries creating few barriers to exit the market.

Traditional broadcasters who provide web TV have an additional competitive advantage. This advantage is that their webcast content parallels their regular broadcast content bringing viewers online as soon as the web address is broadcast. For example, once www.viva.de is broadcast on VIVA, the number of online users jumps higher. Through the interplay of both media, users can receive enhanced offerings (Goldhammer & Zerdick, 1999).

BROADBAND WEBCASTERS IN GERMANY

The broadcast television market and the web TV market will continue to converge. The use of both media allows information providers to reach a larger audience and in conjunction with the possibilities of interactive media, creates a synergy that brings efficiency. This potential for synergy leads to a greater number of providers who offer web TV channels, interactive TV and stream videos.

A wide variety of web TV channels with differing content may be found today—from short comedy films, to a webcam recording of a 10-hour taxi ride in Berlin to traditional news programs by n-tv.de and all genres in between. Today's web TV content providers can be divided into several different categories. The following six classifications are the most useful: streaming agencies, government, service providers, television channels, video-on-demand, and producers.

Streaming agencies are agencies, such as *Pressetext Austria,* that provides live press conferences, events and presentations. The government category is made up of government divisions and agencies, such as Bundestag.de that webcasts debates from the Bundestag.

One example of the "service provider" category is Netscape.com which provides Netscape Newscaster, the typical netcaster service. (University of Leipzig, 2001). Netcaster channels are comparable to traditional radio and television channels (Netscape, 2002). One advantage of a netcaster is that it can operate in the background, providing breaking news while one works on other tasks. The user does not even need to be online as the news can also be read off-line (Netscape, 2002). The category of "service-providers" also includes comprehensive providers such as *fernsehen.tv* which provides links for video content such as movies, tv shows, comedy, news, erotic, lifestyle and advertisements. *Fernsehen.tv* bills itself as the largest German-language iTV portal online (http://www.fernsehen.tv/Sites/).

Television channels are providers who offer web TV in the sense of television watched on a computer. It is possible to distinguish between providers who offer complete movies for free and those who provide on-demand transmissions. There are also web pages for television stations who transmit portions of their programming online, such as n-tv.de and Pro 7 Sat 1 Media Group. Some individual television programs have their own website, like *sportschau* on www.sport.ard.de.

Video-on-demand includes T-Online's video-on-demand service where one can access a program at any time, selecting from a wide variety of programs. The idea of video-on-demand is not new but its availability is enhanced with faster broadband connections. This category also includes niche providers, such as giga.de, which concentrates on online games and films (http://www.giga.de).

Producers are those firms concerned with the production, realization and organization of online media. NeTVision.de is one such firm that provides live webcasts of general shareholders' meetings, press conferences, and IPOs over the internet and the intranet, streaming media-steered internal business communication via streaming by intranet, and digital processing of existing video for streaming applications (http://www.neTVision.de).

ANALYSIS OF DEUTSCHE WELLE (WWW.DW-WORLD.DE)

Introduction to Deutsche Welle

Deutsche Welle has been in existence for fifty years providing serious news coverage since May 3, 1953. The launch of DW-World in 1994, with its new way of distributing Deutsche Welle's multimedia content, was a crucial step toward the future. Diverse web TV content is available on www.dw-world.de through "live video streaming" on either a Real Player or Windows Media Player. One can select from video, audio and text articles on a variety of topics. A broadband connection allows one to access a 24-hour live video stream. The links to the numerous on-demand text, video, and sound files are clearly arranged on the the homepage.

Design and Navigation

It is challenging to present all of DW-World's content in way that makes it easy to find the content. DW-World relaunched its site in 2004 with a new design to make it easier for users to find all of the site's content. Navigating the homepage is now fairly simple and provides the user with a quick overview.

The welcome page for www.dw-world.de allows a user to choose one of the thirty different languages offered. The user is then taken automatically to a "front page" in that language which displays an overview of the leading topics and subsequent menu options (including the option to select a different language).

The pages are generally very simple and clear. The predominant colors throughout DW-World's website are blue and white.

The main menu is located in the left navigation bar. Here, the user can choose among the following major menu options: News; Germany Info; DW-Radio; DW-TV; and Interactive. In the central part of the page the leading topics of the requested information can be found. As soon as one of the menu options is chosen, it is highlighted.

Each selection of an option leads to new options and content. The design of the pages and clarity of the menu make the site very user-friendly.

Content

The content offered on DW-World exceeds Deutsche Welle's TV programming and delivers comprehensive coverage of world events to the user. The content has a Germany-Europe focus. Core languages for DW-World are: German, Arabic, Chinese, English, Portuguese for Brazil, Russian, and Spanish. Each core language has an online editor with the other languages using the corresponding Deutsche Welle Radio editor.

Major sections for English online content are: Current Affairs; Business & Economics; Culture & Lifestyle; and, Science & Technology. The radio and TV sites offer streaming stories and archives of scripts.

Content is not limited to news and information, several information services are also provided. One service is a searchable database of hotels allowing one to research accommodations before departing on a trip. DW-World offers a "mobile" service as well. The "mobile" service will transmit current news and selected content directly to one's mobile device.

Additionally, DW-World offers a wealth of links to useful content related to the different content areas. To illustrate, under the "Study in Germany" section, one link takes the user to the site for the German Academic Exchange Service (*DAAD*) while other links take the user to one of DW-World's five specialized websites, www.campus-germany.de, the portal for students who want to study in Germany. Campus-germany.de is offered in 6 languages. The other specialized DW-World websites deal with culture (www.germanizer.com and www.inspiredminds.de) and history (www.Today-In-History.de).

The features that set DW-World apart from its competition are:

- audio and video on demand
- German and international viewpoints

- independence in selection of news stories
- employees from 70 different nations
- the only uncensored Amharic news service
- multimedia German courses
- the opportunity to foster international dialogue through interactivity

(Guido Baumhauer, DW-World, presentation to the Fulbright German Studies Seminar, June 16, 2004).

Quality of the Webcast

The quality of the webcast programs of DW-World is good. With an appropriate high-speed connection, the images are sharp and the entertainment and information value are high. The rich text content and multitude of useful links on the homepage supplement the webcast.

The information provided is diverse and covers a broad spectrum.

Outlook

DW-World represents an interesting and multi-faceted web TV platform. Those responsible for DW-World carry out their tasks with enthusiasm and engagement. It is always a challenge to find the right media mix (TV, radio, online) for each market. The objective is to allow the target audience to consume the media content with available technological capacity (DW-World.de, 2005).

Future goals for DW are to: Strengthen dialogue with the Islamic world, expand regionalization, strengthen their presence in Asia, facilitate European collaborations, and make use of the new distribution technologies such as mobile internet. Specific online goals include: Strengthening and regionalizing the existing core languages, particularly Arabic, Chinese, English, and Russian; expanding Farsi and Hindu to core languages; introducing Korean as a core language; strengthening and expanding the mobile internet; and offering a language course in order to promote the German language (DW-World.de, 2005).

RESEARCHING THE WEB AUDIENCE

Unlike traditional broadcast audiences, where stations and networks depend on outside companies to measure their audience, webcasters have the advantage of being better able, technologically, to tally their own visitors. DW-World had 10 to 12 million page impressions per month in 2004 with online bringing the youngest audience of their triple offerings (radio, television, online) (Guido Baumhauer, DW-World, presentation to the Fulbright German Studies Seminar, June 16, 2004).

webcasters RTL and n-TV ranked among the top 20 websites in Germany in October 2004 (Werben & Verlaifen, 2004b) with RTL, Sat.1, RTL World and Pro Sieben listed in the top 10 entertainment sites (Werben & Verlaifen, 2004a).

Industry wide audience information is compiled and reported by several companies including Nielsen/NetRatings and comScore Media Metrix.

A NOTE ABOUT WEB RADIO

The focus of this chapter has been on broadband webcasting, i.e. web TV. It is worth noting, however, that web radio is well-established in Germany with over 200 stations available online. Of the 210 stations identified in November 2005, only 3 were internet only stations, with almost all radio webcasting originating with an existing over-the-air station. Popular formats for these stations were contemporary music, news, classical music, and dance music.

CONCLUSION

Although Germany has fallen behind in broadband adoption, it is poised for dynamic growth. New competition among broadband providers is spurring growth. Increased penetration encourages additional broadband-dependent offerings, such as web TV, which further drives broadband adoption.

The internet advertising market is also growing. Despite some losses in advertising revenue by the traditional media, the internet market has grown in the past and all estimations are that it will see double-digit revenue growth.

The German legal landscape makes it easier for one to enter the webcasting market than the traditional broadcasting market. The main reason for this is that internet services are generally not subject to the public broadcasting law, but belong to the sector of media or teleservices. What's more, webcasters always have the option to broadcast from countries with more liberal policies.

Economically, it is also much easier to enter the web TV market than the over-the-air or cable TV market. Germany's web TV market is so new that the providers are relatively unknown. Potential market players have an excellent opportunity to establish a marketable format with attractive contents. There appears to be a special interest among webhosting enterprises to get into the webcasting segment. Web TV also offers content producers and rights holders a vertical integration opportunity as their content can be distributed directly to the end consumer with low distribution costs.

One big question remains: Will television as it is now known ever be replaced?

As for the near future, it is more likely that web TV in Germany will develop a completely new market with niche products. This market will probably be characterized by an international target group operating under globalization.

It is clear that an interesting market exists for web TV that does not necessarily have to be a substitute for traditional TV—web TV may soon become and remain an internationally relevant medium filled with interesting niche content.

In any event, the next five years should see dynamic growth in web TV and in all webcasting applications in Germany!

ACKNOWLEDGMENTS

Special thanks to Isabel Arsoy, Bowling Green State University; Christian Geiger, Stefan Joerger, and Bernd Kleinboetling, San Francisco State University, for assisting with the translation of this chapter and to Ekin Nasuhogullari, San Francisco State University, for research assistance.

REFERENCES

Broadcasting Agreement of the Federal States (Rundfunkstaatsvertrag). BGBI. I, §§2–3, (1991, as amended).
Bundesverband für Informations-wirtschaft, Telekommunikation und neue Medien [Federal Association for Information Technology, Telecommunication and New Media]. (2005). *BITKOM erwartet dynamisches Marktwachstum fuer Online-Inhalte in Deutschland [Bitkom expects dynamic market growth in online content in Germany]."* Retrieved July 27, 2005, from http://www.bitkom. org/de/markt_statistik/ 30739_30744.aspx
Copyright Law (Urheberrechtsgesetz). BGBI. I, §20, (1965, as amended).
Dreiseitl, H. (2004). Rechtlich Aspekte der Medienkonvergenz [Legal aspects of media convergence]. Retrieved July 25, 2005, from http://www.like.e-technik.uni-erlangen.de/download/ Zukunftswerkstatt_Digitales_Radio/Zukunftswerkstatt_Digitales_Radio_2003_WS_03_04/MEDI ENKONVERGENZ%20Powerpoint.ppt
DW-World.de (2005). *Aufgabenplanung 2006–1009: Auf einen Blick [Masterplan 2006–2009: Overview]*. Retrieved August, 2, 2005, from http://www.dw-world.de/dw/article/0,1564,1526207,00. html
Gerhards, M. & Mende, A. (2005). *Offliner: Zwischen interessierte Annaeherung und bewusster Distanz zum Internet [Offline: Between interested nearness and conscious distance from the Internet]*, Retrieved November 17, 2005, from www.ard.de/-/id = 341438/property = downoad/ cw3x8y/index.pdf
Goldhammer, K. & Zerdick, A. (1999). *Rundfunk online. Entwicklung und Perspektiven des Internets für Hörfunk- und Fernsehanbieter [Broadcasting online. Development and perspectives of the Internet for radio and television broadcasters]*. Berlin, Germany: Vistas.
Ha, L. (2004). Webcasting. In H. Bidgoli (ed.), *The internet encyclopedia* (pp. 674–686). New York: Wiley.
HeavyReading.com (2005). *Next generation broadband in Europe*. Retrieved November 17, 2005, from http://www.websiteoptimization.com/bw/0504/

Information and Communication Services Act (Informations- und Kommunikationsdienste-Gesetz). BGBl. I, §§1, 2, 4, (1997, as amended).

Inter-State Agreement on Media Services (Mediendienste-Staatsvertrag). BGBl. I, §2, (1997, as amended).

Mercer Management Consulting (2005a). *Breitbankmarkt: Deutschland ohne Anschluss? [Broadband market: Germany without connection?].* Retrieved August 6, 2005, from http://www.ecin.de/state-of-the-art/breitbandmarkt/

Mercer Management Consulting (2005b). *Kooperation statt konfrontation—wege aus dem werbedilemma [Cooperation instead of confrontation: Ways out of the advertising dilemma].* Retrieved August 6, 2005, from http://www.ecin.de/state-of-the-art/werbedilemma/

Netscape (2002). *Dynamische Informationszustellung fuer Benutzer im Internet und in Intranets [Dynamic information delivery for Internet and Intranet users].* Retrieved August 4, 2005, from http://home.de.netscape.com/de/comprod/products/communicator/netcaster.html

PricewaterhouseCoopers. (2005). *German entertainment and media outlook: 2005–2009.* Retrieved July 20, 2005, from http://www.pwc.com/Extweb/pwcpublications.nsf/docid/C3A3CC7C707F052 E8025709D0030670C

Point Topic, Ltd. (2005). *World broadband statistics: Q2 2005.* Retrieved November 6, 2005 from http://www.point-topic.com/home/press/dslanalysis.asp

Porter, M.E. (1979). How competitive forces shape strategy. *Harvard Business Review, March–April,* 86–93.

Sjurts, I. (2002). *Strategien in der Medienbranche: Grundlagen und Fallbeispiele [Strategies in the media industries: Foundations and case studies]* (2nd ed.). Wiesbaden, Germany: Gabler.

Statistisches Bundesamt [Federal Statistical Office]. (2005). *Informations-Technologie in Unternehmen und Haushalten 2004 [Information technology in businesses and households 2004].* Retrieved August 5, 2005, from http://www.destatis.de/download /d/veroe/pb_ikt_04.pdf

Telecommunications Act *(Telekommunikationsgesetz).* BGBl. I, §§3, 6, (1996, as amended).

Teltarif.de (2005). *Provider verkaufen T-DSL-Anschluss unter eigenem Namen [Providers sell T-DSL connections under their own name].* Retrieved August 9, 2005 from http://www.teltarif.de/i/privatdsl-resale.html

University of Leipzig. (2001). Linkindex Internet Fernsehen: Dienstleister [Links for Internet television: Service providers]. Retrieved July 23, 2005, http://www.uni-leipzig.de/~wehn/Web-TV/bk2site/Anbieter/Dienstleister/

Werben &Verlaifen. (2004a). IVW Online: Zugriffe im neuen Kategoriesystem, Top 10 der Entertainment-Inhalte [IVW Online: Online hits in new category system, Top 10 entertainment sites]. Retrieved November 18, 2005 from http://www.wuv.de/ daten/studien/102004/908/3011.html

Werben &Verlaifen. (2004b). IVW Online: Zugriffe im neuen Kategoriesystem, Top 20 nach Visits [IVW Online: Online hits in new category system, Top 20 according to visits]. Retrieved November 18, 2005 from http://www.wuv.de/ daten/studien/102004/908/3009.html

ZDNet.de (2005). *Breitband Nutzung in Deutschland hinkt* [Broadband use in Germany limps]. Retrieved November 17, 2005, from http://www.zdnet.de/itmanager/kommentare/0,39023450, 39130952,00.htm

ZDNet Research (2005). Broadband penetration in Germany at 8.1%. Retrieved October 13, 2005 from http://blogs.zdnet.com/ITFacts/?m = 20050924

Zimmer, J. (2000). *Media Perspektiven: Interaktives Fernsehen-Durchbruch wieder Internet? [Media perspectives: Interactive television breakthrough via Internet?].* Retreived November 10, 2005 from http://www.ard-werbung.de/showfile.phtml/2000_03_02.pdf?foid = 41

APPENDIX
A Sampling of Web TV Providers

City	TV Station	Web Address	Genre	File Format
Berlin	3sat	www.3sat.de	News & Talk	RealVideo
Berlin	Bloomberg TV	www.bloomberg.de	Business News	WMP TV
Berlin	Deutsche Welle	www.dw-world.de	News	RealVideo
Berlin	Deutscher Bundestag	www.bundestag.de	News	RealVideo
Berlin	Euronews	www.euronews.net	News	RealVideo
Berlin	Eurosport	www.eurosport.de	Sports	RealVideo
Berlin	N24 Live	www.n24.de	News	RealVideo
Berlin	N-TV	www.n-tv.de	News	RealVideo
Berlin	Tagesschau	www.tagesschau.de	News & Talk	RealVideo
Berlin	Viva TV	www.vivaplus.tv	Rock Music	WMP TV
Berlin	ZDF	www.zdf.de	News & Talk	RealVideo
Bonn	GIGA	www.giga.de	General	RealVideo
Cologne	RTL	www.RTL.de	General	Windows

CHAPTER 8

Spain: An Emerging Market Still Taking Its First Steps

Mónica Herrero and Charo Sádaba
University of Navarra

WEBCASTING MARKET ENVIRONMENT

Media Industry Structure

The media industry in Spain started relatively late in comparison with the main European countries. In 1975, after nearly forty years of dictatorship the country started its way to democracy. During those years, the government had a strict control over the media by means of censorship as well as restrictions to the creation of new media. Nevertheless, in a few years, Spain, which accounts for a population of almost 45 million, of population has become in a very active market following very similar tendencies to the rest of the countries in Europe.

Since webcasters are still small players in the Spanish media market, it is worthwhile to consider the environment in which they operate, bearing in mind the nature of the major webcasters. According to our study on the top ten webcasters in Spain, six have an audiovisual off line version (mainly television channels), and five belong to the main multimedia groups in Spain.

In that sense, the liberalization of the audiovisual and telecommunications sector on one hand, and the development of multimedia groups on the other, work as the main forces that drive the market.

THE DEVELOPMENT OF THE SPANISH MULTIMEDIA GROUPS

In the last decade, there has been a strong tendency towards media concentration in the Spanish media market. Mergers and acquisitions have proliferated in these years while established media groups entered into the new media market (Sánchez-Tabernero & Carvajal, 2002). Among the main multimedia groups (multimedia being those groups which own both print and audiovisual media), we will briefly describe the top three groups.

PRISA is the biggest media group in Spain. When Canal Plus, a pay TV channel, was launched in 1990, PRISA was one of the shareholders and owned 25% of the company. Thus, PRISA (which owned the national leader newspaper, El País, and one of the main radio stations, SER) started its activities in the television industry, and is now making an attempt to become a powerful multimedia group. In 1997, Sogecable became the audiovisual division of PRISA, and all the audiovisual affiliated companies were associated under the name of Sogecable. Now, PRISA has a specific unit for the creation and development of content in digital formats, Prisacom. One of the top ten webcasters, los40.com belongs to this business unit (www.prisa.es).

In the last few years Vocento has become the second significant multimedia group in Spain. This group started as a strong regional press group (Correo Group), merged with one of the main national newspapers, ABC, and slowly entered the audiovisual arena. At first, it became shareholder of Telecinco (1996), one of the private television channels. Then Vocento increased its participation in audiovisual production companies, such as Boca or Europroducciones. Moreover, Vocento started the first audiovisual news agency, Atlas, which accounts among the top ten webcasters. Vocento has hence a strong presence in the webcasting market (www.vocento.es).

Finally, Planeta, also originally a publishing group, recently started its activities in media, by acquiring Antena 3 in April 2003, thus becoming one of the main multimedia groups in a short time. Among its main companies, Planeta owns the national daily La Razón, the audiovisual production company DeAPlaneta, and one of the top 10 webcasters antena3tv.com, the online version of Antena 3 Television. There is also a Spanish webcaster under the name www.planetatv.com, but it does not belong to the publishing group. It's just a coincidence that it bears the group's name in its URL.

In order to clarify the position of these groups, Table 8–1 shows the main newspapers groups, radio and television stations in terms of market share or audience.

In sum, multimedia groups are also leaders in the webcasting market. However, due to the nature of webcasting, some webcasters target a specific audience

TABLE 8–1
Media Groups

MEDIA GROUP	PRESS (Percentage)		RADIO (Audience)		TELEVISION (Percentage)	
PRISA	El País	14.0%	SER	5,387,000	—	—
VOCENTO	Vocento*	25.3%	COPE	1,943,000	Telecinco	22.5%
PLANETA	La Razón	5.4%	Onda Cero	2,245,000	Antena 3	20.7%

* Under this name all the regional newspapers belonging to Vocento are considered.
Source: Audit Bureau Circulation (OJD), General Media Survey EGM, and SOFRES, the Spanish Television Rating Service.

in which larger groups do not have interests, as we will discuss later. Some examples of such niche webcasters are www.accine.com and www.spotstv.com.

LIBERALIZATION AND PRIVATIZATION OF COMMUNICATION INDUSTRIES

The television landscape in Spain underwent a complete transformation during the last decade of the 20th century. Until then, there was no television market as such, since the public television service was the only provider (Artero, Herrero, & Sánchez-Tabernero, 2005). Between 1990 and 2000, it went from a system of public television monopoly (TVE) to a system of coexistence between public and private initiatives, with the introduction of private television channels (Telecinco, Antena3 and Canal Plus) in 1990 (Private Television Law 10, 1988). Among these three new channels, Canal Plus—partially owned by Canal Plus France—took the first step towards pay television in Spain (Álvarez Monzoncillo, 1997). All them were terrestrial channels, since cable and satellite television started developing at the end of the nineties, as a result of the legislation.

During this opening-up process, a series of political and managerial decisions were taken, which, in theory, turned the Spanish market into one of the most active in Europe. Moreover, the actual starting signal to the competitive pay television occurred within the last three years of the twentieth century. At the same time, a fundamental expansion to different distribution systems took place, mainly cable television and satellite television (Satellite Telecommunications Law 37, 1995; Cable Telecommunications Law 42, 1995). Due to the late development of cable and satellite television, the new services launched at the end of the nineties were already using digital technology. Thus cable and satellite television services started digital transmission in Spain from their inception.

Digital television was introduced in 1997 with the launch of the first television platform by satellite. The first pay television offers that arose in this new context came as a result of the regulations that enabled competition in the pay television market. It should not be ignored that the new pay television platforms emerged within a different technological context which is characterized by the advance of digital technology. In this sense, any new pay television channel was both a consequence of the liberalization of the distribution sector in which it operated as well as an effect of the development of digital technology, which made possible a multichannel supply service coupled with a better quality of reception. Consequently, there appears to be a close relation between the development of pay television and the implementation of digital television (Brown & Picard, 2005).

In January 1997, the platform of digital television by satellite Sogecable (a company belonging Canal Plus) began its broadcasts under the commercial name of Canal Satélite Digital, and counted on Canal Plus as the driving force for its service supply (Alonso,1999). Vía Digital, the digital television platform led by Telefónica, was the direct competitor of Canal Satélite Digital and started its service in September 1997. The legal battles that both platforms faced, in which the European legislation took part, represent an intricate number of technological difficulties as well as the political interests involved. Therefore, unlike pay television, which arose protected by a monopoly, the digital television by satellite burst directly into a competition environment (Herrero, 2003).

The slow development of cable and the failure of the first experience of digital terrestrial television (a pay television channel called Quiero TV) enabled satellite service providers to be the main competitors for the broadcasting rights of contents. In this way, it was hardly surprising that Canal Satélite Digital and Vía Digital announced their decision to merge in May 2002 under the commercial name of Digital +. The digital satellite market is now a monopoly.

Before considering the cable sector, digital terrestrial television started as fast as it did in other European countries, such as the United Kingdom. The intention of implementing DTT, which involved fewer distribution problems than cable or satellite, led the government to support directly the initiative of Retevisión under the brandname of Quiero TV. Digital terrestrial television started therefore under a pay model, and favored by the government. Quiero TV stopped broadcasting after two years of substantial losses, following the same path as ON digital, the British DTT platform (Brown & Picard, 2005).

Since coaxial cable was hardly implemented in Spain, when the government allowed cable providers to expand their businesses in the middle of the nineties, they started using optical fiber, making use of all the benefits of digital technology. In fact the cable offer was, from the very beginning, a multi-service integrated offer, as cable providers could serve their subscribers with telephone, multi-channel television, and internet access.

Nevertheless, the legislation did not allow big groups to operate in the cable market, and the market structure was very much a regional one, although ONO and AUNA were positioning themselves as the main cable providers. This made difficult for the cable providers to negotiate film and sport rights and therefore to build an attractive television scheduling for potential subscribers. Moreover, the construction of infrastructures was very slow, as previously there had not been any cable structures in Spain.

The uncertainty surrounding the development of cable television services in the near future, even admitting its great potential in the medium- and long-term, became more serious with the merger of the two digital satellite platforms. The green light given by the government to this operation, without satisfying the limitations regarding the control they have on key contents for pay television, caused a great discontent among cable companies. In fact, the position of control granted to Sogecable may well slow down the penetration of the digital television supply by cable operators even further.

Assuming that the pay digital distribution by satellite remains in a monopolistic situation, and that after the failure of the main commitment for DTT, the cable still is the only viable and possible competitor, the likelihood of the integration of both leading operators, AUNA and ONO, is increasing. In fact, both have developed their businesses by acquiring smaller providers in different regions since the legislation has become less restrictive in this sense. By the end of July 2005, the acquisition of AUNA by ONO was just pending on the last approval. That means that both together account for the 24.93% of the pay television market as shown in Table 8–2.

With a single digital platform by satellite (Digital +), a single cable operator of national range, and the recent development by Telefónica of audiovisual pay ser-

TABLE 8–2
Pay Television Subscribers and Market Share 2004

Pay-TV Channel	Distribution	Number of Subscribers	Market Share
Sogecable (Digital +)	Satellite	2,093,817	65.07%
ONO	Cable	434,368	13.50%
AUNA	Cable	367,849	11.43%
Rest of cable operators	Cable	177,484	5.52%
Local cable operators	Cable	135,960	4.23%
Telefónica Cable	Cable	8,388	0.26%

Source: Telecommunications Market Commission, Annual Report 2004.

vices over the broadband (Imagenio), there is little room left for the last means of digital provision in the Spanish market: Digital terrestrial television. However, the government is favoring its development in a regional and local basis. Moreover, all the terrestrial channels have already fulfilled the commitment of starting the diffusion of digital signal content although there are not still digital television sets in the market. The government established this requirement in 2000 in order to prepare the way for the switch from analogue to digital.

Digital providers are now outlining the context in which webcasters operate in terms of audiovisual content, and in terms of competition. However, webcasters are not considered as competitors by cable, satellite, and terrestrial digital providers, but rather as on line versions of the main audiovisual companies, or as new business units within multimedia groups, as we have seen. Since the switch from analogue to digital is planned to be in 2008, television companies are very much involved in the process of digitalization as a priority. Therefore, television companies (either cable, satellite or terrestrial) compete among each other in providing better digital services whereas webcasters are still behind in this battle both in terms of competition and in consumers' perception.

INTERNET USAGE

Internet Penetration

According to the last available data from AIMC (Mass Media Research Association), the most reliable source regarding internet usage and penetration in Spanish market, in May 2005 the medium reached the 33.6% of the population (12,451,000). These figures have been growing firmly for the last years (22.5% in 2002, 26.9% in 2003, 33.1% in 2004). However, according to the same source, only 19% of the total population stated they had used the internet "yesterday," so regular users were still a small minority.

The Spanish internet user profile is an urban man (60.8%), aged 25–34 (30.6%), of a middle economic class (41.3%). The access takes places mainly from home (65.1%), while at work internet usage declines to 32.5%. The World Wide Web (93.5%) and email (82.7%) are the preferred internet applications, with a huge difference with regard to the next one, instant messaging, with 34.2% penetration.

According to the last General Media Survey (EGM) study (2005), the penetration of internet usage is higher among foreigners or immigrants living is Spain than among Spaniards: 39% of the Latin American people living in Spain are using the internet. This could explain why planetatv.com, a foreign-owned webcaster centered in Latin American music and pop culture, has such a strong impact in Spain.

Since home is the main place of access to the internet, the number broadband connections has risen steadily in the last months. Between April 2004 and April

2005, DSL gained almost one million new users, for what now counts as almost 3 million lines. DSL is the main way to access the internet from home although the cost is slightly higher than in other European countries. DSL is not the only successful technology in the Spanish market: Mobile phones have been the quickest technology to gain market share during the last few years. In 2002, the number of mobile phones exceeded the number of traditional phone lines, and as technology evolves from 2–2.5G to 3G, the market is also increasing.

E-commerce activities have also increased significantly for the last years: B2C activities accounted for a total of $290 million in 2000, and in 2004 it reached $1.837 billion (20% more than the previous year). According to the E-Commerce Spanish Association–E-Commerce and Direct Marketing Spanish Federation (AECE-FECEMD) (2005) study, only 27.8% of internet users are active in e-commerce activities.

Beside these internet penetration and usage data, it must be remembered that according to the last *World Economic Forum Global Information Technology Report, 2004/05*, Spain occupies the 29th place among the 104 countries listed in the Networked Readiness Index: Despite its high figures and the increasing popularity of the internet and broadband connections, Spain is far away from other European counterparts as Iceland, Finland, Germany, United Kingdom, or France. Only Portugal ranks after Spain (30th place).

The Internet Users Association (AUI) makes some comparisons between internet penetration in Spanish companies and European ones, with the purpose of showing the weakness of the Spanish information society. According to this source, the percentage of Spanish companies with internet access is 84% while in Europe it is up to 88%. PC usage in companies in Spain is 86.5% versus 94% in Europe. Only 33% of the Spanish companies owns a web site, while in the rest of Europe this figure is 75%. Six percent of Spanish firms sell through the internet (38% in Europe), and 21% of national companies buy goods and services by this medium as opposed to 50% in Europe. The Spanish Internet Users Association pointed out the high connection costs as the main problem to a faster adoption of internet connections.

The situation of the Spanish Information Society is complex, but the positive side is that the potential growth of the internet in Spain is huge, and there is still room for a double figure increase. The enormous adoption of mobile phones and DSL lines ensure the interest of the Spanish market in new technologies, and consumers are ready to adopt them.

Audience Research and Web Traffic Research Data

As in other countries, the audience and web traffic research data in Spain are directly related to the main revenue source for media sites: Advertising. Advertisers

TABLE 8–3
Evolution of Internet Advertising Expenditure in Spain

Year	U.S. Dollars (in Millions)
2002	85.9
2003	87.7
2004	114.12

Source: PwC and IAB Study (2005).

TABLE 8–4
Top 10 Webcasters in Spain

Webcaster	URL
Accine	www.accine.com
Los 40	www.los40.com
3 a la carta	www.3alacarta.com
Atlas News	www.atlas-news.com
Antena3tv	www.antena3tv.com
Spotstv	www.spotstv.com
Planetatv	www.planetatv.com
Ono	www.ono.com
Salud Multimedia (Multimedia Health)	www.saludmultimedia.com
Telecinco	www.telecinco.com

demand information before investing money on the web. According to Infoadex (2005), the unique compiler of advertising expenditure data, in 2004 the internet received only 1% of total advertising expenditures. PricewaterhouseCoopers and the Spanish Chapter of IAB (2005) have offered a closer view of this expenditure as it is showed in Table 8–3. It is still a small medium, but it is has grown firmly the last years, and there exists a common interest in making it as major a medium for advertising as are other traditional media.

There are several sources of data on audience and web traffic in Spain. The AIMC (Mass Media Research Association) publishes the most recognized study on media consumption in this market: The EGM (General Media Survey) is conducted four times a year and provides interesting and updated information about the evolution of media and internet use in Spain. According to this source, between May 2004 and May 2005 the internet gained 450,000 new users. AIMC also conducts a well-known study, *Navegantes en la red*, which in spite of its methodological gaps (it is based on a self-selection sample) is considered one of the main sources about users preferences and attitudes about the internet.

Web traffic research is more complex: Media companies rely on the OJD (Audit Bureau of Circulation) as source of information as the offline media to get information about web traffic. The online version of OJD has an important weakness—not all the media related websites are audited by OJD. OJD's audit includes web platforms as portals, and entertainment sites, and thus offers a varied picture of the traffic.

Nielsen/Net Ratings has developed a system of panels in Spain, based on households. The information emerging from it is very useful but, of course, limited. Advertising agencies and media buying groups develop ad hoc studies, and ad server technology is used to monitor users behavior.

OWNERSHIP AND BUSINESS PERFORMANCE OF LEADING WEBCASTERS

To identify the leading webcasters in Spain, the authors consulted industry and academic experts including Hector Milla, founder of Streaming Strategy S.L., a media consulting company specialized in internet media and digital convergence; Borja Gómez and Manuel Casals, owners of Pulsa TV, a publishing company focused on the interactive digital television market; David Domingo, professor and researcher of internet media at the University Rovira and Virgili; and Pilar Martínez-Costa, professor of digital radio at the University of Navarra. They provided a list of webcasters in accordance with different criteria that bore in mind that Spain is still an emergent market. The results are shown in Table 8–4.

In these results, 40% are pure-play webcasters and 60% are clicks-and-bricks. However, this sample is not representative of the Spanish webcasters as concerns the proportion of pure-plays versus clicks-and-bricks. Nevertheless, as a sector giving its first steps, the experts considered interesting to pay attention to the pure-play models although its market penetration is significantly smaller. They also pointed out the emergence, as in other markets, of ISPs based on DSL services that only recently started offering multimedia services to subscribers. Terra (www.terra.es) is one of the most popular sites in Spain and the third internet service provider. It offers a specific section in the portal with both free and subscription-based broadband multimedia content. The rest of the ISP competitors are also developing similar services for their subscribers, as it is the case of Ya.com (www.ya.com) or Wanadoo (www.wanadoo.es).

The recent development of these new services has led the experts to suggest paying special attention to the main players (clicks-and-bricks) and to some pure-play webcasters offering specialized content. Since the core business of these pure-play webcasters is the webcasting activity itself, it was interesting to analyze

TABLE 8–5
Sources of ISP Earnings

	2003	2004
Internet Services	89.3%	95.8%
Internet access	82.5%	81.7%
Information services	6.8%	14.1%
Inducted traffic	2.6%	1.2%
Advertising	2.7%	2.7%
E-commerce	0.7%	0.3%
Other sources	4.7%	0.0%

Source: Telecommunications Market Commission, *Annual Report 2004*, p. 390.

their performance in making this business profitable. However, for the ISPs the main revenue source comes directly for providing access to internet, as shown in Table 8–5. As DSL subscribers increase, the ISPs will explore new revenue sources including those derived from multimedia content access.

Among the six clicks and bricks webcasters, four of them have parent companies that are publicly listed in the stock market, while the fifth one is planning to go public in two years time and the last one is a regional public service company. The pure-plays belong to small companies, three Spanish owned and one foreign owned.

Media groups own four of the clicks and bricks in the top 10 roster. PRISA is behind loscuarenta.com (the digital counterpart of the leading music radio station in Spain) and also owns a pay television channel in the satellite platform Digital +. It offers pop music and its target is mainly young people. Loscuarenta.com is audited by OJD, and according to the January 2005 data, it has 1,594,643 unique website users.

Vocento controls two webcasters: telecinco.es and atlas-news.com. The first one is the website of the leading television channel we have mentioned earlier. It offers free videos except for adult content which requires sms payment. Short Message System is a payment method by which users send text messages to dedicated commercial numbers; it is exclusively for cell phones and it reaches 79.7% of the population in Spain (Statistics National Institute, 2004). As it for the television audience, its target is a very commercial one and its content strategy supports the most popular television programs with additional content in the web. It is a very active website that incorporate new contents and services frequently. Atlas-news.com is a subscription-based professional streaming news service used by many news websites. There are some free videos, but the majority of its video selection requires payment. Since Vocento has local television stations around Spain, the Atlas-News website can provide audiovisual material to these channels in a very efficient way.

Planeta is behind Antena3tv.com, using the same content strategy as its competitor telecinco.es. According to OJD in January 2005, it registered 715,205 unique website users. Antena3tv.com offers only free videos with decent full screen quality.

ONO is a telecommunications company offering cable internet access. Its website is video-centered web content with free broadband quality videos (except for adult content video which require payment). After the merger with AUNA, the corporation is planning on going public in 2007. ONO stands as one of the most comprehensive websites available in Spain.

The last click and brick webcaster is 3alacarta.com. It belongs to the Corporació Catalana de Ràdio i Televisió Interactiva (CCRTVi) which is the public media corporation in Catalonia. The website concentrates on video content, offers free low quality videos, and subscription or sms payment for broadband quality videos. According to OJD its audience in January 2005 was 421,283 unique website users.

Regarding the pure-plays, two of them are professionally oriented. Spotstv.com is owned by a domestic company and it is targeted to the advertising sector. It commercializes sports, mainly Spanish ones. Saludmultimedia.com is oriented to health professionals and offers real time conferences and congresses, making the content available for visitors after the events.

The other two webcasters are commercially-oriented. Accine.com offers independent cinema, mainly from Spain and Latin America. Its business model is totally based on direct payment. Planetatv.com is a US based website offering news and video clips about the entertainment world. Although it belongs to an American company, the content is fully in Spanish, targeting Spanish-speaking consumers.

Spanish Webcasting Business Practice Models

Revenue sources used by the leading webcasters. Among all the possible revenue sources, advertising, sponsorship, e-commerce, pay per use, and subscription are the most used by webcasters. None of the analyzed sites use content syndication with voluntary contributions as a revenue source.

Advertising and sponsorship reaches 90%. This means that all the webcasters in the sample use advertising except www.accine.com, which is a pure-play webcaster and is funded by subscription only. Following the broadcasting market practice, www.3alacarta.com, a site for a public television channel, also uses advertising as a revenue source on the internet. Six of these sites display more than one ad, and five display more than four ads.

E-commerce is the second revenue source for half of the analyzed sites (50%). Nevertheless, none of the webcasters offering e-commerce include its own products or services for sale. They redirect the users in most cases to third-party e-commerce platforms (such as El Corte Inglés in the case of www.los40.com). Regarding the products retailed in these sites, media entertainment related products have the greatest slaes, followed by music, DVD collections, etc. Two sites sell other commercial products or services such as travel, on line courses, other software, and so on.

Thirdly, pay per use reaches 40% of the sample. For three of the webcasters, it is a secondary source of revenue since it is their way of selling its most exclusive products. Although they could use e-commerce for selling them, they prefer pay per use. Because of the variety of their content, many users could be interested just in specific packs of it, so subscription does not seem to be the best option for them. The amount they charge goes from $1 to $4. As for the methods, only one uses credit cards or other on line payment systems. The others use sms systems for payments. In both cases, an ISP webcast service provider collects the money.

Only 30% of the webcasters offer users the choice of a subscription plan. Only two, atlas-news.com and spotstv.com are professionally oriented. It has not been possible to obtain the subscription fee for atlas-news.com. spotstv.com charges a monthly fee of $24.80. The non-professional site, planetatv.com, charges $9.95 per month. The monies are collected directly by credit card.

Finally, spotstv.com belongs to an affiliation program that redirects the users interested in music to a third platform where they can purchase songs.

Program genres. Before consider the sources of content, Table 8–6 shows the video program genres available on the sites. Neither blockbuster movies nor religious content are provided by these webcasters. All of them offer video content, whereas 60% also offer audio content. Pop music is the most common audio content. Interactive elements, such as games or chat rooms, are not as common as it could be presumed by the nature of the medium. Only 30% of the sites use interactive games. Chat rooms or message boards are only present in 50% of the sites.

Sources of content. Of the examined websites, 60% of the webcasters rely strictly on original content sources. In one of these cases the content is shown exclusively on the website. The other 50% use only repurposed content. The remaining 10% have a greater variety of content sources, including a combination of original, repurposed, and simulcast.

As for the origin of the content, in 60% of the cases it is exclusively domestic production. In two cases, half of the content is domestic and the other half is foreign. When foreign products are provided, they come either from countries of sim-

TABLE 8–6
Video Program Genres

Program Genre	Percentage of Sites Offering the Genre
Sports	60%
TV programs and series	50%
Business news, speech	0
News	0
Music videos	0
Animation or cartoons	40%
TV commercials	30%
Trailers	0
Talk shows	0
Documentaries	0
Pornography	0
Education or instruction	20%
Classic movies	10%

ilar culture or language (Mexico, Argentina, Peru, Colombia) or from the leading media exporters, mainly the United States and the United Kingdom.

Forty percent of the sites organize their content in channels. There is an enormous diversity with regard to the number of channels, it ranges from 5 to 18. Finally, the average number of shows/video clips is not uniform at all. Saludmultimedia.com has 40 video clips and spotstv.com offers 3,000 clips in one channel.

File transmission methods.   According to Ha and Ganahl (2004), it is worth analyzing to what extent the file transmission used by webcasters is related to their revenue sources. In the case of Spain, according to the sample, the main transmission method used is on demand streaming (90%). This system enables users to retrieve the content on demand at any convenient time and it does not constitute ownership, because the video or audio streams cannot be stored on the user's computer system. (Ha et al., 2005).

Although some sites charge for certain kinds of content, 80% of the sites offer the content for free. The use of on demand streaming ensures that ownership is not given to the clients. Only 20% of the sites employ on demand downloading, and they all charge a fee for its use. Moreover, in the case of accine.com this is understandable, as they offer full-length movies that are better watched directly from the hard disk. Live streaming and push are seldom used by webcasters (20% each).

Comparison between pure-plays and clicks-and-bricks webcasters.   The most significant difference between these two sectors is that whereas clicks and bricks webcasters offer general content, pure-plays are highly specialized (except in a single case).

Charging for content is a common practice for pure plays (40% of the sample); they sell their own products and services through the in-ternet as the only distribution channel.

Regarding the webcasters that require registration (50% of the sample), only pure-plays in a great majority (80%) request personal details and contact information. In these cases, the internet is the only way to know and contact the client.

DISCUSSION

Webcasting is not a hot topic in the Spanish market as a whole, neither in professional nor academic publications. Only in the last months is the internet gaining more popularity among users. It is still not regarded as a strategic tool by most media companies. Television companies, for example, are more involved nowadays in the digitalization process rather than in exploring internet business opportunities.

The following three reference points can help us to understand the results.

Firstly, even if DSL penetration has recently increased, and the Spanish market is leading European growth, it is necessary to bear in mind that the situation at the starting point was far below the average in other countries. Broadband connections, so necessary for a good quality webcasting experience, still reach too a low percentage of the entire population.

Secondly, there is little culture of pay per content in this market. The first multi-channel pay television service was launched in 1997, and the development of cable television is considerably slow. As for the internet, media companies are still looking for a proper business model that enables them to sell their own content to users. El País, after two years with a subscription system for its on line edition, (it was the only newspaper in Spain charging such a fee), has opened its content up to all users once again in June 2005.

Finally, e-commerce is not a popular activity for users. This is due, among other reasons, to a lack of culture in distance shopping as well as distrust on on line merchants, etc.

These reasons could explain why the major clicks and bricks players offer their contents for free, and why e-commerce operations, when they do exist, are not very significant and not related to the main content of the webcaster. As in the off line world, advertising is the most important funding system for this emerging market.

Nevertheless, the internet does show itself as a good market niche and highly specialized pure-plays may have a promising future in this environment.

REFERENCES

AECE, FECEMD (2005). *Estudio sobre comercio electrónico B2C* [A study on e-commerce]. Retrieved July 20, 2005, from http://observatorio.red.es/ estudios/documentos/estudio%20_b2c_ 2005.pdf

Alonso, F. (1999). *Sogecable descodificado: cifras y claves empresariales de Canal+ en España* [Decoding Sogecable: Key managerial decisions in Canal Plus Spain]. Madrid: Fragua.

Álvarez Monzoncillo, J.M. (1997). *Imagenes de Pago* [Pay television images]. Madrid: Fragua.

Artero, J. P., Herrero, M., & Sánchez-Tabernero, A. (2005). Monopolio, oligopolio y competencia en los últimos quince años de televisión en España [Monopoly, oligopoly, and competition in the last fifteen years of television in Spain]. *Sphera Publica,* 5, 83–99.

Brown, A., & Picard, Robert G. (Eds.). (2005). *Digital terrestrial television in Europe.* Mahwah, New Jersey: Erlbaum.

Cable Telecommunications Law 42. (1995, December 22). B.O.E. n. 306, December 23, 1995.

Ha, L., Ganahl, R. (2004). Webcasting business models of clicks-and-bricks and pure-play media: A comparative study of leading webcasters in South Korea and the United States. *The International Journal on Media Management,* 6(1&2), 75–88.

Ha, L., Ganahl, R., Arampatzis, A., Allagui, I., Bakker, P., Chausse, M., et al. (2005). Emerging media business models worldwide: A study of leading webcasters in 13 countries. Paper accepted by the Communication Technology and Policy Division, Association for Education in Journalism and Mass Communication Annual Convention (AEJMC), San Antonio, Texas, August 10–12.

Herrero, M. (2003). *Programming and Direct Viewer Payment for Television: The case of Canal+ Spain.* Pamplona: Eunsa.

Infoadex (2005). Estudio sobre la inversión publicitaria en España 2005 [A study on advertising expenditure in Spain 2005]. Retrieved September 1, 2005, from http://www.infoadex.es

PricewaterhouseCoopers (PwC) & IAB Spain. (2005). *Estudio sobre inversión publicitaria de medios interactivos. Resultados del año 2004* [A study on advertising expenditure in interactive media, 2004]. Madrid: PwC.

Private Television Law 10. (1988, May 3). B.O.E. n. 108, May 5, 1988.

Sánchez-Tabernero, A., & Carvajal, M. (2002). *Media concentration in the European market: New trends and challenges.* Pamplona: Eunsa.

Satellite Communications Law 37. (1995, December 12). B.O.E. n. 297, December 13, 1995.

Telecomunications Market Commission. (2003). *Annual Report.* Retrieved September 1st, 2005, from http://www.cmt.es

CHAPTER 9

Italy: The Fastest Growing Broadband Market in Europe

Tiziano Bonini
Istituto Universitario di Lingue Moderne, Italy

ITALIAN MEDIA MARKET ENVIRONMENT

With a population of 58 million people, Italy has a relatively complex and lively media industry. The television and press industry are well established and mature, while the Italian radio world is living a third age of youth (after the golden age of the thirties and the "liberation age" of the seventies). According to Audiradio (the most important Italian audience research company, founded in 1988), radio listeners have passed from 26 million in 1989 to 37 million in 2005 (63% of the population), while television viewers have decreased from 56.8 to 55 million in the last five years.

According to Centro Studi Investimenti Sociali (CENSIS, 2004), one of the major national social research centers, 20 million Italians (35% of the population) read a newspaper at least three days per week, one of the lowest rates in Europe. This figure doesn't include the free press readers. Free press publications have entered the newspapers market in 1999 and, due to the lack of popular press in Italy, have conquered almost 2 million new readers to date.

The first newspapers appeared in Italy after 1840, but their number increased only after the unification of the nation in 1860. Now, *Corriere della Sera* (which belongs to the RCS-HDP group and is moderately center/right oriented), begun in 1876, is the most popular newspaper with around 700,000 copies sold every day. It is followed by *La Repubblica* (controlled by L'Espresso group, center/left oriented), begun in 1976, which sells around 650,000 copies.

Italian radio started to broadcast in 1924, under the fascist regime. In 1944, after the collapse of the regime and the restoration of democracy, a new public broadcaster, RAI, was founded. RAI maintained the monopoly on radio and television until 1976, when a historical sentence of the Constitutional Court gave free access

171

to the ether to private local broadcasters. Television arrived in 1954 and quickly took the place of radio as the "queen" of domestic entertainment.

Nowadays, according to the Minister of Communication (2004), there are 1,686 private local radio stations in Italy, 20 national commercial stations (among which only six belong to big multimedia groups), and 5 national public stations (RAI Radio 1, the most popular, is dedicated to news and talk; RAI Radio 2 has a light entertainment format; RAI Radio 3 is the cultural channel; Isoradio, a station dedicated to traffic news; and Channel Four, an all classical music format). Television is a more concentrated market. There are six national commercial channels (three of them controlled by the same group, Mediaset), three public channels, and almost 200 local channels.

The market of satellite television is controlled by a unique player, the Murdoch-owned Sky television, and counts 9 million subscriptions (16% of the population). The television signal is still widely analog. In fact, 87% of TV households receive an analog signal and, consequently, a traditional offer of contents; 12% have a satellite and only 1% have cable connections (CENSIS, 2004). According to Upa (2004), the total advertising spending increased from $1.65 billion in 1985 to $6.71 billion in 2004 (radio, $374 million; television, $3.2 billion).

RADIO WEBCASTING IN ITALY: FROM FREE RADIOS TO WEB RADIO

"Free radios" are a phenomenon which is part of European culture and history of the 1970s. First there were pirate radios broadcasting from ships anchored in international waters, then free radios were born in France. But it is in Italy that the phenomenon encountered the most fertile ground to grow on. A few months after the historical ruling of the Constitutional Court that ended the public monopoly of the ether, in September 1976, the magazine Altri Media had already listed 700 radios (thirty in Milan alone), while in June 1978 an official research found 2275 radios. Most of them were radios linked to political movements, but there were also all music stations.

But why start so far away in time when telling the history of web radios in Italy? Because Italian online radios after 1995 brought to completion the process of communication deinstitutionalization that was started by free radios; because many experiences of streaming audio came out of the same libertarian spirit; because online radios, like many free radios, were and are chiefly a musical medium; because the democratic potential of both phenomena (in different proportions) has been often exaggerated.

The birth and multiplication of web radios in Italy has been slower and more limited when compared to the United States, due to different new media literacy and to the different penetration of the internet in the two countries. In the U.S., internet users have grown from 62% of the population in 2000 to about 75% in 2004, while in Italy, according to CENSIS (2004) and Eurisko Research (another major national social research center; 2004), the figures went from 17% to 28% (from about 9 million to almost 17 million) over the same time span.

Yet, in Italy as well as in the U.S., the first web radios developed out of individual experiments made by internet enthusiasts. Radio X from Sardinia (which was on air for some months starting in February 1996) aired soul music and rhythm & blues starting at seven PM every night, and it clearly was a hobby, an after work passion in the age of post-fordism. Other radios, like Radio Cybernet, born at the end of 1996, had more alternative connotations and were a direct outcome of the embryonal "digital generation" of hackers, free software programmers, and electronic musicians, that was growing in the internet's shade. In Italy, the first generation of web radios had an essentially amateur connotation. There were radios for almost every kind of passion: Radios with highly specific talk formats, like a station entirely dedicated to UFO and astronomy; radios for fans of a particular Italian artist that would air only music by that artist, such as Radio Dapatas, which aired only the songs of a famous Italian musician, Daniele Silvestri; radios of Neapolitan music, or even the dreadful ones: Stations lacking a real format, which would air heterogeneous selections of music followed by infinite blabberings of the site owner, a sonic counterpart to the unbearable personal sites that were so trendy in the first years of life of the web. In most cases those radios were more similar to simple musical channels which aired one's naive selection of favorites without any awareness of formats and playlists which were a common feature of all the first streaming individual experiments, everywhere: "I stream, therefore I exist." The forces that drove these first free-spirited experimental webcastings were the same ones that paved the way to the advent of private broadcasting in Italy in the mid–1970s: The sudden availability of a brand new channel of communication and its complete freeness. The local ether for the young people of the seventies and the internet for the bit generation of the late nineties represented new and unruled spaces where their young subcultures could finally find home. In fact, the average age of the first generation of Italian webcasters is between 25 and 30. As it happened in the seventies, when almost every day a new station was born while another closed, the life of these first web radios was very short: They could last a single night, or a couple of weeks. Very few of them have been able to survive until the celebration of their first birthday. The enthusiasm generated by these streamings was shared only by a very little portion of the population, people with the same age and the same cultural background of the webcasters.

Afterward, there have been more systematic approaches with commercial intent, like Radio Montenapoleone (owned by some fashion shops), a stream intended for all the shops of the famous Milan fashion symbol street.

Like AOL, Yahoo, and Microsoft in the USA, big editorial and media groups have dedicated themselves to streaming in Italy as well, at a time of huge internet growth and net economy euphoria. Starting in 1999, KATAWEB (portal owned by the editorial group L'Espresso, which controls the second Italian newspaper, *La Repubblica*, and two national radio stations, Radio Deejay and Radio Capital), TISCALI (a telecommunications service company and the second biggest Italian internet provider) and JUMPY (the internet portal owned by the biggest Italian commercial television player, Mediaset, which controls the three most listened to commercial television channels, Canale 5, Italia 1, and Rete 4) have provided for their users streaming services mostly limited to musical offers. KATAWEB radio had sixty different theme channels to attract more listeners. The then-director of KWBroadcast, Ernesto Assante, described the mission of KW Radio saying: "To put it bluntly, I don't need to try to be Raffaella Carrà (a very famous Italian television anchor woman). I don't need to channel ten million people at the same time, this is irrelevant in terms of the net. But I do need an offer that can satisfy all those ten million people and their specific interests." (Perrotta, 2000, p. 156). JUMPY radio only had one channel with both music and speakers with a teenage target (the same as Italia Uno, the Mediaset TV channel oriented towards young people), while TISCALI Musix had thirty theme channels. In these first attempts, web radio was considered as a simple sonic wallpaper to accompany the internet surfer. In a few years, these same offers have changed. With the *sboom*, that is the crisis of net economy, the internet departments of many firms have been shrunken or drastically trimmed, if not completely dismantled. The streaming services offered by the big companies sites has also been rethought. For example, KATAWEB has applied a more selective choice. It doesn't offer theme channels any more but, thanks to its close relation with Radio Capital (owned by the same publisher), just a series of shows (mainly by Italian songwriters) listenable on demand. JUMPY's Radio has vanished, replaced by the much more profitable commerce of mobile ringtones. (Italy has the highest penetration level of mobile phones in Europe. According to CENSIS (2004), active mobile phones are 60 million, more than one per person. 70% of the population claims to use the mobile every day.) TISCALI has kept some thematic channels (very refined soul and urban music) and a program on demand, Vintage Radio, centered around jazz (with a host in the studio featuring interviews, album previews, and concerts). TISCALI is a provider from Sardinia, a region that hosts some of the most important Italian jazz festivals. Vintage Radio, highly enjoyable for jazz lovers, is a "branding" operation that tries to link TISCALI's image to the world of jazz.

Except for a few symbolically relevant experiences that will be described later, the phenomenon of Italian streaming is a bomb that has never exploded, it has rarely hit the headlines, and it didn't manage to take roots before the "dotcom" crisis. The numbers of Italian web radios have not followed the exponential growth of free radio stations or the number of American radio stations. Active web radios have always been far fewer than one thousand.

Between free radios and web radio there is a substantial difference—creativity. Free radios have experimented with the radio's language more deeply, inventing new programs and new styles, freeing the creative potential of the time. Until now, web radios have put emphasis on the technological aspect, experimenting in new ways of connection and communication.

Listeners of free radios would develop such a strong bond with their radios that in some cases they found themselves defending the stations with their own bodies against closure, as it happened for example in March 1977 at Radio Alice, a free radio based in Bologna that was closed down by police because of its political activities. Web radios are more often musical flows kept in the background. It is possible to communicate with one's own online radio by using SMS, email, or mobile phones, but there is often no reason to do so. The most interactive radios are those that manage to involve the listener in the productive process, where the listener is both the transmitter and the receiver, as is the case with collaborative streaming happenings. The NoMusic Festival is a great example of what a collaborative streaming happening is: It was born in 2001 and has reached its eighth edition (www.nomusic.org). It has 24 hour, nonstop streaming in which the source and the authors of the stream change every hour: 48 performers of 24 different countries give life to a 24 hour flow playing directly from their homes. In these kind of projects, authorship and place of transmission are multiple and horizontal. The mass communication model (unidirectional, one-to-many) has been substituted by a network model (bi-directional, many-to-many).

The Message Is the Individual

The dreams and wishes of many "free radios" of the 1970s—freedom of expression, general access to all the communication instruments, the transformation of the communication flow from a vertical dimension (perceived as authoritarian, institutional and hierarchical) to a horizontal one (libertarian, independent, headless)—have been found migrated and extended into the first streaming experiments. To express oneself through a microphone or by choosing one's favorite songs has never been so easy and inexpensive. In the 1970s, one mixer, two vinyl decks, an amplifier, and a transmitter —if ever any were used—were a lot more expensive than a computer and an internet connection are today. For free radios then and for web radios today, what really counts is to have access to a means of communication, to have the possibility of getting one's message through. Free radios were the first to contribute to move the center of gravity of emission from the institutions toward the individuals, through a shared and horizontal management of the communicative action. The encounter between radios and the internet is another step forward in this direction, bringing this process of deinstitutionalization of communication to a completion, allowing the individual to access the necessary means of communication to manage and transmit a message by oneself. If, as in the celebrated McLuhan equation, the medium is the message/massage, now that the individual has become the medium, *he* is the message: Playlists and the words aired on the web (in one word, the message) take on the sense of an individual narration that tells us about the tastes, the life, and the values of the one who selected them and put them online. Through the selected sonic language, the individual transmits his identity.

TWO WEB RADIO CASE HISTORIES

Because of the lack of quantitative audience research on radio webcasting in Italy, I will analyze two cases of web radio that have been acknowledged with numerous prizes for their high quality standard. Also, the two following cases are the best examples of the contemporary Italian web radio market, made of a great number of private independent broadcasters and some small commercial enterprises.

Case History 1:
An Independent Model—Radio Lilliput

Goodbye to the Radio Studio

Radio Lilliput is the most paradigmatic example of the first generation of homemade web radios. Its life was short, and the station doesn't exist anymore. It started broadcasting in September 1999 and closed eighteen months later. Lilliput's listener was not only a participant, he was firstly an "accomplice" of the broadcast.

Radio Lilliput was the first instance of a radio-net already ubiquitous at the source: There was no longer a fixed radio studio from which to irradiate the message, but as many studios as were the connected nodes. The studio had grown nomadic. If the aesthetics of the net is adopted in full, it is pointless to speak of a center and a periphery, of a transmitter and a receiver. There is a center, but it is always on the move, ceaselessly reconfiguring the topography of the electronic territory. The Lilliput experience has surely been marginal, but it is the one that used streaming more efficiently as a technology applied to the net and, more in general, as a real communication tool, in the sense intended by Brecht (1933): He claimed that radio had to become a bi-directional medium, where people could participate more actively to the production of the radio flow. The Lilliput model could be resumed and used for such local micro-communication projects (Lilliputians, in fact) as neighborhood radios, university, or company radios. Or it could be used in difficult contexts, where the only resource available is a telephone line (for example, a reporter broadcasting from his mobile phone), or it could be used to create a global network of independent producers.

Case History 2:
A Commercial Model—DCOD Network

DCOD Network was one of the first web radio projects of a commercial nature born in Italy, and it represents one of the industry's most complete and specialized commercial projects. Antonella De Angelis, DCOD's communication manager, recalls: "From June 1997 the operative management group started to work on the project for the DCOD network. The idea was to realize the first Italian digital media capable of producing and distributing music, information, and entertainment in an audio format targeted to young people, by using the internet's potential. In synthesis, a medium that combined the peculiarities of press, radio, and television, thus allowing the audience to give up the ordinary role of a "passive subject" by gaining access to customized forms of communication" (A. De Angelis, personal communication, February 22, 2004).

DCOD Srl was first set up in June 1998, with the specific goal of dealing with the themes linked to the development of digital media over the internet. The coordination of the project is provided by professionals coming from record labels, publishing houses, and radio and television stations that have realized projects aimed at the "new media" sector in the past. The project was finally launched in March 2000.

Today, the main source of the company's income is represented by the B2B (business-to-business) sector, from which 90% of its revenues are derived. These revenues come from communication services, such as events promotion, management of advertising campaigns, and television formats production, which constitute the real bulk of the revenues of DCOD. These activities are managed by C-Factory, a company incorporated by DCOD to follow the B2B sector more closely. The website counts more than 5,000 visits a day, averaging 12 minutes in duration. The distribution of the users sees 34% from the U.S., 26% from Italy, and the rest divided between Japan, Brazil, and other European countries.

DCOD is appealing for such a global audience because of its special music format, made of a sophisticated playlist of international and Italian indie music.

DCOD offers contents highly tailored on its users, who are aged from 24 to 35 and are looking for the most obscure rock music possible. To satisfy this niche, a single show is broadcasted consisting of a selection of indie rock songs. The services provided by DCOD are divided into six areas of action, each of a different color, all directly linked from the home page. There are two modes of listening, the classic flow, *radiozone* (which is the most popular with the users, especially those at the office), and the on-demand mode, *playbox*, which allows the customization of one's playlist. Besides, there is a *magazine* section that keeps users up to date with the latest news from the world of independent music, the genre chosen by DCOD. A promotional space called *Promozone* is also provided, from which additional information can be obtained about the played groups, and one's favorite records may even be ordered. An area for the "community," *talk talk* (the desire to talk and express oneself), has also been created to provide user interaction. It is a forum of simple conception, arranged in a chronological order, without a moderator to select the themes. Then there is the space for events, *DCOD events*, a little archive where it is possible to listen to the streaming on demand of recordings of events followed by DCOD, such as concerts or shows.

The survival of experiences like the one of DCOD, of a commercial nature but linked to a niche market, depends first on the reliability of the audio, the originality of the contents being offered, the ability of creating a truly unique community, and the development of sources of income that are both online (on the B2B side) and offline (such as agreements with music labels), in addition to parameters independent of the sources, like the broadening of the band and decisions about online copyright rights, because it is impossible at the moment to adopt a pay per listen policy or to survive through just advertising revenues.

COPYRIGHT ISSUES: AN ITALIAN VERSION

In 1999 the SIAE (Italian Society of Authors and Publishers) decided to introduce a license for the online use of music. Under the applicable licensing terms, web radios were divided by SIAE into three categories—commercial, institutional, and personal.

Commercial web radios are radios which "activated by whatever entity, generate revenues through a website created for the diffusion, presentation, promotion and offer of music" (SIAE, 2005). If the music broadcasted from the site is up to 25% of the programming, the web radio will have to pay SIAE 2% of its gross yearly income; from 25% to 75%, the figure rises to 5%, while, if music exceeds 75%, SIAE will get 7% of radio's income. In addition to this annual quota based on transmitted music, the license sets a fixed monthly fee which also varies on the basis of the quantity of music. If the radio broadcasts up to 25% it has to pay around $100 per month. The second segment, from 25% to 75% of music, pays $130. If the music is more than 75%, the monthly fee is $160. In addition, the monthly fee will be increased by $8.50 for each 100 thousand pages visited.

Institutional web radios are the "radios of associations, foundations, public institutions, local authorities, whose websites have the primary aim of illustrating their institutional activities and do not bring about any direct or indirect commercial gains" (SOURCE, 0000, p. 00).

In this case, the tax on yearly gross income is abolished, and the monthly fee, still applied in proportion to the percentage of broadcasted music, are cut by 50%.

Personal web radios are those "radios whose owners are natural persons. Radios that do not generate income and have no commercial goal, not even indirect, such as the amateur web radios." These radios are required to pay a yearly installment of $200 and two half-yearly installments of $145.

FROM ETHER TO THE WEB: PRIVATE COMMERCIAL RADIOS

In which way has the development of the internet been seized by Italian radiophony? In which way have commercial, national, local, and community Italian radios incorporated the net within their communication model? It's not simply a question of finding out when radios started transmitting their FM signal in simulcasting but also of understanding how the instrument of the net has been used according to the different needs of each station.

The first streaming experiences developed in small contexts; local commercial radios and community radios were likely to be (due to their limits in signal covering) more alert to any opportunity for expansion. Local stations saw this new technology as an opportunity to broaden, perhaps only ideally, their coverage. Unlike local American radios, which looked at simulcasting as a way to "bring back home" all those listeners who were members of a local community, but had to live "elsewhere" on a regular basis, this centripetal aspect seems to be absent from simulcasting in Italian local radios, possibly because of the different geographic and cultural configuration of our country, in which distances do not seem as endless as they do in the US and in which people do not seem to have made the culture of perennial mobility their own: Italians are not accustomed to move more than once during their entire life. Most of the people still live close to the places where they have grown up. In the country which has one of the most crowded ether of Europe, simulcasting accentuates a centrifugal aspect. The first radio to start simulcasting its programs was Radio Studio 5, a local radio of Cuneo, on February 29, 1996, while most national radios started streaming only later. RAI started the simulcasting of its programs in 2000. Between 1999 and 2001, all national radios started streaming services. At present, there are 197 national and local stations that transmit their signal in simulcasting on the internet (Mazzei, 2005).

Today, radio websites are complex, virtual places which give the users the feeling of many possible actions (listening to the radio, entering the program's chatroom or forum, writing an e-mail to the speaker, downloading a song, participating to a competition, buying merchandise, *etc.*) but, in the beginning, hybridizing with the net was a lot more superficial. The earliest radio websites were promotional showcases that gave information about the radio, its characters, the programs they aired, and about the frequencies. Paradoxically, those were mute websites. It was a corporate conception of the net, seen as a virtual square where it was necessary to be present like at an international fair. Quite soon however, the radio's internet divisions started expanding and creating ambitious projects of online presence. Private radios were the first to understand the potentiality of the community instruments (chat, forum, mailing list, newsgroups) to attract and keep the audience connected. These virtual instruments of sociality are the base of the strategies of tribal marketing (Fabris, 2003) used by the radios to intercept and capture those tribes of listeners that share the values of the station (in the website of Radio Deejay, the most listened-to commercial radio in Italy, there is a section, "Deejay World" which includes a "fidelity award" to be assigned to the most loyal listeners, chosen among the ones who have filled in a special form with all their personal data). The forums of these stations are places where one can speak about oneself and find people equal to oneself. A place such as this is not public, it's not an Italian town square, it is a private space, the living room of the Deejay's house. Those who participate in these forums have precise expectations about whom they will meet, a little bit like when somebody going to a party wonders about the kind of people he is about to meet. Very often, the access to such a forum is regulated by registration. This is not only very rewarding for the station, but it also marks the crossing of a threshold —those inside are members of the tribe, those outside are not. The forums of public radios, however, apply the radio format. A public radio is a broadcasting service based on a program schedule, made of programs. A public channel does not offer a net forum on its site, but a forum of programs. A public radio listener would rather subscribe to the forum of his or her favorite show (a particularly active forum was that of Golem, a former morning show of Radio Uno, and very active forums today are the ones of cult shows as *Catersport, a* soccer talk radio program, *Caterpillar,* a drive time talk program, *Il ruggito del Coniglio,* a morning time comic show, and *Dispenser,* a music program, all of them broadcasted by RAI Radio Due) than to that of their favorite radio. The forum is an instrument to make the listener loyal to the program.

Radios' websites have quickly evolved from simple showcases to actual portals, rich with new contents and tools—most importantly the customization of the listening and the *community* tools—but not all of them have kept investing on the internet as they did at the start. The general trend, we can observe, has been one of a parabolic kind, with a phase of interest and big investments followed by a steady phase, if not by a drop in the curve of attention. Table 9–1 shows the pattern of the five most listened to Italian commercial stations' presence on the internet over the years ('+" stands for "present" and "–" stands for "not present"; Audiradio, 2004).

RTL is, together with Radio Deejay, one of the private radio stations with the highest listening rate on the internet—some 6,000 to 8,000 daily listeners, with a maximum peak of 1500 simultaneous listeners. These are very good results if we think that, according to Audiradio, only 5.6% (around 2 million people) of all Italian radio listeners has ever listened on line to the simulcasting of their favorite station. The website of RTL sets itself apart from the others thanks to its tools of interaction with the public, which that have evolved over the time, for example through the addition of the possibility of reading the speakers' blogs, a form

TABLE 9–1
Internet Services Offered by the Five Most Listened to Italian
Commercial Radio Stations

Services Offered	RDS	RTL 102.5	Radio Deejay	Radio 105	Radio Italia
First live streaming	1998	1999	1999	2000	2000
Streaming live (simulcasting)	+	+	+	+	+
Streaming on demand	–	+	+	+	+
Registration	+	+	+	+	+
E-mail	+	+	+	+	+
Forum	+	+	+	+	+
Newsletter	–	+	+	+	+
SMS	–	+	–	–	–
Blog	–	+	–	–	–
Web voice (webtelephone)	–	–	+	–	–
Ringtones download	–	+	–	–	–
Competitions and awards	–	–	+	–	+
E-commerce	–	+	–	–	–
Web cam	–	–	–	–	–
Web TV	–	–	+	+	–
News service	+	+	–	+	+

of communication quite trendy these days. Radio Deejay is keener than most websites on communicating its identity and creating the "family-community" spirit that is one of its distinctive traits, through a hyper-stimulation of the listener's loyalty. Simulcasting, the transmission of a perfect copy of the original signal, has become a necessary service but the same does not apply to the offer of material on demand which has shrunk significantly over the years. Radio 105 offers some thematic musical channels on demand, while interviews with artists are the only material available on demand on other sites. Only a few programs, the most successful ones, are available for listening on demand. In general, customization of listening, which at first seemed to be the true added value of the internet, is now relatively marginalized. The absence from all sites of a webcam with which to spy on the speakers is very striking. The webcam was one of the applications used to promote web radios at first. In this sense the radio keeps being a *blind* medium (Arnheim, 1936). Also, there is no need for the radio to show the faces of the speakers since so many of them are on television as well. Most websites don't offer any contents further to what goes on air, they only offer "easy interaction." The textual component has been decreasing with the passing of time, substituted more and more by dynamic graphics in an obsessive attempt to capture attention. The generalist brain-frame of these stations is reflected in their online communication with a few feeble exceptions, as in the

case of both Radio 105 and Radio Deejay. RDS's case is paradigmatic of this de-
terioration of the relationship between private radios and the internet. "At first
we were two working on the website then we quickly became seven plus an in-
tern. From a small room, we moved to an apartment, a space of almost 100
square metres all for ourselves. Words like 'music portal' or 'factory,' started circulating, there were talks about reaching 30 people, then at the end of 2001 we
came back to being only three, back to a small room, our place was taken by the
marketing guys…" (L. Iavorone, personal communication, March 18, 2005).
This is how Luigi Iavarone, contents executive for the RDS website between
2000 and 2003, recalls that short-lived adventure. "At the beginning, the website
was like a skeleton, with a structure in its own right, but still poor in contents,
too static. Then we gave it muscles, we made it dynamic, but then it was as if
this body was atrophying, becoming static again." The number of pages went
down, attention went down, the care in updating the site was lost and the euphoria was gone. "If before the speakers would call me to update their pages, to tell
me to change the title of the last book they'd read because they had read another
one, then they started calling less and less often, and then they just stopped altogether.…" At the moment, RDS's website is one of the poorest ones and, with
the exception of the streaming, it doesn't afford many actions. It looks like a
printed page more than a multimedia page.

PUBLIC BROADCASTING SERVICES ON THE NET

Since February 19, 1996, it had become possible to listen to the radio news from
the site of Radio RAI. The public radio and television station was one of the first to
add streaming to its site, offering the possibility of listening on demand, in an asynchronous mode, to the daily editions of its radio news. Yet, not before four years
had elapsed, did it begin to broadcast its FM channels in simulcasting.

Listening on the net is now regarded by the users of the state-owned radio as a
fundamental service, a natural adjustment to contemporary mobility. Listening
through streaming mainly happens at the workplace, where one doesn't have a portable transistor radio or doesn't want to be a nuisance to his or her colleagues
nearby, or when one is outside the signal coverage. For example, there are many
Italians living abroad who listen to the sports programs on Sundays using the internet. It's a way of temporarily going back home, to feel a part of that world
through the acting of national rituals such as a sports report. The hybridizing of
public radios with the internet does not end with mere simulcasting and community tools, as is the case for private radios. A public radio's website of is a lot richer
than the ones of private radios because the concept has been accepted that the internet is a public resource, a necessary service for the citizen/user. Moreover,
RAI's website is a lot more textual than the private radios' and contains a lot more

TABLE 9–2
Internet Services Offered by Italian Public Broadcaster Compared to the Main
European and International Public Broadcasters

Services Offered	RAI (ITA)	BBC (UK)	R. Fr (FRA)	NPR (USA)	ABC (AUS)	RNE (SPA)
Launch year	2000	1998	1999	1998	1999	1997
Live streaming	+	+	+	+	+	+
On demand streaming	+	+	+	+	+	+
Audio archive	+	+	+	+	+	+
Registration	+	+	+	+	+	–
Email	+	+	+	+	+	+
Forum	+	+	+	+	+	–
Chat	–	+	–	–	–	–
Newsletter	+	+	+	–	+	–
Blog	+	+	–	–	–	–
SMS	+	–	–	–	–	–
Webcam	+	–	–	–	–	–
Ringtones download	+	–	–	–	–	–
Contests	–	–	–	–	+	+
Advertising	+	–	+	–	–	–
E–commerce	–	+	–	+	+	–

of information. Let's compare RAI's internet offer with those from the main European and international public radios.

As the horizontal comparison in Table 9–2 clearly shows, each public channel is present on the net in a different way from the others. To interpret this quantitative table it is necessary to verify the financing methods. The sites that partially depend on the selling of advertising space, like RAI and Radio France, appear to conform to a mixed model of service + entertainment as a result of the double nature of their incomes, both public and commercial. The Radio RAI site is the most "blinking" to the user/consumer, the one with the best "winning smile," while the sites of BBC and NPR are richer in information and service textual contents with a more institutional *look and feel*. The use of community instruments (forum, chat, blog, newsletter) is a lot less accentuated if not almost non-existent on Spanish, Swiss, and American radio. The main difference however can be found in the different application of live and on demand streaming services.

TABLE 9–3
Unique Users per Month for the Live Streaming of RAI Radio Stations in 2002

Public Stations	January	February
RAI Radio 1	12,500	14,800
RAI Radio 2	11,300	13,900
RAI Radio 3	8,800	9,200
RAI (Total)	32,600	37,900

Source: RAI.

Similarly to what happened for private radios the enthusiasm of public radios for internet has been fading after 2001. For the majority of the sites of public channels taken into consideration the structure has changed very little in the last few years. If we exclude periodical graphical renovations, the architecture of these sites, once reached an own face, has remained almost the same if not even reduced in some cases. In spite of this situation of stability the audience, that is the users that connect everyday to these sites to listen to the radio, has grown. Even if the numbers, compared to the figures of ether listening, are still ridiculous it is of some significance that the internet audience has been growing quite quickly and that the listening in internet is growing faster than the access to the internet. This means that always more people, especially among those that already use the net, are getting used to listen to the radio through internet.

In Italy, even if figures remain those of a niche, we witness an increase in the requests for Radio RAI streaming service, especially if compared to the 2002 data in Tables 9–3 and 9–4, that is worth noting.

The live streaming listening has gone from 32,600 in January 2002 to 142,400 unique users in November 2004, not a quick but a constant growth.

While in the UK the asynchronous listening of BBC programs is quite spread, as much as to surpass the live listening, in Italy is the live streaming listening of RAI channels that is more spread. This is likely to be due to the fact that, in addition to a lesser offer of on demand programs from RAI's site, Italian radio programs have more sense if listened to live because that's what they are thought for. BBC produces a lot more radio dramas, documentaries and radio fiction than RAI does and these are all genres which do not have to be listened live and that can have a second youth thanks to on demand streaming.

The RAI radio site is not the richest in contents (BBC and Radio France sites have many more pages), but is surely the most "interactive" one, the one which uses at its best the tools of interactivity (forums, weblogs, webcam, etc.) in order to catch the attention of the user. RAI site is a very "hot" medium, in the sense in-

TABLE 9–4
Unique Users per Month for the Live Streaming of RAI Radio Stations in 2004

Public Stations	January	February
RAI Radio 1	24,000	26,000
RAI Radio 2	22,500	23,300
RAI Radio 3	17,100	20,200
RAI (Total)	63,600	69,500

Source: RAI.

tended by McLuhan, a medium which highly involves the receiver. This high rate of interactivity is due to the fact that the site depends a lot on advertising revenues. Its mixed nature—public and commercial—also influences its mission: Not only does the RAI radio site need to provide a service for the citizens, it also needs to catch their attention for as long as it can in order to deliver precious minutes of the listeners' attention for the advertisers.

Television Webcasting in Italy: The Lack of an Industry

The diffusion of video contents through streaming, more than web radio, is strongly linked to the broadness of the internet connection's band. In Italy the diffusion of broadband connections stayed below the European average until last year. This data has negatively influenced the developing of video contents webcasting. The first experiences of video signals transmissions through streaming were made by amateur, private users—young enthusiasts with the will to experiment the new technology. Among these experiences the most interesting and long-lived was the one of RAGDOLL TV (which was privately owned by two internet fans), which lasted from 1997 to 2002, producing video contents to be shown on demand. Big media groups, public and private, arrived later. After a first phase of enthusiasm extending to 2001 in which the three biggest Italian portals, like KATAWEB, TISCALI, and JUMPY, had all invested much on web TV, a crisis followed that saw the closure of all video streaming services. The reason for this crisis is merely economic: The main income was advertising, but the number of people (the so called "internet traffic") who connected to these services was too low to justify big investments by the advertisers. There was also a problem of contents: What kind of content could maintain its appeal once it was compressed and streamed at low bit rates? In this phase of transition, from 2001 to 2004, only institutional video webcasting services, like RAI, Department of Cultural Goods (Culture web TV) and a few small independent and extremely creative realities remained active. Since 2000 it is possible, from RAI's website, to watch on demand the last edition of the news report of the public channel. RAI has also created a satellite all-news channel—RAInews 24—which is also available through streaming. On RAInews 24 site there is no live streaming but it is possible to watch only a few contents available on demand (interviews, videos, flash news etc). RAI has also created RAI Click, a channel of TV contents accessible only through the net, a truly web TV. With the exception of a few cases, such as RAI Click and MY-TV, the landscape of Italian television webcasting has until now been very poor but the situation is bound to change quickly thanks to a sudden increase of the diffusion of broadband connections.

BROADBAND CONNECTION IN ITALY

Between 2004 and 2005 the diffusion of broadband connections has grown in such an exponential manner that it has given new hopes to the market of television webcasting. A recent study of Forrester Research of Cambridge (Massachusetts), dedicated to the growth of broadband services in our country, states that "the growth of broadband in Italy has been of 100% in respect to the preceding year (2003). Broadband now reaches 20% of Italian homes as it is the European average" (Forrester Research, 2005). According to Eurisko Research (2005), the number of people who now have a broadband connection has passed from 3,3 million at July 2004 to 7 million at July 2005, a figure corresponding to 40% of internet users. According to CENSIS (2004) and Eurisko (2005), there are 30 million computers and almost 15 million internet connections in Italian homes. The total users of the internet in Italy are 17 million people (people that use the internet at least once per month), but, according to data provided by Audiweb (an Italian internet audience research company created by Nielsen/NetRatings; 2005), in June 2005 the Italians to have ever used the internet were 30.7 million (53% of the population). Comparing the data given by CENSIS (2004) and Audiweb (2005), it is easy to find that at least 13 million people use the internet less than once per month, and therefore constitute a potential ground of expansion. Among the 7 million people with a broadband connection, only 400,000 people have a cable broadband connection.

The main reason for the exponential growth of broadband connection in the last two years is the actual govern policy of providing economic incentives for people willing to pass to a DSL connection. Thanks to these incentives people can get the DSL for free, paying only the monthly fee corresponding to their use. Leading the party is Telecom Italia (the former national telecommunication company), which now covers two-thirds of the market (it requires no subscription cost) followed by WIND and TISCALI with DSL (the subscription cost of both services is $15 per month) and Fastweb with optic fiber, with a monthly subscription fee of $14.50. All are interested in pushing in the field of technologic innovation and in the lowering of end user prices. The result is that 40% of Italians (about 24 million people) are expected to have a broadband connection by 2010. Among the major players of the broadband market, only Fastweb seems to make some efforts to take advantage of this quick growth for its webcast services. In fact, it provides the live webcast of the television channels from its website. Fastweb is using sports as a Trojan horse, to enter Italian homes and attract subscriptions. Its strategy—selling sports, selling soccer—is the same used by Sky (the unique satellite service in Italy) to enter Italian satellite market.

TWO WEB-TV CASE HISTORIES

Because of the lack of quantitative audience research on television webcasting in Italy, I chose to analyze two cases of web television that distinguish themselves for the high quality of their contents. MY-TV programs in particular have been the only ones to be re-broadcasted by television channels thanks to their huge internet circulation and success.

Case History 1:
Independent/Commercial Model—MY-TV

Power to Imagine

MY-TV is the first Italian video portal. It is a "metropolitan" TV that "broadcasts" from Milan and Rome featuring music, information about events, clubs, shopping, chat, and forum. Chaired by Salvo Mizzi, it has participations from RCS-HDP Group (which controls the first Italian newspaper, *Corriere della Sera*, and one national commercial radio station, RIN Radio) and Gruppo Ciancio.

MY-TV, which is on demand like other web TV offers, sets itself apart thanks to its contents which range from Flash animated cartoons to fake adverts and satiric programs. MY-TV stands out for the creativity of its animators and the irony of its videos. The reference public is a niche of viewers bored by television. "It's the same public of satellite TV" says Andrea Zingoni, avant-garde artist and creator of Gino il Pollo (Gino the chicken) which has become a successful MY-TV cartoon.

The success of this channel lies in the loyalty inspired in its public through a continuous quality offer and through the email diffusion of videos produced by MY-TV.

In the Italian television webcasting landscape MY-TV, "the TV that brings television to its knees" (one of its catchphrases), surely represents the most creative and successful example.

Case History 2:
Institutional Model—RAI Click

RAI Click is RAInet's (RAI's internet division) web TV and was inaugurated in 2000. Unlike television it doesn't offer any flow of contents but only on demand TV products. Products offered by RAI Click all come from RAI's archives. This means that on this channel can be found only programs already aired on RAI's channels, divided in categories (cinema, entertainment, sports, histories, travels, culture, black and white, news, junior) and chosen according to aesthetic and historic relevance (the most beautiful programs and those that made television history). The access to these programs is free but is in fact limited to those who have a broadband connection.

In this case the internet is used like a large storehouse with a shop-window where the seller, RAI, shows its most valued products as a guarantee of the brand's quality. In addition to offering the most popular shows and series, RAI Click offers many others quality contents (documentaries, films, information) that had little success on TV because of their niche nature. What is a valuable product for the internet is usually not valuable for TV and vice-versa. RAI Click organizes its contents by dividing them and addressing them to distinct niches of the public because on television the same contents are all part of a unique flow. Once its TV life-cycle is concluded the video product gains a second life on the net.

WEBCASTING BUSINESS MODELS

The following is an analysis of the three components of the business models of the webcasters analyzed on this study: Accessibility, content strategies, and revenue sources, based on Ha and Ganahl's (2004) online media business model framework.

Accessibility

Among the 12 webcasters analyzed in this study, a wide majority of webcasters (60%) uses two transmission methods (live streaming and on demand streaming). Only DCOD and RAI offer the additional third method of on demand downloading. MY-TV offers on demand streaming and downloading. One webcaster uses only the live streaming method (Lilliput Radio) while RAI Click is the only webcaster to use on demand streaming as a unique transmission method.

The usability of the sites examined depends on several aspects. First, the internet connection speed accommodation. Only two webcasters (all the video webcasters analyzed) offer more than one choice of internet connection speed to consumers. Ninety percent of the webcasters offer content that can be played only on one media player. Windows Media Player is used by 80% of the webcasters, the remaining 20% use Real Player. None of the webcasters requires additional software and all except one (Radio Italia) have an internal search engine to facilitate users in locating content.

Content Strategies

The majority of Italian webcasters has original content, that has not been previously shown on other media. Only RAI Click offers nonoriginal content whifh has been previously broadcast on television.The median number of channels offered by each webcaster is 3.7, ranging from 1 to 16 channels (corresponding to MY-TV channels). Generally, video webcasters offer more on demand content than radio webcasters. All of them have chosen a very specialised format in order to distinguish themselves from the general offer.

Revenue Sources

Very few webcasters rely on a single source for revenue. The main revenue source still remains advertising, although none of them can survive depending solely on advertising. All are subscription-free and don't use e-commerce. Only 2 of them seek listeners' donations. 80% of the webcasters rely on more than one revenue resource, like public funds in the case of RAI, and B2B (business to business) services, as for DCOD.

CONCLUSION

After a first phase of euphoria and experimentation, and a following phase of crisis and stabilization, the Italian webcasting landscape seems at last to be transforming itself in a real market characterised by three different dimensions: The commercial, the public and the independent, each with its own specific properties.

However, between radio and video webcasting there is a substantial difference due to the different manner of consumption for audio and video web contents. In Italy, listening by streaming of AM/FM radio and web-only radio occurs in the places where conventional listening is not possible. In this case the web is just another diffusion channel. On demand listening, though growing, is still marginal.

The consumption of video contents through the web has an opposite sign if compared to radio contents: On demand fruition is more widespread than live fruition because in the case of web TV, there is the lack of offerings in live streaming. The radio listened through the web keeps its flow characteristics while television flow (Williams, 1974) on the net takes the shape of a text. It's the single program (the text) and not the channel's programs (the flow) that the average user requests for streaming.

Broadband connection growth represents a great opportunity for webcasters, either commercial or independents, to gain new subscriptions and new listeners. But recent history shows that Italian users accept paying a subscription only for specific kinds of content (sports—above all soccer—and films). Webcasting services can become true killer applications, able to push people to get a broadband connection, only if their contents are perfectly tailored on the desires of potential users.

Besides broadband connection, mobility contexts surely represent other new spaces of interest for webcasting, new lands to colonize. In the future, with the increase of communication instruments' pervasiveness and the diffusion of the internet in mobility contexts, it will be possible to watch and listen to programs while in motion or far from home. In particular, with the diffusion of portable audio and video players, it will be easier to download from the net (or to listen to it live) one's favorite radio or television show to watch wherever one wishes. According to Apple sources, for example, in Italy iPod has sold almost a million units. The survival and future diffusion of webcasting, both audio and video, will be more and more linked to the ability of reaching potential users not only in normal fruition contexts like home or office, but also in the transit contexts such as highways, subways, trains, and airports, as well as socialization places like parks, pubs, bars, Italian squares, and shopping centers (Augé, 1995).

REFERENCES

Audiweb. (2005). Retieved November 1, 2005, from http://www.audiweb.it

Augé, M. (1995). Non-places: Introduction to an anthropology of supermodernity. New York: Verso.

Centro Studi Investimenti Sociali (CENSIS). (2005). Fifth Report on Communication in Italy. Retrieved November 1, 2005, at http://www.censis.it

Eurisko. (2005). Retrieved November 1, 2005, from http://www.eurisko.it

Fabris, G. (2003). *Il nuovo consumatore: verso il postmoderno* [The new consumer: Toward a postmodern age.]. Milano, Angeli.

Forrester Research. (2005). Broadband in Italy. Retrieved November 1, 2005, from http://www.forrester.com

Ha, L., & Ganahl, R. (2004). Webcasting business models of click-and-bricks and pure-play media: A comparative study of leading webcasters in South Korea and the United States. *The International Journal on Media Management, 6*(1&2), 75–88.

Italian Society of Authors and Publishers (SIAE). (2005). Copyright and internet. Retrieved November 1, 2005, from http://www.siae.it/UtilizzaOpere.asp?link_page=Multimedialita_DirittoDAutoreEWeb. htm&open_menu = yes

Mazzei, G. (2005). *Il giornalismo radiotelevisivo* [Radio and TV journalism]. Rome: Rai-Eri.

Perrotta, M. (2000). *La radio all'interno di un gruppo editoriale. Il caso di Radio Capital* [Media group doing radio: The case of Radio Capital]. Unpublished Graduate Thesis. Università La Sapienza di Roma.

Williams, R. (1974). *Television: Technology and cultural form.* London: Fontana.

UPA. (2004). Utenti Pubblicità Associati. Retrieved November 1, 2005, from http://www.upa.it

APPENDIX
Leading Webcasters in Italy

Webcasters	Internet URL
Jumpy	http://www.jumpy.it
DCOD	http://www.dcod.it
Tiscali	http://www.tiscali.it
Kataweb	http://www.kwmusica.kataweb.it
RDS	http://www.rds.it
Radio Deejay	http://www.deejay.it
RTL 102.5	http://www.rtl.it
RAI	http://www.radio.rai.it
Radio 105	http://www.105.net
Radio Italia	http://www.radioitalia.it
RAI Click	http://www.raiclick.rai.it
MY-TV	http://www.mytv.it

Radio Search Engines

- http://www.radio-locator.com
- http://www.monitor-radiotv.com/liveradio.htm
- http://www.radiosegugio.it

CHAPTER 10

Greece: Webcasting Is Slowly Taking Shape as an Industry

Alexandros Arampatzis
Edge Hill University, United Kingdom

WEBCASTING MARKET ENVIRONMENT

Media Industry Structure

The Greek media market possesses almost all of the trends that run through the most media-savvy western European markets: It is a highly competitive media market, where (primarily domestic) media conglomerates control the majority of stakes in media outlets across all media sectors. Television clearly occupies the dominant position in the country's media scenery, in terms of accessibility, usage, and social and political influence, whereas the internet is pushed at the lower end of the market, with moderate yearly development and the lowest penetration amongst EU countries (Internet World Stats, 2004).

This is largely attributed to cultural reasons (even a brief look at all available statistics indicates that southern European counties, with Greece at the forefront, lag behind the techno-advanced countries of Europe's north), high connection costs, and an overall poor infrastructure.

The media scenery in Greece changed dramatically after the fall of the military regime in 1974, which, coupled with advances in technology, created the ground for the development of strong, independent, and free from political manipulation media. Alongside the national public service broadcaster, which operated two nationwide TV channels and a handful of radio stations across the country's regions, already established press conglomerates continued to grow while new players entered the market and began to assume a dominant position.

The media companies which assumed the lion's share in the publishing market were DOL, Pegasus, Eleftherotypia, and Kathimerini, with each controlling at least one of the most influential publications in the country. A few years later, when the state monopoly in audiovisual industry was lifted, these companies es-

193

sentially grew into powerful domestic media conglomerates, incorporating under their media portfolio privately-operated radio and TV stations. In the autumn of 1989, they even forged a largely unexpected alliance in order to establish the dominant (until today) private broadcaster, MEGA channel.

In terms of their political standing, Greek print and audiovisual media cover fully all the ground across the two poles of the political spectrum with such efficiency and consistency that pluralism is certainly firmly established. Contrary to what is the case in some norther European countries, both print and audiovisual media choose to take political sides, with print media overtly demonstrating their political disposition. It can also be argued, according to the daily and weekly circulations of the national press that among the papers that top the circulation and readership lists, there is a clear "leftish" leaning.

Regardless of its dominant position, TV in Greece still operates within a largely incoherent and unshaped legal framework that constitutes a permanent cause of dispute and uncertainty among media owners. Since 1989, the country's audiovisual media operate with temporary broadcasting licenses which only exacerbated the messy and convoluted audiovisual field. The consequence of the state's hesitant and opportunistic politics, as far as setting and implementing operating rules and standards is concerned, was the mushrooming of broadcasting, which today consists of a few strong and viable firms and many weak and poorly organized ones (especially at a local level) that essentially litter the fragmented broadcasting field.

In sum, what certainly marks the Greek market is the plethora of operating media enterprises, both print and electronic, for a small country of no more than 11 million people. Despite securing pluralism, diversity of views, and a politically rich public arena, this proliferation of media outlets raises legitimate and timely questions in terms of the quality of the content produced, the degree of independence from the political system in terms of funding (directly or through the advertising of state controlled firms), and the commercial viability of many of these companies within a very competitive business environment.

Press

According to the latest figures, there is a total of 89 newspapers in circulation in Greece: 9 are morning, 15 evening, 23 Sunday, and 17 are published on a weekly basis. In the category of specialized newspapers there are six financial papers and 19 sport newspapers (AADNP, 2004).

Ever since the advent of private television in 1989, the national press has become the second most important source of information for Greeks, and it is highly concentrated in the hands of few publishers (DOL, Kathimerini, Pegasus, and Eleftherotypia). These are all public companies traded in the Greek stock exchange but the majority of shares is concentrated in the hands of a few main shareholders in such a way that their ownership bears, in essence, the characteristics of family businesses.

In terms of circulation, these four publishers occupy more that 60% of the total circulation of daily national newspapers (see Table 10–1).

As mentioned earlier, these four media firms possess the majority of stakes in audiovisual enterprises; at the same time, they control the majority of the leading webcasting outlets as well, creating the paradox of a highly concentrated media market with the publication of an abundance of titles, especially in the area of the leading Athens-based media, along with a national presence and influence.

Total newspaper sale figures show a continued decline from the late 1980s to the beginning of the 1990s, a slide which shows signs of advertising over the past couple of years, with sales moving upwards due largely to the proliferation of titles and the offering of "rich" Sunday editions, beefed up with many supplements. In particular, from 1989 to 1992, as print and electronic media competition peaked, national newspapers lost approximately 28% of their circulation; it fell from a daily average of 2,597,056 copies in 1989 to 1,867,001 in 1992. In 2004, sales rose back again to approximately 2 million copies a day (AADNP, 2004).

Audiovisual Media

Television

The lifeline of Greek Television is shaped by two distinct phases: (a) the broadcasting of Greek state television alone, and (b) the emergence of private TV channels in 1989 that sprang through in a semi-anarchic audiovisual context and radically altered the country's media landscape.

The restoration of democracy in 1974 brought new life to state TV and the Constitution of 1975 defined, for the first time, the social mission and character of Greek broadcasting as a public service. Nevertheless, democratic accountability, pluralism, and objectivity were secured, while ironically, it still remained under direct state control (Terzis & Kontochristou, 2004).

Inevitably, state TV became more of a propagating arm for the government of the day rather than a trustworthy, unbiased, and respectful news source for the public. At the end of the 1980s, the pressure exercised by critical voices, which challenged the credibility, role, and the popularity of state TV, led toward the abolition of the state monopoly and the rather abrupt opening of the media sector to non-pubic television outlets. This was largely favored by the neo-liberal political environment of the day and the lobbying of powerful interest groups such as publishers and radio station owners, who were looking to acquire a pole position in the battle for the promising television market.

Terzis and Kontochristou (2004) describe how the granting of the television licences was not the outcome of a straightforward procedure, but rather the result

TABLE 10–1
Circulation of Greece's Leading Print Media

Company Name	Titles	Daily Circulation	Market Share
DOL	TO VIMA	5,155	7%
	TA NEA	35,788	15%
Pegasus	ETHNOS	24,866	11%
Tegopoulos	Eleftherotypia	32,855	14%
Kathimerini	Kathimerini	22,345	10%

of behind the doors negotiations and intense lobbying which essentially resulted in the granting of provisional licenses to the four major publishers. "Of the two channels that were granted a provisional licence to transmit, Mega Channel (MEGA) started broadcasting in autumn 1989, while New Television never operated. Its place on the television screen was taken by Antenna TV (Ant1), which started to broadcast on New Year's Eve, however illegally as it did not yet have the appropriate provisional licence." In the same way, many other private television channels took advantage of the foggy legal environment and started to operate (mainly in the Greek countryside) without waiting to be granted a franchise and a period of anarchy ensued. In 1993 a law (Law 2173/1993) was finally passed allowing for the setting up of private-commercial television which could transmit across Greece. Yet despite the existence of a basic legal framework that sets out the requirements for setting up broadcast organizations, no Greek TV or radio stations operate under a firm and permanent license.

Today, television has assumed a dominant role in people's lives, shaping the political agenda and playing a critical role in formulating the public atmosphere in Greece. To achieve this high degree of popularity, it was aligned from the outset with market-driven imperatives that favored entertainment and soft news to hard news and current affairs programs. This has elevated TV to the status of the major source of information, entertainment, and culture for the mass public in Greece (See Table 10–2). Currently three public channels and nearly 150 private channels (most of them broadcasting regionally and/or locally) broadcast in the country (Infopublica, 2003).

The public operator in Greece is ERT (Hellenic Radio and Television S.A). ERT is composed of three terrestrial channels (ET–1, NET, ET–3) that have national coverage, one satellite channel, ERT–Satellite, seven national radio stations, two world service radio stations, and 19 regional radio stations[1]. ERT's income is

---

[1]The information was retrieved March 15, 2005 from http://www.ert.gr

TABLE 10–2
Average Daily TV Viewing

Year	Average Daily Viewing Time in Minutes
2000	247
2001	240
2002	247
2003	272
2004	278

Note. Sample = Total viewing population in Athens, Thessaloniki, and in towns with at least 10,000 households, until 30 April 2000. National coverage = Mainland and islands (except Crete), from 1 May 2000.
Source: AGB Hellas, 2004.

threefold. It comes from a unique type of a "licence fee," which is imposed as a surcharge on all consumer electricity bills, regardless of whether consumers own a television set or not. The state also directly subsidizes part of the expenses of ERT, which also employs advertisements to cover part of its operating costs.

In terms of the private channels, apart from the 5 strong channels with national coverage (MEGA channel, ANT1, Alpha, Alter, Star—all but Star channel are affiliated with publishing houses), there is only a handful (out of the 150) of regional TV channels with political and financial clout. Most are parts of larger media groups which incorporate newspapers and radio stations as well.

As far as the development of analogue Pay-TV is concerned, since 1994, Multichoice Hellas has been providing 3 satellite TV services to Greek viewers, namely: Filmnet (films), Supersport (sports), and Fox Kids (for children). Multichoice Hellas was also granted a licence for the provision of subscription digital satellite services under the logo "NOVA" (EIM, 2004, pp. 96–97).

Today, NOVA (owned by Multichoice Hella) is the only pay-TV operator in Greece and by 2004 it had registered approximately 267,000 subscribers (EIM, 2004, p. 96). Its rival Alpha Digital Synthesis platform, which was established in 2001, went bankrupt and closed down in September 2002.

Cable television has not developed as an important distribution system due to poor infrastructure and legal blocks (Iosifidis, 2000). Until recently in Greece, it was forbidden by law for private operators to lay and operate cable infrastructure for telecommunications and/or broadcasting purposes (Law 2328/1995). Law 2644/1998 "on the provision of subscription radio and television services and related regulations" rescinded this restriction (Godard, Bisson, & Aguete, 2003, p. 112). However, this provision has not encouraged the development of cable television since it is considered to be very costly. Cable TV network household penetration is below 1%. In general, Greece has the lowest development not only of cable, but also of satellite television in the EU. Their combined penetration is merely 8.9% (Hellenic Audiovisual Institute, 2003; see Table 10–3).

The biggest challenge for the future of Greek broadcasting involves the developments in satellite and cable television in terms of market shares, profit, and reallocation of power among media players. Moreover, the discussion of the digitalization of terrestrial television and the necessary technological modernization that will be required raises questions around finding financial resources for such an investment and the possible alliances that can be forged for this purpose (Terzis & Kontochristou, 2004).

Radio

Radio is a medium with a strong presence in Greece, as it constitutes a well-trusted source of information and entertainment. Currently, around 1,200 radio stations broadcast regularly in the country. The vast majority of these are private and transmit locally or regionally, and although some do belong to larger media groups, the majority constitute the outcome of the amateur entrepreneurial efforts of individuals. This makes the Greek radio market the least concentrated media market while ownership fragmentation secures pluralism.

Most private stations operate without a licence (only 35 of these have permission to operate and this is a temporary licence, just like TV stations). No government has, as yet, attempted to enforce the existing legal framework and this is at least partly because the legal insecurities within which most of the radio firms operate make them receptive to various kinds of governmental pressure. In terms of program content, most radio stations broadcast news and music programs (EIU, 2003).

Regulatory Framework

The Greek media regulatory framework is largely centred around radio and TV, allowing a great degree of autonomy (in the form of self-regulation) to the press. The new media legal framework is currently taking shape, with the focus lying not on ownership and concentration of outlets, but on issues concerning copyrights and digital protection.

According to Greek legislation, commercial stations are obliged to provide high quality programs, objective information and news reports and promote cultural development. The law gives the power to the National Council for Radio and TV (NCRTV) to request information from radio and television stations regarding their organization and financing.

One of the most contested regulatory fields in the country involves the thorny issue of concentration in the media as well as the involvement of those who control media businesses into public administration contracts. The attempts of the right-wing political party in office to curb the influence of media owners in securing the conduct of business with the state has resulted in a legal dispute between the Greek state and the European Union, on the basis of anti-competitive legislation. This dispute is presently unresolved.

According to the current law, ownership of more than one electronic information media of the same type is prohibited, and every physical or legal person can participate in only one media broadcasting company and only up to 25% of its capital. Furthermore, the capacity of owner, partner, main shareholder, or management executive of an information media enterprise is incompatible with the carrying of the same capacity in an enterprise that undertakes public administration/works or in a legal entity of the wider public sector which carries out works or supplies or provides services. This also includes the activities of all types of related persons, such as spouses, relatives, financially dependent persons, or companies (Emmanouil, 2004).

This piece of legislation was deemed necessary in order to curb the influence of TV station owners. No provision whatsoever is made in Greek legislation for webcasting issues, which is only covered, indirectly of course, by EU internet law. Within this unregulated environment everyone is free to enter the webcasting field without any rules or limitations.

Currently, the owners of a number of dominant media players (Pegasus, DOL, etc.) also undertake contracts that involve the conduct of works or the supply of services for the state (such as construction contracts or printing contracts). This, of course, although it opens a backdoor for potential corruption between state officials and media moguls who may be willing to use their media's clout as a powerful tool in order to exert pressure and secure lucrative state contracts, is the case in many other EU countries (such as France, Italy, or Germany), whereby media firms also possess controlling stakes in firms that supply the state (such as military equipment firms).

Internet Penetration and Usage

The gauging of internet penetration in any given country has proven to be a considerably difficult undertaking. There are multiple sources for the internet-using population and because of differences in methodology, measurements for the same geographic location can vary widely depending on the source used.

In light of this, there is a plethora of local, national, and European oriented sources that survey and analyze the usage of the internet in Greece and the medium's penetration in the local population. Despite the often conflicting results of these sources, what appears to be beyond any doubt is that Greece is lagging behind any other country participating in the Eurozone on most statistics involving the internet and its usage.

Nevertheless, it is also fair to stress that since 2000, and largely due to redrawn governmental policies that were aligned to European Union new-economy and digitization-centered policies, Greece has covered much of the lost ground and achieved significant growth in the highly competitive field of digitization.

Back in 1999, in a study conducted by Forbes magazine, Meland (1999) outlined the dire state of the Greek internet market: "Greece is either a fertile land of unexploited opportunities or an internet wasteland where only a madman would contemplate setting up an online business. One thing is certain: No country in Western Europe—not even Spain or Portugal—is further behind in internet development than Greece. The country's technology infrastructure is years, maybe even a decade, behind the more developed countries in Northern Europe."

Although things have changed ever since, this change has not taken place in a spectacular fashion, as in northern European countries. According to an article by Naftemporiki (2005), the country's leading financial newspaper, "the internet in Greece is growing steadily whereas one observes a rather stagnant growth rate in other countries such as Italy or Germany. But there is still a long way to go" (p. 42).

The statistics describing the penetration of the Internet into the Greek public present large disparities: According to Internet World Stats (2004), and Strategy Analytics (2004), there were 1.71 million Greeks online in 2004, out of a total population of 10.7 million. The number of users drops down to 1.4 million according to CIA's World Factbook (2005), which translates into a 13% penetration of the medium into Greece's population (far below the European average which is 34%), whereas the same index rises significantly to 2.7 million people in surveys published by CLICKZ (Web Atlas, 2005) and which incorporate findings by the Computer Industry Almanac (2004). It seems, given the steady grown of the medium's use in the country, that the truth lies somewhere in the middle and, today, there are around 2 million Greek users of the internet.

However, there are three areas where all sources seem to meet: Broadband penetration in Greece is as low as 0.3%, the number of ISPs is quite high (27), while 54% of Greek businesses have a website. Comparing the internet users, 56% have internet access from home, 34% from work, 7% from schools or libraries, and 3% from internet cafes.

These statistics clearly highlight and reflect the ever-growing gap between the technologically advanced countries of the European north and the digitally underdeveloped European south. In Greece, hopes and prospects for a stronger future growth in the field come from policies such as that of the Ministry of Development which, in line with its aim to create a vibrant information society in Greece, has announced plans to install computers linked to the internet in all schools, provide for the delivery of government services online and connect 50,000 small business to

TABLE 10–3
CATV/Satellite Penetration of Some of the Major European Union Countries,
2003

Country	Level
United Kingdom	39%
Denmark	32%
Sweden	29%
France	23%
Italy	20%
Greece	9%

Source: Strategy Analytics

the internet as well as to equip them with basic skills in e-commerce. A framework of guiding principles, which would regulate the internet sector in Greece, is under review.

The ranking of the most popular Greek radio and TV websites (not necessarily webcasters though, as some play only a promotional role for the medium, without transmitting audio or video content through the web) according to their percentage of average monthly users for 2004, is in Table 10–3.

It is interesting to note that all the webcasters listed in Table 10–3 constitute the online presence of established media companies (bricks-and-clicks). With the exception of antenna.gr, megatv.gr and star.gr, none of the other leading Greek-originating media websites is owned by top-rate traditional media businesses. Consequently, it can be argued that the Greek online media market is clearly very fragmented with primarily medium-sized offline media playing a protagonistic role on the web.

WEBCASTING BUSINESS MODELS

For the purposes of this study and, given the small size of the Greek internet market, a sample of ten webcasters we selected, with the assistance of a group of informants.[2] Taking into account that rich media use is significantly higher among broadband subscribers—with the majority of usage going to unlicenced file down-

---

[2]The informants list comprises of the following people: (1) Nikos Leandros, Lecturer in Media (the Political Economy of New Media), Paneion University of Athens, Greece—nleandr@panteion.gr; (2) Marina Bousiou, Media Research Executive, BARI MRS, FOCUS S.A.—marina@focus.gr; (3) Michalis Meimaris, Professor in New Media, University of Athens, mmeimaris@media.uoa.gr; and (4) Michalis Terzis, editor, Internet Times Magazine, Greece—http://www.internet-times.gr/

loading and audio streaming—and high-speed connectors spend much more time online than those dialing up (Greenspan, 2003), one would expect to encounter a largely undeveloped market in Greece.

Indeed, the coding of the Greek webcasting sites selected reveals a market that, with the notable exception of one or two well-established and forward-looking enterprises—straddles in the uncertain field of inadequate infrastructure and unclear business strategies and objectives. Indicative of the degree of uncertainty and confusion surrounding the webcasting market in Greece is that industry professionals proved to be unfamiliar with the term "webcasting" as such. When asked to assess the state of webcasting in the country, they first wanted to find out "what webcasting is about." When faced with it, they associate webcasting exclusively with the provision of audio and/or video content through the web, overlooking sites which webcast text, still pictures and graphics using push technology (Ha, 2004).

What follows is a brief description of the webcasters selected:

GBC (Greek Business Channel)   It can be argued that this is the Greek equivalent of Bloomberg. GBC is a webcaster with business news and commentary which, obviously, targets primarily the Athens-based business community.

Mad TV   This is a webcaster with very high popularity built to the pattern of MTV. Mad TV targets primarily a young audience and this is conveyed both through the content it webcasts (music audio and video files) as well as the overall look of the site.

E-Radio   This is the most popular Greek radio portal. Very popular with Greeks based abroad who look for a site that aggregates all Greek radio stations that cast their content through the web. Windows Media Player is incorporated in E-radio so that users listen to their selected radio stations via E-radio.

Live24   This is another radio stations' aggregator site that operates competitively to E-radio. Also, Live 24 allows users to access video content as well.

ERT.gr   This is the website through which the video and audio content of the Greek state broadcaster is webcast. The site's provision is rich in politics and culture and, according to its managing director, Christos Stathakopoulos (personal communication, May 20, 2005), "it aspires to be the guardian of the Greek internet," in terms of setting the standards for competition.

ALTER TV   This site webcasts live the content of one of the leading national TV stations in the country. It has gained a competitive advantage over the rest of the TV players on the web, since this was the first TV station to offer its program online for free, a movement that made it very popular with Greek expatriates.

Supersport   The website of the leading Greek sports channel is not the only one to offer comprehensive sports content on the web. However, the depth of its content and the live webcasting of sports events makes it very popular with sports fans.

SKY 100.3   This is the webcaster of the leading Greek news and current affairs oriented radio station. Once again, it is very popular with Greeks who live out of the country and want to access news back home. Sky.com offers a live webcast of its content.

Flash   The third most popular radio station in the country, Flash assumed a comparative advantage over competition since it built one of the first news web portals in the country. Although it is currently seeing its clout diminishing (largely due to financial problems), it is still a very strong player.

CNN   The only foreign site to make it to the top Greek webcasters. This is largely attributed to the high degree of brand recognition and reliability that CNN enjoys in Greece.

Therefore, it becomes clear that the Greek webcasting market is dominated by domestic businesses, with the exception of CNN, and they all originate from a traditional radio and/or TV station, apart from the Greek Business Channel (GBC) which is an online TV platform with several business-oriented channels and E-radio and Live24, two radio station content aggregators that operate web-only. All ten webcasters studied favored live streaming as their preferred transmission method, followed by on-demand streaming and on-demand downloading, for reasons that are clearly related to cost reduction and copyright protection objectives. Only Mad.TV, clearly the most technologically advanced and pioneering (in terms of content, which, vaguely put, constitutes a Greek version of MTV) of the Greek webcasters, used push technology to transmit its content, over all other methods.

Cost imperatives and the very low diffusion of broadband also explain why audio, text, graphics and animation constitute the majority of the content posted on these sites, to the detriment of video. To users without broadband access, viewing video is not only inefficient but a frustrating experience because the gaps between streaming data transmission create garbled and incomprehensive images and audio sounds, says Ha (2004) and the 0.3% figure of penetration of broadband in Greece clearly accounts for the availability of video in only five of the ten webcasters examined.

The limited availability of video content is party reflected on the program genres favored by the leading Greek webcasters, which involve a lot of audio news, sports news, business news, and talk shows and very little provision in the areas of blockbuster movies, TV dramas, comedies, TV series, and classic movies/TV titles (see Table 10–4). However, TV trailers and music videos are a prevalent feature in seven out of ten of the Greek webcasters, possibly due to the relatively small file sizes of these digital products. The program genre that tops the pyramid of popularity featuring in 80% of the sites examined is sports news (primarily football and basketball, not in the form of live video streams of matches though, just plain text or text-based minute-by-minute commentary), whereas religious, porno-

TABLE 10–4
Program Genres of the Leading Greek Webcasters

	Units	Percentage
Video		
Blockbuster movies	2	20%
TV commercials	6	60%
TV programs (entertainment)	6	60%
Education/instruction	2	20%
Trailers/highlights	8	80%
Business (business news/speech/conference)	5	50%
News clips/interviews (non-business)	7	70%
Music videos	7	70%
Documentaries	2	20%
Cartoons/animation	1	10%
Sports 4	8	80%
Pornography (adult content)	0	0%
Other	1	10%
Audio		
Music	8	80%
News	10	100%
Talk/speech/interview	10	100%
Sports	8	80%
Other	0	0%

graphic, and documentary programming occupied negligible space (see Table 10–4).

Since almost all of the leading Greek webcasters are bricks-and mortars rather than pure-plays (see Table 10–5), it is not surprising that nearly none of the content they transmit through the web is original, exclusively produced for this medium. It is either repurposed or simulcast (i.e., shown at the same time as the broadcast). In fact, in the case of three webcasters, Alter TV, E-radio, and Supersport, all of their web content is simulcast, and similarly two of the most popular Athenian radio stations, SKAI FM and Flash FM, use the web primarily as a means to webcast live programming at the same time as the broadcast. Only Mad.TV appears to success-

TABLE 10–5
Top 10 Greek Webcasters

Site Name	Type	Revenue	Ownership	Business Model	User Registration
GBC	PP	n/a	Private	CA	No
MAD TV	CB	n/a	Private	BC	Yes
E-Radio	PP	n/a	Private	CA	No
Live24	PP	n/a	Private	CA	No
ERT.gr	CB	n/a	PSB	BC	No
ALTER TV	CB	n/a	Public	BC	No
Supersport	CB	n/a	Private	BC	No
SKAI 100.3	CB	n/a	Public	BC	No
FLASH	CB	n/a	Private	BC	No
CNN	CB	$23,000,000	Public	BC	Yes

fully be striking a balance in the sourcing of its content: Approximately 40% of content is repurposed from the offline namesake TV channel, 40% is simulcast and around 10% constitute original content available only through the webcast.

In terms of the composition and the originating roots of the webcast content, this is either half domestic and half foreign production, or in any case there is a contribution, of varying degrees, from a non-domestic source. This source is largely dominated by the United States, while the UK comes a close second, and further down the line Germany, France, Italy, and Asian countries in general feed into the Greek webcasters' content. It is important to emphasize that the strong presence of foreign production primarily takes the form of audio files (mainly music) and significantly less the form of video files or, more importantly, text. Clearly, the dominance of the Anglo-Saxon content in the Greek webcasting market can be attributed to two main reasons: first, the language, since English is currently the undisputed world's "lingua franca" and a very popular language in Greece, and second, because the US and the UK (to a lesser degree) have long established a protagonistic (in terms of dominant) role in the distribution of audiovisual content worldwide (largely as a by-product of the domination of the English language).

This prevalent Anglo-Saxon presence in the world's information, entertainment, and cultural industries is transmitted and reflected on the web, a medium which by definition is very receptive to similar influences due to its worldwide span. As for German, French, and Italian production that also to feed into the Greek webcasting market, this is not only due to the geographical and cultural proximity of these countries to Greece but also because they represent some of the strongest audiovisual production pockets in Europe, with strong audiovisual exports.

With the exception of the two radio channel aggregator webcasters (Live24 and E-radio.gr) as well as the Greek Business Channel (GBC) which incorporates 13 distinct channels, all other webcasters are limited to mostly one, rarely two, designated channels, whereas the number of shows/clips offered per channel, despite their clear variations, are roughly around 20 to 22. In terms of sites with audio content, once again the previously established program pattern is repeated, with music, news, talk shows, and sports taking the lead, while non-music and music ringtones are largely overlooked (see Table 10–4).

REVENUE SOURCES—BUSINESS MODELS

Perhaps the area where the infant level of Greek broadcasters is more strongly demonstrated is their business structure—the revenue sources they employ largely shape their business models. Business models are understood and created by stepping back from the business activity itself to look at its bases and the underlying characteristics that make commerce in the product or service possible.

To capture the fundamental importance of a business model in the operation and the viability of a business, one needs to consider that a business model involves the conception of how the business operates, its underlying foundations, and the exchange activities and financial flows upon which it can be successful (Timmers, 1998). The Greek webcasters studied overwhelmingly rely on advertising and content syndication only to recover their operating costs and achieve some profitability. Only Mad.TV (10%) exploits the possibilities opened up by the web in the field of e-commerce by selling CDs, DVDs, and other entertainment related products as well as licensed merchandise of TV shows, stars, characters, and so on. The only leading webcaster (10% of the sample examined) in Greece that ventures to put a subscription tag on (only part of) its content is CNN[3], a foreign webcaster. CNN charges users only for what is tagged as "prime content."

ERT.gr, the Greek public service webcaster, relies on content syndication revenues alone to make some money on the web. As for the amount of advertisements posted on the home pages of the other webcasters, these range from two for Alter TV and E-radio, to seven for the very popular with young users Mad.TV, and eight for the equally popular with male users Supersport. On average each site carried

---

[3]CNN is not listed in the Bari MRS Webit Report, since that lists carries websites originating from Greece only.

four advertisements all in the form of banner ads or pop-ups, none as an audio or video webcast.

The reluctance of the Greek webcasters examined to place some or all of their content behind a subscription wall or make it available through pay-per-use schemes, stems from their belief that the market is not yet mature enough to support such a bold undertaking, Christos Stathakopoulos (personal communication, June 19, 2003), the managing director of ERT.gr, argues.

Yet, the internationally acclaimed CNN has set in place a monthly and yearly subscription scheme on its webcast, which involves only video content (not audio) and starts from $4.95 for the monthly subscription to $39.95 for the yearly one. Direct debit and credit card are the payment options CNN.com offers users in order to carry out the transaction.

Registration

Only two of the leading Greek Webcasters studied (20% of the sample) require user registration to access the webcast content: CNN.com and Mad.TV (see Table 10–5). The former requires users to register their contact and identity information (phone numbers, name, address etc.) and billing information as well as other demographic information such as gender, income, occupation, and hobbies. Mad.TV asks users for all the above but billing information.

In terms of the quality of the transmission, the use of broadband connection secures a reasonably good quality, yet broken transmission problems still persist. This is irrespective of the player used to display the site content, an area where the domination of Microsoft's Windows Media Player is almost absolute. Despite Real Network's Real Player being the most popular webcast player in the United States (Ha, 2004), only two (a percentage of 20%) of the leading Greek webcasters analyzed support Real Player as a second option. As for the file formats used by the webcast services to transmit data, WMP is clearly favoured by them all, mirroring the preference to Windows Media Player.

Finally, only a few sites (30%) require the downloading of additional software in order to acquire full access to the site's content, and this is usually a flash player and only in one case (Mad.TV), chat software.

Added Value Services

Added value services, aimed at enhancing users' experience and facilitating site navigation are rather sparingly incorporated into the sites of the leading Greek webcasters. Only the foreign based CNN.com (10% of the examined sample) provided detailed text description of the content of the video and/or audio with estimated file size in all of the webcast files posted on the site. Similarly, only the Greek Business Channel and Live24 gave users more than one choice of connection speed (e.g.: 56K, 300K etc.) in displaying the webcast. All the other sites analyzed were limited in providing only one connection speed option, regardless of the users' modem capabilities. However, all but two of the Greek leading webcasters carried on their home pages internal search engines or directories of content.

CONCLUSION

The analysis of the content, the features and the business patterns of the leading Greek broadcasters mirrors accurately the state of the Greek internet as a whole: The low broadband penetration weighs heavily on the shoulders of media business ventures whose business plans are necessarily intertwined with advances in technology infrastructure. In light of this, investment in the development of webcasting products that will support viable and forward looking businesses is held at a minimum level, in a market that is almost non existent.

Those webcasters that seem to surface within this business-discouraging context, represent in their majority a bricks-and-clicks business model, through which they essentially expand the delivery platforms for the content of their offline counterparts, adding on the web to traditional radio and video airwaves. Concurring with Ha & Ganahl (2004) findings, Greek clicks-and-mortars enrich their offering with a more varied provision, whereas pure-plays present a horizontally spread but vertically limited content, mainly serving as portals that aggregate radio station content and, usually, simulcast it on the web along with some music videos.

In choosing their revenue sources, bricks-and-clicks and pure-plays don't differ at all. Under the clear influence of the overarching "free" culture of the web, combined with users' perceived (and rarely proven) reluctance to pay for information or entertainment content on the internet, Greek webcasters opt en-masse to charge consumers indirectly as a means of recovering their operating costs, primarily through advertising. In part, the absence of subscription-based payment schemes can also be attributed to the lack of confidence of these media outlets on the value of their content. Similarly, the impact of the poor technological infrastructure is also prevalent in the choice of revenue sources, whereby inevitably pay-per-click options which require a reliable and popular broadband connection to become a viable revenue source are ruled out.

In light of all these, this study found no signs of cannibalization of offline media by webcasters. Since technological restraints impose barriers on the full roll-out of webcasting in the domestic market, one can fairly comfortably assume that leading webcasters find themselves popular particularly with Greek expats, who, in any case, do not have access to offline radio and TV content from home. It is currently estimated that nearly 10 million Greeks live abroad, a figure that constitutes a strong and much-promising market. However, since this is only empirically observed, it is more of a hypothesis that needs further research in order to become an axiom.

Conclusively, if webcasting is still in a nascent stage worldwide (Ha & Ganahl, 2004), then in countries with the specific cultural, economic and technological characteristics of Greece, webcasting is largely a "terra incognita," an unknown and undeveloped new media area. This, alongside confusion and uncertainty, presents a fertile ground for media innovation and business opportunities. As to whether, how and when these will materialize, these depend on the necessary advances in technology and the cultivation of the appropriate business ethos.

REFERENCES

Athens Association of Daily Newspaper Publishers (AADNP). . Statistical information on press circulation. Retrieved July 23, 2004, from http://www.eihea.gr

CIA's World Factbook. (2005). The world factbook—Greece. Retrieved March 18, 2005, from http://
. www.cia.gov/cia/publications/factbook

Computer Industry Almanac. (2004). Internet users by country—Greece. Retrieved March 18, 2005, from http:///wwwc-i-a.com

Emmanouil, N. (2004). Greece—Legal situation. In the *Southeast Europe media handbook 2003/2004*. Vienna: SEEMO.

Godard, F., Bisson, G., & Aguete, M. R. (2003). *European digital pay television platforms: Market assessment and forecasts to 2006*. London: Screendigest.

Greenspan, R. (2003) *Europe poised for high speed surge*. Retrieved March 20, 2005, from http://www.clickz.com/stats/sectors/broadband/article.php/10099_2211141

Ha, L. (2004). Webcasting. In H. Bidgoli (Ed.), *The internet encyclopedia* (vol. 3, pp. 674–686). New York: Wiley.

Ha, L. & Ganahl, R. (2004). Webcasting business models of clicks-and-bricks and pure-play media: A comparative study of leading webcasters in South Korea and the United States. *The International Journal on Media Management*, 6(1&2), 75–88.

Hellenic Audiovisual Institute. (2003). *The audiovisual sector in Greece*. Athens: IOM. (Also available from: http://www.iom.gr).

Infopublica Publicity Guide. (2003). Publicity and communication guide. Retrieved March 12, 2005, from http://www.infopublica.gr

Iosifidis, P. (2000). *Development of digital TV in Greece*. Paris: Institut de l'audiovisuel et des télécommunications, IDATE.

Internet World Stats. (2004). *DSL broadband Internet subscribers—Top 20 countries*. Retrieved March 16, 2005, from http://www.internetworldstats.com/dsl.htm

Meland, M. (1999). Europe: The next frontier: How does Europe stack up on the Internet? A country by country ranking. *Forbes DigitalTool*. Retrieved April 12, 2004, from www.forbes.com/tool/html/99/mar/0329/feat.htm

Naftemporiki. (2005). *Greece is gaining ground in the Internet field*. Retrieved June 12, 2005, from http://www.naftemporiki.gr

Samourkasidou, N. (2002). *Same levels for the Greek Internet market in 2001 before the descending course*. Retrieved February 20, 2005, from www.strategy.gr

Strategy Analytics. (2004). *Broadband penetration in Europe to hit 20 per cent as triple-play era arrives*. Retrieved March 16, 2005, from http://www.strategyanalytics.com/press/PR00121.htm

Terzis, G., & Kontochristou, M. (2004). *The Greek media landscape*. Retrieved March 3, 2005, from http://www.ejc.nl/jr/emland/greece.html

The European Institute for the Media (EIM). (2004). *The information of the citizen in the EU: Obligations for the media and the Institutions concerning the citizen's right to be fully and objectively informed*. Paris: Dusselford.

The Economist Intelligence Unit (EIU). (2003). *Greece: Country Profile 2003*. London: The Economist Intelligence Unit. (Also available from: http://www. eiu.com/schedule).

Timmers, P. (1998). Business models for electronic markets. *Electronic Markets*, 8(2), Web Atlas. (2005). Retrieved March 17, 2005, from http://www.clickz.com/stats/web_worldwide/

Web Atlas. (2005). Trends and statistics: The web's richest source. Retrieved February 20, 2005, from http://www.clickz.com/showPage.html?page=stats/web_worldwide

CHAPTER 11

Norway: The Clicks-and-Bricks Have Taken the Lead

Asle Rolland and Catherine B. Monsen
Norwegian School of Management

WEBCASTING MARKET ENVIRONMENT

Media Industry Structure

Norway's media industry is serving a small but affluent population. According to the United Nations Human Development Index (HDI) the average purchasing power parity (PPP) GDP per capita was $36,600 in 2002 (UN, 2004). Globally, this amount is second after Luxembourg, and if taken into consideration that the latter owes much of its wealth to a workforce commuting from the neighbor countries, the Norwegians may be second to none. The affluence of the market therefore provides Norway with the best environment for becoming number one in webcasting. The size of the market, however, does not. Moreover, the Norwegians are already quite heavy media users, spending 6 hours and 32 minutes engaged in media activities[1] on an average day in 2004, including 34 minutes on the home computer and another 33 minutes on the internet (Vaage, 2005).

Altogether the information sector occupied 4.9% of the Norwegian workforce and accounted for 6.4% of Norway's total economy in 2003 (calculated from Kalvøy & Hansen-Møllerud, 2005). Its information and computer technologies (ICT) sub-sector is however (still) much more important than its content sub-sector. ICT occupies 65% of the total information workforce; almost half of them working in consultancy firms, and accounts for 77% of the information sector's contribution to the total economy. Radio and television occupies 5% of the total information workforce, film and video only 3%. Publishing, with newspapers as the

---

[1]Measured media activities are: newspapers, magazines, cartoons, journals, books, records/cassettes/CDs/MP3, DVDs/videos, radio, television, home computers, internet, cinemas. Media consumption may be overlapping in time.

211

core activity, accounted for 61% of the content sector's value creation in 2002 (Kalvøy & Hansen-Møllerud, 2005). In economic and occupational terms the ICT sub-sector is about as important as building and construction work; the content sub-sector about as important as hotels and restaurants.

Newspapers have traditionally had a strong position in Norway. Their total number in 2002 was 218, plus 13 free papers. Seventy-six of the 218 pay-based newspapers were dailies (defined as published 4 to 7 days per week; Harrie, 2003). The circulation per thousand inhabitants was 543 dailies and 134 non-dailies. More than 200 Norwegian newspapers are on the internet. In 2004 three of four Norwegians read a newspaper each day (Vaage, 2005). The newspapers are also strong in the advertising market, with a 63% share of total advertising revenue in 2002 (Harrie, 2003). In the period 1992 to 2002 newspapers doubled their advertising revenue. However, the Norwegian newspaper industry and readership markets are undergoing profound change. Over the last decades three companies, Schibsted ASA, Orkla Media AS, and A-pressen ASA, have taken control over 34% of the newspapers including 64% of the circulation (Harrie, 2003). Local competition between dailies has almost disappeared (Rolland, 2002). The number and circulation of dailies are decreasing (Harrie, 2003), but non-dailies are in a growth mode. The newspaper share of total advertising revenue is declining and so is daily newspaper reading (Vaage, 2005). This development, however, is partly compensated by increased reading of their internet editions (Vaage, 2004).

With their paper versions in decline, the newspapers must look for new business opportunities, and this has made webcasting interesting. At the turn of the millennium there was great optimism, and a number of newspapers launched, in particular, video news webcasting on their websites (Farmakis, 2005). Some newspapers own local radio and television stations, which means they have businesses to protect and promote by investing in webcasting, as well as having something to rely on in regard to content. An example is the regional newspaper *Stavanger Aftenblad*, which launched video webcasting in 1999 after having bought the local TV station TV Vest (Hauge, 1999). Both TV Vest and its radio station Radio Aftenbladet are currently available at the newspaper's website. Another pioneer around 2000 was Norway's third largest newspaper, the single copy-selling tabloid *Dagbladet*. Shortly thereafter *Dagbladet* ran into economic difficulties due to a severe drop in circulation and had to give up webcasting. In 2005, however, they are about to make a new attempt.

Search on the internet indicates that webcasting has not attracted much interest from the publishers of Norwegian magazines, a market dominated by Danish and Swedish companies (the largest publishing house, Hjemmet Mortensen, is equally owned by the Danish Egmont and the Norwegian Orkla Media; Harrie, 2003). The exception to the rule is the Danish Aller, a major player in the Norwegian magazine as well as web radio markets. However, websites combining instructive videos with consultancies should have the potential to challenge the magazines as content providers, perhaps particularly the special interest magazines. Conversely, webcasting provides magazine publishers with new opportunities.

Although the monopoly was broken in the 1980s, radio broadcasting in Norway is still dominated by the state, operating its own services on basis of a television license fee. The former radio and television monopoly, the Norwegian Broadcasting Corporation (NRK), now operates three national and 16 regional radio channels in addition to a changing but growing number of digital radio channels (7 as of June 2005), partly on an experimental basis. NRK's radio channel P1, once synonymous with "broadcasting" in Norway, is still the giant in Norwegian radio, with a market share of 48% in 2004 (Futsæter, 2005a). NRK's total share of listening was 60%. Its two national private commercial competitors P4 and Kanal24[2], both having public service license agreements with the state, together had a market share of 27%. Despite having lost the license to broadcast nationwide to Kanal24, P4 had a market share of 22%; Kanal24 had 5% per 2004.

NRK's 287 local competitors (Harrie, 2003)—some of them commercial, others owned by non-profit organizations but allowed to carry advertising—had a combined market share of 12% in 2004. According to Radionytt.no, all of the national and 46 of the local radio stations do webcasting.

The magazine publisher Aller's strong involvement in web radio is mainly due to the company's traditional interest and important position in Norwegian commercial radio. From 1990 to 2003 Aller owned 51% of the successful metropolitan Radio1 chain and the nationwide local radio news service Radio Nettverk. In 2003 Aller bought Nordic web Radio (NWR) with activities in Norway and Sweden (serving among others Radio1), and became Scandinavia's largest supplier of internet radio services (www.allerkonsern.no, www.nordicwebradio.no, www.radionytt.no). NWR has gathered the largest radio stations in user-friendly radio players that are made available on the main websites, with the effect that Norway and Sweden now has "the world's highest penetration of internet radio" according to NWR. The company is also responsible for the radio guides Minradio in Norway and Spraydio in Sweden, and has recently established similar services for video webcasting (www.minradio.com).

While still strong in radio, NRK is facing harder competition in television, where it offers two nationwide channels and nine regional programs. Still NRK1 continues to be the market leader with 41% of the total viewing in 2004. The combined market share of the NRK channels was 44% (Futsæter, 2005b). The same year NRK's main competitor, the nationwide commercial channel TV2, also having a public service contract with the state, had a market share of 30%. TVN, reaching 86% of the population, had a market share of 10%. TV2 has in 2005 also

---

[2]Kanal24 was established to compete with the incumbent, P4, for the 2004–2014 license to operate a nationwide, private commercial radio channel. Regional newspapers were the largest shareowners.

expanded its auxiliary offer through TV2 Xtra—from September 5, 2005 TV2 Ze-bra—into a full-fledged television channel based on satellite and cable distribu-tion. Xtra/Zebra is however destined to become the pay-TV channel of the TV2 system (Berg, 2005).

The Swedish Modern Times Group (MTG) has greater success in Norway with the radio station P4, where it owns 33%, than with its TV stations (TV3, ZTV, Viasat). The most popular MTG television offer, TV3, with 62% penetration, had a market share of 6% in the second quarter of 2004.

AC Nielsen's Reklame-Statistikk AS, using the rate-card method, and Mediebyråenes Interesseorganisasjon (MIO), using the survey method (Mediefakta, 2003), are measuring the Norwegian advertising market. The two methods yield widely different results, with AC Nielsen's turnover figures being more than the double of MIO's, the difference however partly explained by AC Nielsen measuring gross and MIO net values. According to Arne Inge Christophersen of Initiative Universal Media even the AC Nielsen figures are too low. At Mediaforum's conference in October 2005, Christophersen said that the Norwegian advertising market has a total value of close to $4.6 billion, or almost the double of AC Nielsen's and five times MIO's estimate (Giske, 2005). Advertis-ing on the internet is booming. In August 2005 alone there was an increase of 62% in brand advertisements on the internet. The increase from July 2004 until July this year was 51% (Sandengen, 2005). The estimate for the end of 2005 is that $92 mil-lion will be used on internet advertising (INMA, 2005). One argument for this great increase in internet advertisement is that the media and media bureaus today are able with better certainty to prove the effect and value that the advertisers expe-rience by entering the internet (Larsen, 2005a).

COMPUTERS, INTERNET, AND BROADBAND USAGE

The consumption of webcasts depends absolutely on access to a computer, almost entirely on access to internet via broadband (Ha & Ganahl, 2004), however, less on access to these products and services at home as the consumption may also be for instance at school or work. Nevertheless, in 2004, 72% of the Norwegian house-holds and 79% of the Norwegians age 9 through 79 had access to a PC at home; 60% of the households and 66% of the persons had access to internet at home (Rød, 2005; Vaage, 2005). A recalculation of figures from Gallup Intertrack (a monthly study made by the market research firm TNS Gallup) indicates that in June 2005, 72% of the Norwegians age 12+ had access to internet at home, 13% at school, and 43% at work. According to Eurostat only Iceland (81%) and Denmark (69%) had higher household penetration of internet in Europe in 2004 (Rød, 2005). In Norwegian firms access to internet has culminated at close to 90% (Pilskog, 2005). Almost all of the public sector is on the net (Hansen-Møllerud, 2005).

In accordance with recommendation from OECD, Norway (like most OECD countries) has adopted a policy of state stimulation and encouragement but otherwise absolute non-interference in broadband, leaving it to the market forces and local initiatives including the initiatives of local public authorities (St.meld. nr. 49, 2003). As a result the Norwegian broadband development is slightly above average for the OECD (and EU) countries (Nielsen/NetRatings 2003, 2004)[3]. By March 2005, 35% of the Norwegian households had access to internet via broadband (Solberg, 2005), 30% via dial-up. Furthermore, 80% of the Norwegian households have a broadband offer from at least one supplier, estimated to rise to 85% at the end of 2005 (Intech, 2005). This makes Norway one of the leading countries in Europe. A study of European household broadband penetration indicates that Belgium, the Netherlands, Switzerland, Denmark, and Norway lead, with the penetration in Belgium calculated to 37.4%. Trailing were Greece, Ireland, and Germany (HeavyReading.com, 2005). The average broadband penetration among all households in Europe per Q1 2005 was 28% (Stokke, 2005).

Digital subscriber line (DSL) is the leading broadband platform in the 30 OECD countries. A breakdown of broadband technologies in 2004 shows that DSL represents 60%, cable modem 33.5%, and other technologies 6.5% (e.g., fiber optics, LAN, satellite, and fixed wireless). Canada, Portugal, and the United States are the only OECD countries that have more cable modem than DSL subscribers. In Norway, DSL is by far the leading broadband platform with 12.3 subscribers per 100 inhabitants, leaving only 2 subscribers per 100 inhabitants to cable modem and 0.5 to others. One reason for DSL being more prominent than cable is the wide spread of ISDN in Norway, making it very convenient for people to keep their original supplier of ISDN, most commonly a telephone operator, when switching to broadband—i.e., DSL. Telenor has done a remarkable job in order to keep their customers when switching from ISDN to broadband services. Additionally, the main cable operator in Norway—UPC—could profitably work even harder to promote their broadband services.

By April 2005, there were 130 broadband operators registered in Norway compared to about 50 suppliers in the autumn of 2001. The growth in the number and geographic spread of the new entrants has been characterized as impressive. However, most of the new, mainly local suppliers of broadband are still very small and do not represent true competition to the main broadband operators in Norway. The incumbent telecom operator Telenor operates the original fixed network in Norway, currently holding a 50% market share. Second and third are the mobile operator NextGenTel with 17% and the cable operator UPC with 10% of the broadband

---

[3]According to OECD 2004 the Norwegian penetration in December 2004 was 14.9 per 100 inhabitants. The OECD average was 10.3. In countries with active state interference, like South Korea and Canada, broadband development is by far above average (Nielsen/NetRatings 2003, 2004)

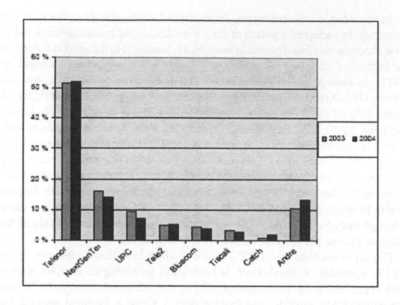

FIGURE 11–1   The operator's market shares of broadband subscriptions. Source: Intech, 2005.

market (Intech, 2005). Among other suppliers of broadband in Norway are Tele2, Bluecom, Tiscali, and Catch Communications (see Figure 11–1). However, different types of radio systems and even electricity firms[4] are constantly capturing more customers. In addition it is also possible to offer broadband solutions over satellite and via networks for distribution of digital TV.

Most of the key broadband operators in Norway have established cooperation with content suppliers, and vice versa, typically represented by a telecommunications operator having customers on mobile telephony and broadband, but little content, which can be provided by a TV producer. As an example, TV2 and Telenor are cooperating on video streaming, archives, pay-TV solutions, and distribution of TV2's webcasting to Telenor's broadband customers. The agreement between the TV channel and the Norwegian incumbent telecommunications operator implies that TV2 is the content provider and Telenor provides the technical distribution of the services TV2 webcast features. Moreover, the services can be

---

[4]For examople, Lyse Broadband (https://www.lyse.no/produkter/bredband/) and Tafjord Energy providing broadband through its subsidiary company Tafjord Mimer (www.mimer.no).

bought through Telenor's payment solution "Mobilhandel," i.e., payment over the mobile telephone (Veseth, 2004).

Furthermore, NextGenTel has established a content portal, BroadPark, where their customers are offered Video-on-Demand from SF Anytime—a Swedish content aggregator (www.sf-anytime.com)—as well as the portal provides webcasting and an overview over news channels, internet radio stations, etc. Also as regards energy firms providing broadband, cooperation with a content aggregator is the most common development. Tafjord Mimer for example, collaborates with the content aggregator iVisjon (www.ivisjon.no) and Lyse Broadband collaborate with NRK as a distributor of a 24-hour TV channel (both video webcasting and broadcast TV), focusing on local news and entertainment from one particular county of Norway—the home county of Lyse Energy. Content concentrating on news and the like from the local city or county is argued to become a successful business in the future webcasting market of Norway.

AUDIENCE RESEARCH ON WEBCASTING

At the time when internet and webcasting were put on the research agenda the London-based global market research company Taylor Nelson Sofres (TNS) had bought the Norwegian Gallup Institute, renamed it TNS Gallup, and made it the market leader in Norwegian commercial audience research. TNS Gallup has sought the position of "official currency supplier" [5] even for webcasting. It started by introducing Gallup's Web Top, part of their large continuous interview and fill-in *Consumer & Media survey*, originally set up for the newspapers but subsequently expanded to cover radio listening and local television viewing, as well as several commercial activities[6]. Then TNS Gallup acquired Red Sheriff's international browser measurement WebMeasure, passively capturing the online behavior of panelists using proprietary technology, and announced it to replace Web Top as the "official Norwegian currency" from 2002 onwards (Skaugerud, Anderson, & Futsæter, 2001, p. 8). At Christmas 2003, TNS' global competitor Nielsen/NetRatings acquired Red Sheriff. The uncertainty this caused in the Norwegian market in regard to what it would imply for the service was immediately calmed down by TNS Gallup, assuring it would be business as usual as they had a contract with Red Sheriff until the end of 2006 (Berg, 2004a, b, c). However, in June 2004, TNS Gallup announced that great changes in their internet measurement were on their way (Schreurs, 2004) and February 2005 marked the end of WebMeasure as the

---

[5]The "official currency supplier" is the only supplier whose data are accepted by the stakeholders and used in their financial transactions.

[6]TNS Gallup is measuring national television viewing in a TV meter panel and will measure radio listening with the personal portable meter or PPM from 2006 onwards.

"official currency" in Norway. For a while it was the end of measurement of internet traffic altogether, as no figures were published for the next four months (Schreurs, 2005). However, in June TNS Gallup returned with figures based on TNS Metrix (Gram, 2005), a result of the 2002 alliance between comScore Networks—the deliverer of the competing measurement system Media Metrix—and TNS subsidiary CMR (TNS Gallup, 2002). According to TNS Gallup the differences between Red Sheriff/WebMeasure and TNS Metrix are of a technical character. For instance, TNS Metrix does not at all use Java applets, treats non-cookie browsers differently and uses a different filter to avoid measurement of non-human traffic (spiders, robots, etc.; TNS Gallup, 2005).

OWNERSHIP AND BUSINESS PERFORMANCE OF LEADING WEBCASTERS

Leading Video Webcasters

TNS Gallup has not yet published consumption figures for Norwegian video webcasting. The most likely reason for that is the absence of an industry or a market mature enough to demand such a service. But Norwegian video webcasting definitely does exist. The TNS Metrix chart for week 31/2005 (August 1–7) ranked 60 websites according to traffic, and on 10 of the sites video webcasting was offered (Appendix A). Three of the offers were on the websites of the national television stations NRK (www.nrk.no), TV2 (www.tv2.no), and TVN (www.tvnorge.no), and a fourth was the broadband supplier Telenor, collaborating with TV2 (www.online.no). Another four webcasting offers were local television stations available from the websites of the local or regional newspapers owning them (www.bt.no, adressa.no, aftenbladet.no, and agderposten.no). All of these offers must be considered clicks-and-bricks.

The two remaining webcasting offers, however, are pure-plays. One is available at the website of the financial news service www.imarkedet.no and contains mainly video presentations of business enterprises, made either by the companies themselves or by iMarkedet on their behalf. The other is BabyTV.no, the common video portal for BarniMagen.no and DinBaby.no. BabyTV.no offers educational and instructive videos to its target group, pregnant women and parents, especially mothers with small children. Incidentally, iMarkedet pioneered webcasting in Norway, at least in the sense of submitting the first live transmission, on August 16, 2000, beating another pure-play supplier—the online newspaper Nettavisen—by 15 minutes (Sørensen 2000a, b). Nettavisen was later bought by TV2, the webcaster pioneer among the clicks-and-bricks. In September 2000, TV2 transmitted from the Sydney Olympics on demand in a closed network reaching fifteen thousand households as the European Broadcasting Union (EBU) had banned open net transmissions from the event (Sontum, 2000).

A pure-play channel not yet measured by TNS Metrix is Norwaylive.no, claiming to be the first Norwegian commercial internet and broadband television channel when it started webcasting on May 2, 2005. Norwaylive.no is an advertising-financed free video-on-demand service streaming its content to a presumably young audience (14–40) at two different speeds in Windows Media Video format. Market analysts are, however, skeptical to its chances of success, due partly to its lack of interesting content, partly to the track record of the interests behind it (Ertnes, 2005; Harvestpartner.no, 2005; Larsen 2005b,c; Propaganda, 2005; Veseth, 2005).

On its way from click-and-brick to pure-play is NRK's broadcast television program *Bokbadet* containing in-depth interviews with novelists. About to be dropped by NRK in the fall of 2005 it was taken over by the leading book club Bokklubben and re-launched as a video webcasting (Hauger, 2005).

None of the ten TNS-Metrix measured websites offering video webcasting are exclusively devoted to webcasting, and neither the traffic figures nor the ranking indicate who are the leading Norwegian video webcasters. However, observers like the head of the internet department of TNS Gallup indicate that probably NRK television has the largest audience, and probably TV2 is most profitable, both for the same reason: While NRK's offer is mostly free of charge, TV2's is pay-TV or video-on-demand (Dag Andersen, personal communication, May 15, 2005).

NRK is owned entirely by the state, with the State Secretary for Culture as general assembly. Established in 1933 to administer the state's broadcasting monopoly, its current vision is to obtain a reputation for being innovative, interpreted as testing and implementing new technology, new production- and distribution forms, new business areas, and new sources of revenue. In the market the aim is to hold a "leading position" in radio and television, and a "strong" position in the digital multimedia market (NRK, 2004).

The TV2 Group is owned with equal shares by the two Norwegian (multimedia) press groups Schibsted ASA, A-pressen ASA, and the Egmont Group in Denmark. TV2 AS owned 49% of the semi-national TV channel TVN from 1997 to 2004, when it sold to the majority owner SBS and increased its ownership share in the new national radio channel Kanal24 from 34 to 49%. The strategy of the TV2 Group is to be leading content supplier on all electronic media platforms (www.TV2.no). Luxembourg-based SBS Broadcasting S.A. owns 100% of TVN and of the Radio1 chain. August 22, 2005 the two private investment companies Permira and KKR bought SBS for 2.1 billion USD according to a press release from SBS 22.8.05.

Leading Audio Webcasters

The turmoil resulting in change of measurement technology is probably the reason why the most recent figures for web radio at the time of writing are from the last week of February 2005 (week 8, See Appendix B). That week six of the ten most visited web radio stations belonged to NRK (in positions 1, 3, 4, 5, 8, and 10). Holding the highest positions were NRK's three national radio channels, and although some digital stations appeared lower on the list none of the NRK offers were exclusive for internet listeners. In fact only two stations on the web radio Top Twenty list were truly pure-plays, Boogie 75 in position 15 and B2000 in position 20, both delivered by Nordic Web Radio. Although P4 Hits in position 19 is an exclusive internet station, it is the click-and-brick radio station P4 that offers it. However, new pure-play internet radio stations continue to pop up, the newest at the time of writing being Hit Norway, starting transmitting from a small town in northern Norway on August 1, 2005 (Dahl, 2005).

By far the most visited web-radio station in week 8 was NRK's P1 with more than twice as many unique visitors as the station in position 2, and more than 12 times as many as the station in position 10. In fact the concentration of visits was so great that it becomes difficult to characterize more than the top five a "leading audio webcaster"; the stations in position 6–20 clearly resembled the non-leading stations more than the leading ones in terms of audience attendance (station 20 had 29 unique visitors more than station 21).

All the leading internet radio stations represent well-established clicks-and-bricks. Although the popular click-and-brick station P4 had four unique web-offers to their internet listeners (P4 Hits, P4 Oldies, P4 Norsk, and P4 Ballade), the traditional radio station P4 had more than twice as many unique visitors as the four unique web-offers combined (P4 in position 7, the others in positions 19, 23, 30, and 32).

The most important effect of internet is its impact on the ranking of click-and-brick radio stations. In position 2 week 8 was the local commercial radio station Radio1 Oslo, and in position 6 another local commercial station, NRJ Energy. The national commercial stations P4 and Kanal24 were in positions 7 and 9. On the internet these four commercial stations are competing on equal terms, as the distinction between national and local stations does not make sense, and winners in week 8 were the stations otherwise restricted to serve local audiences. It has been estimated that about 30% of Radio1 Oslo's and 20% of NRJ Energy's total listening stems from the internet, but Radio1 Oslo also profits from an internet service where the station is automatically turned on (digi.no, 2004).

WEBCASTING BUSINESS MODELS

Most of the leading Norwegian webcasters, both video and audio, are (still) based in Norway and fully owned by Norwegian companies or individuals. Moreover, most of the webcasters in Norway are commercial, e.g., TV2, Telenor Online, TV Norge, Norwaylive.no, Radio1, P4, Kanal24, and Nordic Web Radio, even though few report making profit from their webcast activities. Even NRK is allowed and expected to make a profit from its activities besides operating the license-financed public service broadcasting channels[7], which in fact is the reason why, in 1996, it was turned into a limited company (Syvertsen & Karlsen, 2000).

In the following an analysis of the accessibility, content strategies, and revenue sources components of the business models of leading webcasters in Norway is presented, based on Ha and Ganahl's online media business model framework (2004). Each component is discussed relative to the two most common webcasting business models, branded content model and content aggregator model (Ha & Ganahl 2004). The "branded content" is the model most commonly used by leading Norwegian webcasters, indicating that they have their own branded content that is distributed to their media brand. However, there are also some "content aggregators" in the market.

The Branded Content Model

The two click-and-bricks operators NRK and TV2 both supply web-TV services. TV2 provides access to its most popular programs both through live streaming and on-demand downloading. Downloading of TV programs is included in subscription packages with prices varying from about $4.60 per week to $90 on a yearly basis. In addition, TV2 supplies free content on the internet. TV2's webcast-supply can only be played on one media player; the Windows Media Player.

---

[7]The license-financed public service broadcasting is there in order to secure what in Europe is referred to as Universal Service Obligations (USO). The Universal Service concept is an essential element of the global information society. This dynamic and evolving concept strives to extend access to electronic services to all members of society rather than just to the part of the population that enjoys access to the service through the market forces. The EU focuses on the importance of the social implications of technology and that the Information Society should be designed for "All of Us." The European Union has identified the common scope of Universal Service obligations in Europe (e.g., http://europa.eu.int/information_society/policy/ecomm/todays_framework/universal_service/index_en.htm)

NRK's video webcasting is also supplier of a broad assortment of the channel's programs through live transmission and on-demand downloading. Its selection ranges from news, sports, entertainment, as well as a broad choice of children's and youth's programs. Also NRK's programs require registration, but most of the content is free of charge. Like TV2, NRK web-TV requires the use of Windows Media Player for live streaming or on-demand downloading.

TVN's video webcasting, in cooperation with MPS Nordic, is restricted to content from entertainment programs and series that previously have been broadcasted. Most of the content requires payment. Moreover, Telenor Online provides its broadband customers internet based VOD (Video On Demand) services through its entertainment portal iCanal. ADSL customers can watch movies by making a selection from a web-library and then log on with an ADSL username and password before the movie starts playing. Payment is required and is demanded through Telenor's internet invoice.

Among the video webcasters working on the branded content model there is also Norwaylive.no. Unlike the above-mentioned webcasters, Norwaylive.no is a pure-player, but still focusing on branded content; self-produced programs are thematically sorted as topicalities, culture, fashion and trend, food, traveling, movie, music, and games. This service is financed through advertisement. Transmission requires a web-browser that supports Windows Media Player.

Most of the leading audio webcasters in Norway are working on the branded content model, both the clicks-and-bricks as well as the pure-plays. There exists a full range of radio stations offering the usual mix of programs from the FM bandwidth. Most of the pure internet radio stations (i.e., pure-plays) specializes on a specific content, like news, rock, classic music, jazz, Latino, talk shows, religion, sports, etc. With regard to content, the program features are often more comprehensive than what is broadcasted via traditional TV programs. Both NRK and P4 provide a package consisting of several internet channels with live transmission as well as access to archives. In addition, these internet radio stations offer services like text-based information connected to the content transmitted. Kanal24's web radio offer on the other hand, is much simpler, restricting itself to parallel live streaming on the internet of what is broadcasted on air. Radio1 is originally a local radio station chain broadcasting in the four largest cities of Norway; however, now that it provides internet radio, it reaches out to a large extent of Norwegian listeners. As Kanal24, Radio1 does parallel live streaming, but in addition it offers additional features that take advantage of the interactivity of the internet like chat room, message board, play list rating and opinion polls. P4, Kanal24 and Radio1 all obtain their revenues from advertising.

The Content Aggregator Model

A few Norwegian webcast suppliers focus on the content aggregator model. Media Network is a Norwegian company delivering distribution of IPTV (internet Protocol TV) in cooperation with Viasat. The service includes of up to 40 channels and the customers are operators who want to reforward IPTV. Moreover, as for audio webcasters focusing a strategy on content aggregation the internet contains several portals helping users finding radio stations sorted after category or geographic criteria. MinRadio.com, owned by Nordic Web Radio (NWB), is an example. NWB is also a leading provider of digital content services with the main focus on web radio. The company develops and operates solutions for several internet radio stations on behalf quite a few media firms. Two of the largest Norwegian newspapers, *Dagens Næringsliv* and *Aftenposten*, as well as Telenor's iCanal and TV2 are among the companies receiving tailor-made internet radio features from NWB. Their consumers then use the webcasting service for a wide selection of content. These are accurately the characteristics of the content aggregator model referring to the operation of the webcaster as an entertainment or information portal. The webcaster serves as a one-stop entertainment or information source to provide consumers with convenient service (Ha & Ganahl, 2004).

An explanation why most webcasters in Norway (still) represent the branded content business model may be the one offered by earlier studies claiming that all clicks-and-bricks webcasters work on the branded content model because they will not carry the media content of offline and online competitors (Ha & Ganahl, 2004). As already observed the traditional electronic media, i.e., clicks-and-bricks, provide most webcasting in Norway. At the outset this was the case also in the United States, but there the pure-plays are now dominating (chapter 2). It is not unfair to recognize the American market as more mature than the Norwegian, which could be an explanation for these differences. In contrast to the clicks-and-bricks, pure-play webcasters have a choice between the branded content model and the content aggregator model. Since it could seem like the content aggregator model is particularly common in a more mature market (like the U.S.) than a more undeveloped market (like Norway), it could be argued that the dot-com media operators (pure-plays) do not (yet) have a reliable supply of content and therefore have to count on the convenience and comprehensiveness of the content to consumers and assemble a portfolio of content suppliers from various sources as content aggregators and operate like cable system operators (Ha & Ganahl 2004).

OUTLOOK OF THE WEBCAST INDUSTRY

In Norway, as well as in other European countries, one can hardly discuss the future of electronic mass communication without taking the State into consideration. Webcasting clearly evades the existing state regulatory regime. From that point of view webcasting is beyond public, political control. Furthermore, the webcasting industry does not need state intervention in order to regulate access to its own market. Webcasting does not depend on the utilization of limited resources like frequencies, nor does it cause signal interference, which are reasons why state regulation of broadcasting may be in the interest of the producers or the industry itself. Thus webcasting deprives the state of reasons to interfere in electronic mass communication. Within broadcasting the industry's own need for access regulation has provided the state with an opportunity to regulate content[8]. All Norwegian nationwide private, commercial radio and television channels licensed by the state must sign a contract obliging them to broadcast in accordance with public service principles similar to those governing the state's own broadcaster NRK. The licensee must act completely independent of the owners or other interest groups of political, economic or other character, and as part of the yearly report the licensee shall each year give a public service account to the state for its program activities. However, to what extent the Norwegian state will consider this lack of opportunity to control webcasting a problem most likely depends on webcasting's audience success. The state does not control the content of the numerous local radio stations, and for cable and satellite broadcasting the license system was replaced in 2003 by merely requiring the broadcasters to register at the authorities.

On the other hand, the state is also operating its own broadcasting, and webcasting does threaten the state broadcaster NRK's main source of income—the license fee on television receivers. In August 2005 it became known that NRK wanted the concept of "television receiver" expanded to cover all terminals capable of receiving televised signals, which would now include personal computers and cellular phones. Since almost all Norwegian homes already pay the broadcasting license fee, due to possession of at least one TV set (in 1968 the license duty was transferred from the set to the household) the immediate impact of this upon the households' economy and NRK's revenue would be negligible. What the NRK obviously wants to forestall is a situation where the households replace their TV sets with personal computers and watch television programs for free. One could argue that this should be of no concern for the NRK, because unless the state broadcaster itself enters the internet it will not have a free-rider problem. There is also no

---

[8]An immense future challenge will include to what extent and how to regulate content. This is one of the main focuses in the EU as regards the further work on the new regulatory framework for electronic communications (http://europa.eu.int/information_society/policy/ecomm/todays_framework/index_en.htm).

societal reason why the company should be represented on the internet, as the main justification for its existence was the need for an institution to administer the state's broadcasting monopoly at a time this was deemed necessary. However, the present state-owned limited company NRK has its own economic interests. Its worst scenario must be that webcasting without NRK, perhaps dominated by pure-players, becomes sufficiently popular for large segments of the audience to drop the traditional TV set and thereby avoid paying the license fee. Thus while the monopoly NRK argued that the license fee must be considered a subscription for its offer, competitive NRK has persuaded the authorities to accept that the fee is a duty on the receiver as such, to be reserved for NRK's use. This is the principle the company now wants to expand. Forestalling this development is probably also a major reason why NRK has started webcasting and has a company strategy of being present on "all important media platforms" (NRK, 2004, p. 6). The company obviously takes into consideration that without an NRK offer an attempt to impose the broadcasting license fee on the owners of personal computers and cellular phones would lack social and political legitimacy (Rolland, 2005).

Being on the internet the NRK has a competitive advantage in the superior size of its program archive, due to the many decades of monopoly. However, this advantage will be gradually reduced as the archives of the competitors grow and the audience segment interested in old-time NRK programs shrinks. Moreover, this change in audience segment interest triggers the discussion of international influence. There is little doubt that the internet and webcasting provides tremendous amounts of content available for people all over the world, as long as one has admission to a PC with internet access. However, culture and language represent significant restrictions as regards people's interests. Even though Norwegian people in general speak very well English[9], the experience from television is that access to English or other foreign channels has negligible impact upon their viewing habits. Although it is hard to argue how the cultural phenomenon on webcasting will develop in Norway, the analysis in this chapter shows that so far as regards clicks-and-bricks the international influence is marginal.

Until now, the internet has not been especially friendly to content providers, who have made large investments to establish online presence and received little financial payback; faced consumers who have shown little willingness to pay for content distributed over the internet; and have seen widespread copyright violations diminishing their revenues (Baya & Berg, 2004). Consumers have shown themselves to be very price sensitive relative to adopting broadband, making pricing a significant impact on adoption rates. Up until now therefore, advertising is still the most common revenue source for European—and also Norwe-

---

[9]Most Norwegians know how to speak English, and most at age 50 and downwards speak English pretty well. Many Norwegians also learn German or French at school, however this is nowhere near the high number of people who speak English (http://wikitravel.org/en/Norway).

gian—webcasters. As regards the future of commercial webcasting in Norway, we may return to the predictions of Arne Inge Christophersen for advertising on the internet (Giske, 2005). His estimate for the Norwegian advertising market in 2006 was $900 million for newspapers, $400 million for television, $200 million for internet, $100 million for magazines and periodicals, and $80 million for radio. He expects internet to pass television and establish itself as the second most important advertising medium in 2007 to 2008. If Norwegian webcasting is able to build a solid audience base that can attract advertising or obtain sufficient subscription revenue internet has a fair chance to pass television. For the moment it seems like the clicks-and-bricks have taken the lead.

REFERENCES

Baya, V., & Berg, E. M. (2004). *The broadband future—Interactive, networked, and personalised, Europe, January 2004.* Retrieved August 1, 2006, from http://www.pwcglobal.com/imges/ infocom/ Broadband%20UK.pdf

Berg, H. (2004a). Nielsen kaprer nordiske nettmålinger [Nielsen captures Nordic net ratings]. *Propaganda,* January 6. Retrieved August 18, 2005, from http://www.propaanda-as.no/php/ art.php?id = 97745&versjon = utskrift

Berg, H. (2004b). Gallup—Ingen endringer i norske nettmålinger [Gallup—No change in Norwegian net measurements]. *Propaganda,* January 6. Retrieved August 18, 2005, from http://www.proaganda-as. no/php/art.php?id = 97788&versjon = utskrift

Berg, H. (2004c). INMA vil ha TV-målinger på nett [INMA wants TV ratings on the net]. *Propaganda,* March 15. Retrieved August 18, 2005, from http://www.propaganda-as.no/php/art.php?id = 101392 &versjon = utskrift

Berg, H. (2005). TV2 Xtra starter med daglige programmer [TV2 Xtra starts daily broadcasting]. *Propaganda,* May 19. Retrieved August 9, 2005, from http://www.propaganda-as.no/php/art.php?id = 214653&versjon = utskrift

Dahl, K. (2005). Ny norsk nettradio på lufta [New Norwegian net radio on the air]. *Radionytt.no,* August 15. Retrieved August 5, 2005, from http://www.radionytt.no/05175.htm

digi.no (2004). *Radio over internett øker kraftig* [Radio over the internet increases rapidly]. November 11. Retrieved August 19, 2005, from http://www.digi.no/php/art?id = 112070

Ertnes, A. K. B. (2005). Norwaylive.no lansert i dag: Åpner ny, norsk TV-kanal på nettet [Norwaylive.no launched today: Opens new, Norwegian TV channel on the net]. *digi.no,* May 2. Retrieved August 24, 2005, from http://www.digi.no/php/art.php?id = 213146

Farmakis, N. (2005). Web-TV har blitt viktig. [Web-TV has become important] *Computerworld.* Retrieved April 27, 2005, from http://.www.computerworld.no/index.cfm/fuseaction/artikkel_utskrift/ id/49075

Futsæter, K.-A. (2005a): *Radiolytting 2004. Sterk økning for radio* [Radio listening in 2004: Strong increase for radio]. Retrieved January 12, 2005, from http://www.tns-gallup.no/medier

Futsæter, K.-A. (2005b). *TV-seing 2004. Økt TV-seing* [TV viewing in 2004: Increased TV viewing]. Retrieved January 12, 2005, from www.tns-gallup.no/medier

Giske, A. (2005): Mener mediemarkedet er verdt 30 milliarder [Believes the media market to be worth 30 billion]. *Kampanje,* October 7. Retrieved October 12, 2005, from file://E:\Home\rol\LOCALS~1 \Temp\198\BH7NILYG.htm

Gram, T. (2005). Gallup klar med nye nettall [Gallup ready with new net figures]. *Propaganda,* June 30. Retrieved August 15, 2005, from http://www.propaganda-as.no/php/art.php?id = 218441&versjon = utskrift

Ha, L., & Ganahl, R. (2004). Webcasting business models of clicks-and-bricks and pure-play media: A comparative study of leading webcasters in South Korea and the United States. *The International Journal of Media Management, 6*(1&2), 74–87.

Hansen-Møllerud, M. (2005). Informasjons- og kommunikasjonsteknologi i offentlig sektor [Information- and communication technology in the public sector]. In Pilskog, G. M., Hansen-Møllerud, M., Kalvøy, A., & Rød, H. (Eds.), *Nøkkeltall om informasjonssamfunnet 2004, Statistical analyses 71* [Key figures about the information society] (pp. 89–104). Oslo-Kongsvinger: Statistics Norway.

Harrie, E. (2003). *The Nordic media market: Media companies and business activities.* Gothenburg: Nordicom: Göteborg University.

Harvestpartner.no. (2005). *Web-TV er tema i media Norge* [Web-TV is a topic in media Norway]. Retrieved August 24, 2005 from http://harvestpartner.no/index.php?option = com_content&task = view&ide = 34&Itemid = 1

Hauge, K. A. (1999). Aftenbladet starter web-TV [Aftenbladet starts web-TV]. *Computerworld.* Retrieved April 27, 2005, from http://.www.computerworld.no/index.cfm/fuseaction/artikkel_utskrift/id/16136

Hauger, K. K. (2005). Sender Bokbadet på egen web-tv-kanal [Sends Bokbadet on own web-TV channel]. *Kampanje.* Retrieved August 15, 2005, from http://www.kampanje.com/00/53/06/1.html

HeavyReading.com. (2005): *European broadband penetration rates—Percentage of households, March 2005.* Retrieved August 15, 2005, from http://www.heavyreading.com/

INMA. (2005): *Reklamerevolusjon på Nett* [Revolution in advertising on the net]. Retrieved August 19, 2005, from http://www.inma.no

Intech. (2005): *Tjenesteutvikling og regulering på konvergerende tele—medie- og internett- plattformer* [Service development and regulation on converging telecon, media, and internet platforms]. Retrieved September 20, 2005, from http://www.abelia-innovasjon.no/pub/config/dir_struc_root/2712_1127292776_IntechRapport.pdf

Kalvøy, A., & Hansen-Møllerud, M. (2005). Informasjonssektoren [The information sector]. In Pilskog, G. M., Hansen-Møllerud, M., Kalvøy, A., & Rød, H. (Eds.). *Nøkkeltall om Informasjonssamfunnet 2004, Statistical Analyses 71* [Key figures about the information society] (pp. 19–45). Oslo-Kongsvinger: Statistics Norway.

Larsen, V (2005a): Reklamerevolusjon på nett [Advertising revolution on the net]. *Dagens Næringsliv.* Retrieved August 20, 2005, from http://www.dn.no/forsiden/etterBors/ article575210.ece

Larsen, V. (2005b). Tviler på web-tv-mål [Doubting the aim of web-TV]. *Dagens Næringsliv.* Retrieved August 24, 2005, from http://www.dn.no/forsiden/IT_Telekom/article453848.ece?action = print

Larsen, V. (2005c). Han bløffet meg [He bluffed me]. *Dagens Næringsliv,* June 6. Retrieved August 24, 2005, from http://www.dn.no/forsiden/etterBors/article529131.ece?action = print

Mediefakta. (2003). Informasjon fra medienorge [Information from MediaNorway (www. medienorge.uib.no)].

Nielsen/NetRatings. (2003). *June bandwidth report—Korean broadband penetration breaks 70%, US broadband growth lags.* Retrieved August 20, 2005, from http://www.websiteoptimization.com/bw/0306/

Nielsen/NetRatings. (2004). *US narrows Canadian broadband lead—US broadband penetration grows to 46%—April 2004 bandwidth report.* Retrieved August 20, 2005, from http://www. websiteoptimization.com/bw/0404/

NRK. (2004). *Noe for alle. Alltid. Overordnet strategi for NRK 2002–2006* [Something for everyone, always: Superior strategy for NRK 2002–2006]. Retrieved August 20, 2005, from http://www.nrk.no

Pilskog, G. M. (2005). Informasjons-og kommunikasjonsteknologi i næringslivet [Information and communication technology in trade and industry]. In Pilskog, G. M., Hansen-Møllerud, M., Kalvøy, A., & Rød, H. (Eds.), *Nøkkeltall om Informasjonssamfunnet 2004, Statistical Analyses 71* [Key figures about ht einformation society], (pp. 77–87). Oslo-Kongsvinger: Statistics Norway.

Propaganda. (2005). I gang med kommersiell web-TV [Commerical web-TV has started]. May 2. Retrieved August 24, 2005, from http://www.propaganda-as.no/php/art.php?id = 213118&versjon = utskrift

Rolland, A. (2002): *Mediemakt og mediemonopol* [Media power and media monopoly]. BI: The Norwegian School of Management, Research report 2002/01.

Rolland, A. (2005): Kringkastingsavgift for PC og mobiltelefon [Broadcasting license for personal computer and cellular phone]. *Medieverden, 13*. PAGE SPAN.

Rød, H. (2005). Informasjons- og kommunikasjonsteknologi i husholdningene [Information and communication technology in the households]. In Pilskog, G. M., Hansen-Møllerud, M., Kalvøy, A., & Rød, H. (Eds.), *Nøkkeltall om Informasjonssamfunnet 2004, Statistical Analyses 71* [Key figures about the information society], (pp. 63–76). Oslo-Kongsvinger: Statistics Norway.

Sandengen, B. (2005): Nettreklamen vokste 62 prosent [Net advertising grew by 62 percent]. September 27. Retrieved August 20, 2005, from www.mediacom.no

Schreurs, N. (2004). Gallup varsler endringer i nettmålingene [Gallup announces changes in net measurement]. *Computerworld,* June 9. Retrieved August 20, 2005, from http://.www.computerworld.no/index.cfm/fuseaction/artikkel&id = 09881C68-D96D—3

Schreurs, N. (2005). Ingen trafikktall fra TNS Gallup [No traffic figures from TNS Gallup]. *Computerworld,* August 18. Retrieved August 20, 2005, from http://.www.computerworld.no/index.cfm/prioritert/artikkel/id/51494

Skaugerud, T., Andersen, D., & Futsæter, K.-A. (2001). *Gallup WebMeasure*. December 2001. Retrieved August 20, 2005, from http://www.gallup.no/Internett

Solberg, E. L. (2005): *Bredbånd i Norge—Utfordringer, ambisjoner og tiltak* [Broadband in Norway—Challenges, ambitions, and efforts]. Moderniseringsdepartementet, April 5. Retrieved April 27, 2005, from http://odin.dep.no/mod/norsk/aktuelt/taler/politisk_ledelse/050001–090045/dok-bn.html

Sontum, E. (2000). Beskjeden start og høye mål for TV2 Interaktiv [Modest start and high aims for TV2 interactive]. *Propaganda*, September 20. Retrieved April 27, 2005, from http://.www.propaanda-as.no/php?ide = 71222&versjon = utskrift

St.meld. nr. 49 (2003) *Breiband for kunnskap og vekst* [Broadband for knowledge and growth]. Det kongelige nærings- og handelsdepartement [The Royal Ministry of Trade and Industry].

Stokke, O. (2005). *Bredbåndsmarkedet—fokus på fremtidens produkt—og innholdstilbud* The broadband market—Focus on the future product and content offer]. NextGenTel presentation at the broadband conference Bredbånd Norge 2005. Retrieved August 20, 2005, from http://www.nextgentel.no/ressurser/presentasjoner/2005–09–14_Olav_Stokke.pdf

Syvertsen, T., & Karlsen, G. M. M. (2000). The Norwegian television market in the 1990s. *Nordicom Review, 21*, 71–100.

Sørensen, R. (2000a). På jakt etter tv-looken [searching for the "TV look"]. *Computerworld,* August 23. Retrieved April 27, 2005, from http://www.computerworld.no/index.cfm/fuseaction/artikkel_utskrift/id/19973

Sørensen, R. (2000b). Tar det som det kommer [Taking it as it comes]. *Computerworld,* August 23. Retrieved April 27, 2005, from http://www.computerworld.no/index.cfm/fuseaction/artikkel_utskrift/id/5352

TNS Gallup. (2002). *COMSCORE and CMR extend strategic alliance through acquisitions of media metrix and evaliant (US)*. Press release July 18. Retrieved August 20, 2005, from http://www.tns-global.com/corporate/Doc/0/VE6RTCQBGTJ417OGT9G5AE6IC3/59

TNS Gallup. (2005). De første offisielle tallene fra TNS Metrix [The first official figures from TNS Metrix]. Retrieved August 18, 2005 at http://www.tns-gallup.no/arch/img.asp?file_id207472&ext = ppt.

United Nations (UN). (2004). Human Development Report 2004. New York: UNDP.

Vaage, O. F. (2004). Internettavisene demper nedgangen i lesing av papiraviser [Internet newspapers moderate decline in printed newspaper reading]. *Samfunnsspeilet, 6,* 49–52.

Vaage, O. F. (2005). *Norsk mediebarometer 2004, Statistical Analyses 68* [Norwegian media barometer 2004]. Oslo-Kongsvinger: Statistics Norway.

Veseth, B. (2004): TV2s web-TV fra Telenor. Teleavisen AS, 14.01.2004 [TV2's web-ITV from Telenor]. Teleavisen, January 14.

Veseth, B. (2005). TV-kanal på bredbånd [TV channel on broadband]. *Megaband,* May 2. Retrieved August 24, 2005, from http://.www.megaband.no/print.asp?page = 121&article = 15268&msgpage = 0&msgpost = 0

APPENDIX A
TNS Gallup: Video Webcaster figures, TNS Metrix week 31/2005

Website	URL	UV	US	PI	UV +/-	US +/-	PI +/-
TV2 Nettavisen	www.tv2.no	709,094	2,842,307	22,465,273	13.81	18.06	24.28
NRK.no	www.nrk.no	329,316	778,065	5,136,264	16.59	16.44	12.82
Online	www.online.no	298,361	1,866,289	3,297,764	8.01	10.73	10.37
Bergens Tidende	www.bt.no	171,879	534,332	2,727,143	28.87	21.78	27.66
adressa.no	www.adressa.no	131,782	422,516	2,087,752	27.49	32.88	32.91
Aftenbladet.no	www.aftenbladet.no	83,430	251,904	1,318,359	15.65	9.14	-2.64
TVNORGE	www.tvnorge.no	27,719	40,166	202,272	12.1	12.07	12.49
BarniMagen	www.barnimagen.com	23,815	60,908	1,035,828	9.89	11.53	4.80
iMarkedet	www.imarkedet.no	19,555	75,470	270,699	24.87	27.29	33.97
DinBaby	www.dinbaby.com	12,426	36,033	680,601	9.63	11.39	5.42
Agderposten	www.agderposten.no	11,131	24,033	96,597	n/a	n/a	n/a

Notes. UV = Unique Visitors; US = User Sessions; PI = Page Impressions.
Source. Norsk Gallup Institutt AS, Oslo. Retrieved August 15, 2005, from http://www.tns-gallup.no

230

APPENDIX B
TNS Gallup: Audio Webcaster figures,
WebMeasure week 8/2005

Net Radio	UV	+/–	PI	+/–
NRK P1	65.819	59,63p	211.762	74,5p
Radio1 Oslo	29.985	0,56p	148.984	10,81p
NRK P3	29.366	11,37p	80.100	5,41p
NRK P2	19.907	33,66p	46.331	17,08p
NRK mPetre	17.344	–2,6q	45.055	–3,81q
NRJ–Energy	10.183	–9,91q	30.489	–9,87q
P4 Norge	10.092	2,57p	27.559	0,09p
NRK Alltid Nyheter	8.134	18p	15.712	12,28p
Kanal24	6.392	6,34p	13.827	0,33p
NRK Alltid Klassisk	5.322	1,91p	11.309	–3,75q
Klem FM	4.449	–4,28q	12.369	–8,79q
Radio1 Bergen	3.719	–14,86q	8.797	–20,68q
The Voice	2.710	–9,82q	5.891	–9,8q
Radio1 Trondheim	2.709	–3,9q	5.957	–17q
Boogie75	2.317	–4,89q	4.603	1,52p
Radio1 Stavanger	2.136	–7,85q	4.461	–7,81q
Radio Fredrikstad	1.955	22,72p	4.601	38,71p
RadioAdressa	1.765	25,71p	4.756	49,75p
P4 Hits	1.718	–2,05q	3.773	–0,79q
B2000	1.692	–10,48q	2.776	–13,03q

Notes.   UV = Unique Visitors; US = User Sessions; PI = Page Impressions.

Source.   Norsk Gallup Institutt AS, Oslo. Retrieved August 15, 2005, from http://www.tns-gallup.no

CHAPTER 12

Denmark: Smooth Sailing (For Now)—The Public Service Legacy in Danish Webcasting

Kyle Nicholas
Old Dominion University

OVERVIEW

The Danish webcasting scene is marked by very high access to internet resources and limited diversity in ownership and programming. Although Denmark boasts some of the highest rates of internet connectivity and broadband subscribership in the world, webcasting in the small Nordic nation is concentrated mainly in the hands of the key broadcasters, with reliable audience numbers available only for the main public service webcaster. In fact, it is the nationally-owned DR Corporation that appears to be the most innovative and aggressive pursuer of web audiences, primarily through simulcasts and rebroadcasts of existing content.

Very few "pure-play" webcasters specifically aimed at Danish audiences exist. Of the handful discussed in this study, the most interesting resemble the "pirate" radio stations that disrupted Danish broadcasting several decades ago. The Danish government once responded to radio pirates by opening up Danish broadcasting, at first creating new networks then eventually liberalizing secondary networks and inviting commercial competition (Jauert, 2001). In 1958, the private commercial station Radio Mercur began broadcasting into Copenhagen from international waters off of the coast of Denmark (Mishkind, n.d.). It was aimed at young people and featured American popular culture, a threat to the centralized, paternalistic (and nationalistic) culture of Danish radio. A few years later, another pirate station, Danmarks Comercielle Radio (DCR) started up, eventually merging with Mercur. Although not strictly illegal at the time it began broadcasting, the Danish government eventually responded by outlawing the station. The combined station was shut down in 1962, but its brief existence changed the face of Danish broadcasting. Mercur challenged the public service notion that radio was to be used for serious culture and information matters. As Per Jauert (2001, n.p.) notes, "the Danish radio audience had tasted the forbidden fruit, and anxiety among the politicians grew when audience research proved that the listeners preferred Radio Mercur" to Danish public radio. That anxiety spurred DR to offer more channels with more variety and over the next 40 years led to steps toward liberalization and commercial broadcasting.

Will that pattern repeat itself in globalizing online world of webcasting? There are a few independent webcasters plying the commercial media sphere, and undoubtedly many who remain beneath the surface, exchange webcasts via private and unseen networks. But, while it is tempting to see the intrusion of webcasting itself as the "new pirate" disrupting the Danish public service model, it appears for now that changes in the public and commercial spheres that are the target of this chapter are coming from within. Although minimal transmission costs can allow webcasters to pursue economies of scale globally, first copy costs for original programming are still quite high compared to repurposed content. This equation gives a huge advantage to webcasters with ready-made content; in Denmark that advantage is with the public and commercial broadcasters who can stretch their content dollars across platforms and exploit cross-marketing opportunities in radio, television, and the web.

One interesting factor to watch in Danish webcasting then will be the development of pure-play outsiders, those not affiliated with the major broadcasting companies, on the established networks. To date, these would-be competitors present less sophisticated interfaces, fewer consumer options, and at least some frankly admit that they have no revenues (for example, Club FM). But these same webcasters also appear to be very focused on their audience, featuring narrowed content choices distinct from more mainstream rebroadcasts and supporting more connection options. The public service broadcasters, if not particularly innovative in content, are certainly strategizing to maintain their central role in Danes' "life on the screen." DR[1] has created a strong online presence, with some attempt at diversity, particularly in musical offerings. Other broadcasters with public service obligations are innovating as well, as discussed below.

How effectively either privately-owned or public webcasters are able to reach and deliver audiences will depend on how they meet some key challenges in the near future. Although some relief may be on the way, copyright restrictions on webcasting content continue to hamper repurposing audio and video materials, and increase the costs of original productions. Indeed, in an interview Claus Thor Nielsen, Managing Director of DR Interactiv, cited copyright as the key obstacle to expanding online offerings (personal communication, July 18, 2005). Another

---

[1]DR is the acronym for the Danish Broadcasting Corporation, the umbrella company for Danish Radio, Danish Television, DR Multimedia and DR Interaktiv webcasting efforts.

challenge will be creating consumer demand for online offerings, particularly rebroadcasts and streamed content. Online consumers increasingly demand more interactive content, and audio-visual materials that can be manipulated—ripped, mixed and burned—into new combinations for redistribution on the web. The same web-savvy producer-consumers that may be most likely to be early adopters of webcasting want content they can repurpose to create identity and community in the web (Nicholas, 2005). Streamed media simply does not lend itself to these activities (indeed, it is easier for the average consumer to rip music from the radio or video from the television). A third challenge for Danish webcasters will be the emergence of global competition without geographic or regulatory constraints. As the chapters in this book demonstrate, the variety of national broadcasting models combined with new, strictly online players creates asymmetrical opportunities for webcasting success. Danes, the Nordic region, and Europe will have to consider outside pressures as they continue to refine their internet regulations and refocus their online strategies.

To that extent, a review of Danish webcasting is a case study of what occurs as the public service broadcasting tradition and nascent efforts toward media liberalization encounter and adapt to the emerging mediascape. Barely a quarter century ago, Danes encountered electronic news, culture and entertainment through a single, state-owned source. In 2005, Danes enjoy the same plethora of broadcasting options as in most advanced nations: terrestrial and satellite radio; terrestrial, cable and satellite television; regional, national and international networks; and independent stations, many with some web presence. Like the other nations mentioned in this volume, Denmark is adjusting to the emerging multichannel universe. But in addition to these technological or channel options, Danes must also respond to commercialization as both an opportunity for more choices and as a disruption to carefully planned (and very popular) cultural programming. In a country of 5.5 million people about half the size of the U.S. state of Maine, it remains to be seen how webcasting—a transitional technology linking the broadcast past with the infinitely targeted and multimodal future—will develop.

DANISH BACKGROUND

Denmark is a constitutional monarchy; Queen Margaret II assumed the largely ceremonial throne in 1972, becoming the first female monarch since the early 15th century. In 2004, Denmark ranked with Finland and New Zealand as the least corrupt governments in the world (Transparency International, 2004). Despite their commitment to European liberalization, Denmark remains outside the Eurozone, holding onto its Danish Kroner. The Nordic countries, comprising Denmark, Sweden, Norway and Finland, have a long history of both independence and interrelationship. Denmark, Sweden and Norway form a cultural-linguistic market for media goods, but Danish culture clearly has global appeal. Danish architecture and furniture decorate the world. Some of the most heralded Danish entertainers have strong appeal across the region and throughout Europe, including the author Karen Blixen (*Out of Africa*; *Babette's Feast*) and the director Lars von Trier (*Breaking the Waves*; *Dancer in the Dark*). The folk-pop stars Aqua, wildly popular in Europe, reflect the sensibility of many Danish cultural exports, interpreting a unique Danish form known as *fano* for a global audience.

WEBCASTING MARKET ENVIRONMENT

Danish webcasting, to the extent it exists, has evolved out of a Danish mediascape dominated technically and culturally by a few players. The public service companies originally sanctioned by the Danish government, DR, TV2, and P radio (including P1, P2, P3, and P4) are the dominant entrants in terms of sites offered, sophisticated interfaces and content variety. While reliable information on actual viewership—and in the case of TV2, revenues—is scarce, the domination in radio and television appears to extend to the web, at least for now.

An extensive survey of webcasts originating in Denmark reveals that almost all media outlets—newspapers and radio stations in particular—have refrained from broadcasting audio-visual content via the web. There are several possible explanations for this. First, as of this writing, obtaining copyright permission for transmission of music via the web is a complicated and expensive process in Europe. New rules for webcasting music are being developed at the European Union in the autumn of 2005 that may alleviate this problem, but the current situation gives a distinct advantage to large organizations with the resources to either originate programming or negotiate copyrights (Tilak, 2005). A second reason for concentration is the brand dominance of DR, P1–4, and TV2. These networks not only have national brand strength, but their content is redistributed through local and regional radio, television and newspapers throughout the country. Third, their market dominance reflects their position at the center of Danish culture; they are not only "the old standby" but have been responsive to cultural trends as well. Finally, Danish media outside of these firms is very local and relies heavily on local public subsidies and local advertising. It may not make sense for such local players to bother with webcasts, particularly in such a small and sparsely populated country.

Newspapers

There are at least 45 local and regional newspapers in Denmark, including the English-language *Copenhagen Post*, but Danish readership is dominated by three regional dailies. The combined circulation of regional broadsheets *Berlingske*

Tidende, Morgenavisen Jyllands-Posten, and *Politiken* is about one third of all Danish readers (Ceiling & Lesion, 2001). As elsewhere, new technologies including web-based distribution has caused "old media" like newspapers to adapt. In 2002, district weeklies—free, advertising supported papers featuring local news coverage—began distribution to virtually every Dane, and about 90% read them (Ceiling and Lesion, 2001). The success of strategies like this might help explain why Danish newspapers have not yet felt pressured to make their Webster more interesting and interactive.

Although papers use the web to increase circulation, particularly through games and other promotions, very little webcasting activity takes place in their online editions. The most common webcasts are streamed 10 to 15 second news bites offered through Reuters. Four online papers, *Berlingske Tidende* and it's sibling *BT Online, Ekstrabladet,* and the *Jyllands-Posten* offer what they term "web TV" featuring the Reuters snippets in English. Two other papers, *SJ Nyheder* and *Herning Folkblad* offer short promotions for "15 minutter," a current events production of TV Danmark.

Berlignske and *BT Online* are owned by Orkla Media, the fourth largest media company in the Nordic region, which also owns more than 50 local papers. The papers provide news to SBS owned radio stations, and Orkla also owns several stations in Jutland and around Aarhus, the third largest city in Denmark. It owns printing presses and has part ownership in a photo agency. The company also owns Metropol Online, which produces Webster for a number of media companies (Orkla, 2004). Based in Norway (*Berlingske's* offices are in Copenhagen), Orlka reflects the fact that Denmark commercial media tend to be horizontally and vertically integrated, and that Nordic companies tend to own media across the region, rather than within national borders. This integration actually reduces the number of "media faces" that Danes encounter, as detailed below, and works to reduce content variety across integrated outlets.

Radio

Public service radio.   Until very recently, the Danish broadcasting market consisted entirely of public broadcasters and remains dominated by the public service model. Danish Radio was formed in 1925; DR television came along in 1951. Despite recent liberalization and competitive entrants, Danes remain committed to DR programming. DR is financed almost entirely through mandatory license fees; it carries no advertising, but about seven percent of revenues come from various sponsorships and co-productions, and about two percent from merchandise sales. Annual license fees for households with a color television and radio average about $214 in 2005, or about $0.89 per day plus tax. About 93% of all Danish households pay the fee. Revenues for DR exceeded $543 million in 2004 (Facts on DR, 2003).

DR is an independent, publicly financed institution with a workforce of more than 3,400. Created by the Danish government, it has an independent board of directors and a public service mandate requiring that it provide "the Danish population with a wide selection of programs and services comprising news coverage, general information, education, arts and entertainment. Quality, versatility and diversity must be aimed at in the range of programs provided." Public service guidelines also require an emphasis on Danish language and culture and "freedom of information and of expression (is) a primary concern" (Facts on DR, 2003, p. 5).

The Danes' preference for DR programming has remained high, even in the face of liberalization and the introduction of competition and new media alternatives. Nearly 85% of all Danes listen to Danish Radio and about 81% watch Danish Television in a typical week (DR, 2005). DR radio comprises four stations, each with its own public service mandate. Stations P1 and P2 feature classical music and cultural programming; P3 is aimed at young audiences. The fourth "station," P4, is actually nine separate regional channels, featuring news and cultural programming. This multimodal, regional model was adapted to Danish television when it was liberalized in the late 1980s.

More than 300 local radio stations broadcast some programming, although most are part-time and many rebroadcast either public service or commercial programs. Most local radio stations are community-based and municipally-subsidized. Local broadcasters in Denmark are generally overseen by community and regional boards; the great majority of them are non-commercial. This arrangement of boards assures "localness" in radio that is not seen much in the United States, or countries with similar commercial models. For most of these stations, the expanded audience scope offered by webcasting likely would not justify the expense of the enterprise.

Commercial radio.   Commercial radio is dominated by four international firms: SBS, Sky, Talpa, and ABC. Formerly Scandanavian Broadcasting, SBS' Danish offerings include *Radio 2* and *The Voice*. SBS claims that *The Voice* is the most popular Danish station in its genre (pop music). These stations, featuring European and American pop music, are among the few commercial webcasters in the market. SBS owns interests in 10 television networks and 53 radio stations in northern Europe. The company reported operating income of more than $87 million in 2004 (SBS agreed to be acquired by two investment firms for $2.5 billion in August 2005).

Sky Radio, part of NewsCorp's Sky satellite broadcasting firm covering much of Western Europe, broadcasts a digital signal to 24 regional stations throughout the country. Sky purchased the rights to radio P5 in 2004 for $8.6 million; it reaches about 80% of the country. In 2005, Sky claimed to be the most popular commercial radio network in Denmark, with more than 1.1 million listeners, or ten percent of the population (SkyRadio, 2005). Holland's Talpa International purchased the rights to radio P6 in 2004 for about $3.6 million. The satellite network covers about 36% of the country, including Copenhagen. Unlike the Sky deal, Talpa's purchase of P6 did not come with public service obligations. Talpa (which means "mole" in Latin) is part-owned by billionaire John de Mol, creator of the groundbreaking reality television series "Big Brother" and "Fear Factor." The Dutch firm Rabobank purchased 20% of Talpa in 2005 (AFX, 2005). Also in 2005, Sky and Talpa became the first commercial broadcasters on digital radio (DAB) in Denmark, joining what had been an exclusively DR realm. Only about 135,000 Danes (3%) own digital audio receivers, but that number is expected to rise sharply, driven in part by new commercial participation (Worldlab, 2005). The ABC group has 24 terrestrial stations named either *Radio ABC* or *Radio Alfa*. Neither the ABC nor Alfa groups webcast, however.

Television

Public service television. The introduction of TV2 in 1988 changed the television broadcasting picture for Danes. Where once there was a single face, a single visual authority in the country, TV2 created an alternative to the iconic news, culture, and quality programming of DR. TV2, much in the model of P4 radio, consists of a central station and eight regional stations (TV Syd, TV Fyn, TV Ost, TV Nord, TV Lorry, TV Mid-Vest, TV Ostylland, and TV Bornholm) which both distribute and produce some programming. Originally, the network was publicly funded through license fees, with a directive to become advertising supported. Although public oversight and some public service obligations remain with TV2, they operate more independently and are more susceptible to consumer trends. Since 2000, that privatization has accelerated as the Rasmussen government has moved to liberalize Danish media. The stations receive about 20% of their operating revenues from national license fees, but must depend on advertising for the remainder. In 2002, TV2 was reorganized into an independent government-owned company so that it could be privatized; the TV2 national channel is now entirely financed through commercial means. The regional stations retain the old public-private formula, but they are now financially independent; each receives a direct share of license fees from the Danish government and can contract their own advertising. The eight regional stations continue to carry TV2 programming in daily "broadcast windows," specific dayparts dedicated to national programs. Since 2003, TV2 has added two demographically targeted stations. *TV Zulu* targets teens and young adults with a combination of music videos, reality shows, and brash comedies like BBC/HBO's "Ali G," and other international fare. The second spin-off, *TV Charlie*, aims at baby boomers and skews toward the upper end of that demographic with programs like "Twist and Shout" featuring stars of the 1970s.

These stations, available through cable and satellite, are financed entirely through subscription fees and advertising.

The emergence of TV2 cut into DR TV's audience substantially, and DR reacted by creating a DR1 and DR2 in 1996. DR1 is the traditional, terrestrial television broadcast; DR2 is available mainly via satellite and programming is generally available during prime time and the evening hours (Jauert & Prehn, 2000). The two stations reflect DR's strategy of "something for everyone." DR1 is the place to find traditional Danish cultural programming, documentaries, news, and public affairs. DR2 features more specialized genres, with both children's programming and edgier fare for adults.

Danes watch an average of two and half hours of television daily (Ceiling and Lesion, 2001), with the two DR channels and the two TV2 channels each garnering about a third of the audience, a slightly smaller share than the public networks in Norway, Sweden and Finland (Facts on DR, 2003). There are about 50 local television stations broadcasting at least part of the day in Denmark. Local stations are financed through membership and subscription fees, and to a lesser extent through municipal subsidies and sales of transmission time. All stations are controlled by local boards, similar to the national boards that supervise DR and TV2, and the local newspaper boards (Danish Cultural Ministry, 2005).

Commercial television.   Since 2002, cable and satellite stations, no longer require licensing, only notification to the government (Lett, Vilstrup, et al., 2003). This agreement positions cable and satellite systems at the leading edge of liberalization in Denmark, as demonstrated by the purchase of P5 and P6 radio channels and international entry into television. The private television landscape is dominated by three cable and satellite players, including TV3 and 3+, brands for Kinnevik's Modern Times Group. These stations are broadcast from London and are also available in Sweden, reflecting a more international sensibility. The Modern Times Group (MTG) operates, Viasat, the largest satellite service in Denmark, and claims to be the "the largest Free-to-air and Pay-TV operator in the Nordic and Baltic regions and the largest commercial radio operator in Northern Europe" according to its website (www.kinnevik.se). TV3 doubled its operating income to more than $8 million in the first half of 2005 (MTG, 2005).

Canal+ is the leading pay TV channel cluster in the Nordic countries (Denmark, Sweden, Norway and Finland) with more than 725,000 subscribers (Canal Plus, 2005). Canal+ emerged in 1997 as a joint venture between Norway's telecommunications provider, Telenor, and Vivendi-Universal's French subsidiary Canal+. In 2001, Vivendi sold its shares back to Telenor, which operates its cable and satellite systems as Canal Digital DK in Denmark (Forrester, 2003). It distributes Danish and international television as well as exclusive film and sports programming. Offerings in Denmark feature five premium channels including an original programming channel, three film channels and Canal+ Sport. Canal+ owns Nordic satellite broadcast rights to most Hollywood studio productions and exclusive rights to distribute Europe's premier football (soccer) leagues in the Nordic region. Viewers can receive Canal+ throughout Denmark via satellite, cable or the emerging digital terrestrial network.

Completing Denmark's private television broadcasting picture is TvDanmark, principally owned by SBS. In 2000, the TvDanmark signal was split; TVDanmark 2 consists of 15 regional affiliates situated in the largest cities in Denmark, broadcast via UHF and satellite out of Copenhagen, and TvDanmark 1 is broadcast via satellite from London. All Danish television networks must carry DR1, DR2, TV2 and TVDanmark 2.

As more Danes subscribe to cable and satellite packages, the traditional national networks are recontextualized within a growing set of offerings with an increasingly international flavor. Increased competition in broadcasting generally provokes new strategies for both content and distribution. Commercial broadcasters in the United States and elsewhere secure audiences by using genre as a branding strategy, and by using the web to aggregate audiences in communities of interest. Online communities use network Webster to both consume and participate in the brands, reinforcing their identification with the programming (Edgerton & Nicholas, in press). Danish public and quasi-public networks must find ways to create more niche programming while preserving their unique public service role. There is some evidence that both DR and TV2 are developing more niche programming, and indeed that DR is using the public service "genre" as a brand. Both networks are aggressively pursuing online audiences as a way of both extending their brand and reinforcing connections with their audiences. Given these imperatives and the natural advantages of incumbents, it is not surprising that they are the early leaders in Danish webcasting.

WEBCASTING IN DENMARK

Internet Penetration and Use

The Danish telephone system KTAS (now TeleDanmark) did not reach one million subscribers until 1978, despite opening its first exchange 97 years earlier. Today, internet penetration and use is quite high and Denmark is a European leader in broadband access. Denmark tops Europe in internet and mobile phone penetration and in e-business implementation, and leads the world in information technology spending per capita (MAIT, 2004). According to the European Commission, Denmark is the "information society global leader" (eGovernment News, 2004). More than three out of four Danes use the internet and 56% of them go online daily. Internet connectivity is expected to rise to about 4.3 million by 2007, out of a total population of less than 5.5 million (CIA Factbook, 2005). The Danish telecommunications market was liberalized in 1995, and TeleDanmark, the incumbent monopoly provider, reduced its broadband charges by up to 65% shortly thereafter (Point-Topic, 2005); Danes can access broadband from TDC for about $47 month (512/128 mbps). As a result, ADSL broadband is almost universally available in Denmark, and individual broadband subscriptions (both cable and ADSL) have surpassed 36%; about two-thirds use ADSL (ITU, 2005).

Nearly all (97%) Danish businesses and organizations are connected to the internet and more than 80% of Danish enterprises connect via the high speed networks (Eurostat, 2005). Danes may be even more connected in the future. A joint study by IBM and *The Economist* magazine business intelligence unit ranked Denmark as the top "e-ready" country in the world in 2004 (Greenspan, 2004). The study ranks countries in six categories including: connectivity and infrastructure, business climate, consumer and business technology adoption, social and cultural environment, legal and policy climate, and supporting e-services. Denmark's technological sophistication reflects a deep public commitment historically to communicating with the world as well as its more recent cautious invitation to bring the world to Denmark. The appendix shows the list of the leading Danish webcasters.

Public Service Webcasting

DR. The Danish webcasting landscape is dominated numerically by DR. The state-owned broadcaster claims more than 800,000 weekly visits to its consolidated site, the only firm audience figures available. DR simulcasts its radio programming and streams multiple channels of "web only" audio programming, in addition to producing a few programs exclusively for the web (see Table 12–1). According to Claus Thor Nielsen, Managing Director of DR Interactiv, DR's site receives more than 1.1 million requests for rebroadcasts each week (Nielsen, 2005). DR offers programming on demand, but restricts offerings to those television and radio shows produced by DR. As with most other webcasters, copyright restrictions appear to be the most limiting factor in content offerings. "Rights issues are a huge problem to us…(including) rights to archived programs" Nielsen notes. "Most of our streamed content is produced by DR. Sometimes we buy rights to other programs, but usually it is too expensive for us. The return on investment is simply too low" (C. T. Nielsen, personal communication, July 18, 2005).

DR streams all audio channels via a sophisticated Flash-based program module titled "DR NetRadio." The NetRadio module allows users to quickly scan channels and stream with a single click. In addition to DR radio, the four "P" stations are simulcast. P1 features news, debate, and social programming in half hour and 1 hour segments. P2 is known as "kvalitetsbetonede" or quality radio. Its programming consists of classic jazz, "root music," arts, and culture, with lengthy discussions wrapped around bits of performance and recorded music. DR's newest radio offer-

TABLE 12–1
Revenue Source by Webcaster Type

	Clicks-and-Bricks		Pure-Play	
Revenue source	n	%	n	%
License fees	6	40.0	20	83.3
Advertising/sponsorship	8	53.3	2	8.3
Subscription	1	6.7	0	0
Pay-per-view	0	0	1	4.2
E-commerce	0	0	1	4.2

ing, P3, streams uncensored rap, dance, and club music, all very international in flavor, aimed at a younger audience. The national P4 Danmark station, as well as the nine regional P4 stations, are all simulcast. The stations are not very diverse, except when it comes to regionally focused news reports. All feature a combination of news, music and talk radio.

In addition to simulcasts and a few on-demand programs, DR produces 18 specialized audio web streams spanning a broad range of demographics and taste publics. These include the fancifully named *Barometer* and *Barracuda*, along with *Boogieradio, Gyldne Genhor* (Golden Oldies), a children's cartoon music stream, and specialized culture, news, and sports programming.

DR1 videostreams four news updates each day, except Saturday. Each pre-recorded clip lasts from about 20 seconds to 2-1/2 minutes. Additional updates and special reports on news, business, weather, sports and entertainment are of similar length. Each are captured directly from news broadcasts and streamed at 256 kbps (DR says they will increase to 1 mbps by early 2006). Streams also feature original in-studio interviews. DR's second station, DR2, features on-demand "gyldne klip," or "best of" videos dating back as far as 2002 (see Table 12–2). The videos feature cultural "evergreen" stories. Contemporaneous video offerings available via the DR2 website are identical to those offered on DR1. DR also features "mobile casts" for mobile phones with subscription to DR Mobil services. News, culture, and music from DR programming is available in a variety of formats for mobile devices, including GSM and Bluetooth. In all, DR offers a broad set of transmission modes through which consumers can receive programming that is more targeted, though perhaps no less familiar, than its various broadcast offerings.

TV2.   The public-commercial TV2 network has created the "Sputnik" service for downloading television and film programs, in partnership with Nordisk Film, a

TABLE 12–2
Content Source by Webcaster Type

Content Source	Clicks-and-Bricks		Pure-Play		Total	
	n	%	n	%	n	%
Original	1	5.0	19	95.0	20	48.8
Repurposed	9	45.0	1	5.0	10	24.4
Simulcast	10	50.0	1	5.0	11	16.8

subsidiary of the Danish media giant Egemont. TV2 Sputnik charges for both television and film streams. Sputnik television is available by subscription for about three dollars per day, prorated for longer subscriptions. The on-demand service allows users to select from many of the programs available via TV2 regular broadcast programming and a host of domestic and international films.

Sputnik is the primary webcaster of Hollywood, international and Danish films in Denmark. In 2005, Nordisk increased the number of films available to Sputnik subscribers to nearly 400 through an arrangement with Scanbox, a Danish corporation that controls rights to about 2,000 international and 300 local films (Scanbox, 2005). Charges for each film viewing range from as low as three dollars for some documentaries to seven dollars for premier films. Typically, a feature film or documentary is available for streaming for 24 hours, although some films may be viewed multiple times, depending on copyright terms. Due to copyright restrictions, films viewed through Sputnik cannot be shared outside the original computer (nor can films be viewed on computers located outside of Denmark). Sputnik also makes film clips, trailers and other promotional material available for free. Films and television are shown via "broadband" but no reference to actual delivery speed is available.

Browser Dominance

Both DR and TV2 videostreams are available only through the Microsoft Explorer web browser (Netscape Navigator and Firefox, the Mozilla open-source browser, for instance, do not work). In fact, many DR and TV2 video links first prompt users to acquire various Microsoft multimedia software, including incessant prompts to upgrade to Windows Media 9 (despite that fact that Windows Media 10 is available in the United States). This close integration of content and software when combined with copyright restrictions leaves a narrow channel of opportunity for potential users. Users of public webcasts must acquire and utilize branded (non-Danish) software for most programming, and at the same time they must demonstrate their connection from a Danish ISP to acquire films and presumably other independently produced programming via TV2. Although there are likely technical reasons for the tight integration of Danish public broadcasting and Microsoft products (it is easier to support one platform than multiple platforms) the practice would seem to run counter to European Union legal decisions regarding Microsoft in other spheres, and certainly inhibits competition from other browsers and multimedia software. (This integration is not the case with DR or TV2 mobile services, which support multiple software platforms, including the Real Player, nor is it a problem with music streaming from DR's multi-channel NetRadio, which meshes seamlessly with both Navigator and Firefox browsers.) Nevertheless, Danish webcasting presents an interesting—and typical—case where the "openness" of the web is constrained by invisible technical and legal barriers (Lessig, 2002).

Commercial Webcasting

The list of private and independent webcasters in Denmark is neither long nor especially varied. Webcast programming consists chiefly of simulcast audio streaming punctuated by brief video snippets. Although the presence of media-related Webster is high, none of Denmark's more than 100 daily newspapers have created audio streams, and only a handful of top broadcasting firms feature any streaming at all. Rather, broadcasters are more likely to offer informational pages, with some e-commerce opportunities for ringtones, concert tickets, and logo paraphernalia. Design energy on these sites is high, but stream offerings are slim.

TV Danmark (SBS) broadcasts mainly independently produced television, primarily American and European series, including *South Park*, *CSI*, and *Will & Grace*. Because of copyright issues, these mainstays cannot be webcast. TV Danmark streams a short news and events oriented program called *15 Minutter*, and *Seerforum*, a consumer news program. The shows collect material from TV Danmark's eight regional stations and are available only to those who have created a member profile. Both stream at more than 2 mbps in Windows Media Player.

The Voice FM and Radio 2 simulcast the SBS-owned satellite and terrestrial radio services. The stations feature mainly pop music, with a few news updates sprinkled throughout the day, typical of music-oriented FM radio. Music at both sites is easily accessible via a 96kbps stream on either Windows Media Player or Real Player. The trans-Nordic stations take a pass on some obvious e-commerce opportunities. Despite their hip and technologically trendy appearance, The Voice and Radio 2 offer surprisingly few avenues for users to interact with each other or purchase media. Their chief offerings cross-promote concerts, albums, DVDs, films and other media purchase opportunities not sold directly from their sites. Both The Voice and Radio 2 advertise their SMS (Short Message Service) dating service, but the service was not running at the time of this writing. Ringtones are also advertised but consumers must dial up an outside service to purchase them.

SkyRadio offers a remarkably static website, with a SkyRadio player supported by T-Mobile systems at 96 kbps, which requires a separate plug-in in most browsers. Like the SBS stations, Sky simulcasts its digital satellite signal—featuring mainly soft hits from the U.S. and Europe—promotes its on-air offerings, and abstains from most e-commerce(they do sell concert tickets in their "VIP Section"). The Sky site is used primarily for promoting its on-air offerings and introducing listeners to the faces behind the radio voices. The lack of interactivity at SkyRadio.dk may seem perplexing at first, but in fact it is typical of the satellite broadcasters, who tend to focus on geographic footprint and exclusive distribution deals. Sky's position may change soon, however. Parent company NewsCorp, who has previously shown remarkably little interest in new media, has spent more than $1.5 billion on internet properties in 2005. The company recently made a series of moves to invest in internet enterprises, including the purchase of interactive gaming firm IGN for $650 million (BBC, 2005), and deals for Scout Media, a sports information website, MySpace, a social networking site, and the Blinkx search engine (Hoffmeister, 2005).

The nascent webcasting efforts of these two international conglomerates clearly do not match the depth and breadth of their organizations. To date they have failed to press their presumed advantages in brand recognition and resources in the web realm. This leaves an opening for smaller, independent organizations to capture market share. But to date, few have stepped up to fill the gap.

The Independents

While the big corporations rely on repurposed radio content and the visuals aimed at the broadest audiences, the ghost of Radio Mercur may rise again in the form of a small handful of savvy independent webcasters. For now, only one, Jubii, appears to be profitable, but others may prove disruptive in the short term. RiseFM calls itself "Denmark's #1 Underground Radio." The RiseFM site is produced entirely in English and, as might be expected, this pure-play station spins non-stop dance music. The station is ad supported, but claims on its site to have "no income at all." RiseFM's stream is available at 128 kbps on Windows Media, RealOne, Winamp, or Xbox media players. The station partners with various dance and rap Webster, including Danskrap.dk and Trancedjs.dk, but those stations do not webcast. RiseFM features both resident and guest DJs that program music and features a chat room.

Although neither site explicitly mentions the other, RiseFM and ClubFM are clearly closely related. Both sites feature virtually the same FAQ and the stations have identical explanations of their business (both claim no profits). Both are pure-play stations featuring dance and club music. One technical difference is that ClubFM works only through Windows Media Player and currently streams at a lower bitrate (changing to 128 kbps in September 2005). Each site does have its own personality, however. ClubFM features "band battles" pitting musical styles in a popularity contest, each pushed by its own web DJ and subject to listener comments. The station also plays a broader mix of hits, while Rise FM sticks mainly to trance and rap favorites. Both stations are frankly political; RiseFM has aligned itself with the Danish anti-child pornography movement, while ClubFM features news and photos from the popular "We Are Not Afraid" anti-terrorist campaign.

TABLE 12–3
Program Genre Comparison by Webcaster Type

Program Genre	Clicks-and-Bricks		Pure-Play		Total	
	n	%	n	%	n	%
Video						
Movies	1	1.8	1	6.3	2	2.7
TV Commercials	4	7.0	2	12.5	6	8.3
TV programs (entertainment)	4	7.0	2	12.5	6	8.3
Education/instruction	3	5.3	1	6.3	4	5.5
Film trailers/highlights	2	3.5	2	12.5	4	5.5
Business	10	17.5	1	6.3	11	15.2
News clips/interviews	10	17.5	1	6.3	11	15.2
Talk shows	10	17.5	1	6.3	11	15.2
Music videos	2	3.5	1	6.3	3	4.2
Documentaries	3	5.3	2	12.5	5	6.9
Cartoons/animation	3	5.3	2	12.5	5	6.9
Sports	1	1.8	0	0	1	1.3
Danish Culture	3	5.3	0	0	3	4.2
Audio						
Music	6	40.0	19	42.2	25	41.7
News	4	26.6	13	28.9	17	28.3
Public affairs/culture	4	26.6	13	28.9	17	28.3
Sports	1	6.7	0	0	1	1.7

RiseFM's tenuous existence combined with programming that speaks directly to urban youth gives it an edginess lacking in most Danish webcasts. Its international flavor and reliance on English only, also distinguish it from both the public service and blandly commercial alternatives (see Table 12–3). It remains to be seen whether alternatives like RiseFm and ClubFM can stimulate enough imitators to diversify ownership and programming in Danish webcasting.

Completing the small group of independents is the quirky Jubii, a pure-play unique to the Danish webcasting scene. Unlike most of the other sites described in this study, Jubii resembles an online media store, with both downloads and direct sales of media artifacts. Content on Jubii ranges from ringtone and single song downloads (about $1.45 each) to DVD purchases, online dating and matchmaking services, online gaming, pornography and live chat. Those services most relevant to this study—music downloads and adult films—are provided via the pay per download model. Users can create a purchase profile and use major credit cards, similar to Amazon or other media purchase services. While users download songs, the films are streamed at the time of purchase. Jubii sets itself apart from other Danish webcasters in its variety of games, music and videos, and its broad target audience. Only on Jubii can one both stream adult videos and download ringtones and games clearly aimed at children and teens. Jubii serves its various publics by segmenting its site offerings, dividing up chatrooms, online debates, and topical news areas among others. Jubii features online dating, job searches, photo processing, and animated greeting card services. It offers special sections for women, travelers, investors, and other groups. Appeals to these groups depend on the e-commerce model, with limited advertising for special offerings, for instance, travel specials.

OUTLOOK OF THE WEBCASTING INDUSTRY IN DENMARK

Today, DR clearly dominates Danish webcasting, offering 31 of the 44 webcasts located for this study. Perhaps expecting a 21st century "pirate effect," DR has anticipated Danish reaction to the "forbidden fruit" of pure-play webcasters. This time, DR appears to be expanding before serious competition strikes and its operating guidelines call for continued upgrades and new offerings (DR, 2004). An analysis of the webcasting picture in Denmark indicates that a combination of the public service broadcasting tradition and the "freerider" web culture combine to make commercial exploitation of webcasting relatively rare within its borders. The most common routes to revenues among Danish webcasters are the license fee (67%) and advertising (26%); pay-per, subscriptions and e-commerce structures are each used by less than three percent of webcasters. Advertising is indeed the most common revenue stream for commercial broadcasters (77%), which feature ads both in-stream (usually through simulcasts of radio programming) and on the site. E-commerce strategies are a key feature of only one site, Jubii, although several others are designed to exploit this opportunity in the future. The most common commercial strategy is the promotion of off-site purchasing opportunities, particularly ringtones. As the revenue stream for ringtones, games, icons and other one-off downloadables shrinks, however, commercial webcasters will need to develop more consistent and identifiable value on their sites (Young, 2005). Only two webcasters, Jubii and TV2, have any real marketing presence. TV2 uses both subscription and pay-per offerings, while Jubii delivers a variety of purchasing opportunities including pay-per and direct sales. Of the 13 commercial non-public webcasts studied, two (RiseFM and ClubFM) claim to make no profits at all.

What are we to make of a highly-educated, culturally-sophisticated, extremely well-connected society with so little indigenous webcasting? The Danes' global leadership in digital lifestyle indicators, including digital media adoption rates and wide availability of broadband connections, suggests that the Danish webcasting market should be ready for expansion. One of the key barriers to growth, copyright protections that in many instances make re-transmission prohibitively expensive, may be eased by new rules and the creation of uniform markets. The European Union was scheduled to release new copyright rules pertaining to transmission of audio and visual programs via the internet in August 2005, and DR expects that it will abide by those conventions (C. T. Nielsen, personal communication, July 18, 2005). The new rules will be designed to create single copyright market, alleviating the need for rights holders and webcasters to negotiate fees nation-by-nation. EU Internal Market and Services Commissioner Charlie McCreevy noted that the EU has to "improve the licensing of music copyright on the internet. The absence of pan-European copyright licenses makes it difficult for new European-based online services to take off. This is why we are proposing the creation of Europe-wide copyrights clearance" (Tilak, 2005). The initiation of this license should free up DR to offer more content, and make it easier for commercial webcasters to proliferate, provided license fees are reasonable.

Beyond regulatory obstacles, there are a few cultural conditions that account for slow growth in webcasting. To ascertain why a nation might not jump into webcasting, we must first ask why people use webcasts as opposed to other media. Beyond the novelty of seeing something in a new medium, four key conditions structure the utility of webcasting. First, webcasting has emerged as convenient way to get audio-visual materials that are transmitted in other channels. The inferior quality of most webcasts (tinny-sounding computer speakers, small video windows) means that webcasting is a second choice in these instances. One key reason to use webcasting is to overcome time and/or location barriers. Some webcast users time-shift media, listening or viewing on demand, rather than according to a broadcaster's schedule. They effectively shift locations too, by tapping into broadcasts via the web that are not available in their area. This shifting is one key motivation to use webcasts. A second reason is to obtain programming available only via webcasts. Compelling original and exclusive programs will draw webcasts audiences provided they have serviceable equipment and bandwidth. Third, consumers will be drawn to webcasting when it provides a value vis-à-vis other means of transmission. If webcasts are cheaper to acquire at similar quality, they may be preferred over other means of distribution. If copyrighted material can be acquired for free, as in some peer-to-peer and private networks, this value soars. Finally, some consumers may find webcasts particularly convenient, especially those that tend to place networked computers at the center of their personal communication and information sphere. These users are already busy blogging, using peer-to-peer networks to find music and video, mixing and burning their own media products, and performing other tasks. Webcasting becomes a component of a multi-windowed media sphere for these multitasking users.

In light of these conditions for use, the cultural environment in Denmark may make webcasting less immediately useful for many users. The quality of Danish radio and television is quite high, due in part to the public service model and to restrictions on the number and duration of advertisements in other networks. All Danes who own radio or television must pay license fees, and virtually all Danes own these devices, so in effect they have already paid for much of the content that would be repurposed for webcasts. Cable and satellite penetration give the average Dane access to additional variety of audio-visual content from both domestic and international sources. Although Danes are highly productive, and the culture of work is changing in Denmark, they are hardly the workaholic culture of their cousins in America, for example. Danish culture places a high value on family time and Danes seem to be more successful at segregating work and home life than many American families. While broadband penetration to Danish homes is nearly 37%, most Danes still access high-speed internet at work, where watching or listening to webcasts is less desirable. Webcasts would represent a market value only if they were original to the web, or if the potential viewers did not already subscribe to a cable or satellite network. Finally, the very "localness" of Danish broadcasting may also limit any experimentation with webcasting.

None of these cultural attributes is universal among Danes, of course. With an extensive infrastructure already in place, we should expect to see accelerated diffusion of webcasting as it takes hold in the Danish popular imagination. Meanwhile, it is very likely that a lot of webcasting takes place outside the realm of traditional broadcasting structures and beneath the surface easily accessible via search engines. One of the major limitations of this study is its focus on public and commercial webcasting, whereas the true pirates and pioneers of the web are navigating the waters of what is often referred to as the deep web or "darknet" (Biddle, England, Peinado, & Willman, 2002). In these networks, which generally do not use common web protocols and do not publish web addresses, people connect only to those they trust. Darknet participants share media in a variety of ways including via streaming and events, one time webcasts of original creations (Lassica, 2005). In an era of regulatory uncertainty in Europe and in a nation with a tradition of centralized media, the creative people that would broaden the webcasting scene in Denmark may devote their resources instead to darknet outlets. Unlike Radio Mercur, which floated within view of the Danish coast and broadcast via standard frequencies, darknet webcasting functions like a submarine, beneath the surface and always in motion. If the Danish commercial and independent webcasting scene remains undifferentiated, the dominance of DR may force Danes to seek out darknet webcasters or look outside their borders for the next set of "pirates" to provide juicier, if not strictly forbidden, fruit.

REFERENCES

AFX (2005, September 23). *Newsbrief.* Retrieved September 26, 2005, from http://uk.biz.yahoo.com/050912/323/frtyr.html

BBC (2005, September 8). NewsCorp to buy internet firm IGN. *BBC News UK Edition.* Retrieved September 28, 2005, from http://news.bbc.co.uk/1/hi/business/4226170.stm

Biddle, P., England, P., Peinado, M., & Willman, B. (2002). The darknet and the future of content distribution. Paper presented to the *ACM Workshop on Digital Rights Management*, November 18, 2002. Retrieved October 1, 2005, from http://crypto.stanford.edu/DRM2002/prog.html

Canal Plus (2005, August). *About Canal Plus.* Retrieved July 22, 2005, from http://www.canalplus.dk/page.asp?guid = 42D5705B—EE62–4D25–958A—45849859ED53

CIA Factbook. (2005) *Rank order population.* Retrieved July 18, 2005, from http://www.cia.gov/cia/publications/factbook/rankorder/2119rank.html

Danish Cultural Ministry. (2005). *Three levels of broadcasting.* Retrieved from September 12, 2005, from http://www.kum.dk/sw3205.asp

DR. (2004). *Danish Broadcasting Corporation annual report, English summary.* Retrieved July 5, 2005, from http://www.dr.dk/omdr/pdf/2004-DR-ANNUAL_REPORT.pdf

DR. (2005). *Facts on market share.* Retrieved July 15, 2005, from http://www.dr.dk/omdr/index.asp?aid = 33

Edgerton, G., & Nicholas, K. (2005). I want my niche TV: Genre as networking strategy. In Edgerton, G. & Rose, B. (Eds.), *Thinking outside the box: Television genres in transition* (pp. 247–267). Lexington, KY: University of Kentucky Press.

eGovernment News. (2004, November 10). *Denmark is the new information society global leader, says IADBC.* Retrieved July 12, 2005, from http://europa.eu.int/idabc/en/document/3462/5648

Eurostat. (2005, May 13) *Half of individuals and nine out of ten enterprises used the internet in 2004.* Retrieved July 17 2005, from http://europa.eu.int/idabc/en/document/3462/5648

Facts on DR 2003. (2003). Retrieved July 26, 2005, from http://www.dr.dk/omdr/pdf/FACTS—2003-PDF.pdf

Forrester, C. C. (2003, April). Nordic exposure. *World Screen.* Retrieved September 15, 2005 from http://www.worldscreen.com/featuresarchive.php?filename = 0403scan.txt)

Greenspan, R. (2004, April 27). Denmark deemed most 'E-Ready'. *Clickz Stats and Geographics.* Retrieved July 15, 2005 from http://www.clickz.com/stats/sectors/geographics/article.php/3345751

Hoffmeister, S. (2005, September 9). Murdoch adding to online empire. *Los Angeles Times, section 1.* Retrieved September 20, 2005, from http://www.latimes.com/business/la-fi-newscorp9sep09,1,6119093.story?ctrack = 1&cset = true

International Telecommunications Union (ITU). (2005, April 13). ITU's new broadband statistics for 1 January 2005. *ITU Strategy and Policy Unit Newslog.* Retrieved October 22, 2005, from http://www.itu.int/osg/spu/newslog/ITUs+New+Broadband+Statistics+For+1+January+2005.asp

Jauert, P., & Prehn, O. (2000). *Danish media landscape.* Retrieved July 18 2005, from http://www.ejc.nl/jr/emland/denmark.html#2

Jauert, P. (2001, December). *Formats in radio broadcasting: The American-Danish connection. p.o.v,* V.12. Retrieved June 21, 2005, from http://imv.au.dk/publikationer/pov/Issue_12/section_3/artc2A.html.

Lassica, J. (2005). *Darknet: Hollywood's war against the digital generation.* New York: John Wiley & Sons.

Lessig, L. (2002). *The future of ideas*. New York: Random House.

Lett, Vilstrup, & Partners. (2003) *New media policy accord, new radio and television broadcasting act in Denmark and act on TV2 Denmark A/S*. Retrieved July 15 2005, from http://www.legal500.com/devs/denmark/tm/dktm_003.htm

MAIT. (2004, February) Danish ICT industry. *E-News*, vol. 23. Retrieved October 10 2005, from http://www.elcot.com/mait-reports/danish%20ICT.pdf

Mishkind, B. (n.d.) *Old radio: Danish broadcasting*. Retrieved August 5, 2005, from http://www.oldradio.com/archives/international/denmark.html

MTG (Modern Times Group). (2005). Financial results for the second quarter and six months ended 30 June 2005. Retrieved on September 7, 2005, from http://wpy.observer.se/wpyfs/00/00/00/00/00/06/0A/A9/release.html

Nicholas, K. (2005). Dig that cowboy: textual networks in the adaptation process. In Nicholas, K. & Christensen, J.R. (Eds.), *Open windows: remediation in global film adaptation* (pp.16–40). Aalborg, Denmark: Aalborg University Press.

Nordic Capital. (2003). *Nordic Capital and Baker Capital acquire Canal+ Television AB —the leading premium pay-TV provider in the Nordic region*. Retrieved September 14, 2005, from http://www.nordiccapital.se/press/030909%20en.pdf

Orkla. (2004). Orkla media report. Retrieved July 22, 2005, from http://www.orkla-media.no/dav/49AC93F12F.pdf

Pedersen, J. F. (2000). The role and function of public service broadcasting in Denmark. Speech given at the *Transformation of Broadcasters* in Fry, Belgrade, Yugoslavia, December 10–12, 2000. Retrieved June 14, 2005, from http://www.b92.net/events/conference/speach-denmark.html

Point-Topic. (2005). *Denmark broadband overview*. Retrieved July 12, 2005, from http://www.point-topic.com/content/operatorSource/profiles/Denmark/Denmark.htm&comp_id = 761&g = 1

Scanbox. (2005). Corporate information web page. Retrieved from October 2, 2005 http://www.scanbox.dk/intl/2005.htm.

SkyRadio. (2005, May). *Sky Radio er den mest populære kommercielle radio*. Retrieved August 1, 2005, from http://www.skyradio.dk/index.aspx?FilterId = 974&ChapterId = 1753&ContentId = 29233

Søllinge, J. D., & Leksikon, G. (2001). *Danish mass media*. Retrieved from September 22, 2005, from http://denmark.dk/portal/page?_pageid = 374,477822&_dad = portal&_schema = PORTAL

Tilak, J. (2005, July 11). Commission proposes pan-European online music licensing. *Digital Media Europe*. Retrieved August 4, 2005, from http://www.dmeurope.com/default.asp?ArticleID = 8985

Transparency International. (2004). *Corruption perceptions index*. Retrieved October 1, 2005, from http://www.transparency.org/cpi/2004/cpi2004.en.html#cpi2004

Worldlab. (2005, July 1). Commercial broadcasters Sky Radio and Radio 100FM (Talpa) on DAB in Denmark from 1/9. Retrieved September 17, 2005, from http://www.worlddab.org/images/DR-Pressrelease-new_services—01–07–05.pdf

WPY Observer. (2005, July 25). *Financial results for the second quarter and six months ended 30 June 2005*. Retrieved September 5, 2005, from http://wpy.observer.se/wpyfs/00/00/00/00/00/06/0A/A9/release.html

Young, K. (2005, August 1). Ringtones fall flat. *Forbes.com*. Retrieved August 1, 2005 from http://www.forbes.com/technology/2005/08/01/ringtone-sales-flat-cx_vnu_0801ringtone.html.

APPENDIX
List of Leading Webcasters

DR Group & (P1–4)

- http://www.dr.dk/netradio/

TV2

- http://tv2.dk/

Jubii

- http://www.jubii.dk/

Sky Radio

- http://www.skyradio.dk/index.aspx

Club FM—streaming

- http://www.clubfm.klubsider.dk/

Rise FM

- http://www.risefm.com

Kanal 5/TV Danmark

- http://www.tvdanmark.dk/

SBS Group

Radio 2

- http://www.radio2.dk/

The Voice

- http://www.thevoice.fm/#

Radio ABC Group

Radio ABC

- http://www.radioabc.dk/

Radio Alfa

- http://www.radioalfa.dk/

Radio Silkeborg

- http://www.radiosilkeborg.dk/

PART IV

Webcasting Business Practices and Dynamics in the Asian Pacific

CHAPTER 13

China: The Largest Broadband User in Asia and the Second Largest Broadband Market in the World

Min Hang
Jönköping University, Sweden

Dahong Min and Binyan Yang
China Academy of Social Science, China

Recent years have witnessed remarkable increase in the development of webcasting business in China. As the largest broadband user in Asia and the second largest broadband market in the world, China holds great potentials to explore business opportunities brought by the emerging webcasting business. This chapter reviews the market environment and the status quo of the webcasting business practices in China; it also discusses the pertinent issues facing the market in order to seek for suggestions for future development.

WEBCASTING MARKET ENVIRONMENT

The Growth of the Media Industries in China

Since the founding of the People's Republic of China in 1949, a communist media system introduced from the former Soviet Union had been established and prevailed for a quite long time in China. Constrained by a very strict policy control, media had been considered merely a tool for political propaganda. All the media entities were owned, operated, and financed by the government, and the media sectors were operating totally outside the economic world.

The media liberalization and deregulation took place in China after the adoption of the policy of "reforming and opening to the outside world," initiated by the

257

late Chinese top leader Deng Xaioping in the late 1970s. Commercial advertising emerged in 1979, and TV stations started to gain their revenues from advertising and sponsorship. During the 1980s, the socio-market economy mechanism was introduced and the media industries grew substantially. Since the 1990s, more consolidation and industrialization occurred, and especially after getting into the new millennium, tremendous changes happened in the media field.

Nowadays, with the economic boom and the rise of the advertising expenditure, the media industries have become increasingly prosperous. According to a study conducted by Tsinghua University (Cui, 2005), the total revenue of China's core media business reached $39.3 billion in 2004. The major revenue sources include advertising, broadcasting services, book publishing, newspaper and magazine issuing, box-office value of films, sales of audiovisual products, wireless services, games, and other related services.

The study shows that there were 570 publishing houses in China in 2004, generating a total revenue of $13.2 billion. There were 9,047 types of periodicals and 2,119 types of newspaper published, generating $6.03 billion. In the audiovisual media sector, the gross income of the national radio and TV industry was $9.3 billion in 2004, an increase of $719 million over 2003. The income of the motion pictures reached $43.3 billion (not including income of film AV products, fees paid by TV stations, incomes of network film services, and incomes of issues in the secondary market), and the box-office value of domestic films reached $18.4 million, an increase of $7.2 million over the year before.

By September 2004, there are over 1,900 radio and TV stations in China, providing 1,800 sets of radio programs, 2,200 sets of analog TV programs and 48 sets of digital TV programs. The annual feature-length film production reached 200 in 2004, and the TV series production reached 11,500 episodes (Sun, Huang, & Hu, 2005). The cable TV subscription has totaled 100 million households by 2004 and there are 6,000 cinemas and over 10,000 movie screens in the country. In addition, The internet industry is also growing significantly, and the whole media industries are in the midst of rapid changes while many of the traditional media services are going to digital.

INTERNET USAGE AND BROADBAND PENETRATION IN CHINA

With a population of 1.3 billion, China contains the biggest market potential to develop the digital media services. According to a recent survey conducted by the CNNIC (2005) on internet usage in this world's most populous nation, there were 103 million people in China who became internet users by June 30, 2005. The number represents a year-on-year growth of 18.4 % netizens. In addition to the increasing internet usage, the number of PCs online reached 45.6 million, and the number of broadband users reached 53 million, an increase of 23.8% over the previous year. It is the first time in China that the number of the broadband users surpassed the dial-up users; and the number of netizens and broadband users in China is the second largest in the world as of June 30, 2005, following the United States. According to figures published by the market analyst Point Topic Ltd. (Sayer, 2005), China is predicted to have more broadband internet subscribers than the U.S. by the end of 2005, assuming the number of subscribers to broadband internet continues to grow at the current rates.

As to the access services, most subscribers used broadband by ADSL. In 2004, 75% of broadband subscribers use the ADSL services, and this market share is still growing. Next to ADSL are the access services by LAN, XDSL, Cable modems, LMDS, LEO, and PLC (iResearch, 2004). The broadband access service market is emerging to be very competitive in China. Telecommunication companies are continuously launching different marketing strategies to attract broadband users and to stimulate the expansion of the broadband market. However, despite the fast growth of the broadband market, the bandwidth deployment is still limited. For example, Beijing Telecom offers only two bandwidths for the ADSL users: 512KB and 1MB (Min & Yang, 2005). It is thus expected that the technological environment could be improving with the development of network infrastructure in the following years in order to meet the growing market demand for the webcasting services.

Policy Environment

China's webcasting business is strictly regulated by the state government. The major responsible authority for webcasting administration is the State Administration of Radio, Film and Television (SARFT). From 1999, the SARFT has issued a series of policies to regulate the transmission of audiovisual programs. In October 1999, the *Notice on the Enhancement of Administration of the Transmission of Audiovisual Programs to the Public via Information Networks* was issued, which stipulates that "the transmission of audiovisual programs via internet or other information networks within the Chinese territory is subject to the approval by the SARFT" and that "'web radio,' 'web television,' and 'web movie' are not allowed to broadcast without permission given by the government" (SARFT, 1999, Article 1). It is further provided in the *Notice* that news program to be delivered through information networks shall be produced by Chinese radio and TV stations.

In November of the same year, the *Provisional Regulations on Approval and Administration of the Establishment of Precedent Platform for Web Audiovisual Program Transmission* was issued. And in April 2000, the *Provisional Regulation on Supervision and Administration of Web Audiovisual Program Transmis-*

sion was promulgated. In January 2003, the *Regulation on the Administration of Transmission of Audiovisual Programs via Information Networks* was issued as the SARFT Decree No. 15, which took effect on February 10, 2003. And in July 2004, a revised version of the Decree No. 15, which was renamed as SARFT Decree No. 39, was issued and took effect on October 11, 2004. The frequent issuing and revision of the administration regulations on webcasting reflect the constant changes in the transmission of audio and video contents brought by the rapid technological advancement and the dynamic media environment. Another reason for the revision from the SARFT Decree No. 15 to No. 39 was that the *China Administrative Permission Law* was promulgated by the central government in March 2004, and all the ministerial decree articles that are in contradiction with this Law required revision.

In Article 2 of the SARFT Decree No. 39, it is stipulated that "the regulation is applicable to all the information transmission services and related activities, which use IP as the main technical means and various electronic devices such as computers, TV sets, and mobile phones as terminals, transmitting information through mobile communications networks, fixed communications networks, microwave communications networks, cable television networks, satellite or other urban domain networks, broad domain networks and intranet" (SARFT, 2004, Article 2). In addition, it stipulates that "the 'web audiovisual programs' referred by this regulation are those containing continuously moving pictures or continuous sounds, in a form similar to a radio program, TV program or motion picture" (SARFT, 2004, Article 2). The regulation divides web audiovisual programs into four categories: (a) news; (b) movies and television dramas; (c) entertainment programs including music, traditional operas, sports and recreations; and (d) professional programs related to technology, education, medicine, finance, broadcasting, military, and law.

It is also explicitly stipulated that all the webcasters must apply for a "License to Broadcast Audiovisual Programs via Internet" (SARFT, 2004, Article 6). And to get the "License," webcasters should meet the following basic criteria: (1) the webcasting must be in accordance with the planning, technical standards and management requirements for broadcasting public programs; (2) the webcasters must have adequate funds, equipment, and premises to engage in the broadcasting business; (3) the webcaster must have adequate audiovisual program resources; (4) the broadcaster must have the necessary professional staff; and (5) the broadcasting must be in compliance with other relevant laws and regulations. Moreover, webcasters who will provide news, movies, or television dramas are subject to additional requirements. For example, a news webcaster must, in addition to the criteria above, satisfy the following requirements as well: (1) the webcaster must be approved by the Information Office of the State Council as a provider of news programming; and (2) the broadcaster must have held a License for Broadcasting for more than three years, or have been approved as a news agency for more than three years. Apart from this, the regulation provides that "wholly-foreign-owned institutions, Sino-foreign joint ventures and Sino-foreign cooperative entities are not allowed to engage in the webcasting business" (SARFT, 2004, Article 8).

LEADING WEBCASTERS IN THE MARKET

Although strictly regulated by the policies, the webcasting business opportunities still attracted much interests from media and telecommunication companies because it offers many benefits to individuals and organizations that need to disseminate information and content. According to a report from the Guangzhou Dayang Net (2005), the number of the online movie and TV customers had reached 13 million in China in 2004, and it is predicted that the number will increase to 21 million in 2005. The whole webcasting market generated approximately $13.5 million in 2003, and the revenue is predicted to reach $24.5 million in 2005, with an increase of 82%.

The current chapter on webcasting business practices in China is based on two surveys. The first is a content analysis on 20 leading webcasters, and the second is a questionnaire survey on webcasting consumers. For the first survey, to identify the leading webcasters in China, the authors consulted industry experts, competent authorities, and research institutions that include the director of China Internet Labs, officials from the SARFT, and a senior researcher of the China Academy of Social Science. However, it is very hard to provide a comprehensive and precise list of the leading webcasters as the whole industry is still developing and is in its infant stage. However, with the recommendations given by the informants, it is possible to identify several major clusters of webcasters that are active in the market:

Radio and Television Stations

The first cluster of webcasters includes those central and local radio and TV stations that are traditional media industry players. Holding the great advantages of the audiovisual program resources, radio and television stations moved early and fast in getting into the webcasting market. Among this cluster, the most influential webcasters include the V.CCTV, the Inte Radio and the Yinghe Online Radio.

The V.CCTV (http://v.cctv.com/CCTVPortal/) was launched in May 2004 as a new web channel of the China Central Television (CCTV). During the first day of webcasting, it attracted 680,000 clicks on the site, and at the peak there were 3000 users online at the same time. In spring 2005, it webcast the Spring Festival Evening Party. The program attracted a total of 200 million clicks within 5 hours,

180,000 viewers were watching the program at the same time, and the peak bandwidth reached 12G with the support of CDN technology.

The Inte Radio (http://www.chinabroadcast.cn/) is a multi-language online radio station of the China Radio International, the most internationalized radio station in the country. The Inte Radio was launched formally on July 13, 2005, after a half-year's trial operation that began the proceeding October. The Inte Radio offers online audio services in 42 different languages, providing news, music, entertainment, and foreign language education programs.

The Yinghe Radio (http://www.radio.cn/) is an online radio station of the China National Radio, the largest domestic radio network in China. In 2004, the CNR launched the CNR Online, offering 8 channels for live streaming and 60 programs for downloading or streaming on demand. On July 28, 2005, it further opened the Yinghe Online Radio, broadcasting a large variety of interactive audio programs.

News Agencies and Newspaper Companies

The second cluster includes news agencies and newspaper companies. Xinhuanet.com is a news site affiliated with the Xinhua News Agency, the national news agency in China. As early as 2001, Shanghai Branch of Xinhua News Agency, together with Shanghai Municipal Telecommunication Company, established a joint venture: Shanghai Xinhua Telecom Network Co. Ltd. Later, Xinhua Net TV (http://xintv.xinhuanet.com/) was launched in June 2001. During the annual sessions of the China National People's Congress (CNPC) and the Chinese People's Political Consultative Conference (CPPCC) in 2005, the Xinhuanet.com had provided over 60 hours of audiovisual programs, 52 interviews totaling 30 hours, and 110 audiovisual clips. Interestingly, Xinhua News Agency had planned for the expansion to the audiovisual media business for a long time, but failed at the very beginning because of the policy restrictions. The development of internet and webcasting business once again provided it an opportunity to diversify its print media business to the audiovisual spheres. At present, Xinhuanet.com has grown to be one of the largest webcasting sites offering news content.

People.com.cn is a news site of the People's Daily, a state newspaper with subscriptions in many different countries and regions. People.com.cn has established its own multimedia channel (http://av.people.com.cn/GB/index.html), providing video news, interviews, talk shows, and other kinds of news content.

Portal Sites

The third cluster comprises portal sites offering audio and video content. In response to the new changes brought by the broadband network, popular portal sites such as

Sina.com, Sohu.com, and Qianlong.com started to launch special channels to webcast their content. Most portal sites use webcasting as an approach to strengthen the provision of their news and entertainment programs. For example, during the visit to mainland China by the Taiwan's Kuomintang Delegation led by the president Lian Chan in late April and early May of 2005, the Sina Broadband created a column providing over 100 video news items to update the most recent information of the visit. Usually, the audiovisual content on the portal sites are broadcast first in the live streaming format, and later they become available online for more days in the VOD format.

Telecommunication Companies

The fourth cluster of active webcasters includes telecommunication companies that provide video and audio media content. Telecommunication companies hold great advantages of network connection, particularly the broadband connection. In recent years, these companies are seeking to play more roles in the content market. Until now, many telecommunication companies have set up their own broadband content service sites, such as Tiantian Net TV of China Netcom (www.116.com.cn), internet Star Sky of China Telecom (www.chinavnet.com) and Dream Net of Greatwall Broadband (www.gwbn.com.cn). The Tiantian Net TV, for example, positions itself as the site providing the most fashionable internet experiences for audiences, and offers a variety of TV, movie, and entertainment webcasting products both for free and for pay.

Others

In addition to these major clusters of webcasters, there are also some other players that are active in the market. Some of them have traditional offline media counterparts and the others are holding content advantages in certain specific fields. For example, Wuzhou Media Press and Shanghai Meiya Media Group established the Wuzhou Net TV (www.cnitv.com) in March 2004, providing programs in over ten channels. Relying on the advantages of its offline book store, Beijing Xinhua Jindian Audio and Video Co. Ltd opened a professional audio readings website: Audio-books (www.audio-books.cn), selling more than 100 audio reading materials, and providing over 1000 books for pay downloading. Shenzhen Security Information Corporation set up the China Panorama Net TV (http://market.p5w.net/sib/), providing video and audio stock market news and financial programs.

To acquire more understandings about the webcasting practices, the authors identified 20 leading webcasters for further study. The selection of the leading webcasters is, however, not restricted by the quota for each cluster; rather the popularity of the webcasters is the most important criterion in making the list (see Appendix A).

WEBCASTING BUSINESS PRACTICES

Analysis of the 20 Leading Webcasters

According to Ha and Ganahl et al. (2005), webcasters can be categorized into three types: clicks-and-bricks, pure-plays, and ISPs. Clicks-and-bricks are those terrestrial broadcasters that already have an offline TV or radio station/network and an additional service online, or established organizations with an online presence. Pure-plays are organizations that provide audio and or video service online with no other counterpart offline. And ISPs are internet service providers with their own audio and video content services in the internet service. Among the 20 leading webcasters, all three types of webcasters are present. The click-and-brick is of the highest proportion as 9 of the 20 leading webcasters fall into this category, 7 webcasters are pure-players, and the other 4 are ISPs.

Applying the Ha and Ganahl (2004) taxonomy for webcasting content strategy, 11 of the 20 webcasters employ the content aggregators strategy, and 9 apply the branded content model strategy. The following is a more detail analysis of the business strategies of the leading webcasters.

Accessibility.   For content transmission, most of the leading webcasters use more than one transmission method, only one uses merely one transmission method, 13 webcasters use two transmission methods and 6 use three transmission methods. Among all the methods of transmission, the "on-demand streaming" is the most commonly used by the leading webcasters.

For the internet connection, most webcasters provide 2 speeds. The two commonly available speeds are 512KB and 1MB. As to the media players displaying the content, Windows Media Player and Real Player are the two major applied software programs. Windows Media Player is used by 75% of the webcasters and Real Player is used by 60% of the webcasters. A majority of the webcasters does not require any additional software to view or to listen their program, however, some webcasters require flash and chat software for the music content and chatting room services. In addition, most webcasting sites (90%) have text description of the audiovisual content and the information of the estimated file size or playing time, but most of them do not have search engine or a directory to facilitating users to locating content.

Content strategy.   As regards to the webcasting content, most of the leading webcasters (85%) provide more than one program genre. And 63% of the content is repurposed and has previously been shown in other media; only 15% of the content is original and exclusively shown on the websites. 65% of the webcasters have primarily domestic production with only a little foreign production, and 35%

use exclusively the domestic content. For those with foreign content, Korea, American and Japanese productions are the most commonly seen.

A variety of channels are shown on the webcasting sites, ranging from 1 to 50, and the average number of channels is 5. Among those with only one designated channel, the average number of shows and video clips is 15. Among the 9 sites providing audio content only or both audio and video, 56% of them offer more than one type of audio content, which indicates a lower level of variety comparing with the video webcasters.

Revenue source.   For webcasters that mainly provide news, technology, education or financial content, most of their webcasting services are free of charge. However, for most webcasters that offer movie, TV, radio, and other entertainment content, the subscription or another type of paying model is used. Among all the 20 leading webcasters, there are 8 free webcasters and 12 providing services with charge.

The major revenue sources of the 20 webcasters are advertising (80%) and subscription (55%). Next popular revenue source is pay per use (30%), and e-commerce is also applied by two webcasters. The average number of revenue sources is 1.9, meaning that most webcasters apply more than one revenue source. The pricing structure is composed of charges per use and/or charge by a subscription fee that is either monthly or annual. The average monthly subscription fee is $2.50, and the average charge per use is about $0.12.

The payment method varies from credit card, telephone debit, paypal, or other online payment services, cash card, or bank transfer. The most commonly used methods are the online payment services (55%) and telephone debit (35%). In most cases (8 out of 12), the ISP on behalf of the webcast service provider collects the fees from users, while two pure-play webcasters and two ISP webcasters collect money directly from customers.

For the sites displaying advertising, an average of 15 ads appear per site. For sites offering e-commerce services, the products being sold online include videos, CD albums, and other commercial commodities.

In addition, the broadband has created a new kind of advertising: online video and audio advertising. The use of online audio and video advertising can be seen in some portal sites with extensive traffic. For example, Coca-Cola launched a 4-episode video advertising program in the biggest Chinese news portal, Sina.com; customers can either download or view them by streaming.

International influence.   Restricted by the policies, all identified leading webcasters are domestic by ownership and most content provided on the sites is domestic content. Thus, the international influence is not very visible in these leading webcasters at present. However, with the further opening up of China's media market, more foreign capital and media content will get in, and the webcast industry will be influenced to a larger extent by the international media.

SURVEY ON THE WEBCASTING CONSUMER BEHAVIOR

The analysis of 20 leading webcasters offers an understanding of webcasting business practices from the content point of view. To examine the consumers' perception on webcasting services and acquire more knowledge from the audience' perspective, the authors conducted another survey, aimed at finding out the consumers' behavior in using the webcasting services.

The survey was conducted by posting an online questionnaire on 6 websites: www.xinhuanet.com (the state news site), www.116.com.cn (the ISP), www.bjradio.com.cn (the local radio site), www.btv.com.cn (the local TV site), http://ting.pcpro.com.cn/ (the online audio site), and www.tom.com (the popular portal site) in March 2005. During one week, the survey received a total of 1279 valid responses and 279 comments. Among all the responses, 937 respondents claimed to have webcasting consuming experiences, they were sampled as the users of webcasting service. 324 respondents answered that they had not used the webcasting service, and were thus sampled as the non-users of the webcasting service. The users' consuming behaviors and non-users' reason for not making use of the webcasting services were studied. However, as the questionnaire was posted on the popular websites, the respondents are netizens whom are more familiar with internet services than the average population, and the findings may show mostly the netizens' consuming behavior on the webcasting services. The followings are our findings from the survey (see Appendix B for survey questionnaire).

Demographic Features

Gender.   Among all the 937 users of the webcasting services, 803 of them are male and 134 are female. The male users account for 85.7%, taking the dominating majority.

Age.   32.7% of the webcasting users are aged between 33–45, 28.9% of them are aged between 25–32, and 26.6% of them are between 18–24. There are very few older than 60 (9.4%) or younger than 18 (1.7%). It is thus obvious that most webcasting users are young adults, aging from 18 to 45 (88.2%).

Education.   684 users (73%) hold degrees higher than bachelor and 218 have high school education or below. 35 users didn't answer this question, though it is still very clear that people with the university education are the majority of the webcasting users.

Consumer Behavior

Audio or video content. Among all the 937 webcasting users, 871 of them used both audio and video content, which translates to 93.7%; 3.2% used only the audio content, and 3.8% used only the video content.

Usage frequencies. The survey shows that the users have quite high frequencies of using the webcasting services. 45.6% of the users retrieve webcasting content in a daily basis; 41.3% of them use it every week, and only 10% use it every two weeks or even longer.

Types of content. Among all types of webcasting content, the music content is used the most often, by 79.2% of the users. The next popular content is the movie and TV programs, which have been used by 73.9 % of users. The news programs are used by 61.3% of users, education program are used by 40.3 % and the entertainment programs such as traditional opera, talk show and other recreation content are used by 17.3% of users. So, the music, movie and other entertainment products are the most welcome by the consumers, news content is also frequently retrieved, and the learning and education program is the other type of popular content received.

Use of different types of webcasters. To retrieve the webcasting content, 52.9% of users go to the pure-play webcasters, 40% of users use the bricks-and-clicks, and 39.3% position themselves on the ISPs. Only 8.8% of users utilized webcasting services provided by the foreign webcasters.

Method of file transmission. As to the methods of file transmission, 842 users said that they prefer the live streaming or on-demand streaming, and 612 users like to download the content and watch/listen later. The reason for streaming content's preference is because technologically, the streaming content is much easier to use than the downloading content.

Displaying software. According to the informants, the most commonly used displaying software are Windows Media Player and Real Player, with the using rate of 80.7% and 80.6% respectively. Next is the Winamp, the software to play the MPS, with the using rate of 23.9%.

Reception devices.   As to the reception devices, in addition to computer, the MP3 is used the most often, 57.3% of the users use the MP3 to retrieve the webcasting content. 24.6% of them make use of the mobile, and much fewer users use the PDA, which only accounts for 5.4%. Also, 35.3% of the users have other devices, such as MP4 and game player to receive information.

Re-transmission of files.   For the downloaded content, the survey shows that most users (74.5%) downloaded the content for self-view, a part of them (35.5%) re-transmitted the files to friends, and there are also some users uploaded the content to internet for others to share.

Paying behavior.   Among the 937 users, only 131 persons (14%) had paid for the webcasting content, the rest 806 persons (86%) only used the free content. This result indicates that most people are still not adapted to the paying model of the webcasting services.

Quality of the webcasting content.   Very few users (6.3%) agreed that the quality of the current web audio and video services is satisfying. 46.5% of them felt that "the transmission of the image or sound is broken, the audio is incomprehensible, or the images are garbled." The remaining 47.2% of users said that the quality is medium for continuously viewing or listening.

Comments and Suggestions Given by the Customers

The survey also invited the informants to give comments and suggestions for the current usage and future improvement of the webcasting services. A total of 279 informants made comments and suggestions, which are summarized as follows: (1) many users commented that the broadband transmission speed is still slow which has affected the usage of the webcasting services; (2) the sound and image quality of webcasting content is not satisfying; (3) consumers are still expecting far more free content; (4) the content richness and diversity also needs improvement; and (5) some of the users suggested that there should be more downloading services provided in the webcasting sites.

The Reasons for Not Using the Webcasting Services

As indicated before, the authors found 324 non-users out of the 1279 informants. As to the reasons of not using the webcasting service, most of the non-users answered that they don't know much about the webcasting service or they are not familiar with the technological issues concerned. 26.6% of them answered that the net speed is still too slow to retrieve the webcasting content, and only a few of them said they are not interested in webcasting at all. So, most non-users are mainly frustrated by the technological and information limitations. If the technological conditions are further improved, and people get to know more about the webcasting, more customers will be attracted into the market.

OUTLOOK OF THE WEBCAST INDUSTRY

Fueled by the fast economic growth and the technological advancement, the webcast industry will keep rising in China, providing more opportunities for media and telecommunication companies to explore. However, challenges emerge concurrently with opportunities. Restricted by the policies and specific country media conditions, China's webcast industry is also confronted by some challenges. Pertinent issues that are challenging the future development include the following.

The Regulatory Issues

In China, the development of webcasting business is strictly administrated by the government policies. The regulatory factors are determinant for the development of the webcast industry. As introduced before, the SARFT has stipulated a series of regulations to administer the webcast market. However, the webcasting business operation involves several more administrative authorities other than the SARFT. For example, the internet content transmission of webcaster is under the supervision of the Ministry of Information Industry, and the provision of news programs needs to be approved by the Information Office of the State Council. These parallel authorities bring some overlapping administrations on the webcasting business, and it is required to have more coordination between different departments. To avoid conflicts caused by the "multi-channel administration," the SARFT, for example, is now seeking to make a higher level of administrative law promulgated by the State Council to harmonize the regulating of the whole webcast industry.

Illegal Webcasters in the Market

Despite the strict regulations, there are still many illegal webcasters operating in the market, providing erotic or illegal audiovisual content. According to a survey conducted by the iResearch (2004), among all the webcasters operating in the market, only 30% of them are holding the official license given by the responsible authorities; almost 70% of the market income has gone to the illegal webcasters in 2004. The existing black webcast market has hindered the development of the whole industry. Many content providers are thus hesitating in getting into the market as they are afraid of piracy.

To prevent revenue loss due to illegal duplication of the webcasting content, some service providers adopted the DRM (Digital Rights Management) scheme to control or restrict the use of the digital media content. However, an efficient market system is the most urgently needed to create a healthy market environment for the webcasting business.

The Business Models

According to the survey on the consumers' behavior, a large majority of consumers still prefer the free webcasting content. Thus it is not easy for the webcasters to establish a subscription model to support the webcasting practices, especially at the present stage because the webcasting content transmission is not guaranteed by good quality as it is restricted by the technological capacities. So, discovering an effective business model is one of the pertinent issues facing the future development.

Content Diversity and Richness

For most media businesses, "content is the king"; how to improve the content diversity and richness is the key issue to increase the webcasting consumption. The market has seen more alliances and cooperation between the service providers and media content providers in recent years. By utilizing the respective advantages, the pertinent challenge ahead is to develop more high-quality content and interactive programs.

The IPTV Issues

The development of webcasting is closely linked with the IPTV licensing issues in China. IPTV is TV and radio services based on the IP protocol. In such services, TV sets and personal computers are used as terminals. Connecting to a broadband network by set-top-box, audiences can receive digital radio, television, VOD, and video recordings programming.

The IPTV licensing is a very sensitive issue in China, as the growth of the IPTV will bring big challenges and competition to the traditional media sectors. At present, the SARFT has taken very cautious steps in approving the IPTV. By the end of April 2005, there is only one media company, Shanghai Wenguang News Media Group, received the license for the IPTV operation. However, many other companies including the telecommunication companies are still seeking to enter the IPTV market. IPTV will create significant volume of web audiovisual content transmission. Thus, how to deal with the IPTV issues is pertinent for building the future landscape of the webcast industry.

Podcast and Vlog Issues

The future webcast landscape is also largely influenced by the rapidly advancing online video and audio transmission technologies. For example, the current spread of the Podcast and Vlog in China has brought many new changes to webcasting.

Podcasting is a method of publishing via the internet, allowing users to subscribe to a feed of new files. It became popular in late 2004, and it enables independent producers to create self-published radio shows, and gives broadcast radio programs a new distribution method. The same technique can also deliver video files. (Apple, 2005) The Vlog or video blog is a weblog which uses video as its primary presentation format. It is primarily a medium for distributing video content produced by individuals, and it is the next step from text blog and Podcasting. (Videoblogging, 2005)

Podcasters and Vloggers appeared in China in the late 2004. During the next six months, these new technologies have attracted great attentions from both individual netizens and media companies. The current popular Podcast and Vlog sites in China include the China Boke (www.imboke.com), Toodu.com (www.toodu.com), the China Video-blog (www.vvlogger.com/plog/index2.php), and the Bokee Podcast Channel (http://podcast.bokee.com/). These sites provide customers with 30MB–100MB free space, and some of them also offer the recording services and the RSS reader for customers to feed and subscribe to files (iResearch, 2005). The technological advancement has made the transmission of individual or independent-produced audiovisual content more accessible in terms of time and cost, though on the other hand, it also adds difficulties for the market administration.

CONCLUSION

To conclude, the future development of the webcasting business is confronted with many challenges as stated above. Major challenges include the strict regulatory control imposed by the government; the hostile competition brought by the existing illegal webcasters; the immature business models; and the increasing demand for the content richness and diversity. The webcast industry will develop continuously, though also very cautiously without too many threats to the traditional media sectors, as the example given by the current IPTV licensing. In addition, the emerging technologies bring difficulties for webcasting administration and management. However, despite of the challenges, the increasingly growing broadband market and fast rising media industries will further provide the webcast industry with the potential to develop. With a proper handling of the pertinent issues, a prosperous future may be seen in the years to come.

REFERENCES

Apple. (2005).*Podcasting, the next generation of radio*. Retrieved June 27, 2005, from http://www.apple.com/podcasting/

CNNIC. (2005). *The 16th CNNIC statistical report on China's internet development*. Retrieved July 27, 2005, from http://www.cnnic.net.cn/html/Dir/2005/07/20/3046.htm

Cui, B. G. (Ed.). (2005). *Blue book of China's media: Report on development of China's media industry (2004–2005)* [in Chinese]. China: Social Science Academic Press.

Guangzhou Dayang Net. (2005). *Statistics shows that the market revenue for online movie and TV has reached 200 million RMB*. Retrieved March 28, 2005, from http://www.dayoo.com

Ha, L., & Ganahl, R. (2004). Webcasting business models of click-and-bricks and pure-play media: A comparative study of leading webcasters in South Korea and the United States. *The International Journal on Media Management, 6*(1&2), 75–88.

Ha, L., Ganahl, R., Arampatzis, A., Allagui, I., Bakker, P., Chausse, M., et al. (2005, June). *Worldwide webcasting business models: A comparative study in 13 countries/regions*. Paper presented at the meeting of The First Oriental Television Forum, Shanghai, China.

iResearch (2004). *Research report on China internet Access, 2004*. Retrieved July 27, 2005, from http://www.iresearch.com.cn

iResearch (2005). *China is following the international trend of podcasting and vlogging*. Retrieved July 27, 2005, from http://www.iresearch.com.cn/Movie_Music/detail_news.asp?id = 19459

Min, D.H., & Yang, B.Y. (2005, June). *An analysis on transferring webcasting content via internet*. Paper presented to The First Oriental Television Forum, Shanghai, China.

SARFT. (1999). *Regulations issued by state administration of radio, film and television* (SARFT). Retrieved June 30, 2005, from http://www.sarft.gov.cn/downstage/page_3.jsp

SARFT. (2004). *Regulations issued by state administration of radio, film and television* (SARFT). Retrieved June 30, 2005, from http://www.sarft.gov.cn/downstage/page_3.jsp

Sayer, P. (2005). *China could over take US in broadband access this year.* Retrieved March 27, 2005, from http://www.thestandard.com/movabletype/datadigest/archives/001181.php

Sun, X.H., Huang, W., & Hu, Z.R. (2005). (In Chinese). 2004 China radio, film and television industry report. In B. G. Cui (Ed.), *Blue Book of China's Media*. China: Social Sciences Academic Press.

Videoblogging. (2005) *What is Videoblogging?* Retrieved July 27, 2005, from http://www.videoblogging.info/

APPENDIX A
Listing of the 20 Leading Webcasters in China

No	Webcasters	Site	Type	Business Model
1	V.CCTV	http://v.cctv.com/CCTVPortal/	Clicks-and-bricks	Branded content
2	Xinhua Net Video	http://www.xinhuanet.com/video	Clicks-and-bricks	Branded content
3	China National Radio	http://211.89.225.2/	Clicks-and-bricks	Branded content
4	Beijing Radio Online	http://www.bjradio.com.cn/2004	Clicks-and-bricks	Branded content
5	China Radio International	http://www.chinabroadcast.cn	Clicks-and-bricks	Branded content
6	My CCTV	http://www.mycctv.com.cn/	Clicks-and-bricks	Branded content
7	North Net	http://video.enorth.com.cn/	Pure-play	Content aggregator
8	Huaxia Net	http://www.hxnetwork.com	Pure-play	Content aggregator
9	SMGBB	http://www.smgbb.cn	Clicks-and-bricks	Branded content
10	Wuzhou Net TV	http://www.cnbb.com.cn/maya/	ISP	Content aggregator
11	Panorama Net	http://market.p5w.net/sib/	ISP	Content aggregator
12	Tiantian NetTV	http://movie.116.com.cn/116/tt	ISP	Content aggregator
13	Chinese Police Report	http://www.cnitv.com/mayavod2003/chinapolice/	ISP	Content aggregator
14	Dream Net	http://www.bbvod.net	Pure-play	Content aggregator
15	Qianlong NV	http://www.qianlongnv.com/defa	Pure-play	Branded content
16	JNGD	http://www.jnnc.com/	Clicks-and-bricks	Content aggregator
17	CCTV Online	http://www.cctv.com/tvonline/i	Clicks-and-bricks	Branded content
18	Sports Online	http://sports.people.com.cn/	Pure-play	Content aggregator
19	Oriental TV Multimedia	http://www.pemi.com.cn	Pure-play	Content aggregator
20	China Web TV	http://www.cwtv.com.cn/	Pure-play	Content aggregator

APPENDIX B
Questionnaire on Webcasting Consumer Behavior

Dear Sir/Madam,

The following investigation is conducted in order to improve the webcasting service. We appreciate your participant in the investigation, and thank you for your kind cooperation.

[Website Name]

Questions

1. What methods do you use to access to the internet? (select as many as are applicable)

    ___ Dial-up
    ___ ISDN
    ___ ADSL
    ___ Cable modem
    ___ LAN
    ___ LMDS
    ___ LEO
    ___ PLC

2. Have you used the webcasting services? (select one)

    ___ Yes (if yes, please go to the question 4)
    ___ No (if no, please go to the question 3)

3. If you haven't used the webcasting services, can you specify the reason? (select one)

    ___ Do not know about this service
    ___ Not familiar with technical issues
    ___ The net speed is too slow
    ___ Not interested in it

4. What kind of webcasting services have you used? (select one)

    ___ Only audio
    ___ Only video
    ___ Both audio and video

5. How often do you use the webcasting services? (select one)

    ___ Every day
    ___ Every week
    ___ Every two weeks
    ___ Every month
    ___ Every half year

6. What types of content do you use? (select as many as are applicable)

    ___ Music
    ___ Movie/TV
    ___ News
    ___ Education
    ___ Entertainment programs including traditional opera, talk show and
        other recreation content
    ___ Others

7. What transmission methods do you use? (select as many as are applicable)

    ___ Live streaming or on-demand streaming
    ___ Downloading

8. Where do you find the webcasting services? (select as many as are
    applicable)

    ___ The ISPs
    ___ The clicks-and-bricks
    ___ The pure-players
    ___ Foreign sites

9. What displaying software do you use? (select as many as are applicable)

    ___ Media player
    ___ Real player
    ___ Quick time
    ___ Winamp
    ___ Footbar
    ___ Media Player Classic
    ___ Others

10. What reception devices do you use to receive the webcasting content except computer? (select as many as are applicable)

   ___ MP3
   ___ PDA
   ___ Mobile
   ___ Others

11. How do you deal with the downloaded webcasting content? (select as many as are applicable)

   ___ For self-use
   ___ Retransmit to friends
   ___ Upload the content to internet and share with others

12. Have you paid for the webcasting content? (select one)

   ___ No, I only use the free content.
   ___ Yes, I have paid for the webcasting content.

13. How do you think about the quality of the webcasting content? (select one)

   ___ Very satisfying
   ___ Medium for continuously viewing or listening
   ___ Broken sound, incomprehensible audio or garbled image

14. Please provide us the following personal information

   (a) Gender
      ___ Male
      ___ Female
   (b) Age
      ___ Younger than 18
      ___ 18–27
      ___ 28–38
      ___ 39–45
      ___ 46–59
      ___ Over 60

(c) Education
    __ University degree and above
    __ High school education and below

14. Please send us your further suggestions and comments to the following address: [email or URL]

CHAPTER 14

Hong Kong: The Crown Jewel of Broadband for China With the Second Highest Broadband Penetration in the World

Alice Y. L. Lee
Hong Kong Baptist University

Clement Y. K. So
Chinese University of Hong Kong

The rapid advancement of the internet technology has made webcasting a common practice in Hong Kong. Many entertainment and non-commercial sites have become multimedia portals and are providing audio and video clips for convenient consumption. In fact, Hong Kong is one of the leading communication centers in Asia. Even in the colonial period (from the late 19th century up to 1997), it had already established itself as an important exporter of movies and television programs. Particularly during the years of 1970s and 1980s which signified Hong Kong's rapid economic growth, the moving image industry flourished in the colonial city. Its telecommunications infrastructure was also well built.

Since the handover of sovereignty to China on July 1, 1997, Hong Kong has striven to stay at the forefront in the development of information technology. The former Chief Executive, Tung Chee Hwa, stated his vision of making Hong Kong a leader, not a follower, in the information world in his 1997 policy address. In November 1998, K. C. Kwong, the Secretary of Information Technology and Broadcasting, put forward the Digital 21 IT Strategy, which aimed at positioning Hong Kong as a leading digital city in a globally connected world. Guided by the policy, great effort has been made in putting in place the right environment, infrastructure, skills and culture to encourage the development and adoption of IT by the whole community (HKISPA, 1999).

279

By 2004, 65% of households were connected to the internet (Census and Statistics, 2005). In April 2005, household broadband penetration rate was 62.4% (Communications and Technology Branch, 2005a). The high internet penetration rate and the popularity of the use of broadband lay a good foundation for the development of webcasting in Hong Kong.

WEBCASTING MARKET ENVIRONMENT

As an international city, Hong Kong's population was 6.9 million by the end of 2004 while the household number was around 2.3 million (Census and Statistics, 2005). Hong Kong's population is mainly composed of Chinese, and foreigners are only 7.7% of the total. The top three foreign nationalities come from the Philippines, Indonesia, and the U.S. Chinese and English are the official languages. English is widely used in the government, the legal system, and by the professional and business sectors. Cantonese is the major dialect spoken by the local people.

The development of webcasting in Hong Kong is closely related to the city's vibrant media industry. Although Hong Kong is geographically small, 52 daily newspapers, a number of electronic newspapers, and 864 periodicals are published (HKSAR Government, 2003a). The Hong Kong newspapers that were registered at the end of 2003 included 28 Chinese-language dailies, 11 English-language dailies, 8 bilingual dailies, and 5 dailies in other languages. The top three newspapers in Hong Kong are the Chinese popular press, namely the *Oriental Daily*, the *Apple Daily,* and the *Sun*. Together they have a lion's share (almost 70%) of the total newspaper circulation. The *Oriental Daily* distributes around 400,000 copies on a daily basis and has been the number one newspaper in Hong Kong in terms of circulation for many years. Newspapers in Hong Kong are all commercially run with diverse political orientations. Some are pro-China while some are pro-Hong Kong with special concern on local political rights. Lately, three tabloid-sized newspapers emerged in Hong Kong and they are delivered to the citizens free of charge. The total circulation of these three free newspapers is around 1 million.

In broadcasting, Hong Kong has two terrestrial commercial television companies, 5 subscription television licensees, 12 non-domestic television program licensees, 1 government radio-television station and 2 commercial radio stations. The top four broadcasters are Television Broadcasts Limited (TVB), Asia Television Limited (ATV), Hong Kong Cable Television Limited (i-CABLE), and Radio Television Hong Kong (RTHK). Apart from RTHK, all the broadcasters in Hong Kong are privately run. The broadcast and print media are two separate systems and cross-over in ownership is not encouraged.

In the radio industry, the public broadcaster RTHK and two commercial broadcasters, Hong Kong Commercial Broadcasting Co. Ltd. and Metro Broadcast Corporation Ltd., broadcast 13 radio channels in Cantonese, English, and Putonghua.

Programs in Philipino and Bahasa Indonesia are also broadcast to cater for the needs of the largest minority groups in Hong Kong (Communications and Technology Branch, 2005b).

In terms of television, Hong Kong viewers can receive over 200 television channels, including pay and free television channels and other free to air satellite TV channels. The channels are diverse with a global outlook, and most of them have imported foreign programs. They include CCTV, CNN, CNBC, BBC, NHK, TV5, Deutsche Welle, Arirang, HBO, ESPN, Discovery, National Geographic, Turner TCM, and the Cartoon Network. However, the most popular television stations in the territory are still the two domestic free television broadcasters, ATV and TVB. Each broadcasts one Chinese and one English television channel. Free domestic television is received by more than 99.6% of the population (Census and Statistics Department, 2005; Communications and Technology Branch, 2005c).

Lately, the popularity of free terrestrial television has been challenged due to the rapid development of new communication technology. According to the 2005 Asia-Pacific Broadcasting Union (ABU) seminar held in Bangkok, in the near future free domestic television broadcasters in Asia will face an increase in competition from cable, broadband, and internet television. Their profits will decrease and their operations will need significant changes (P. W. Kwan, personal communication, May 20, 2005).

Domestic pay television broadcasters in Hong Kong have increased in recent years. In Hong Kong pay television recipients are domestic households and hotel industry. Hong Kong Cable Television Limited (i-CABLE), Hong Kong Broadband Network, PCCW VOD Limited and SuperSUN (formerly known as Galaxy Satellite Broadcasting Limited) are currently providing pay service. The first three are broadband television services while the last is a satellite television service (OFTA, 2005). SuperSUN will soon also provide a broadband service through the Hutchison Global Communications. i-CABLE is, at this point, the market leader in the broadband television service.

The Hong Kong government has decided to liberalize the television market. The new services have introduced many more television program channels. The government is also set to introduce digital terrestrial broadcasting in Hong Kong and is reviewing the broadcasting regulatory regime to facilitate technological convergence. The Chief Executive in council, the top government policy making body, has set a policy which states that the two incumbent terrestrial television broadcasters, ATV and TVB, must launch digital terrestrial television services by 2007 at the latest. The objective of launching the digital terrestrial television (DTT) broadcasting is to enhance Hong Kong's broadcasting infrastructure (Communications and Technology Branch, 2005d). From the policy maker's point of view, a vibrant television market will not only widen the viewers' choice but also enhance Hong Kong's position as a regional broadcasting hub (HKSAR Government, 2003b).

The success of the move of television broadcasting into cyberspace very much depends on the sophistication of Hong Kong's telecommunications system. In the past decade, the government has been quite eager to build up a world-class telecommunications infrastructure. The aim is "to have a competitive, advanced and high bandwidth telecommunications infrastructure that is capable of supporting demanding, new and innovative services to meet future needs and challenges, thereby furthering the goal of developing Hong Kong into a leading digital city" (HKSAR Government, 2003c, p. 1).

Internet and Broadband Penetration in Hong Kong

Internet services are very popular in Hong Kong. There were 186 internet service providers in Hong Kong in April 2005 (Communications and Technology Branch, 2005a). They are all privately owned and their operators are optimistic about the profit return of the internet business. According to data from the Census and Statistics Department (2005), 64.9% of households with personal computers at home were connected to the internet and 56.4% of people aged 10 and over had used internet services during the previous year. In the business sector, half of the local companies and organizations had internet connections. Of internet users aged 12–64, 63.6% used the internet daily and 25.3% used it several times a week (Nielsen Media Research, 2004).

By 2004, virtually all households and commercial buildings were covered by the broadband network. The number of broadband accounts increased significantly over the years. In April 2005, the household broadband penetration rate reached 62.4%. Broadband internet subscribers have out-numbered dial-up subscribers since 2003, which reflects the high popularity of broadband in Hong Kong. Government statistics indicate that in January 2005, 1.5 million customers used broadband services with a speed of up to 10 Mbps (Megabytes per second), accounting for over 21% of the total population. There were only 1.0 million registered customer accounts with dial-up access, far less than the broadband users. Table 14–1 shows that in the residential market broadband usage had grown quickly from 2002 to 2004 (Nielsen/NetRatings, 2004a). All local primary and secondary schools are connected to the internet with broadband. In other words, the broadband penetration rate in the education sector is 100%.

Internationally, Hong Kong is second only to South Korea in terms of broadband penetration rate. In addition to the high penetration rate, Hong Kong has the most affordable broadband internet service. Based on the data for 2002, broadband service charges accounted for only 1.9% of real disposable income in Hong Kong, compared to 7.0% in South Korea (Communications and Technology Branch, 2005e). Hong Kong ranked number one in the world in the International Telecommunication Union's (ITU) Digital Access Index published in No-

TABLE 14–1
Broadband Penetration Rate in Hong Kong (2002–04)

	% of Household with Internet Access	
Time Period	Narrowband	Broadband
Quarter 1, 2002	42%	58%
Quarter 3, 2002	24%	76%
Quarter 1, 2003	19%	81%
Quarter 3, 2003	16%	84%
Quarter 1, 2004	11%	89%
Quarter 3, 2004	13%	87%

Source. Nielsen/NetRatings-GNETT.

vember 2003, in terms of the affordability of internet access (HKSAR Government, 2003c). Broadband service charges in Hong Kong have been lowered further in the past two years due to keen competition. A survey conducted by a Swiss management school in 2005 reported that Hong Kong's competitiveness is ranked second in the world, just behind the United States. Among the many advantages of Hong Kong, "broadband usage" and "internet cost" are important positive factors (*Apple Daily*, 2005).

The high use of the internet, the high broadband penetration rate, the low cost of broadband internet services, the well-developed broadband television market, and the digitalization of terrestrial broadcasting provide a favorable environment for the development of webcasting in Hong Kong.

Webcasting Companies in Hong Kong

Webcasting started in Hong Kong in the late 1990s as the internet became prevalent. Many local media companies established online counterparts and carried multimedia material on the web. Broadcast companies such as radio and television stations were particularly interested in putting their programs on the web to reach audiences far beyond Hong Kong. The dot-com bubble burst in 2000 frustrated local webcasters at the time. Many dot-com companies could not survive because of the downfall of the new economy. However, the growing popularity of broadband technology and the low cost of broadband service charges then injected life into the development of webcasting. In the new millennium, more webcasters are available and their content has become more substantial. Comparatively speaking, the

TABLE 14–2
Audience Data on Leading Webcasters in Hong Kong

Parent/Brand/Domain	Unique Audience (000)	Web Page Views (000)	Sessions per Person	Web Pages per Person	Time per Person (hh:mm:ss)
tvb.com	692	18230	3.23	26	0:16:58
881903.com	212	6805	3.75	32	0:14:53
RTHK	342	10027	3.13	29	0:22:19
NOW	283	8115	2.89	29	0:18:00
i-CABLE.com	163	8731	3.96	53	0:22:42
hkatv	162	2660	2.00	16	0:09:19
Metro Broadcast	158	3601	2.71	23	0:10:23
HKedCity	461	8890	3.01	19	0:06:28
tdctrade.com	75	194	1.17	3	0:01:19
Breakthrough	no data				

Notes. NetView only covers Hong Kong at-home internet usage. Office, school, and internet café or overseas traffic is not included.

Source. Nielsen/NetRatings-NetView.

broadcasters in Hong Kong are far more enthusiastic about developing webcasting than their newspaper counterparts.

Table 14–2 shows some audience data on the leading webcasters in Hong Kong. Individual online audiences spend an average of 14 minutes on a single site (Nielsen/NetRatings, 2004b). Primetime for online surfing is from 11:00 pm to 1:00 am (M. Chow, personal communication, May 17, 2005). Ten leading webcasters in Hong Kong, as listed in Table 14–3, were selected for investigation. They were chosen because they have a high rate of usage or are well known among Hong Kong citizens. The selection was based on the information obtained from the AC Nielsen Hong Kong Report and the consultation of local webcast professionals from TVB, Breakthrough, Hong Kong Education City Limited, and RTHK.

Among the leading webcasters, tvb.com and hkatv.com are the online sites of the two domestic free television broadcasters, Television Broadcasts Ltd. and Hong Kong Asia Television Ltd., respectively. i-CABLE.com is the online site of a broadband television broadcaster. 881903.com (Commercial Radio) and Metro Broadcast are the online versions of two local radio stations. NOW belongs to PCCW IMS Limited and is the online platform of the local ISP Netvigator. RTHK on the internet is the online site of the public broadcaster RTHK. HKedCity is a government-funded

TABLE 14–3
Leading Webcasting Companies in Hong Kong

Site Name	Web Site	Site Nature*	Business Model**
tvb.com	www.tvb.com	CB	BC
RTHK	www.rthk.org.hk	CB	BC
881903.com	www.881903.com	CB	BC
NOW	www.now.com.hk	ISP	CA
i-CABLE.com	www.i-cable.com	CB	BC
hkatv	www.hkatv.com	CB	BC
Metro Broadcast	www.metroradio.com.hk	CB	BC
HKedCity	www.hkedcity.net	CB	BC
tdctrade.com	www.tdctrade.com	CB	BC
Breakthrough	www.breakthrough.org.hk	CB	BC

*CB = clicks-and-bricks, ISP = Internet service provider
**BC = branded content, CA = content aggregator

one-stop educational portal that serves about 1,300 local schools. Breakthrough is a multimedia youth site that targets local youth. Tdctrade.com is run by the Hong Kong Trade Development Council and its webcast programming serves local and international business users. The first six webcasters are commercial entertainment sites, whereas the last four are non-commercial sites. According to Nielsen/NetRatings, tvb.com, RTHK and HKedCity have the highest web page views (see Table 14–2). These top webcasters provide both audio and video clips.

WEBCASTING BUSINESS PRACTICE MODELS IN HONG KONG

Many media organizations, government agencies, NGOs, and educational organizations in Hong Kong are now providing commercial or non-commercial webcasting services. They offer audio and video content that is made by both professional and amateur producers. Although the cost of internet access in Hong Kong is not that high, webcast production is an expensive operation. Obtaining enough funding is crucial for the acceptance and maintenance of the service. Hence, webcasters in Hong Kong are seeking feasible business models with which to run their webcasting services.

In analyzing webcasting in Hong Kong, we have adopted the Ha and Ganahl (2004) framework to analyze the business models and development strategies. Content strategies, transmission methods, and revenue sources are identified as the three common components of a webcasting business model. The first part of our investigation weaves around these components, and the second part explores the uniqueness of the Hong Kong webcasting service.

The Domination of Branded Content Business Model

Table 14–3 shows that the leading webcasters in Hong Kong are clicks-and-bricks sites. There is only one internet service provider, NOW, on the leading webcaster list.

In Hong Kong, most of the clicks-and-bricks sites are the online divisions of existing broadcast organizations such as tvb.com, i-CABLE.com, hkatv.com, RTHK, 881903.com, and the Metro Broadcast Corporation. The audio and video web programs that they provide mostly originate from their offline radio and television stations. They naturally employ the branded content model. Other clicks-and-bricks sites such as HKedCity, Breakthrough, and tdctrade.com also offer web content that is mainly produced by related companies and departments. They also offer branded content.

In contrast, Netvigator, an internet service provider, runs NOW and adopts a content aggregator model. As it does not have an offline division, it obtains its content from different media companies. For example, it buys webcasting programs from tvb.com broadband, Commercial Radio, Disney, the BBC, Bloomberg, and other foreign producers. The result in Hong Kong matches that of the international findings perfectly. Clicks-and-bricks webcasters employ the branded content model while the ISP webcasters employ the content aggregator model.

Clicks-and-bricks webcasters in Hong Kong are more likely to repurpose or simulcast their audio-video content online than ISP webcasters. In Hong Kong, all of the clicks-and-bricks webcasters simulcast their programs, particularly their newscasts. For example, tvb.com and i-CABLE.com broadcast their news programs live both online and offline. Radio station sites such as 881903.com and Metro Broadcast transmit their programs live all day. RTHK also provides live webcasting. Therefore, for the clicks-and-bricks webcasters, the difference in webcasting content between online and offline is not great.

Content Strategy—Localization or Globalization?

Web sites are generally defined as global media. Yet, this perceived status is becoming contestable. Halavais (2000) finds that although there are no national borders on the World Wide Web, invisible social and cultural borders are still apparent. Other studies indicate that many online sites still have strong attributes of the countries or regions to which they belong. Therefore, although online news media seem to be global, they are actually local tools and are mainly used domestically. It is likely that webcasters will develop business models based on the marketing strategy of localization. The localization of webcast programs has the advantage of cultural proximity on the one hand and meets the local language requirement on the other.

We find that all of the leading webcasters in Hong Kong are domestic sites, and that local content dominates the market. Half of the leading webcasters offer purely domestic content. Radio sites in Hong Kong usually do not import programs, perhaps due to language constraints. Sites such as 881903.com, RTHK, and Metro Broadcast produce their own programs and put them on the web. HKedCity and Breakthrough, as educational and youth sites, only provide local web programs. The other half of the leading webcasters—tvb.com, NOW, i-CABLE.com, atv.com, and tdctrade.com—have primarily domestic content, with only a small portion of foreign content which is usually syndicated and provided by foreign media corporations.

The executive managers of the webcasters that we interviewed all said that local content is much welcomed by their online users. As webcasters such as HKedCity and Breakthrough serve local students and youth, it is natural for these sites to provide relevant local programs (J. Cheng, personal communication, April 21, 2005). Television sites such as tvb.com, hkatv, and i-CABLE.com play supporting roles for their offline stations and serve the local television audience. There is no point in bringing in too much foreign content (M. Chan, personal communication, April 27, 2005). As mentioned before, radio sites are very much localized. Although tdctrade.com brings in foreign content for local businessmen, its webcasts place heavy emphasis on the Hong Kong perspective.

Among all of the leading webcasters, NOW seems to have the most foreign content. It provides BBC World news, Bloomberg financial news, CNBC Market Watch, Disney movies, Japanese cartoons, and fashion shows from Europe. However, all of these international programs have become the second layer of the site since 2002. When the site first launched its pilot project in September 2001, it brought in foreign content to strengthen the brand. However, very soon the company found that most of the foreign content had little attraction to local online users. The site has shifted to providing more local content (M. Chow, personal communication, May 17, 2005). Industry wisdom and market research both indicate that news, current affairs, drama, music, and movies are the most popular webcasting genres. These web programs are mainly local productions in Hong Kong.

In terms of content diversity, webcasters in Hong Kong provide a wide variety of audio and video clips for their online audience. NOW and i-CABLE.com offer the most diversified video content. RTHK, hkatv, and tvb.com also display many different types of video clips. The video content on these sites commonly includes movies, TV programs, TV commercials and trailers, drama series, comedies, variety shows, educational materials, business information, news programs, talk shows, music videos, documentaries, cartoons, sports, and adult movies.

Metro Broadcast provides the highest variety of audio clips. 881903.com, RTHK, and NOW are also top audio content providers. Music, news, talk shows, interviews, sports, and ring tones are common audio content. In terms of popularity, music and interviews rank first, news ranks second, and sports ranks third.

For the limited amount of foreign web programs, the major sources are the leading media exporters such as the United States, Europe, and Japan. The United States provides cartoons such as Disney programs, Hollywood movies, music, and television programs. The European countries offer current affairs programs such as BBC news, television series, and fashion shows. Japan supplies cartoons, television drama, and adult movies. In recent years, more programs have come from Taiwan, Korea, and mainland China. Their music programs, television dramas and movies are particularly popular among the young online audience.

Transmission Modes and Revenue Models

Windows Media Player, Real Player, and Quicktime are the three main media players for accessing audio and video web content. In Hong Kong, Windows Media Player is the most popular device and all of the leading webcasters use it. RTHK, 881903.com, and HKedCity also use Real Player. HKedCity is the only site that also uses Quicktime. It is expensive to provide more than one media player. However, the Deputy Head of the New Media Unit of RTHK (M. Cheung, personal communication, April 21, 2005) insists that it is worthwhile providing both Windows Media Player and Real Player because it broadens the reach of the website's audience. HKedCity also tries its best to provide technical convenience to the thousands of school teachers and students that it serves. Its online users can choose any of the three media players.

At present, there are four main file transmission methods used for webcasting: Downloading on demand, streaming on demand, live streaming and push (Ha, 2004). In Hong Kong, the most common transmission method is streaming on demand. Every major webcaster uses this method. Among our 10 leading webcasters, 8 also use downloading on demand with the exception of RTHK and tdctrade.com. RTHK, a government-funded broadcaster, has a very strict copyright policy and does not allow any downloading from its site. Downloading on-demand is very much related to subscription services. For example, online audiences can download music, ring tones, and video games after they have paid the webcasters. NOW online subscribers can download programs from the Avatar Mall to give their online icons a new cyber look.

Live streaming is also a common device, but not every webcaster uses this method frequently. The radio station websites, such as 881903.com, Metro Broadcast, and RTHK, simulcast their radio programs around the clock. While tvb.com and i-CABLE.com broadcast their news programs live several times a day, NOW only provides live service on rare occasions. Live streaming requires more resources and technical support. Some of the local webcasters provide this service only when it is necessary (M. Chow, personal communication, May 17, 2005). The "push" device, or the automatic sending of content to subscribers, is not popular in Hong Kong. Only i-CABLE.com uses it to provide an online news service.

Professionals in the Hong Kong web industry have realized that the viewing habits of media users today have changed a great deal. Users are no longer interested in watching television or listening to radio programs at a fixed time. In particular, web users no longer follow program timetables. They watch web programs when they have time or when they are in the mood to go online (M. Chow, personal communication, May 17, 2005). Therefore, video-on-demand programs are required more than live-streaming programs. The streaming on-demand device matches the consumption pattern of web users and facilitates their need to seek information. In comparison, live-streaming still follows the mass-broadcasting concept and no longer suits the habits of local users. Of course, some of the live programs are still attractive to overseas web users who watch the special live programs across the globe.

Webcasting in Hong Kong is not a profit-making business. It plays a supporting role in providing a service for commercial and non-commercial sites. For entertainment sites, webcasting serves a supplementary function to their offline counterparts. For non-commercial sites, webcasting is a public service for the community. The primary target of the business model is not to make a profit but to generate enough revenue to maintain the site (M. Chan, personal communication, April 27, 2005; M. Chow, personal communication, May 17, 2005; C. Wong, personal communication, April 20, 2005). For example, tdctrade.com does not regard its business model as revenue seeking but as "expenditure recovery" (C. Wong, personal communication, April 20, 2005).

Government funding and financial support from religious institutions are the major revenue sources for non-commercial sites. Breakthrough receives funding from religious groups, and also encourages online contributions. HKedCity and tdctrade.com receive support from the government and also conduct e-commerce to generate income. For example, HKedCity operates an e-commerce mall for educators and students. It sells educational products and services such as teaching resources, books, magazines, computer goods, software packages, and online learning services. The aim of the mall is not only to sell goods, but also to introduce new educational products. Tdctrade.com operates a TDC Cyber Market Place, an online business platform for matching local and foreign business companies. The Cyber Market Place generates income through its *Sourcing Guide*, which is easy online sourcing for products, services, and brands from Hong Kong, mainland China, and Taiwan. Members of tdctrade.com can subscribe to the *Guide* to obtain access to the product database.

The non-commercial sites have no external funding and must explore different kinds of revenue sources. Online advertisements, e-commerce and commercial sponsorship are the most common sources of revenue for entertainment sites. Online advertisements are found on almost all of the entertainment sites, and commercial sponsorship is also visible. Occasionally, tvb.com puts magazine-type advertisement programs that are sponsored by various commercial companies on its site. These include keep-fit, new property promotion, and travel programs. Although online shopping is not yet popular in Hong Kong, many commercial sites are still using their platforms to do e-business. For example, tvb.com runs an eShop, which sells TVB videos and products. The merchandise includes TVB drama programs, TVB brand-related souvenirs, and Miss Hong Kong bears. NOW sells Korean online computer games and generates a sizable income, and 881903.com links its online audience to the cyber shopping mall of yesasia.com.

Chyi (2005) shows that the online audience in Hong Kong is still not prepared to pay for online content. Her survey in Hong Kong shows that only 12% of the respondents are willing to pay for online news. Therefore, most of the webcasting programs in Hong Kong are offered free of charge. Some webcasters, such as 881903, i-CABLE.com, and NOW have launched a subscription model, and their online audiences gain access to webcasts by monthly or yearly subscription. These webcasters also offer pay per use services such as movies on-demand or ring tone downloads on-demand.

COMMERCIAL WEBCASTING VERSUS NON-COMMERCIAL WEBCASTING

In Hong Kong, 4 of the 10 leading webcasters are non-commercial sites. Webcasting development has the following unique characteristics. The goal of webcasting is not to generate revenue, but to serve a website's parent company or the community. Webcast programs are better developed in non-commercial sites than in commercial sites. Webcast content focuses on informational, educational, and cultural materials. Webcasting targets the local youth audience.

In other countries, webcasting can be a profit-generating media product for websites such as CNN.com. However, in Hong Kong, webcasting is a service rather than a product for sale. Leading commercial webcasters in Hong Kong can be divided into two groups: ISP-related and non-ISP-related. For both, webcasting is not an independent business but a means to an end for their parent companies. They are established to either help their parent companies promote broadband business, or to extend the audience market for the entertainment programs.

Leading webcasters NOW and i-CABLE.com are closely related to the broadband business of their ISP parent companies, PCCW IMS and i-CABLE Broadband respectively. Webcasting services are helpful in boosting broadband business in two ways. Firstly, webcasting can attract broadband customers to subscribe to more expensive packages. All broadband companies in Hong Kong hope that their customers will subscribe to advanced packages such as higher bandwidth services or unlimited broadband access. From a marketing point of view, webcasting is a good way to "burn" bandwidth. If more webcast programs are provided for a broadband customer, then the customer will be more willing to subscribe to a more expensive broadband package. Although webcasters are not able to generate profit directly, their ISP parent companies can. Secondly, webcasting is a retaining tool for pleasing and keeping broadband customers. Broadband business in Hong Kong is highly competitive. Although Hong Kong is a geographically small city, more than 14 companies provide residential broadband services. To compete for more clients, broadband companies have to provide their users with a better value service. Special webcast programs are offered to users, which is an effective way to attract and retain customers.

Practitioners in the webcasting industry admit that webcast services are a useful way to promote broadband business (M. Chan, personal communication, April 27, 2005; M. Chow, personal communication, May 17, 2005). Over the last few years, using webcasting to "burn" bandwidth and encourage subscription to expensive broadband packages has been a very effective strategy. However, the rapid development in broadband technology has made unlimited broadband access very common. By mid–2005, most broadband users in Hong Kong used high bandwidth services. The need to use webcasts to sell more expensive packages has decreased. Instead providing high quality webcast entertainment has become important. Take NOW as an example, its webcast service is exclusive for Netvigator broadband users. The web service is "added value" to the Netvigator subscription. Netvigator users only have to pay a small monthly fee ($30 HK) to access the website and enjoy a wide variety of web shows. NOW's in-house survey indicates that its web service is able to retain customers. Most Netvigator users who discontinued their broadband service did not subscribe to NOW. Meanwhile, Netvigator users who subscribed to NOW at the same time seldom left the broadband company (M. Chow, personal communication, May 17, 2005). Therefore, NOW values its webcast service and periodically updates its web programs to entertain its Netvigator customers.

The non-ISP related commercial webcasters in Hong Kong, such as tvb.com, 881903.com, and hkatv, are basically supplementary to their offline counterparts. These webcasters maintain an entertainment site structure to promote their counterparts' broadcast programs, provide entertainment for online users, and create interactive platforms for communicating with audiences (M. Chan, personal communication, April 27, 2005). They do not develop independently but work closely with their offline broadcast stations. Their role is to expand the market for the offline radio and television programs.

The goal of the leading non-commercial webcasters in Hong Kong is also to assist their parent organizations in serving the community. For example, the webcast service of tdctrade.com is regarded as a means to promote trade for the Trade Development Council (C. Wong, personal communication, April 20, 2005; B. Liu, personal communication, April 20, 2005). HKedCity, a government-funded site, helps the government to serve the educational community. Its webcast programs aim at enhancing the quality of teaching and learning in Hong Kong schools (J. Cheng, personal communication, April 21, 2005). The objective of RTHK's webcasting is to offer "added value" to RTHK's programs with the aim of expanding its reach in Hong Kong and to the rest of Greater China. Breakthrough promotes the activities of its offline youth organization and provides an interactive webcast platform for local young people.

As the leading commercial webcasters in Hong Kong regard their webcasting operations as cost instead of profit centers, they have reservations about investing heavily in their webcast services. Very little original webcast content is developed. Even tvb.com, the leading webcaster in Hong Kong, clearly states that it will continue its promotions and supportive role for the TVB station, but it has no plans to launch any exclusive online programs (M. Chan, personal communication, April 27, 2005). In contrast, leading non-commercial webcasters consider the web to be an effective platform upon which to promote public services. They are willing to invest more resources in developing webcast programs and produce more original web content. As a result, webcasting flourishes in non-commercial sites rather than in commercial sites. The 10 leading webcasters in Hong Kong provide more than 30,000 audio and video clips daily for online users. RTHK is the top provider, offering 9,061 clips, far more than the other entertainment sites. On average, each leading non-commercial site offers 3,697 clips, while each commercial site only has 2,552 clips.

The leading non-commercial webcasters in Hong Kong have seen the advantages of webcasting in delivering useful information and promoting education and culture. To them, webcasting messages are entertaining, interesting, direct, easy to understand, and efficient to retrieve. Online users can listen to and watch webcasts at anytime, from any place and with any device. Webcasting can add value to existing programs and extend the market to a global audience (M. Cheung, personal communication, April 18, 2005; L. Yau, personal communication, April 9, 2005; C. Wong, personal communication, April 20, 2005). HKedCity is willing to expend resources and effort on studying how to use the characteristics of webcasting such as interactivity, connectivity, global access, and immediacy to build high quality learning platforms for the local educational community (J. Cheng, personal communication, April 21, 2005). HKedCity has recently set up two new web programs: Teacher TV and English in the Media. These programs integrate short video clips, written texts, worksheets and forums to share good teaching practices and promote interactive English learning.

The non-commercial webcasters in Hong Kong provide an abundance of informational, educational and cultural web programs for their online users. For example, there is a huge volume of current affairs and documentary programs on the RTHK website. The site also offers mini-educational programs such as One-minute Online Chinese Language, One-minute Online Reading, Cultural Travel Logs, Classic Speeches, and Online Chinese Culture. Tdctrade.com offers market intelligence and trade promotion materials for Hong Kong. HKedCity not only provides 1,000 educational television programs, it webcasts speeches, songs, animations, teaching tips, curriculum materials, educational activities, cultural workshops, and teachers and students' productions. Breakthrough is a website that showcases creative work from young people. Many youngsters submit their audio and video productions and share them with their peer groups. The site also produces special original web programs for cultivating a healthy youth culture.

In terms of audience, half of the RTHK users are Chinese living overseas, while the other half are local Hong Kong citizens (M. Cheung, personal communication, April 18, 2005). Tdctrade.com serves businesspeople from Hong Kong, mainland China and the international business community (B. Liu, personal communication, April 20, 2005). With the exception of these two sites, most of the leading webcasters in Hong Kong target the local audience, particularly young people. Over the years, NOW has realized that young people are very interested in watching web programs and they are sensitive to innovative ways of information delivery (M. Chow, personal communication, May 17, 2005). Tvb.com found that young people are their most frequent visitors. HKedCity and Breakthrough cater to mainly the younger generation. 881903.com, hkatv, and Metro Broadcast also concentrate on serving local radio and television audiences, and their online users are mostly young.

FUTURE OUTLOOK

In Hong Kong, webcasting has developed rapidly with the advancement of broadband technology. In April 2005, the Hong Kong Broadband Network began to offer an ultra-high speed one gigabit per second broadband service (SCMP, 2005). With high connection speed, high broadband penetration rate, and low prices, webcasting is becoming more accessible.

However, webcasting does have limitations. Many broadcast audiences have not yet familiarized themselves with watching movies, drama and sports on the web. They are not patient enough to remain in front of a computer or other device for a long period of time (S. Wang, personal communication, April 9, 2005). Moreover, for many audio and video genres such as football matches, MTV, and soap operas, audiences still prefer to watch together with friends and family members instead of enjoying them in isolation. Only a limited amount of entertainment programs are sellable to web users (M. Chow, personal communication, May 17, 2005). Moreover, online audiences prefer short clips. When webcasters repurpose existing radio and television programs, they have to expend resources on repackaging. Hence, local commercial webcasting will not be profitable in the near future.

In contrast, non-commercial webcasters have less concern about the cost of webcasting. They only see the advantage of the web for public services and are very optimistic about the future. Their audiences are more willing to go online in solitude to consume educational and cultural information. Apart from songs and movies, the most popular web programs in Hong Kong are general news, business news, educational programs, documentaries, and informational materials. Local online users seem to prefer to use webcasting for learning and information seeking rather than pure entertainment. Non-commercial webcasters see the great potential of webcasting for information sharing and training, and are designing short clips for their users. It is expected that in the coming years, webcasting will continue to grow in the non-commercial sector.

The latest development of webcasting in Hong Kong is on wireless devices such as mobile phones and video iPod. The mobile phone penetration rate in Hong Kong is the highest in the world. In March 2005, mobile subscriber penetration per capita reached 119.1% (Communications and Technology Branch, 2005a). Some local broadcast stations such as TVB and i-CABLE are already delivering their newscasts through 3G mobile phones. As more people access the web from their wireless devices, the market for webcasting is growing. In the media industry, many innovative projects are in progress to produce short web audio and video clips for mobile phone users. For example, tdctrade.com is developing a mobile edition of its webcasting. HKedCity is considering how to upgrade its webcast service to match the wireless school campaign that was launched by the local educational authority. The aim of the campaign is to facilitate students' learning through their lap-top computers, 3G mobile phones, video iPod, and other internet devices in any location in their schools. Right now, when students are in schools, they can only go online in computer laboratories. With the advancement in wireless technology, the future of webcasting in Hong Kong is full of opportunities.

ACKNOWLEDGMENTS

The authors gratefully acknowledge funding support for this study by Competitive Earmarked Research Grants (CUHK4320/01H and HKBU2022/00H) from the Research Grants Council of Hong Kong.

REFERENCES

Apple Daily. (2005, May 13). Rising up, just behind the U.S., Hong Kong competitiveness ranks second in the world, p. A06.

Census and Statistics Department. (2005, March). *Hong Kong in figures*. Hong Kong: Hong Kong Special Administrative Region Government.

Communications and Technology Branch. (2005a). *Key telecommunications statistics*. Commerce, Industry and Technology Bureau, Info.gov.hk. Retrieved May 16, 2005, from http://www.citb.gov.hk/ctb/eng/telecom/ks.htm

Communications and Technology Branch. (2005b). *Sound broadcasting in Hong Kong*. Commerce, Industry and Technology Bureau, Info.gov.hk. Retrieved May 16, 2005, from http://www.citb.gov.hk/ctb/eng/broad/sound.htm.

Communications and Technology Branch. (2005c). *Television broadcasting in Hong Kong*. Commerce, Industry and Technology Bureau, Info.gov.hk. Retrieved May 16, 2005, from http://www.citb.gov.hk/ctb/eng/broad/tv.htm.

Communications and Technology Branch. (2005d). *Hong Kong to launch digital terrestrial TV broadcasting in 2007*. Commerce, Industry and Technology Bureau, Info.gov.hk. Retrieved May 16, 2005, from http://www.citb.gov.hk/ctb/eng/press/pr09072004.htm.

Communications and Technology Branch. (2005e). *Telecommunications, Hong Kong: The facts*. Commerce, Industry and Technology Bureau, Info.gov.hk. Retrieved May 16, 2005, from http://www.citb.gov.hk/ctb/eng/press/pr09072004.htm.

Chyi, H. I. (2005). Willingness to pay for online news: An empirical study on the viability of the subscription model. *Journal of Media Economics, 18(*2), 131–43.

Ha, L. (2004). Webcasting. In H. Bidgoli (Ed.), *The internet encyclopedia* (pp. 674–682). New York: John Wiley & Sons.

Ha, L., & Ganahl, R. (2004). Webcasting business models of click-and-bricks and pure-play media: A comparative study of leading webcasters in South Korea and the United States. *The International Journal of Media Management, 6 (*1&2), 75–88.

Halavais, A. (2000). National borders on the World Wide Web. *New Media & Society, 2*(1), 7–28.

HKISPA. (1999). *An environment for competitive broadband and internet development in Hong Kong—An HKISPA position paper*. Hong Kong: Hong Kong Internet Service Providers Association.

HKSAR Government. (2003a). The mass media. *Hong Kong annual report*. Hong Kong: Hong Kong Special Administrative Region Government.

HKSAR Government. (2003b). Introduction. *Hong Kong annual report*. Hong Kong: Hong Kong Special Administrative Region Government.

HKSAR Government. (2003c). Telecommunications. *Hong Kong annual report*. Retrieved May 16, 2005, from http://www.info.gov.hk/yearbook/2003/english/chapter17/17_09.html.

Nielsen Media Research. (2004). *2004 Nielsen media index: Hong Kong report* (Jan-Dec 04). Hong Kong: AGB Nielsen Media Research.

Nielsen/NetRatings. (2004a). *Nielsen/NetRatings—GNETT*. Hong Kong: AGB Nielsen Media Research.

Nielsen/NetRatings. (2004b). *Nielsen/NetRatings etView. Hong Kong: AGB Nielsen Media Research*.

OFTA. (2005). *Pay TV services, Industry focus*. Info.gov.hk. Retrieved May 16, 2005, from http://www.ofta.gov.hk/en/broadcast/tv-pay-whatisit.html

SCMP. (2005, April 21). Broadband service sprints to a faster connection. *South China Morning Post*, p. B1Z.

APPENDIX
List of Interviewees and Dates of Interview

- *Marcus Chan*—Principal Editor, TVB.COM Limited (April 27, 2005)
- *Jacqueline Cheng*—Chief Executive Officer, Hong Kong Education City Limited (April 21, 2005)
- *Mayella Cheung*—Deputy Head, New Media Unit, Radio Television Hong Kong (April 18, 2005)
- *Ming Chow*—Project Management Manager, Internet Services, PCCW Limited (May 17, 2005)
- *Peter W. Kwan*—Senior Vice President (News), Asia Television Limited (May 20, 2005)
- *Brian Liu*—Senior Webcast Producer, E-commerce, Hong Kong Trade Development Council (April 20, 2005)
- *Lawrence Yau*—Senior Communication Manager, Hong Kong Trade Development Council (April 9, 2005)
- *Sing Wang*—Chief Executive Officer, TOM Group Ltd. (April 9, 2005)
- *Clare Wong*—Head of Publications and E-Commerce, Hong Kong Trade Development Council (April 20, 2005)

CHAPTER 15

Taiwan: Bandwidth, Connection, and Access—Analyzing the Business Models of Webcasters in Taiwan

Yu-li Liu
National Chengchi University, Taiwan

MEDIA INDUSTRIES IN TAIWAN

The Kuomingtan (KMT) government of the Republic of China established its capital in Taiwan in 1949. Taiwan's population is 22.61 million (Taiwan Yearbook, 2004). Two ethnic groups, Fujianese and Hakka, constitute about 85% of the population. Mandarin is the common language for communication; however social pluralization has been accompanied by a growing emphasis on native languages such as Taiwanese, Hakka, and others.

Taiwan has a hybrid TV system, with both commercial and public TV. There are four commercial terrestrial TV stations, one Public TV Service (PTS), 63 cable operators, and 128 satellite channels in Taiwan. In 2003, the Legislative yuan revised three broadcasting related laws and asked all the political parties, government, and the military to withdraw their shares from the terrestrial TV stations, cable systems, and satellite TV by the end of 2005. China Television Company (CTV), mainly owned by the committee, was sold to the owner of one newspaper group, China Times. Chinese Television System (ITS), primarily owned by the Ministry of National Defense, was transferred to become a member of the public broadcasting group. Taiwan Television Enterprise (T.V.) is still partially owned by some state banks. It has not divested its government shares completely by the deadline because of some legal questions.

The cable television penetration is 80% (GO, 2005). The cable subscribers can receive almost 100 channels by paying less than $600 in New Taiwan (NT) dollars or around $18 per month (in U.S. dollars). The cable TV industry has been trying to provide video on demand (GOD) since the mid–1990s, but has not succeeded. Interestingly, it is webcasting service that has provided GOD first. Most satellite

TV channels are privately owned. There are 54 domestic and 14 foreign companies offering 128 satellite channels in Taiwan (GO, 2005). More than 100 channels compete for cable TV subscribers; most of the subscribers receive more than 90 channels, including domestic channels and such foreign channels as NHK, Jet TV from Japan, HBO, Disney, and Discovery from the United States.

Although webcasting has become a global medium, it still targets local audiences. While there are three types of webcasters, namely, clicks-and-bricks, pureplays, and ISP providers, only the two leading content aggregators, hiChannel and webs-tv, are able to make webcasting a promising business in Taiwan. The offline channels such as the terrestrial channels and satellite channels are unable to generate more revenues online because of a lack of bandwidth, different mindsets, and diverse program sources. Therefore, they mostly use webcasting as a supporting medium rather than as a business in itself.

The two major webcasters began to develop in 1999 and 2000 when the broadband industry started to grow in Taiwan. According to a Point-Topic report conducted in June 2005, Taiwan has the fourth highest broadband penetration in the world, being surpassed by South Korea, Hong Kong, and Israel (Point-Topic, 2005). Taiwan has been making great efforts to promote the fulfillment of its National Information Infrastructure with broadband network technology as its application has been rapidly developed in recent years. Does the development of broadband promote the use of broadband content or vice versa? The ways in which the leading webcasters in Taiwan position themselves and how they adapt their business models are very unique compared to other countries. For instance, hiChannel made good use of its high ADSL penetration strength while webs-tv established partnership relations with many ISPs. Their content providers all agree to share the revenue after they collect the fees from the users. Therefore, the webcasters do not have the pressure to pay the content providers royalty fees before they collect the fees.

As in many other countries, the internet users are not accustomed to paying for the audio/video services they receive on the web (Chyi, 2005; Lin, 2004; Mings & White, 2000). It thus takes time for the webcasting services to motivate users to pay for their services on the web. This chapter seeks to analyze how webcasters started their services, why the two major content aggregators dominate the webcasting market, and what business models they are using to generate their revenues. (Many statistics are not present in the chapter but are presented in the accompanying CD. Please refer to the CD for data analysis.)

AUDIENCE RESEARCH ON WEBCASTING

In 1999, there were three research companies including AC Nielsen that provided internet survey services. However, they terminated their services in 2002 because of a lack of subscriptions and the limited size of the market. Currently, a new company, InsightXplore, is the only research company conducting research on internet user behavior on a regular basis. InsightXplore has established strategic alliances with many portals and websites. It obtains data from the meters it installs on panel users' computers. It employs a panel of 20,000 users with software meters installed on their computers, and uses ARO as an index, where ARO represents access, reach and opportunity.[1]

This chapter analyzes the business models of the top 20 webcasters. To identify the top 20 webcasters in Taiwan, the author considered selecting them on the basis of revenue and traffic. Since revenue data were not available, the author consulted with InsightXplore, AC Nielsen, Yam, and HiNet regarding the traffic of the webcasters.[2] It was found that none of them could provide an authoritative list of the top 20 webcasters. Based on AC Nielsen's study, the top eleven most visited websites are portals, e-newspapers, and search engines. Only seven websites account for more than 10% of visits. The author has selected four websites, which are also included in the list of the top 11 websites provided by AC Nielsen.[3]

InsightXplore analyzes different categories of websites. Because the AROs of the webcasting sites are very low, it only announces the top three webcasters, namely, webs-tv, WindowsMedia, and hiChannel (InsightXplore, 2005). ISPs such as Asia Pacific Online (APBB) are also included. APBB belongs to a new fixed network or telephone company.[4] It provides both ADSL and cable modem services. Gamebase and Gamer are two important game websites. KingNet is an entertainment website. Channel 5 is connected to hiChannel, and can be linked to the hiChannel website. One major shareholder of hiChannel owns Channel 5. Three commercial terrestrial TV channels (T.V., C.V., and ITS) and one public TV channel are included. The Broadcasting Corporation of China (BCC), the largest radio station, is selected. A satellite TV channel TVBS is included, as well as RealMa, a content aggregator. The selection criteria for the top 20 webcasters are mainly based on traffic flow. The author consulted with many industry people and checked all the well-known webcasters and selected 20 webcasters based on the traffic ranking provided by Alexa, a web search company.[4] (See Table 15–1.)

---

[1] AC Nielsen only conducts communication behavior surveys in which the internet is included every three months. Yam conducts web surveys every year.

[2] HiNet has provided a list of the high-traffic websites with 20,000 or more users on January 19 and 20, 2005.

[3] AC Nielsen conducts the nationwide communications behavior survey every three months. It has the data for the popular websites ranked in its samples.

[4] Alexa internet was founded in April 1996. It provides related links and traffic rankings of the websites.

TABLE 15–1
Top 20 Webcasters in Taiwan

Web Type / Website Name	URL	Business Model	Traffic Rank
Clicks-and-Bricks			
Chinatimes	http://news.chinatimes.com	Branded content	624
ETtoday	http://www.ettoday.com	Branded content	945
TVBS	http://www.tvbs.com.tw	Branded content	4,328
CTV	http://www.chinatv.com.tw	Branded content	4,930
TTV	http://www.ttv.com.tw	Branded content	6,391
MTV	http://www.mtvchinese.com/Index.html	Content aggregator	16,616
PTS	http://www.pts.org.tw	Branded content	21,343
BCC	http://www.bcc.com.tw	Branded content	22,075
Pure-play			
CTS	http://www.cts.com.tw	Branded content	26,930
Yahoo!kimo	http://tw.yahoo.com	Content aggregator	1
hiChannel	http://www.hiChannel.hinet.net	Content aggregator	83
WindowsMedia	http://www.windowsmedia.com	Content aggregator	234
Gamer	http://www.gamer.com.tw	Content aggregator	487
Webs-tv	http://www.webs-tv.net	Content aggregator	858
Gamebase	http://www.gamebase.com.tw	Content aggregator	882
Channel 5	http://www.ch5.tv	Content aggregator	11,625
KingNet	http://movie.kingnet.com.tw	Content aggregator	11,951
ISP Provider			
RealMa	http://www.realma.com/guide	Content aggregator	52,016
Hinet	http://www.hinet.net	Content aggregator	83
APBB	http://www.apbb.com.tw	Content aggregator	8,258

BROADBAND PENETRATION AND USAGE IN TAIWAN

Webcasting services require high bandwidth from the provider. The users also need to have a broadband internet connection in order to enjoy the quality of the webcast (Noam, Groebel, & Gerbarg, 2004). The ROC government has a clear broadband policy. In May 2002, it announced the *"Challenge 2008"* Six-year Na-

tional Development Plan to transform Taiwan into a high-tech service island. One of the objectives of this plan is to develop a "Digital Taiwan." To this end, one of the most important aspects of the plan is to install broadband internet in every household, with a goal of reaching six million households by the end of 2007 (CEPD, 2002).

There are seven million households in Taiwan. Approximately 4.91 million households (HH), or 68.34% of the household population in Taiwan, use the internet, and 4.08 million households, or 56.84% of the HH population, use broadband (TWNIC, 2005). Chunghwa Telecom (CHT) is the dominant fixed network in Taiwan. Its branch company HiNet also dominates 82% of the ADSL market. Seednet, an ISP, is the second biggest provider of ADSL service. In addition, three new fixed networks have offered ADSL services also since they began their operations. Eastern Multimedia Company (EMC) and Hoshin GigaMedia Center, Inc. also provide broadband service via a cable modem. The broadband strategies they adopt include promotion, bundling, advertisements, and price competition, etc. CHT's strategy has been to focus on branding and reliability, and so its ADSL price is higher than that of the ISPs. Seednet's strategy has been to focus on good service and lower prices.

Eastern Broadband Telecommunications (EBT) is a new fixed network that also has a family affiliation with the cable MSO EMC, and so it provides both ADSL and cable modem services. It has acquired an ISP named Asia Pacific Online (APOL) and is now the second largest provider in the Taiwanese broadband market. GigaMedia not only provides cable modem service but also provides ADSL service. The reason why it provides both ADSL and cable modem services is because it wants to provide full broadband services to its customers. It is so-called one stop shopping. Because GigaMedia hesitated to invest in upgrading to two-way cable in 2001–2002, it lost some of its one-way cable modem subscribers (Liu, 2003). In recent years, realizing the drawbacks of the one-way cable modem service, it no longer promotes one-way cable. Altogether, the cable modem penetration is only 3.98% of the broadband penetration.

Other new fixed networks include Taiwan Fixed Network (TFN) and SPARQ (New Century InfoCom Tech Co., Ltd.). Because they are new entrants and still have problems regarding access to the last mile, they prefer to promote broadband to small and medium businesses and also the buildings which have access to high speed internet. Other ISPs such as Seednet and SoNet also actively promote ADSL. For instance, SoNet encouraged HiNet subscribers to switch to its service with gifts such as computers and digital cameras.

During the first stage of broadband deployment, fast speed was important to the wide diffusion of broadband. At that time, the broadband operators provided many promotions regarding speed and lowered their prices to attract users. During the first quarter of 2003, the growth of broadband slowed significantly, and therefore the content of broadband was considered the next important driving force (Liu, 2003).

Broadband Usage

Among the phone survey interviewees who are broadband users, 63.52% use it as a tool to browse web pages, 43.82% use it for e-mail, and 29.59% use it for information searching. The percentage watching videos and TV online is below 2% (TWNIC, 2005).[5] According to many studies, most broadband users are still reluctant to pay for audio and video services on the internet. However, according to a survey conducted by InsightXplore in October 2004, 58.9% of users were willing to pay for online music, and 74.2% of them had experiences of paying for the online music or downloading the music. Users between 21 and 30 years of age were more inclined to pay for the online music.

Webcast Consumption

According to InsightXplore (2004), 50% of internet users have visited the online video websites. Although there are many webcasters, there is no research or survey reporting the full activities of webcasters. In 2004, the web advertising revenue was NT$2 billion (US$60.2 million) (or 2.25% of the total advertising revenue) (Brain, 2005. 2).[6] The total revenue for webcasting was NT$0.45 billion ($13.55 million) a year.

Because webs-tv and hiChannel are the two biggest webcasters, their customers' consumption can shed some light on the webcast consumption in Taiwan. According to an internal study conducted by webs-tv in November 2004, news constitutes the largest content viewing category with an audience share of 27.1%, followed by adult programs (24.3%), drama, (15.5%), variety shows (12.1%), music (5.5%), and movies (4.6%) (M. Chen, personal communication, January 17, 2005). However, hiChannel's customers watch TV programs the most (36.83%), followed by entertainment (10.3%), movies (6.59%), and simulcast (1.99%) (S. Chen, personal communication, June 9, 2005). 33% of the customers only watch less than 10 minutes of TV, 21% watch 31–60 minutes, and 24% watch more than 90 minutes of TV. 52% of the customers paid less than NT$100 ($3.01), and 42% paid between NT$101 (US$3.01) and NT$1,000 (US$30.12) online (Liu, 2003).

Half of the hiChannel customers are 25–35 years old. Male customers account for 70%, and female customers for 30%. The majority of customers of webs-tv are

---

[5]The survey was conducted between May 30 and July 31 2005. There were 3059 samples.

[6]$1.00 U.S. is approximately equivalent to $33.20 NT. The exchange rate varies according to the date.

also 25–35 years old. Male customers account for 65% of them, and female customers for 35%.

WEBCASTING MARKET ENVIRONMENT

Taiwan's audience enjoy a multichannel TV environment. The two major webcasters, namely, webs-tv and hiChannel, developed in 1999 and 2000. As they grew in the market, the telephone companies and ISPs started to promote high-speed internet. The reasons why they could grow included: (1) the big bandwidth of the content aggregators; (2) the promotion of broadband connections; and (3) the support of the content providers.

When the webcasters emerged in the market, the existing television channels hesitated as they debated whether to provide content to the webcasters. In fact, there was a debate between the programming department and the information department of some television stations regarding whether webcasting services would hurt their ratings and advertising revenues.[7] The programming departments of the television systems or channels did not want to provide their programs to webcasters, because they were afraid that the ratings of their programs might be affected by their online counterparts. The information departments thought that the internet viewers were different from those of the television viewers. Therefore, more access meant more opportunities and more revenue.

The five terrestrial stations and most of the leading satellite channels have their own websites. However, they have not made many efforts in regard to having their own webcasting services. They mainly use webcasting as a supporting medium. In the beginning, newscasts and dramas were delayed on purpose. Now, news and dramas are simulcast. Since they do not provide complete programs on their websites, their ARO (hits) are relatively low. The five terrestrial stations all have e-commerce with the exception of C.V. Most of them sell DVDs. T.V. even sells hotel packages. Some have advertisements embedded with each piece of news. FTV On Demand adopts a subscription model, and also provides some free programs. Although PTS is a public service, surprisingly its dramas are not free of charge. Webs-tv and hiChannel provide many channels and are content aggregators. All the branded leading channels are willing to have more exposure and access to users via their websites.

---

[7]The programming department is in charge of programming strategies. The information department is in charge of the news automation and web sites maintenance.

Unlike other countries, most branded content webcasters in Taiwan are not good at managing the webcasting business. They do not think webcasting service is their core business, so they pay more attention to the offline media. Even though many radio stations and TV channels have their own websites, they are willing to provide their content to the aggregators in order to have more access to internet users.

BUSINESS PERFORMANCE OF LEADING WEBCASTERS

Leading Video Webcasters

According to a report announced in October 2003 by InsightXplore, the three most popular webcasters are webs-tv.net Inc., Microsoft's WindowsMedia.com, and HiNet's hiChannel. Webs-tv.net is a content aggregator. Having established strategic alliances with the fixed networks, ISPs, and portals, it brings the whole webcasting service to the platforms of the fixed networks and ISPs. Their cooperation model is that the fixed networks and the ISPs collect the fees from the customers, which they subsequently share with webs-tv. The way webs-tv cooperates with the portals varies. It sometimes provides video clips of the movies to MSN, or else it buys advertisement spots on Yahoo's website (M. Chen, personal communication, January 17, 2005). As for the e-newspaper UDN.com, webs-tv provides it with TVBS news. It also helps Formosa TV to build its webcasting-on-demand site. (See Table 15–2.)

Webs-tv has also established strategic alliances with many ISPS such as SeedNet or portals such as Yahoo!Kimo, Sina, and Yam. In order to make the users feel that they (portals and ISPs) have webcasting services, they provide links to webs-tv on their webpage (the second layer). This phenomenon is very different from that of other countries (Ha et al., 2005).

WindowsMedia.com is also a content aggregator. It does not collect money from the users, but is positioned to be a portal of webcasting users. Thus, it has links with many other content aggregators or providers of branded content. Its content includes TV, radio, movies, music, etc. It also has links with Windows Media Player. Whenever the Window Media Player users start the program, they can view the website of WindowsMedia.

HiChannel is a content aggregator that was established by Chunghwa Telecom (the biggest telephone company) and Elta (a content aggregator). It has strategic ties with SeedNet, Gamebase, and Gamer. Elta established its own webcasting service which is referred to as Ch5. There are many overlapping content sources between the two webcasters, however Ch5 targets younger users.

TABLE 15–2
The SWOT Analysis of hiChannel and webs-tv

	hiChannel	webs-tv
Strengths	1. Enough bandwidth. 2. CHT's branding. 3. CHT has more operating money. 4. HiNet is the biggest ISP. 5. More exclusive content.	1. Cooperates with many ISPs; consumers have more access to its content. 2. Diverse payment mechanism. 3. Provide other services such as diary and blog.
Weaknesses	1. Has less platform. 2. Consumers have less access to hiChannel content.	1. Branding is not strong. 2. Its strategic partners have less ADSL penetration.
Opportunities	1. The development of IPTV and 3G. 2. The Chinese market is still big. 3. The users will be willing to pay for the web content.	1. The development of WiMax can solve the problem of the last mile. 2. The Chinese market is still big. 3. The users will be willing to pay for the Web content.
Threats	1. P2P download. 2. Growth of webs-tv.	1. P2P download.

Online News Webcasters

There are two major news webcasters in Taiwan: ETtoday.com and China-times.com. ETtoday.com is a clicks-and-bricks webcaster that has positioned itself as an internet data center. It belongs to Eastern Broadcasting Company (EBC) which has eight cable channels. In 2004, ETTV's eight channels secured the highest cable viewer ratings in Taiwan—averaging 14.77% of market share (AC Nielsen, 2005). In terms of revenue, EBC also led the field in 2004, earning US$180 million through television, radio, the internet, and newspaper enterprises. EBC also has two overseas satellite channels which can be seen in 66 countries. ETtoday itself is one of the top three e-newspapers. Its offline channel ET News Channel receives the highest rating among the various news channels, and its rating is the third among all the channels (AC Nielsen, 2005). It is used to integrate all the news platforms such as radio, TV, newspaper, and the internet within its media group. It employs an integrated marketing strategy, making good use of advertising production, radio ads, internet ads, market surveys, marketing, public relations, news coverage, image ads, product ads, sponsorship, program production, projects, etc (Y. Chang, personal communication January 21, 2005; Fetschrein & Knolmayer, 2004). It also originates some news for ETtoday. However, its original content is only in text and graphic form. Its webcasting service is "repurposed" and "simulcast" from its own TV channels.

As in other websites, people who come to ETtoday are more interested in its e-newspaper than its ETTV channels.

The *China Times* is one of the leading newspapers in Taiwan. It owns a group of TV channels (CTiTV) such as news, entertainment, and full service channels. Its e-newspaper Chinatimes.com used to provide a webcasting service CTiTV on the front page of its website. Now, it has moved to the second layer. CTiTV also has its own website, but it does not provide links to the *China Times*. Surprisingly, the *China Times* also has a link with webs-tv. Chinatimes.com has also originated some audio or video interviews with art or cultural celebrities or those that are based on its online polling topic (V. Kuo, personal communication, August 16, 2005).

UDN.com is part of the United Daily News Group, and its e-newspaper is widely received. Since it does not own any video content, it has established a strategic alliance with the TVBS-N channel. Because webs-tv owns the exclusive rights for TVBS-N online, UDN.com has a link with webs-tv as well. Even though UDN.com is a branded e-newspaper, it is not considered as a webcaster.

Game Webcasters

Gamer is ranked among the top 20 websites, and is the most popular game website (InsightXplore, 2004). More than one million non-repeated people visit its website each month and the average usage time is 20 minutes. In November 2000, Gamer spent NT$400,000 dollars (US$12,048.19) each month, but its financial source depended on advertising dollars only. Since its users are loyal to the website, it tried to adopt e-commerce to generate revenue. In November 2001, Gamer started to break even. Since 2003, Gamer can make NT$1 million (US$30,000) dollars from advertising, and between NT$1 million (US$30,000) and NT$5 million (US$150,000) dollars from e-commerce annually. It has been making profits since the end of 2001. 64% of Gamer's users are students (Shih, 2004).

Another famous website is Gamebase which is the number two game webcaster. It was founded in 2000 by a computer magazine of a publishing conglomerate group. Gamebase has gathered enormous amounts of game-related data such as game critics, game strategies, game skills, game introductions, etc. It aggregated a large quantity of game information in order to become a game portal. In June 2004, Gamebase started to provide a webcasting service by cooperating with many domestic game companies. Its webcasting service provides information regarding new games, exclusive games, etc. It also gives away prizes to attract more visitors. Nearly one million non-repeated people visit its website each month. The average usage time is 24 minutes. 77.5% of Gamebase's users are students and 67% of the users are 16–25 years old.

Portal Webcasters

Yahoo!Kimo is the only portal webcaster. Yahoo and Kimo were merged in February 2001. They have built strategic alliances with ETtoday and Giga in video service and with Rose Record Company, Money KTV and the Voice of Taipei in audio service. Most of Yahoo!Kimo's visitors are between the ages of 15 to 29.

Music Webcasters

There are two kinds of music webcasters. One is an online music service, the other is web music radio station. For music online, the users need to download the software. Since Kuro started to adopt a subscription scheme, QBand, iMusic, HiMusic, and KKBox have considered the web as an important platform for generating revenues. KKBox's core business is to provide professional music online. It has more than 65,000 members. HiNet's online music is supported by KKBox, so it provides link to KKBox.

A web music radio station does not require the users to download the software. All the major record companies provide similar webcasting services. The popular radio stations such as BCC, UFO, New 98, ICRT, and the Voice of Taipei all have their websites. They all use RealNetwork's Real Player, Microsoft's Media Player, and Apple's Quick Time to provide simulcast and audio on demand services.

Animation Webcasters

Ah-kuei is an animation webcaster. It created the figure Ah-kuei just for its website. All the stories online revolve around Ah-kuei, and the contents is all original. After Ah-kuei became popular, the web figure was introduced to TV and movies. Ah-kuei also does commercials for some products as a spokesman. Its major revenue comes from members' subscription fees. It also extends its business to places overseas such as Japan. More than two million people have visited Ah-kuei's website. Half of the visitors are students. Because Ah-kuei's traffic ranking is low, it is not included in the top 20 webcasters list.

WEBCAST BUSINESS MODELS

Business models can coexist and one model is not necessarily better than another (Ha & Ganahl, 2004). Some webcasters aggregate different content sources to provide webcasting services. Some share profits with ISP and content providers. Some provide video clips of entertainment for service, not for profits, but as a service or for complimentary purposes (Ha, 2003; Ha, 2004).

Ward (2000) classified the online business models into two kinds of models: Improvement-based and revenue-based models. The improvement-based model does not aim to make a profit. Its website purports to cut down the cost of service, improve product and corporate image, increase the level of customer loyalty, and adopt the products of its company. The revenue-based model seeks to improve the service quality and to make profits by selling products or services online.

Ha & Ganahl (2004) used content aggregator and branded content models to analyze the webcasters' business models. They pointed out that the webcasters can be classified as two kinds: Clicks-and-bricks and pure-play. A clicks-and-bricks model means that there are offline media such as ESPN.com. A pure-play model means that it exists only online as in the case of Real Network. This chapter analyzes the business model of the webcasters in Taiwan based on the ACR framework.

OWNERSHIP AND BUSINESS PERFORMANCE OF THE TOP 20 WEBCASTERS

Altogether, nine webcasters adopt the branded content business model. The nine clicks-and-bricks webcasters all adopt the branded content model except MTV. The Pure-play and ISP providers all adopt the content aggregator model. Although A-Kuei, a pure-play provider, adopts the content aggregator model, it is not included in the top 20 webcasters.

None of the top 20 webcasters are publicly listed on the stock market. This chapter next analyzes the three dimensions, namely, accessibility, content strategies and revenue sources related to the webcasting business model.

Accessibility

Some webcasters provide two kinds of speed (narrow speed and high speed) for their users. The average connection speed is 512k. Since HiNet and some other ISPs provide higher speeds such as 1 or 2 mps, broadband content transmission becomes easier. The media player is also important. If the users experience difficulties playing the videos with their media players, they will abandon the service. 95% of webcasters use Windows Media Player, and 25% of webcasters use Real Player. No one uses other proprietary players. The top 20 webcasters except RealMa and MTV all provide search engine or directory services within their sites.

As for the transmission method, 90% of webcasters all use on demand streaming, 60% of webcasters use the live streaming transmission method, and 15% of webcasters use on demand downloading. Only one webcaster uses the push transmission method.

Content Strategies

Nearly 45% of the top 20 webcasters are clicks and bricks and 45% are pure-play. While 90% of webcasters repurpose their content, 50% of webcasters simulcast their content. And 15% of webcasters use original content. The webcaster A-Kuei has unique content on its website, and has positioned itself as an Asian Disney. By employing rich media characteristics, it created an animated figure named A-Kuei. After being shown on the internet, it was later introduced to TV and movies. Because of the limited capital and budget, the A-Kuei webcaster did not expand its business and had less influence in the webcasting industry. Its content is very focused. All the stories revolve around the figure A-Kuei. The webcaster provides entertainment, games, and an educational service on its website. HiChannel and Ch5 share some of the content. When they started their services, they initiated a program called the "Anchorwomen Wearing Underwear Show." In the show, a woman reported the news wearing only a bra and underwear. Because hiChannel is partially owned by a state-owned fixed network Chunghwa Telecom, it terminated the show because of the pressure from the legislators and the public. Although hiChannel and Ch5 are content aggregators, they still have a variety show that originated for their internet customers. Their competitor webs-tv also holds two big events annually in order to attract the users' attention (M. Chen, personal communication, October 6, 2005).

As for the video genres, news clips/interviews, cartoons/animations, and TV commercials are the most popular ones, followed by business, trailers/highlights/video clips of entertainment content, and TV programs/series. With regard to audio genres, music, talks/interviews, and news are the most popular ones.

According to hiChannel, the killer application is the adult programs. The adult programs played by the webcasters still have to apply for permission from the regulator under the TV rating regulation and the Videotape Law. Since hiChannel is partially owned by a state-owned telephone company CHT, it will be under pressure when promoting its adult programs. Webs-tv believes that the killer applications for webcasting are news, variety shows, and adult programs (M. Chen, personal communication, January 17, 2005).

Revenue Sources

Most of the webcasters' revenue is generated from advertising/sponsorship, followed by e-commerce, content syndication, subscriptions, and pay-per-view. Content aggregators tend to have more advertising, while branded content webcasters seem to have more content syndication and e-commerce. Eight of the top 20 webcasters do not provide e-commerce services.

With e-commerce, more webcasters sell media/entertainment-related products and other commercial products. Few webcasters sell the licensed merchandise of TV shows/stars.

With regard to the payment methods of leading webcasters, credit card payment and telephone debit are used mostly. Content aggregators tend to be more likely to adopt telephone debit and credit card payment methods. However, branded content webcasters like to use credit card and direct debit payment methods.

International Influence

The international webcasters do not have much influence on the webcasting market in Taiwan. The international contents do not bring much revenue to the webcasters either. If the foreign programs do not have Chinese subtitles or dubbing, the programs are not widely received (M. Chen, personal communication, October 6, 2005). Of the leading 20 webcasters, only 10% have foreign ownership and 15% are joint ventures. The rest are domestic webcasters. Yahoo!Kimo, RealMa, and TVBS are joint ventures. Windows Media and MTV are foreign-owned webcasters. Yahoo! previously led the international market. Because it could not beat Kimo in Taiwan, it merged with Kimo. Yahoo!Kimo is the most popular website, but it is only a pure-play webcaster.

CASE STUDIES

HiChannel

Founded in July 2001, hiChannel is one of the two leading content aggregators. Owned by CHT and Elta, its media database acts as a platform for all of the contents. In July 2005, it had 90 partners and 150 channels, including terrestrial channels, cable channels, and other movie channels. HiChannel does not have to pay the royalty fees before it collects money from the users. Its business model is to split the revenues with the content providers on the basis of a 3:2:5 ratio (CHT, Elta, content providers). CHT, the largest telephone company, is responsible for the video server, storage, bandwidth, and billing; Elta, the largest audio-video content aggregator, is responsible for marketing, aggregating the content, and digitizing the content; the ICP is required to provide the content with the copyright. (See Figure 15-1.)

Like most of the television stations and satellite channels, the fixed networks and the cable modem operators each have their own websites. They all provide content, but are not as attractive as hiChannel. HiChannel is an open platform and has the advantage of CHT's last mile and branding. Thus, many content providers

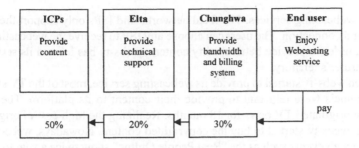

FIGURE 15-1   HiChannel business model. *Source*: Elta.

are willing to come to this platform because CHT's high ADSL penetration can help them reach more broadband users.

HiChannel owns 250,000 hours of content in its video server, of which 81% is reproduced content, 9% is original content, 6% is simulcast, and 4% is outsourcing (S. Chen, personal communication, June 9, 2005). Its server capacity can allow 24,000 people to watch the same film or program online. Its content includes five categories:

1. Simulcast: news, entertainment, elections, singer's show, etc.
2. GOD: The paid movies can be viewed repeatedly for 48 hours.
3. Video commercials: They are played before the free content.
4. Monthly subscription: The subscribers can pay NT$88 (US$2.65), NT$188 (US$5.66), or NT$288 (US$8.67) monthly for the movies, dramas, variety shows, and adult programs.
5. Package service: The users can choose to pay for specific packages of programs or movies.

In addition to the above webcasting services, hiChannel also provides video chatting, e-learning and audio/video space rental services (S. Chen, personal communication, June 9, 2005).

Webs-tv

Webs-tv was established in April 1999, positioning itself as a web multiple system operator (MSO). It has formed strategic alliances with seven partners including fixed networks and ISPs such as anet.tv, sparq.tv, GigaTV, SonetTV, BTV, avplus.tv, and estv. Webs-tv is responsible for aggregating the contents and managing the webcasting services. The fixed networks and ISPs only support the bandwidth and connection. The users can choose any ISP to receive the webcasting service. In order to provide better quality content, webs-tv has located its servers in each partner's territory.

When webs-tv started to provide its webcasting service, most of the TV stations and channels were reluctant to provide their content to its platform. Therefore, webs-tv originated TV news for 18 months. Realizing the high cost of originated content, webs-tv started to buy the copyrighted content. Nowadays, webs-tv will hold big web events such as the "Real People Online" show twice a year to attract web users.[8] It owns 200,000 hours of content in its video servers.

Webs-tv's major revenue source is subscription fees. Its annual net profit is currently NT$20 (US$0.60) million, and it has been making a profit for two years. The revenue sharing model of webs-tv with other ISPs and ICPs is similar to that of hiChannel. The ratio is also based on the 3:2:5 ratio (ISPs, webs-tv, content providers). The difference between webs-tv and hiChannel is that webs-tv has servers in all of the ISPs' territories, while hiChannel only cooperates with one ISP—HiNet. The ISPs have their own websites, so they have some control over their own websites. Since webs-tv needs to use its partners'—the ISPs'—billing systems, it has to pay transmission fees to the ISPs. By cooperating with all the ISPs, webs-tv also has bargaining power when it pays the royalty fees to the content providers.

In addition to providing content similar to HiChannel, webs-tv also tries to provide some exclusive channels such as TVBS, TVBS-N, TVBS-G, ETV, Videoland Sports, Videoland Movies, Ctitv, Ctitv News, and Ctitv Variety channel on its platform. Because webs-tv's competitor—HiChannel—is partly owned by CHT, webs-tv cannot use its brand to cooperate with CHT's branch company HiNet. Therefore, webs-tv has established a branch website—Broadband TV—in order to use HiNet's billing system. In other words, webs-tv cooperates with almost all the ISPs, either directly or indirectly. Webs-tv has access to almost all the broadband users.

Webs-tv believes that the development of other digital platforms such as digital TV, CHT's MOD and SeedNet's DFC will not threaten its own growth, because it can cooperate with them. [9] Webs-tv will enter the IPTV market. It believes that with the technology of WiMax, it can solve the problem of the last mile and reach more broadband users. It can also save some circuit fees paid to the ISPs. Its international users account for 30% of its customers. Most of the international users are Chinese residing overseas. A comparison of the strengths, weaknesses, opportunities, and threats (SWOT) of hiChannel is shown in Table 15–1.

---

[8]"Real People Online" is a show to invite people to challenge themselves online. The show is unedited. It is composed of 24 hours activities of the participants.

[9]SeedNet's DFC means Digital Family Center. It is an IPTV. Subsc:ibers can receive video services via a TV plus a set-top-box.

CONCLUSION: OUTLOOK FOR THE WEBCASTING INDUSTRY IN TAIWAN

The webcasting market is not big in Taiwan. Only the two largest webcasters can survive and generate a profit The leading webcasters believe that the percentage of people who are willing to pay for webcasting service will grow to 10% of the broadband users; therefore, there is still room for them to grow. In order to increase the economic scale, the webcasters should consider providing content not only to PC end-users but to TV audiences and 3G users as well. When they discuss the royalty fees with the content providers, they will acquire three kinds of rights at one time.

During the first stage, the leading webcasters adopt a revenue-sharing model. There is no risk for the webcasters. When they reach a certain economic scale, they have to adopt the minimum guarantee model. It means the webcasters have to guarantee to pay a certain amount of royalty fees annually or monthly. In addition, when they are able to compete with other platforms, they start to buy the exclusive rights to play the programs shown on their platform. Even though the leading webcasters are content aggregators, they also have several original programs such as variety shows, Real People online shows, sports games each year to make it look unique to other platforms.

Does broadband service help webcasting services develop or vice versa? What are the real killer applications for webcasting? Some webcasters think that adult programs are the killer applications. However, they cannot provide too much publicity for the service because of their social image. They have even relocated the adult programs to the second layer in order not to provoke the parents' groups.

According to past research, broadband users have been reluctant to pay for on-line video or TV. Only the big webcasters are optimistic about this market. The small players only use it as a supporting medium. Strictly speaking, there are no successful clicks-and-bricks. While ETtoday is one of the ten big websites, its webcasting service is insignificant in the webcasting market. People visiting the ETtoday website do so mostly for the text-and-graphics news instead of its offline channels.

Although most of the major TV channels have their own websites, they do not have good performance in webcasting. They lack bandwidth and have different mindsets. People like to go to the content aggregator websites, because they can be satisfied with one-stop entertainment. Almost all the popular channels are provided on that platform.

Although webcasting is a global medium, most of its customers still prefer domestic programs. The webcasters usually do not reproduce the foreign programs because they do not have enough manpower or budget to do it. Thus, the foreign program sources account for only 30% of the two major content aggregators and the domestic content still dominates the webcasting market.

Bandwidth is important for both the webcasters and the users. If they are big enough, the quality will be better and more stable. Users will become more and more willing to pay for the web content. With more people connected to broadband, more content providers will invest in this platform. However, the content providers should not limit their content to exclusive use so that they can have more access to the users.

REFERENCES

AC Nielsen. 2005. *Rating measurement studies*. Unpublished raw data.

CEPD. (2002). *The economy*. Retrieved December 15, 2005, from http://ww.cepd.gov.tw/2008/index. htm

Chan-Olmsted, S., & Lee, Y. (2003). Internet business models for broadcasters: how television stations perceive and integrate the internet. *Journal of Broadcasting and Electronic Media, 47*(4), 597–617.

Chang, B., Lee, S., & Lee, Y. (2004). Devising video distribution strategies via the internet: Focusing on economic properties of video products. *International Journal on Media Management. 6*(1&2), 36–45.

Chyi, H. I. (2005). Willingness to pay for online news: An empirical study on the viability of the subscription model. *Journal of Media Economics, 18*(2), 131–143.

Fetschrein, M., & Knolmayer, G. (2004). Business models for content delivery: An empirical analysis of the newspaper and the magazine industry. *International Journal of Media Management, 6*(1&2), 4–11.

GIO. (02005). A brief introduction to Taiwan. Retrieved December 10, 2005, from http://www.gio. gov.tw

Ha, L. (2003). Crossing offline and online media: A comparison of online advertising on TV web sites and online portals. *Journal of Interactive Advertising, 3*(2). Retrieved October 6, 2005 from http://www.jiad.org/vol3/no2/ha/index.htm

Ha, L. (2004). Webcasting. In H. Bidgoli (Ed.), *The internet encyclopedia* (pp. 674–682). New York: John Wiley & Sons.

Ha, L., & Ganahl, R. (2004). Webcasting business models of click-and-bricks and pure-play media: A comparative study of leading webcasters in South Korea and the United States. *The International Journal of Media Management, 6*(1&2), 75–88.

Ha, L., et al. (2005). Emerging media business models worldwide: A study of leading webcasters in 13 countries. Paper to be presented at the annual conference of the Association for Education in Journalism and Mass Communication, San Antonio, Texas, August 10–12.

Hoskins, C., McFadyen, S., & Finn, A. (2004). *Media economics: Applying economics to new and traditional media*. Thousand Oaks, CA: Sage.

InsightXplore. (2004). *ARO web measurement studies*. Retrieved December 17, 2005, from http://www.InsightXplore.XXX

InsightXplore. (2005). *ARO web measurement studies*. Unpublished raw data.

Lin, C. (2004). Webcasting adoption: Technology fluidity, user innovativeness and media substitution. *Journal of Broadcasting and Electronic Media, 48*(3), 477–500.

Liu, Y.L. (2003). Broadband use, competition and relevant policy in Taiwan. *Journal of Interactive Advertising 4*(1). Retrieved December 3, 2005, from http://jiad.org

Liu, Y.L. (2004). *Telecommunications*. Taipei: Yeh-Yeh.

Mings, M. S., & White, B. P. (2000). Profiting from online news: The research for viable business models. In B. Kahin & R. H. Varian (Eds.), *internet publishing and beyond: The economics of digital information and intellectual property* (pp. 62–97). Cambridge, MA: MIT Press.

Noam, E., Groebel, J., & Gerbarg, D. (Eds.). (2004). Internet *television*. Mahwah, NJ: Erlbaum.

Picard, R. G. (2002). *The economics and financing of media companies*. New York: Fordham University Press.

Point-Topic. (2005). Broadband analysis. Retrieved December 15, 2005, from http://www.point-topic.com

Shih, T.H. (2004). Game can be a interest. *Cheers, 4*, 80–81.

TWNIC. (2005). Internet broadband usage in Taiwan. Retrieved November 30, 2005, from http://www.dgbas.gov.tw/public/Data/59616412471.PDF

Ward, H. (2000). Principles of internet marketing. Cincinnati, OH: SouthWestern.

APPENDIX
In-depth Interviews

- *Yu-cheng Chang*—Director, ETtoday (January 21, 2005)
- *Morse Chen*— CEO, webs-tv (January 17, 2005; October 6, 2005)
- *Sally Chen*—CEO, hiChannel (June 9, 2005)
- *Teddy Jin*—Research Manager, Nielsen Research (January 18, 2005)
- *Vincent Kuo*—Editor in Chief, ChinaTimes.com (August 16, 2005)
- *Sislley Yu*—Marketing Manager, InsightXplore (January 18, 2005)

CHAPTER 16

Korea: The Country With the World's Highest Broadband Penetration— Popular Video Webcasters and User-Generated Content Models

Sora Park
Hanyang University, Korea

WEBCASTING MARKET ENVIRONMENT

Korea's webcasting industry was able to develop steadily because of its fast growing media markets and its advanced IT infrastructure. The media market is one of the most dynamic markets in the world. New media are being introduced aggressively by both market forces and governmental policies. While traditional media are still heavily regulated,[1] less regulation exists in the new media sector. Often new media and telecommunications industries are launched under governmental protection. Audiences and readers quickly absorb new media services, causing financial difficulties for major newspapers and broadcasters. Most of the major newspapers have been experiencing financial losses during the past few years. Major broadcasters have been slowly losing audience share from over 90% to under 70% during the past decade.

For instance, DMB (digital multimedia broadcasting), a new mobile content delivery service, was launched in 2005 and delivers multi-channel video, audio, and data channels to mobile phones. Major telecommunication companies are ready to

---

[1]Traditionally the media sector is heavily regulated. The amount and price of TV advertising is still regulated by the government as well as the program content that is shown on major TV. Cross-ownership rules between broadcasting and newspaper still exists as well as restriction of ownership rules of foreign companies (49%).

introduce IPTV into the market soon[2]. The internet has already been accepted by the majority of media users, and online newspapers have attracted many news readers. New business models have been experimented with and have succeeded.

On the other hand, the traditional media sector is experiencing a slow down in revenues and is also losing readership and viewership. The four major traditional mass media—i.e., television, radio, newspaper, and magazine—experienced an 8.2% decrease in revenues in 2004. Among them, the newspaper market suffered the largest decrease in revenues. However, it is not always the case that print-media is on the downturn. Only recently introduced, free dailies have already experienced a two-fold increase in revenues.

The total advertising volume across all media in 2004 was approximately $5.8 billion[3] (670 billion won), a decrease of 1.5%. Despite the fact that the ad market did not perform very well in 2004, internet advertising revenues nevertheless increased by 45.4% from the previous year.

In 2001 the proportion of total television advertising exceeded newspaper advertising, which shows that electronic media had become the most popular form of information and entertainment consumption. In 2004 television generated 48.4% of the advertising revenue earned by all four major media markets. The newspaper market's share was 36.9%. More and more people are getting used to electronic or digital media, which are often viewed as providing new media services just entering the market an opportunity to compete with existing mass media. (See Table 16–1.)

THE MEDIA MARKET OVERVIEW

Korea has 3 major television networks, KBS, MBC, and SBS. SBS is privately owned and is affiliated with 9 local commercial broadcasters. The other two are public broadcasters. There is also an educational network, EBS, which has nationwide coverage. Korea has one direct satellite service provider, SkyLife, 418 cable system operators, 159 cable networks and 540 daily newspapers as of 2004. The

---

[2]DMB (Digital Multimedia Broadcasting) is a satellite or terrestrial distribution service that delivers mobile content to cell-phones or vehicle mounted monitors. The largest mobile telco, SKTelecom, launched satellite DMB service in May 2005; other companies including major broadcasters will start terrestrial DMB services early next year. DMB service is unique in the sense that people can now view video content on the go. IPTV (Internet Protocol Television) is a video delivery service (mainly VOD) via broadband networks. In Korea the major telecommunication companies, KT and Hanaro Telecom, are investing in this area.

[3]All dollar values were calculating by using the mid-year exchange rate for every year as reported by the Korea Exchange Bank (www.keb.co.kr).

TABLE 16-1
Change in Advertising Revenues of Each Media (%)

Year	Newspaper	TV	Radio	Magazine	Cable	Internet	Total
1980	29.7	30.0	14.0	31.8	—	—	25.9
1990	38.9	13.7	52.3	41.4	—	—	27.8
2000	17.5	38.6	43.0	25.6	35.5	67.5	28.8
2001	−17.5	−5.6	−5.3	181.9	−4.9	−5.8	12.8
2002	15.4	24.9	17.2	18.7	42.0	44.4	1.9
2003	−6.4	−3.0	−0.7	−8.4	26.9	45.9	−0.6
2004	−7.7	−5.6	−3.9	−15.0	34.4	45.4	−2.0

Source: *Advertising Yearbook*. Cheil Communications, 2005.

total over-the-air broadcasters' revenue in 2003 was $2.3 billion (283.4 billion won), with profits totaling $20 million (24,820 million won).

In 2004 there were approximately 1400 movie screens. A total of 279 movies were released in theaters, 78 of which were domestic and 201 foreign. While there are more foreign movies released, the box office shares of domestic movies are well over 50% since the year 2002.

The Korean market first saw new media services introduced in the 1990s. In 1995 cable television was launched and direct satellite services arrived in 2002. Cable TV household penetration reached 73.4% (12.8 million HH) in 2004, having begun in 1995 with a mere 3.8% at year's end. Due to the deregulation in the cross-ownership of system operators and cable networks, we now see large MSOs owning multiple cable networks such as ON Media and CJ Media, which are the largest cable networks in Korea. The cable industry is becoming more and more concentrated. In 2004, the market share of total revenues of MSOs (multiple cable system operators) was 72.8% of all cable system operators. The market share of cable networks that own two or more channels were 48% (Korea Broadcast Commission, 2005).

The telecommunications market has also been well received in Korea. In 2004, 36.6 million people had a mobile phone, making that market larger than the one for landlines. The internet has also had a rapid diffusion rate. As of December 2004, 31.6 million people—approximately 70% of the population—use the internet according to the National Internet Development Agency of Korea (2004). The broadband penetration rate reached 24.7 persons per 100, which means over 71% of the households (HH) subscribe to broadband services (12.3 million HH) in January 2005, with most broadband users (8.7 million) having DSL-based services. DSL services are more popular compared to cable modem services since cable penetration reached 50% in 2003 and is not as popular. KT is the major provider of DSL services with a market share of 51% in the broadband markat, followed by Hanaro Telecom (22.8%) and the third is the cable modem service company Thr:net (10.7%).

The younger generations in Korea have very high usage rates of 96.2% in the 6–19 age group and 95.3% in the 20–29 age group. In the years to come, virtually everyone will be using the internet. The quick adoption of internet technologies occurred recently. In 1995 only 366,000 people were using the internet, just 0.8% of the population. This usage rate increased to 22.4% in 1999, 56.7% in 2001, and 68.4% in 2004.

Characteristics of Webcasters in Korea

A few factors created a favorable environment for webcasters in Korea. The first is the rapid growth of the internet industry compared to other industries. Second, the high broadband penetration facilitated the easy delivery of multimedia content to users. Third, although the traditional media sector is undergoing deregulation, it remains unable to fully adapt to rapid technological and market changes, whereas the new media sector benefits from being governed by more flexible regulatory conditions.

Internet VOD services were launched by the major broadcast networks (KBS, SBS, and MBC), but many small webcasters had already been experimenting with a diverse range of content. At first, video services were regarded as complimenting original TV broadcasts, a perk for loyal television viewers. In some ways they were an extension of bulletin boards and chat rooms about major television programs. But the market demand for internet VOD services in recent years has increased with broadband penetration. With the emergence of this new market as a primary source of revenue (except for the public broadcaster KBS which receives license fees from viewers), broadcasters quickly began to charge for their formerly free services.

Due to the quality and popularity of the content they provide, the major broadcasters have the greatest stake in the webcasting industry. Although producers of experimental programs and low budget movies also use the internet as a venue to market their products, not many have succeeded.

The major broadcasters' sites and other portals offering major movies and TV shows receive the lion's share of both revenue and user traffic. Although webcasters primarily offer repurposed major movies and TV shows, the viewing population differs somewhat from traditional broadcast viewers. The viewing occurs within hours or days after the original broadcast.

People often suppose that information distributed on the internet should be free of charge, but high quality entertainment VOD services may be changing this assumption. According to a survey conducted by KISDI (2004), among internet users over the age of 15, only 20.1% have ever used pay services on the internet. By category, the most popular pay services were music (70.8%), news and information (67.3%), and movies and TV programs (54.5%). On average users spent 17,700 won (approximately $15) per month. As the penetration of broadband services reaches the saturation point, internet pay services have grown accordingly. In 2002, pay service revenue exceeded $127 billion (156 trillion won), a 56% increase over the previous year (Korea IT Industry Promotion Agency, 2003).

Portal sites provide VOD to entice users to logon to their sites. Most of them have blockbuster movies, popular TV shows, and adult content. ISPs are also aggressive in obtaining rights for webcasting major movies and TV shows. Megapass (owned by the major telecommunications company KT) and Hanafos (owned by Hanaro Telecom) are DSL services that package broadband connectivity with access to their database of movies and TV shows. Cable modem services likewise often promote VOD services to compete for broadband consumers. However, there is a limit to portal sites or broadband providers in distributing major TV shows because the broadcasters all have their own webcasting companies, which are all competing for the best content.

To summarize, the market for new media services including webcasting is growing in Korea due to the high broadband penetration and early adoption and easy acceptance of digital media services. The participation of major media companies in the webcasting business is also a positive factor.

WEBCASTING BUSINESS MODELS

There are several hundred internet VOD service sites in Korea. KORWA (Korea Webcasting Association) reports that approximately 570 webcasters are operating in 2005. The majority of them are music sites or adult movie sites. Those sites, however, have a very limited subscriber or viewer base and provide content of limited quality too. Successful VOD sites are run by the major broadcasters, KBS, MBC, and SBS. These networks' internal sites provide real-time news and radio shows as well as VOD services for dramas, sitcoms, variety shows, and documentaries, drama reruns being the most popular.

KORWA defines webcasting as "an interactive multimedia on-demand service that uses the internet to deliver text, images, audio, and video to end users" (2005). Webcasting is not an extension of broadcasting but rather a new content delivery system on the internet. There are four major business models within the industry.

The first is portal sites that provide an array of services including e-commerce and webcasting. In the second, the aggregated webcaster model, content is acquired, packaged, and then distributed on the web. This model can also be called the content aggregator model. The third, the clicks-and-bricks model, entails major broadcasters repurposing their own content originally broadcast on TV. The clicks-and-bricks model is often equivalent to the branded content model, which likewise repurposes existing content. The fourth model is the producer model, where webcasters use the internet to exhibit their original programs. The fourth category mainly consists of adult content and educational webcasters. The clicks-and-bricks model is by far the most successful in terms of revenues and the number of users. In the following sections, the clicks and bricks model and the content aggregator model will be analyzed in detail.

Just under one in four (22.5%) webcasters offer entertainment, including movies, music, and animation. Another 16.4% of webcasters provide current affairs, religious, and cultural programming. 28.8% have educational programming and 13.7% offer local news and information.

Video content delivery is relatively easy due to the broadband infrastructure, and in recent years watching a movie or TV program downloaded on PCs has become very popular among the younger generation. This phenomenon is due in part to the peer-to-peer (P2P) services that are pervasive in Korea. There are different kinds of P2P services that are popular in Korea but the majority of them share a web-drive space to share content ranging from software to video content, which operates similarly to the freeware sites. Although it is unknown how much of the population uses these shared file services, for the younger generation, it is certainly well accepted.

Over-the-air broadcasters understood that the internet VOD market would be a fruitful aftermarket, especially for the younger audiences, so the major television networks invested heavily in building internet sites that provide VOD services.

On these sites the drama genre accounts for the majority of consumption, but viewing demographics are not consistent with those for over-the-air viewers. That is, the internet VOD market serves as a complementary market to broadcast TV.

Responding to this new demand for high quality content, the major broadcast networks each have their own webcasting services whose content is mostly paid-VOD.

Pure play models are adopted by major portal sites such as NHN. ISPs like Hanafos, for example, are also actively engaged in pure play webcasting services. Since the clicks-and-bricks sites provide BBS (online bulletin) services and other free content such as video trailers, they attract more users than pure-play services that have a more diverse range of content that comes from several different channels. The online communities and bulletin boards that the major broadcasters provide free of charge as a complementary service to their paid VOD serve as a feedback route for TV show fans where they discuss issues about the show, send comments to writers and actors, download photos and scripts, etc.

There are a few major internet rating companies that regularly report on internet traffic. Launched in 2000, KoreanClick (www.koreanclick.co.kr) randomly selects people to participate on panels that take web surveys. Rankey (www.rankey.com)

has volunteers selected to correspond to population demographics, who use the internet and provide rankings in a wide range of web categories. Rankey is a subsidiary of Mediachannel, an internet research and consulting company established in 2000. Metrix Corporation (www.metrixcorp.com) was founded in 1999 and provides the most comprehensive web user data with the largest online panel.

I consulted the Metrix Corporation ranking data in selecting the top 20 webcasters. Metrix Corporation ranks various categories of internet sites. It has been reporting weekly and monthly website user traffic data since April 2000.

According to the data, portal sites dominate other internet sites in general and easily earn the top rankings. Gauged by the number of unique visitors, Media Daum, NHN, Yahoo Korea, and SK Communications lead the internet industry. Portal sites' domination of the internet market seems to be a universal trend. Koreans' use of these portals, however, is unique. Media Daum has succeeded in attracting users to its online community services, where people meet with people according to hobbies and interests. Other portal sites have also invested heavily in communication-based services like weblogs, emails, and bulletin boards. An enormous amount of user-generated content is gaining popularity, and users' communication techniques are becoming increasingly sophisticated. For seamless usage, some internet community sites offer linkage with mobile phones, where users can update their own blog through their mobile phones.

OWNERSHIP AND PERFORMANCE OF LEADING WEBCASTERS

Using the Metrix Corporation internet site ranking data, the top 20 webcasting sites during the second half of 2004 were selected for analysis.

Among the top 20 webcasters, 12 used the branded content model, 8 were content aggregators. Some of the content aggregators offered user-generated content or educational aids.

Nanpasun is a non-profit, small-scale radio service that started out as a radio channel for an educational institute. Saycast is the subsidiary of an online chat service, Sayclub. Saycast enables members to livecast their own music selection to a wider audience while chatting. V-TV provides real time relay services of television and radio channels from all over the world. There are also popular education websites that webcast online courses. 1318 Class is a service that provides K1 to K12 subject courses for school aid.

In the the branded content model group, five of the webcasters were major over-the-air broadcasters' online sister companies (SBSi, KBSi [Conpia], iMBC, and EBS), two were private local broadcaster sites (PSB and TGMBC), four were cable channels (CBS, YTN, FoodTV, and Onuri TV), and one was a foreign cable network (CNN). Among the webcasters owned by domestic cable networks, one is a 24 hour news channel (YTN), two are religion channels (Onuri TV and CBS), and the fourth is a culinary information channel (Food TV).

Most major broadcasters' pay VOD content is programming that has already been aired on TV, offered after a slight time lag (which varies from 30 minutes to a few hours). Local broadcasters or cable networks, on the other hand, usually provide real time streaming services of their original broadcast content, mostly free of charge. For those providing content free of charge, advertising is the main source of revenue, whereas webcasters with pay VOD services are less dependent on advertising money.

Examples include:

- Tong Tong TV, a content aggregator oriented toward adult content, providing a diverse range of services including Japanese animation, movies, adult games, and adult movies;
- NGTV is a music video and TV commercial repurposing website that shows trailers and cuts not shown during the airing of the original content on TV;
- Qwiny provides animation VOD, TV program guides and games; and
- 24cast, a web-based radio service with realtime radio channels and blockbuster movies.

Webcasters' business models differ according to whether they are pure-play or clicks-and-bricks webcasters. (See Tables 16–2 and 16–3.)

The over-the-air branded content providers by far have the highest concentration in terms of user traffic and revenues, so they are analyzed in more detail to gain a more precise understanding of the webcasting industry as a whole.

The three major broadcasters launched their subsidiary webcasting sites in 1999 and 2000 to complement their over-the-air TV broadcast, but during the last few years the market for webcasting content has grown dramatically and the broadcasters are eager to identify this additional distribution channel for their TV shows. Broadcasters upload their TV shows shortly after their original broadcast on national TV. The peak usage of VOD viewing occurs right after the original broadcast, meaning that people who cannot get to their TV in time for the original broadcast use their computer to watch it as soon as it's available. It could also mean that certain viewers, particularly those from the younger generation, prefer to watch programs on a personal computer rather than a shared TV. The majority of VOD users are in their 20s, and this does not vary much by genre or program. For television, the viewership's age demographics would be different for all programs. VOD viewers are more or less homogenous regardless of content.

Financially, clicks-and-bricks webcasters performed better than their parent companies in recent years. Since 2003 over-the-air broadcasters have experienced decreases in both revenues and profits, and their cable networks and webcasters have outperformed them financially. Over-the-air broadcasters have suffered fi-

TABLE 16–2
Business Models of the Top 20 Webcasters

Business Model	Type	Parent Company	Webcaster
Branded content model	Clicks-and-bricks	Major TV networks	www.sbs.co.kr www.kbs.co.kr www.imbc.com www.ebs.co.kr www.conpia.com
	Clicks-and-bricks	Major cable networks	www.cbs.co.kr www.ytn.co.kr www.foodtv.co.kr www.onnuritv.com www.cnn.com
	Clicks-and-bricks	Local broadcasters	www.psb.co.kr www.tgmbc.co.kr
Content aggregator	Pure-play	Entertainment	www.ngtv.net www.tongtongtv www.24cast.net www.qwiny.com www.v-tv.co.kr
	Pure-play	User-generated content	www.saycast.com
	Pure-play	Education	www.1318class.com

nancial losses due to the overall downsizing of the advertising market and competition from newcomers, such as cable, internet, and satellite. MBC, the parent company of iMBC, has been slowing down in terms of revenue. In 2003, its revenue was down 5.13% from the previous year, and its revenue decreased by another 1.37 % in 2004. Profits decreased by 22.49% in 2004. SBS, the parent company of SBSi, saw its profits drop by 57.99% in 2004. Revenue was down 4.1% in 2003 and 3.23% in 2004. So, there is a decreasing trend for both revenue and profits of major broadcasters.

Company Strategies

Webcasters have been hesitant to go public, and since the industry is relatively new, not many companies have made an IPO. The companies listed in KOSDAQ are SBSi, iMBC, YTN, CJ Homeshopping, CCS (Choonbuk Broadcasting), DCC (Korea Cable Dongjak Broadcasting, a cable system operator), Hankook Kyongjae TV (cable network), and Hanvit I&B (cable network). Most of them are clicks-and-bricks companies but are not ranked highest among the webcasters.

TABLE 16–3
Internet VOD services of the Three Major Broadcasters*

	KBSi	iMBC	SBSi
Parent Company	Korea Broadcasting System (KBS)	Munwha Broadcasting Company (MBC)	Seoul Broadcasting System (SBS)
Established	April 2000	March 2000	August 1999
Number of employees	Approx. 150	Approx. 80	Approx. 83
VOD price	Free of charge, but has an affiliated pay VOD service site, conpia.com	500 won/1000won (approx 35/70c) per viewing	500 won/ 1000won (approx 35c/70c) per viewing
Upload time	30 minutes after original broadcast	1 hour after original broadcast	Within 1~2 days after original broadcast
Primetime	23:00~01:00,	23:00~01:00, 14:00~18:00	23:00~01:00
Users	20s, 41.9%; 30s, 23.8%	20s, 34%; 30s, 28%	20s, 50%; 30s, 25%
Other	Operates a subscription base site conpia.com for pay services	Switched to pay services on April 2003	Switched to pay services on September 2001; IPO February 2003

*In compiling data about the major webcasters, S. Kim (CEO, KBSi), Y. Moon (Director, iMBC), and J. W. Kim (Director of Strategy & Management, SBSi) provided data and insight on the Korean webcasting industry.

Among the 20 leading webcasting companies, only 3 are publicly listed. All 17 others are privately owned, but some of them report financial data, which are summarized in Table 16–4.

Most of these companies are affiliated with or owned by major media companies. All of them fit in the category of branded content model.

IMBC's revenues in 2004 totaled $16.12 million (18.628912 billion won) which represents a 10.9% increase from the previous year. In 2003, revenue increased by 23.4%, reflecting iMBC's decision to make its free VOD into pay services. The revenue collected from paid programming (VOD) increased by 75.9% while ad revenue decreased 0.6%, staying constant. The ad revenue in 2004 was $2,109,469 (2.437492 billion won). VOD services accounted for a majority of iMBC's revenue, 59.2%. IMBC's relatively low level of dependence on advertising (13.1%) is a recent phenomenon. In 2002, 29.7% of its revenue came from advertising and only 5.9% from selling programs. The revenue structure is changing to a "pay" model rather than the ±free content with advertising" model long used by traditional broadcasters.

TABLE 16–4
Financial Performance of Publicly Listed Webcasting Companies (in $ million)

		Revenues			Profits		
	IPO date	2004	2003	2002	2004	2003	2002
SBSi	2/5/03	19.27	16.87	17.00	3.57	3.18	1.61
iMBC	1/21/05	16.12	12.32	7.45	2.95	1.63	0.21
YTN	9/4/01	57.23	49.96	41.40	1.25	1.74	–4.89
Hanvit I&B	8/10/00	51.17	37.26	22.16	–11.92	–31.87	0.43
Hankook KyongJae	7/30/04	22.52	20.85	—	3.48	2.81	0.00
DCC	6/11/99	11.76	10.21	9.15	2.48	2.34	1.30
CCS	5/30/03	12.81	12.10	10.93	0.25	2.45	1.97

Source: www.kosdaq.com; www.imbc.com; sbsi.sbs.co.kr

SBSi is more aggressive and therefore has had more success generating profits from VOD services.

Even though its revenues are smaller than iMBC's, its profit margin is greater. SBSi also adopts a diversification strategy in order to prepare for the uncertain future—it has positioned itself as a consolidated company that produces, packages, and repurposes content.

The relatively high portion of web agency revenues reflects the fact that webcasters provide web design tools and services for other websites because it initially set out to share risks of the highly uncertain market for paid content on the internet. Since Koreans often regard web content as free and find it hard to pay for content, early business models in the webcasting market were not as optimistic as today. Refer to Table 16–5.

Major clicks-and-bricks webcasters have the largest market share in the industry by far. The smaller and less successful webcasters have a more diverse range of strategies and outcomes, though. The 20 top webcasters in 2004, according to the Metrix Corporation's ranking, were used for this analysis.

Transmission Method

Some of the webcasters analyzed (30%) provide on-demand downloading services, and 19 out of 20 provide on-demand streaming services. Only Qwiny does not. Qwiny's parent company is On Media, a large entertainment and media company with several cable networks and system operators. Qwiny's main online content is its

TABLE 16–5
Revenue Source for Major Clicks-and-Bricks Webcasters (in $)

Category	iMBC		SBSi	
	Revenues	Proportion	Revenues	Proportion
Advertising	2,109,469	13.1	1,218,520	6.3
Ecommerce	—	—	18	0.0
VOD/programs	9,540,871	59.2	10,138,468	52.6
Other sources of revenue	469,669	2.9	4,870,619	25.3
Revenue from other fees	120,064	0.7	—	—
Web agency	3,881,875	24.1	3,025,530	15.7
Total	16,121,949	100.0	19,271,311	100.0

cable channel specializing in games, OnGameNet. Qwiny provides online games, game instruction manuals, and user bulletins. It also provides pay animation VOD services targeted at gamers. Only 25% of webcasters—CBS, SBSi, KBSi, PSB, and Nanpasun—have streaming services of scheduled programs. Major broadcasters with news content offer real time news to users. None of the webcasters analyzed used the push method.

Webcasters promote themselves as alternatives to home video or VOD services, providing people with content they can view at their own convenience. Usually VOD streaming gives the paying user at least three hours to watch the show, and some make the show available for an entire day after payment, affording users considerable viewing flexibility.

Most webcasters provide additional interactive features. 90% of the 20 webcasters analyzed have chatrooms or message boards, 30% have interactive games, and there are also other interactive features such as e-commerce, ringtone downloads, and so forth. Enormous amounts of viewer feedback on the message boards and in the online communities of popular TV dramas are known to have caused the networks to change the shows' storylines. The webcasting page not only serves an interactive function for the webcaster, it is also a valuable interactive tool for the sister media company.

Original Content Proportion

Webcasting content is either original or repurposed. Only a small proportion of content is simulcast with an offline media. Repurposed movies and TV shows are the most common products on webcasting sites. Of the 20 leading webcasters analyzed, on average, 47.05% of content is original and 42.65% is repurposed. Only

9.5% is simulcast. However, the actual usages among users are highly geared towards repurposed content of popular TV shows.

Revenues

The most common method of generating revenues for the leading webcasters is advertising. Only one webcaster has no ads. All others rely heavily on advertising. The next most common source of revenues is subscription fees, either collected on a per viewing basis or for access over a designated period of time. 75% of the webcasters analyzed have subscription plans of one sort or another. E-commerce is less popular. Only 40% of sites had this option. Another less popular but increasingly important method is selling content to other distribution channels such as mobile companies.

The 3 webcasters affiliated with major broadcasters mainly rely on subscription and PPV/VOD. They count less heavily on ecommerce and advertising.

Genre

Most of the leading webcasters provide general TV shows, news, and adult content, and a lesser number offer full length movies and TV dramas. About half provide previews, trailers, and commercials. Most webcasters deal in multiple genres—only a few specialize in a single genre. Educational webcasters often provide both tutoring and instructional programs, while other webcasters usually have a mix of entertainment, news, and movies.

INTERNATIONAL INFLUENCE

Korea is unique in that domestic movies and TV shows are most popular with general audiences. The market share of domestic movies in 2004 was 57%. Foreign programming constitutes less than 5% of national TV networks' programming. The webcasting market reflects this domestic popularity.

Foreign Webcasters in Korea

As in other countries, the top webcasters in Korea are predominantly domestic. Of the 20 webcasters studied, only CNN, a U.S. news channel, was a foreign webcaster. The market does not attract foreign content as much as do other media sectors like movies or the internet in general.

Foreign Content on Domestic Webcasters

Most webcasters provide domestic content. 90% of the leading webcasters primarily provide domestic TV shows and movies. Domestic webcasters, though, do also provide a considerable amount of foreign content, especially movies. If some portion of the content is foreign, that content is most likely a Hollywood movie. For 86.7% of the webcasters, U.S. films are their most dominant foreign products. The other 13.3% were Japanese animation and movies. No webcaster promotes other countries' cultural products as being of substantial interest.

WEBCAST INDUSTRY OUTLOOK

Transient Model vs. Niche Market for Specialized User Generated Content

Webcasters are trying to find business models that best fit their content, technology, and costs. But communication and information technologies are changing rapidly, making it difficult for newcomers to define long-term strategies. Currently webcasters' comparative advantage shapes both their content emphasis and their delivery of services to consumers. In the future several different paths may evolve from the current mixed strategy business models.

The leading webcasters in Korea depend substantially on repurposed movies and TV shows, and most webcasters provide high quality mass appeal content that has already been tested out in other distribution windows. This generalization is especially true for the internet sister companies of major broadcasters. However, it is evident that their webcasting is a transient technology and that the services developed are therefore transient too. Webcasting video content is mostly a VOD service based on broadband delivery. Since broadband was a pervasive new technology, webcasting reached its audience, creating a market for VOD. New technologies, though, are expressly geared towards the VOD market. In 2004, some of the cable system operators began offering digital cable services. DBS is also providing NVOD at a low cost, which allots several channels for one show that is shown at different times so that the viewer can choose when to start watching a show. Although higher in cost and lower in quality (due to the small screen size), mobile services now also provide video services. IPTV will be introduced into the market shortly and will compete directly with webcasting services.

Webcasters now strive to find new business models that will make them the strongest in the market for user friendly, user initiated video viewing. Webcasting via the internet has certain advantages that will generate new business strategies in the ever competitive media market.

First, user generated content will succeed in the long run. User generated content, text based and image based weblogs, for example, is a stable market. Music and video content will be another new area of development in the near future. Some webcasters in Korea have already capitalized on this demand. Several audio sites allow users to create their own internet radio stations, webcasting music to their peers. Some provide space for sharing home video footage with friends and families.

Second, we can foresee that repurposing movies and TV shows will continue to be a very important sector of the webcasting market. This area will probably compete and merge with new distribution technologies, both telecommunication and media based services. Major webcasters are investing heavily in content repurposing for mobile media and other new distribution outlets, trying to fit themselves into the content production and aggregation model. Their advantage is their experience acquiring and modifying digital content. Since internet services are based on digitalized media, major webcasters have a comparative advantage over traditional media companies in transforming and delivering content to other digital media platforms.

For traditional media companies, especially the broadcasters, webcasting is becoming a new business model. In Korea, broadcasters face fierce competition from new media such as cable television, direct satellite, and new mobile services like DMB. In the near future interactive digital services such as IPTV will threaten established companies. The broadcasters' audience share has dropped from over 95% 10 years ago to just over 60% in recent years. This downward trend will soon accelerate since the young generation prefers the internet to TV (Park, 2004). However, these new technologies can become a new opportunity for traditional television networks. Broadcasters can expand their audience using these new windows of distribution as conduits for video products like blockbuster movies and dramas.

According to the executives at iMBC, KBSi, and SBSi, the clicks-and-bricks webcasters have been very aggressive studying and investing in digital content distribution technology and services. IPTV, the delivery method closest to webcasting but which offers better quality and is simpler to use, is an area that webcasters are already planning to participate in, either directly or through corporate alliances. According to IMBC Director Youngsam Moon, major webcaster iMBC's vision is in developing digital content, as it is a company that specializes in the distribution of media content (personal communication, July 6, 2005). In the near future, DMB, WiBro (Wireless Broadband internet)[4], and IPTV will be new opportunities

---

[4]WiBro is a new service to be launched in 2006. It is also known as the 3.5 generation mobile telecommunication device which uses the 2.3 GHz bandwidth and can provide 1Mbps broadband internet services via cell phones.

domestically as well as internationally. IMBC is initiating a partnership with Japanese media companies to explore these opportunities.

Partially owned by the largest telecommunication company in Korea (KT), KBSi is trying to keep up with the information and communication technology markets. In 2003, KBSi started converting its parent company KBS's popular TV shows for mobile services, and these shows are now available for viewing on any mobile phone serviced by the major Korean telecommunications companies. In 2004, KBSi reached out to Japan's NTT DoCoMo mobile services, and it is currently providing content in Japan. The market outlook for VOD services is optimistic, according to the CEO of KBSi. This is true for KBS and KBSi, as decades of being in the TV business have allowed it to accumulate vast stores of high quality content. In 2002, KBS also began aggressively exporting Korean dramas to other Asian countries in both analog and digital formats. And like their competitors, it is currently moving forward with DMB, WiBro, and IPTV services, according to KBSi CEO Songho Kim (personal communication, May 3, 2005; July 1, 2005).

SBSi focuses on mobile services. It currently provides its dramas and shows to SKT's and KTF's mobile VOD services. Mobile services will be a major source of revenue and profit in the short run. SBSi also plans to invest in new digital services like IPTV and WiBro. Its market position in the long run is as a digital content packager and distributor, not as a broadcaster or a TV station. So, the new business models will be based on the value added to original video content via digital technology, and on the range of different outlets that companies can use for distribution. Companies will not rely solely on either the internet or broadcast TV, but will explore opportunities in mobile, satellite, and other digital services that can deliver video content. Companies choosing to specialize in webcasting alone would not have a very bright outlook according to Jin Wook Kim, SBSi's Strategy and Management Section Leader/Director (personal communication, June 10, 2005; June 14, 2005).

On the other hand, webcasting is also serving experimental, independent webcasters, allowing them to test a wide range of content online. Although the audience is much smaller, this niche market will allow new video products to be tested and further distributed to other channels. The way that digital music enabled independent and experimental music to be introduced into the mainstream market will become an exemplary case for video webcasters studying market potential. Although both company performance and usage patterns are highly concentrated, even more so than in the traditional media sectors, there is still room for new ideas and content that will compete with each other for the attention of internet users.

According to industry specialists, the prospects for webcasting alone are not bright due to fierce competition from alternative multimedia services now coming onto the market. Industry personnel interviewed for this study regarded themselves as content aggregators, content providers, or content producers, not broadcasters.

They think of internet webcasting technology merely as a device that extends the distribution channels for their content. So it seems that this technology will be temporary and transient, and that it will be replaced rapidly by some new, more advanced digital multimedia technologies.

ACKNOWLEDGMENTS

The research on which this chapter was based was conducted by the Kwangwoon University Research Grant 2005.

REFERENCES

Advertising Yearbook. (2005). Seoul, Korea : Cheil Communications.
Korea Broadcast Commission. (2005). *Report on the state of the broadcast industry.* Seoul: KBC.
Korea Webcasting Association. (2005). Retrieved January 30, 2005, from http://www.korwa.or.kr
National Internet Development Agency of Korea. (2004). *Survey on the computer and internet usage.* Seoul: NIDA.
Park, S. (2004). Pricing strategies of internet VOD services and its impact on television viewing in Korea. Paper presented at the 6th World Media Economics Conference, Montreal, Canada. May 15, 2004.

APPENDIX
List of Leading Korean Webcasters

- www.kbs.co.kr (www.conpia.com)
- www.sbs.co.kr
- www.imbc.com
- www.ebs.co.kr
- www.tongtong.tv
- www.ytn.co.kr
- www.cbs.co.kr
- www.foodtv.co.kr
- www.onnuritv.com
- www.ngtv.net
- www.nanpasun.net
- www.cnn.com
- www.qwiny.com
- www.24cast.net
- www.saycast.com
- www.1318class.com
- www.v-tv.co.kr
- www.tgmbc.co.kr

CHAPTER 17

Japan: Mobile and Broadband— Two Emerging Business Models in the World's Third Largest Broadband User

Kenichi Ishii
University of Tsukuba, Japan

Morihiro Ogasahara
The University of Tokyo, Japan

The webcaster is the marriage of broadcasting and broadband network. However, despite many new entrants to the webcasting service, Japan has not yet seen a successful marriage, especially on the PC. A well-known failure is Tresola, a joint company set up in 2002 by three major commercial TV broadcasters in conjunction with the NTT Group, SONY, Hitachi, and major Japanese movie companies. This company started to webcast TV programs through the internet, but it suspended the service in 2004 because the number of subscribers was much smaller than expected (Harada, 2004).

In contrast, the webcasting business thrives on mobile phones in Japan. Third-generation (3G) mobile phones enable users to download music, browse websites, make videophone calls, and even view videos via their mobile phone. The unique business model has promoted a variety of content business on the mobile internet. This chapter describes the present circumstances of the webcasting services and explores what factors promote or harm the development of the webcasters in Japan.

WEBCASTING MARKET ENVIRONMENT IN JAPAN

Content Industry Structure

As of 2002, the market size of the Japanese media industry is ¥12.8 trillion ($119 billion), which is estimated to account for 10.3% of the world content market and 2.5% of Japan's GDP (Commerce and Information Policy Bureau, 2004). Of the total content industry market, visual content occupies 34.6%, music 13%, games 9%, and printed content 44%. According to the estimates by the Commerce and Information Policy Bureau (2004), the market size of digital content is ¥2.1 trillion ($19 billion), or 17% of the total market of the content industry. The webcasting content, which is our research target, occupies only about 1% of the total content industry in Japan. What is surprising is that, unlike most countries in the world, mobile internet has a much larger (about seven times) market size for webcasting content than the PC. (See Table 17–1.)

One of the characteristics of the Japanese content industry is the oligopolistic market structure. For example, the major four newspapers, the *Yomiuri*, the *Asahi*, the *Mainichi*, and the *Nikkei*, issue 66% of the total circulation of morning newspapers in Japan (Dentsu Soken, 2003). The dominant position of the major newspapers is supported by the unique systems such as home delivery and price-maintained merchandise. With regard to commercial TV broadcasting, four nationwide TV networks, Nippon TV, TBS, TV Asahi, and TV Tokyo, have control over the domestic market. Also, three of the four major TV stations, Nippon TV, TV Asahi, and TV Tokyo form a capital and business alliance with the major newspapers, the *Yomiuri*, the *Asahi*, and the *Nikkei*, respectively. In addition, two large agencies, Dentsu and Hakuhodo, dominate the advertising market handling more than half of the TV advertisements in Japan (Dentsu Soken, 2003). Such a closed market structure in the Japanese mass media, which has not basically changed since the 1960s, has harmed the growth of webcasting business by keeping new entrants out of the market, since these traditional media have no incentive to proceed with a new business.

Despite the recent advent of a variety of new media, terrestrial TV broadcasting maintains an important place in daily life. According to a nationwide survey conducted in 2000 (Institute of Socio-Information and Communication Studies, 2001), the daily TV viewing time was on average 190.3 minutes, accounting for 47% of the total time spent on information activities. In 2005, according to a JWIP (World Internet Project Japan) survey,[1] the amount of TV viewing time was 180.3

---

[1]The World Internet Project Japan Survey was conducted nationwide in Japan in 2000, 2001, 2002, 2003, and 2005. The respondents were chosen from a probability sample whose ages ranged from 12 to 74 years. The data collection method was a self-administered questionnaire. The number of successful respondents in 2000, 2001, 2002, 2003, and 2005 are 2555, 2816, 2333, 1520, and 2029, respectively.

TABLE 17–1
Market Size of Content Industry in Japan (billion ¥)

	Market Size (billion ¥)	Percentage	Usage Time per Day (minute)
Visual			
Visual package (DVD and video)	582.8	4.6	8.0
VOD on PC internet	14.7	0.1	
VOD on the mobile phone	38.3	0.3	
Broadcasting	3580.4	28.0	202.4
Movies	203.2	1.6	
Total	4419.4	34.6	
Music			
CD	489.4	3.8	10.0
PC internet downloading	3.6	0.0	0.8
Mobile phone downloading	90.7	0.7	—
Karaoke	872.6	6.8	1.1
Concerts	206.0	1.6	
Total	1662.3	13.0	
Games			
Total	1124.4	8.8	7.4
Printed Media			
Books (including magazines and comics)	2696.3	21.1	11.4
Newspapers	2397.9	18.7	25.0
Content on the mobile phone	71.6	0.6	0.5
Content on the internet	376.8	2.9	8.2
Others	41.9	0.3	—
Total	5584.5	43.7	
Total	12790.6	100.0	

Source: Commerce and Information Policy Bureau (2004); Institute of Socio-Information and Communication Studies (2001).

minutes per day, while the amount of time spent on the internet was only 38.1 minutes[2] (World Internet Project Japan, 2005). As demonstrated by these figures, the internet has not gained a position as a competitive threat to TV broadcasting in Japan.

Internet Penetration and Usage

The growth rate of internet users in Japan has been rapidly accelerating since 2000. The number of internet users at the end of 2003 was 77.30 million, and the penetration rate in the total population was 60.6% (Ministry of Public Management, Home Affairs, Posts and Telecommunications, 2004).

Mobile Internet

In this chapter, *mobile internet* refers to the internet via mobile phones. One of the unique characteristics of Japanese internet is a high penetration rate of mobile internet users. According to the JWIP survey conducted in 2005, 67% of Japanese internet users accessed the internet via PCs, 72% via mobile phones, 38% via both a PC and a mobile phone, 33% only via mobile phones, and 28% only via PCs in March 2005. As of 2005, 44% of the sample used mobile phones to access the internet (The World Internet Project Japan, 2005; see Appendix 1 in accompanying CD).

Japan enjoys the most advanced mobile internet services in the world. The number of internet-enabled mobile phones is 69.7 million, occupying 86% of total phones as of December 2003 (Ministry of Public Management, Home Affairs, Posts and Telecommunications, 2004). Japan has unique mobile internet services, such as picture/video mail and picture characters in e-mail. These services are used to express emotion in character-based text messages (Ishii, 2004). Cultural factors in communication patterns, such as a tendency to avoid direct communications, may partially explain why these unique uses are embraced in Japan (Ishii, 2004; Ishii & Wu, 2006).

Major Japanese carriers (NTT DoCoMo, KDDI, and Vodafone) provide a variety of advanced mobile internet services, including GPS (global positioning system), Java application, picture/video mail, MP3 (Mpeg) player, and electronic money (non-contact prepaid cards), as well as standard e-mail and web browsing service. In the end of 2004, the number of subscribers to internet provider systems

---

[2]These averages were computed based on the total population, giving non-users the value of zero.

on mobile phones reached 73 million people, which is 85%[3] of mobile phone users in Japan (Telecommunications Carriers Association, 2005).

In October 2001, NTT DoCoMo launched 3G (third-generation) mobile communication services in Japan, which was the first of its kind in the world. The 3G service, named IMT–2000 (International Mobile Telecommunications–2000), is a high-quality digital, new-generation mobile communications service that enables up to 384K bps data communications on a global basis. Following NTT DoCoMo, the KDDI Group launched its IMT–2000 service, known as CDMA 2000–1x, in April 2002. The number of 3G mobile phones reached 24 million in December 2004 (Telecommunication Carriers Association, 2005).

PC Broadband Users

Along with increased internet use, there has also been a dramatic growth in the diffusion of PC broadband since 2000. According to a quarterly survey by the Ministry of Public Management, Home Affairs, Posts and Telecommunications (2005), the number of subscriptions to broadband services totaled 19.51 million in March 2005. Specifically, the number of subscriptions to DSL increased 2.6% from December 2004 to 13.67 million, and the number of subscriptions to FTTH (fiber to the home) increased by 17% to 2.85 million. For the first time, the increase in the number of FTTH subscribers exceeded its counterpart of DSL subscribers (Ministry of Internal Affairs and Communications, 2005).

DSL. The recent growth of DSL was encouraged by Yahoo!Japan's entry into the ADSL service in September 2001. The government's decision to let third party companies bypass Nippon Telegraph and Telephone Corp. (NTT) switches and access its subscribers' phone lines directly cleared the way for the commercialization of DSL connections. Due to the fast access speed and low monthly charge, ADSL subscribers for Yahoo!Japan reached about 5 million in September 2005 (Yahoo!Japan, 2005b).

FTTH. Fiber-to-the-home reliably provides a very high speed internet access (up to 100Mbps), whereas the connection speed of DSL (500K–30Mbps) diminishes the further one get down the line from the telecom's central office. Japan has begun offering commercial FTTH (fiber to the home) services utilizing fiber optic networks designed for general users. The initial development of FTTH was upheld by the launch of Usen Corp., a cable music distributor for karaoke parlors, by beating NTT to the punch with a 100Mbps priced at $40 per month. NTT lowered its

---

[3]The number of mobile phone users is based on the subscribers to the three major carriers (NTT DoCoMo, KDDI, and Vodafone).

rates in response to Usen's move. Later Yahoo!BB also launched FTTH services. NTT recently launched 100Mbps services for a competitive price: $48 (¥5200) per month. Due to the lowered charge, NTT has obtained more subscribers to FTTH services than those to ADSL services since the summer of 2004.

Cable network. Japan lacked good cable network systems because of strict regulation by the government, based on the local community-oriented strategy. In the 1980s, the government placed the development of CATV as local IT projects which would bridge the economic gap between urban and rural areas (Ishii, 2003). Thus, CATV operators were allowed to operate only in a local community. Even though the regulations against MSOs (multiple system operators) were lifted in 1993, the penetration rate of cable TV was only 20% in 2000 and 34% in 2003 (Ministry of Public Management, Home Affairs, Posts and Communications, 2004). There are 2.95 million subscribers to internet connection services via cable networks as of March 2005 (Ministry of Internal Affairs and Communications, 2005.)

Public wireless LAN (local area network). Many broadband operators and mobile phone carriers launched a wireless LAN service, including Yahoo!Japan, NTT East, NTT West, NTT DoCoMo, NTT COM, and other companies. As of March 2005, however, only 117 thousand users subscribe to the service, according to the quarterly report released by the Ministry of Internal Affairs and Communications (2005).

The Japanese government proudly described Japanese broadband as the "world's highest levels" in its white paper (Ministry of Public Management, Home Affairs, Posts and Telecommunications, 2004, p. 3). According to an ITU report, monthly broadband fees per 100kbps in Japan are $0.09, which is at the world's lowest level as of 2003, as compared to $3.53 in the U.S. and $0.25 in South Korea (Frieden, 2005). FTTH fees are currently only $0.048 per 100kbps ($48 for a 1000Mbps service. See Appendix 2 in accompanying CD).

Factors Accounting for the Use of the Webcasting Services

Despite advanced broadband technologies, Japanese internet users rarely use the webcasting service on their PC. According to a JWIP survey, 9% of the sample downloaded music files on PC, 19% downloaded music (mostly ring tones) on mobile phones, and 14% played videos on PC (World Internet Project Japan, 2004; Appendix 3 in accompanying CD). To explore what factors determine the use of webcasting services, the logistic regression was conducted. Table 17–2 indicates that significant variables vary between the different services. Males and non-workers are more likely to download music files on PCs, while younger people are more

TABLE 17–2
Logistic Regression Coefficients

Dependent Variable	Downloading Music Files on PC (PC Internet Users Only)	Downloading Music Files on Mobile Phones (Mobile Phone Users Only)	Downloading or Streaming Videos (PC Internet Users Only)
N	450	455	450
Constant	.893	1.104	1.927
Gender[a]	−.838 **	.466	−.622 *
Age	−.010	−.066 ***	−.042 ***
Education[b]	−.386	−.054	.250
Student[c]	−.741	−.252	.217
Work[d]	−.685 *	.346	−.219
Income[e]	.018	−.054	−.012

[a]Male = 1, female = 2. [b]College or higher = 1, else = 0. [c]Student = 1, else = 0. [d]Full-time worker = 1, else=0. [e]¥1 million ($9260).
$*p < 0.05$, $**p < 0.01$, $***p < 0.001$.

likely to download music files (mostly ring-tones) on mobile phones. Males and younger people are more likely to download or stream videos on PCs. These results indicate that the users of webcasters differ between PCs and mobile phones.

WEBCASTING BUSINESS MODELS IN JAPAN

Major Webcasting Companies

In order to identify leading webcasters in Japan, access rates (monthly reach) for Japanese webcasters were estimated based on one-month access data, which was collected by Video Research Interactive[4] in November 2004. Table 17–3 lists the top 20 webcasters based on the estimated access rates (Also Published as Appendix 4 in accompanying CD). Note that this ranking does not include websites for mobile internet, because access rates for mobile phone websites were not available at the time of the study.

---

[4]Video Research Interactive is the leading company for internet access ratings in Japan. This company regularly surveys website access rates, using the software built in 10,000 respondents' PCs. An access to webcasters is defined as an access to HTML pages that had a link to video or music files, because it was not possible to measure directly an access to the video/music files.

TABLE 17–3
Top 20 Webcasters on the PC Internet in Japan

Rank	Name	URL	Typology[a] (content)	Access Rate (monthly reach)	Approximate Number of Available Videos[b]
1	Yahoo!Japan	http://www.yahoo.co.jp/	ISP portal	14.2%	1,000
2	Caribbeancom.com	http://caribbeancom.com	SD (adult)	6.7%	800
3	99bb.com	http://www.99bb.com/	SD (adult)	5.1%	6,000
4	Goo	http://www.goo.ne.jp/	ISP portal	4.3%	5,500
5	Real Guide	http://japan.real.com/guide/	SD	4.2%	100
6	Shockwave.com	http://jp.shockwave.com	SD	3.9%	150
7	1pondo	http://sample.1pondo.tv	SD (adult)	3.7%	600
8	dmm.co.jp	http://www.dmm.co.jp	SD (adult)	3.3%	10,000
9	Anime X-press	http://tv-tokyo.co.jp/anime/	DBC (TV anime)	2.6%	15
10	eroxjapanz.com	http://eroxjapanz.com	SD (adult)	2.5%	20,000
11	MSN Music	http://music.msn.co.jp/	SD (music and movies)	2.3%	500
12	Biglobe	http://www.biglobe.ne.jp/	ISP portal	2.3%	2,000
13	Showtime	http://showtime.jp	SD (movies)	2.3%	8,000
14	pinkeys.com	http://pinkeyes.com	SD (adult)	2.2%	500
15	0721.com	http://0721.com	SD (adult)	2.1%	1,000
16	x-gallery.tv	http://x-gallery.tv	SD (adult)	2.1%	800
17	NHK	http://www.nhk.or.jp/	DBC (TV news)	1.8%	100
18	Web Gendai	http://kodansha.cplaza.ne.jp	SD (movies)	1.7%	10
19	Oricon Style	http://www.oricon.co.jp	SD (music)	1.7%	200
20	tokyonights.tv	http://tokyonights.tv	SD (adult)	1.7%	400

[a]SD: specialized distributor, DBC: distributor with branded content. [b]These numbers were estimated in April 2005.

The most popular portal site in Japan, Yahoo!Japan, also ranked number 1 in the ranking. Following Yahoo!Japan, however, many websites do not rank high in the general ranking. For example, there are as many as nine adult websites in the ranking, including caribbeancom.com, 99bb.com, 1pondo, dmm.co.jp, eroxjapanz.com, pinkeys.com, 0721.com, x-gallery.tv, and tokyonights.tv. All of these adult websites are operated in foreign countries (eight in California, and one in the Netherlands), which accounts for the exceptionally high rate (56%) of foreign webcasters in Japan as compared to other countries (See Figure 2–3, Chapter 2). However, these websites mostly offer Japanese videos in Japanese language.

The unexpected popularity of these adult webcasters should be understood in light of the regulation against adult contents in Japan: Some adult videos, which include highly obscene materials, are prohibited from being sold or broadcast in Japan. For such materials, only an expurgated edition is available in Japan. Hence, in order to escape from the regulation, foreign-based companies offer an unexpurgated edition of Japanese adult videos through the internet, where regulations are relatively loose. More interestingly, in all of these adult websites, users are allowed to download videos, whereas downloading services are uncommon in other Japanese webcasters (only 5 out of 11 other websites offer any downloading services). This denotes that the customers regard adult webcasters as an alternate to DVDs.

The ranking denotes that clicks-and-bricks companies play a limited role in the webcasting market in Japan. Two TV broadcasting companies are listed in the ranking (Anime X-press and NHK), but these companies utilize webcasting sample programs free of charge to promote their TV programs. Subscription webcasting services by TV stations have not been very successful yet, although some TV stations plan to webcast TV programs.

Lastly, some content aggregators (Ha et al., 2005) are listed in Table 17–3. Three ISP (Internet Service Provider) portal websites (Yahoo!Japan, goo, and Biglobe) provide webcasting services. Additionally, there are more specialized content aggregators in the ranking. For example, Showtime provides a variety of movies on the internet. Oricon provides music and ring tones with the original music ranking information.

Webcasters on Mobile Phones

As compared to webcasting on PCs, webcasting on the mobile internet is in its more advanced stages in Japan. Among Japanese youth, downloading music through the mobile internet is very common by virtue of the widespread use of internet-enabled and high-speed 3G mobile phones in Japan. 19% of the total population downloaded music on mobile phones in 2003. The market size of downloading music for mobile phones amounts to ¥129 billion ($1.19 billion), approximately 30 times larger than its counterpart for PCs (Table 17–1).

According to a survey by Video Research Interactive[5] (2003), 37% of mobile phone users browsed the internet on their mobile at least once a week in 2002. Among mobile internet users, the most popular website type was ring-tone downloading (54.1%), followed by weather forecast (32.5%), and mobile phone wallpaper (31.7%). According to an NTT DoCoMo's annual report (NTT DoCoMo, 2005a), the most accessed program genre was ring-tone and screen/ wallpaper (30%), followed by entertainment information (24%), game and horoscope (22%), information (12%), database (4%), and transaction (8%). The carriers offer various services on the mobile phone. For example, i-mode (mobile content service offered by NTT DoCoMo) users have access to various services, such as e-mail, sports results, weather forecast, games, financial services, and ticket booking.

ISPs on mobile internet have developed a different business model as compared to their counterpart on the PC internet. Mobile phone carriers play a dominant role in the mobile internet market, because the carriers are the only ISPs on the mobile internet, and operate the major portal website called "official sites," which are directly linked to the ISP's menu page. For example, i-mode handsets have an "i-mode button." When users press the i-mode button, the "i-mode Menu" appears. The menu includes an entry to a directory of all official sites. Users can access directly "unofficial" sites, which are not directly linked to the menu, by keying in the URL[6]; but users do not usually pay for the unofficial sites because the carrier does not collect the bill for these sites.

Official sites can charge an information fee with its connection fee charged by ISPs. Carriers handle billing of those charges on behalf of the content provider. To manage the mobile internet business on the network, the carriers design handsets and give strong editorial and usability rules to content providers. For example, adult websites are not allowed to register in the official sites.

As the competitor to NTT DoCoMo—which operates an i-mode service for the largest number of subscribers in Japan—the second largest carrier, KDDI, promoted 3G mobile phone services. Currently, KDDI gained more 3G subscribers than NTT DoCoMo (Appendix 5 in accompanying CD). As compared to the 2G service, the 3G service generates a higher percentage of total ARPU (Average Revenue Per User) from data communications. KDDI offers webcasting services on the 3G mobile phones utilizing the faster speed of 3G service CDMA–2000 1x (2.4 Mbps). KDDI's EZ Channel service offers video content, including news, weather, movies and music information via push technology. In the end of 2004, 282 official sites registered in the official menu of KDDI's network, webcast videos. Taking

---

[5]This survey was conducted in the metropolitan area in July 2002. The number of completed respondents was 1,039 (response rate 86.8%).

[6]For the users' convenience, some unofficial websites send email in response to an empty mail from users. Users can connect to the website by clicking on the link in the email.

full advantage of the largest number of 3G subscribers, KDDI looks for a way to differentiate their service from NTT DoCoMo's text-based i-mode service.

In 2004, KDDI also launched the music distribution service called Chaku-uta Full (ring tone songs in full). This service sends the entire tune instead of the 30-second sample (Uranaka, 2004). Currently, ten websites offer 13,000 songs for the service as of March 2005 ("Ikkyoku marugoto daunrodo," 2005). It normally takes 30–40 seconds to download a song on the mobile phone. At present, the Chuku-uta Full service seems very successful. In the first three months after the launch of the service, over three-million songs were downloaded, despite relatively higher charges (about ¥300 or $2.80) as compared to Apple's iTunes for $0.99 ("Ikkyoku marugoto daunrodo," 2005). Using multifunctional mobile phones equipped with an MP3 player, KDDI challenges Apple's i-POD dominance[7].

Mobile phones use a small screen and a different operating system as compared to PCs, thus many venture companies recently launched to produce content specialized for the mobile internet. In contrast, there are few venture companies for webcasting services on PC-based internet, because existing media companies mostly produce content for PC-based internet. In response to the growing demand for mobile internet content, more venture companies launched content services on the mobile phone (Appendix 6 in accompanying CD). In spite of tough competition, these companies have gained substantial profits from the mobile content business.

Webcasters on PC Portals

Three portal sites rank in the top 20 webcasters (Table 17–3). They include Ya-hoo!Japan (in top position), Goo (4th), and Biglobe (12th). These webcasters occupy an important position in providing a variety of video content excluding adult content. Recently leading FTTH operator Usen Corp. has also begun the webcasting service via website GyaO (http://www.gyao.jp/) and the number of subscribers has exceeded 5 million as of December 2005[8]. With regard to business model, these portals are content aggregators who operate the webcasting service, as a one-stop entertainment or information source, to provide a convenient service for consumers, collecting and packaging content from a number of different sources. Consumers use the webcasting service for a wide array of content (Ha & Ganahl, 2004).

What are the business strategies of PC portals in Japan? Why does Japan lag behind the major countries in the webcasting business within the PC-based internet

---

[7]NTT DoCoMo also acquired an approximate 42% stake in Tower Records Japan Inc. to develop a music distribution service via a mobile phone (NTT DoCoMo, 2005b).

[8]"GyaO" is not listed in Table 17–3 because it began the webcasting service in April 2005.

market? To explore these problems, this study analyses related publications and information from interviews with informants from major PC portals[9].

BUSINESS STRATEGIES OF MAJOR PC PORTALS

Following is a comparison of the business strategies of the three major PC portals for the webcasting business. These three companies run an ISP service and operate a portal website with the largest amount of traffic in Japan. According to Nielsen/NetRatings (2005), monthly reach for portal sites of Yahoo!Japan, NIFTY, and Goo is 83.7%, 48.3%, and 30.4%, respectively. The number of ISP (mostly DSL) subscribers to these companies is around five million (Appendix 7 in accompanying CD).

Case 1—Yahoo Japan Corporation

Yahoo Japan Corporation operates Yahoo!Japan, the biggest portal site in Japan. There were 26-billion page views to Yahoo!Japan in March 2005. Also Yahoo!Japan Streaming, one of the services of Yahoo!Japan, provides consumers streaming video content on demand. Yahoo!Streaming provides video content on two different modes. Some programs are offered on pay-per-view basis. The other programs are free-of-charge to Yahoo!Premium (content service of the portal site) members and Yahoo!BB (ISP service) subscribers.

Since both services are fee-based, the revenue source of the free video content service is based on the subscription mode, where the content is bundled as a package so that all is available to the subscribers (Ha & Ganahl, 2004). Yahoo!Premium members can use a bundle of several services offered by Yahoo!Japan, including video programs, an auction service, and a webmail service, for a monthly fee of ¥294 ($2.70). Yahoo!BB is the broadband Internet Service Provider (ISP) service by Yahoo Japan Corporation. The number of Yahoo!Premium members is over 5 million, while Yahoo!BB has 4.9 million subscribers. Of the 10 most popular video programs listed on Yahoo!Japan, six belong to the adult genre, one to the sport genre, one to the movie genre, one is an animation program, and the other is a comedy show, as of December 2005. All of these programs are offered as a bundled service with Yahoo! Premium members. In sum, as of December 2005, 1,900

---

[9]The authors interviewed three informants from Portal Business Headquarters, Digital Contents Business Dept. of NTT Resonant Inc. (Hiroki Matsumoto, Hiroyuki Aiba, and Kazuomi Akao, personal interview, March 9, 2005). The second author interviewed an informant from Nifty Co. (Shinji Yatsu, personal interview, March 10, 2005).

video content programs are available to members free of charge, while 3,100 are pay-per-view programs[10].

The free streaming video content service does not seem to occupy a central position in Yahoo!Japan. For example, Yahoo!Auction achieved seven billion page views (27.1% of the total page views of Yahoo!Japan) in March 2005, and it is one of the most accessed as well as profitable services among Japan's portal sites. Yahoo!Japan obtains most of its profits from advertising, listings, internet service (FTTH and ADSL) and auctions. In contrast, video content generates only limited amount of profits. According to the second quarter interim report 2005, the total sales amount of fee-based content services (movies, music, and games) was ¥779 million ($7.2 million) for the quarter, which is only one ninth of the turnover of the advertising business (¥6,971 million or $64.5 million) (Yahoo!Japan, 2005b). However, a bundle of packaged services has been successful in terms of attracting more visitors to the portal site. The highest monthly reach rate is supported by a wide variety of useful content and information. In other words, the purpose of Yahoo Japan Corporation's investment in free content provision is not to obtain a profit directly from that service, but to capture a membership, thus maintaining ascendancy in its portal and ISP operations[11].

Case 2—NTT Resonant

NTT Resonant Inc. operates a portal site named "Goo." NTT Resonant is a subsidiary wholly owned by NTT Group, which is the dominant telephone carrier in Japan. NTT Resonant provides portal services, including searching, e-mail, weblog, shopping and distributing digital content through Goo, which is one of the top 5 internet portal sites in Japan. This company chooses a combination of two revenue sources, a pay-per-view mode and a subscription mode, on the webcasting business. Subscribers choose between the two options.

An estimated 8,000 video programs are available to the audience on the pay-per-view service, as of December 2005. Subscribers to the pay-per-view service are mostly males in their 30s or females in their 40s. Animations are most popular among males in their 30s, while Korean TV dramas, which are currently enthusiastically viewed by many Japanese women, are most popular among females in their 40s. Meanwhile, these subscribers view programs in a limited number of genres. That is to say, a niche audience only views niche programs on the

---

[10]Yahoo! announced to offer some 100,000 titles on Yahoo!Douga (http://streaming.yahoo.co.jp/) in December 2005 (Yahoo!Japan, 2005c).

[11]According to IR information of Yahoo!Japan, the missions of the media business department are (1) to "provide users with a variety of desired content and service, thereby stimulating page views and increasing advertising sales" and (2) to "provide fee-based content and services" (Yahoo!Japan, 2005a).

site. An informant from NTT Resonant said that the audience could take advantage of viewing video programs via the webcasting service, especially in some niche genres. For example, Korean dramas are offered in dubbed Japanese on TV, while their counterparts via the internet are offered in Korean with Japanese subtitles. For ardent fans, it is essential to enjoy the fresh voice of their favorite Korean actors. Additionally, the company provides a VOD service on a monthly subscription basis named BROBA, with approximately 100,000 subscribers, as of March 2005. The service offers its subscribers 100 packaged video programs for a monthly fee of ¥315 ($2.90). The monthly subscribers view more diversified programs than a pay-per-view user.

NTT Resonant attempts to fill the lineup of video content program to attract more members to the VOD service. To increase the variety of video programs, NTT Resonant has established a collaborative relationship with content product companies. The number of programs, especially in the popular genre, is a key to success in the competition with other portals. Since pay-per-view users usually consume only a small number of programs, it is more important for NTT Resonant to gain more monthly subscription members.

Case 3—NIFTY Corporation

NIFTY Co. is a subsidiary wholly owned by Fujitsu Co., one of the largest electronic companies in Japan. NIFTY is one of the biggest ISPs in Japan, but it is not in the top 20 webcasters because the site has no specialized channel for webcasting. An estimated 600 video programs are scattered on several pages in the portal site, thus the site is not very attractive as a one-stop webcaster. Since NIFTY lacks human and financial resources for the right clearance, this company has focused its webcasting business on the ASP (Application Service Provider) services and has shared the fee income with content holders without having to purchase the webcasting right. As opposed to Yahoo!Japan and NTT Resonant, NIFTY chooses the pay-per-view mode as a revenue source on the webcasting business rather than the subscription mode.

Webcasting users at the portal site @NIFTY are mostly in their 30s or 40s. The most popular content is animation and Korean dramas. Animation occupies about 70% of paid streaming video services in sales. NIFTY offered fee-based video content programs exclusively to @NIFTY members, thus the webcaster plays a limited role in the content business. Video content occupies less than 10% of the total sales of fee-based content. NIFTY aims to make the portal site more attractive by increasing the number of video programs, especially dramas.

BUSINESS STRATEGIES OF PC PORTALS
FOR THE WEBCASTERS

Currently, Japanese consumers pay almost an equal amount of money for a streaming movie and a video/DVD rental. However, most of the consumers prefer watching video/DVDs on TV rather than watching the webcast on PC. Exceptions are Korean dramas and animations. Many people watched niche genres, such as Korean TV dramas, via the webcasting service, because some Korean TV dramas were not available in video/DVD rental shops. Also, some animations were watched via the webcasting service, because these animations were often not in stock in the rental video/DVD shops due to their extraordinary popularity. In other words, the webcasters tend to complement video/DVDs rather than to compete with them.

These three cases demonstrate that the payment mode, or choice between the pay-per-view mode and the subscription mode, differentiates the business strategies. These three PC portals have different business strategies regarding the webcasting business. Yahoo!Japan adopts the subscription mode for the revenue source, utilizing 1,900 titles of free video programs. Yahoo!Japan positions the webcasting service as a way for the dominant portal site to increase the number of visitors. This is the e-commerce revenue mode, where free content is the bait (Ha & Ganahl, 2004). Like Yahoo!Japan, the leading FTTH operator Usen's webcasting service ("GyaO") is free to registered subscribers. Usen earns profits from targeted advertising toward a specified age/gender group (Kuramoto, 2005).

Unlike Yahoo!Japan, NTT Resonant does not regard the webcasting service as the bait. NTT Resonant positions the webcasting service as a profitable e-commerce enterprise. NTT Resonant adopts the subscription mode, but this company prefers the paid subscription rather than the pay-per-view mode. In contrast, NIFTY adopts only the pay-per-view mode. NIFTY positions the webcasting service as the bait. Although the three companies commonly aim to attract a large base of users to their portal sites, the specific strategies for their webcasting businesses are very different.

CONCLUSIONS

Four Webcaster Typologies

In Japan, many webcasting services coexist. We classify the webcasters into four typologies, namely: integrator, ISP portal, distributor with branded content, and specialized distributor. These four typologies are located according to the following two dimensions: (1) whether the company holds network infrastructure, and

TABLE 17–4
Webcaster Typologies and Business Models in Japan

Webcaster Typology	Example	Network (ADSL and/or FTTH)	Content Production	Business Model
Integrator	Sony Group	Y	Y	CA or BC
ISP portal	Yahoo! Goo GyaO Mobile phone carriers	Y	N	CA
Distributor with branded content	itv24.com Tresola Content providers on the mobile phone	N	Y	BC
Specialized distributor	MSN Oricon (mobile phone)	N	N	CA

Notes. CA = content aggregator; BC = branded content (Ha & Ganahl, 2004).

(2) whether the company produces branded content. Table 17–4 demonstrates these typologies. Note that these typologies should be understood as pure ideal-types, because these dimensions are continuous rather than discrete, and some companies may be located on the boundary. However, these typologies are useful for understanding the differences in the business models between the mobile internet and PC internet in Japan.

Integrators hold network infrastructure for customers (ADSL or FTTH) and produce branded content by themselves. The Sony group is one of few examples in Japan. The Sony group operates an ISP and produces movies and music, however its portal site called So-net (http://www.so-net.ne.jp/) is not very popular. Although no integrators rank in the top 20 (Table 17–3), some ISP portals in the PC internet market attempt to become an integrator through acquisitions and mergers, as will be described below. With regard to business models (Ha & Ganahl, 2004), integrators have the choice between the branded content model and the content aggregator model depending on the relative importance of the content production.

ISP portals hold network infrastructure, but they do not produce content. In Japan, NTT group's Goo and Yahoo! are the major ISP portals on the PC internet. Usen Corp., the leading FTTH operator, operates a portal on the webcasting service with the largest number of subscribers in Japan. Mobile phone carriers, such as NTT DoCoMo and KDDI, also operate their portals on the mobile internet, although their business model considerably differs from their counterparts on the PC internet, as described previously. To gain more subscribers to their ISP services and more customers to their site, ISP portals usually attempt to offer a wide variety of services and content, including the webcasting services. Thus ISP portals generally work on the content aggregator model.

Distributors with branded content do not own a network infrastructure, but distribute and produce their branded content. They employ the branded content business model. An example is the above-mentioned failed case of Tresola. Some small creative production companies seek to merchandise their content on the internet to escape from the dominance of the major mass media. Itv24.com (http://itv24.com/) is an example of these companies. Itv24.com is operated by a small TV production company, which creates TV programs for TV stations. This company seeks to merchandise its programs on its own channel through the internet. The major advertising agency Dentsu Inc. and five Tokyo-based TV broadcasters also plan to run the webcasting business based on free television broadcasts directly to the internet. Unlike Tresola, which charged for their on-demand content, this service is to simultaneously transmit reruns of TV programs via multiple channels on preset schedules (Nihon Keizai Shimbun, 2005). Distributors with branded content presently still occupy a minor position in the PC internet market, while they lead the webcasting business in the mobile internet market (Appendix 5 in accompanying CD). The competition structure in the mobile internet market facilitates the entry of many distributors with branded content into the market, as will be described below.

Specialized distributors do not either hold their networks or produce branded content. They employ the content aggregator business model. These companies offer a distribution system utilizing advanced software technologies or unique information systems[12]. In other words, an excellent distributor system is their advantage. MSN (Microsoft Network) Japan is an example of specialized distributors. Unlike MSN U.S., MSN Japan does not operate an internet connection service in Japan. This company utilizes the advanced software technology to help many companies distribute content through the internet. Oricon is another example. Oricon is a unique marketing research company that has regularly published music ranking information based on its unique surveys. In 2005, Oricon launched an online-music distribution service associated with its ranking information.

Webcasters in the Mobile Internet

In contrast to the webcasting business on the PC internet, the webcasting mobile business seems much more successful in Japan. Why is the webcasting business so successful on the mobile phone, while it is not on the PC?

---

[12]Adult content providers are classified into the specialized distributors, because the programs these adult webcasters distribute via the internet are actually not original ones except for being an unexpurgated edition.

A number of factors, including technological factors, psychological factors, and the market structure, can explain the difference between the two markets. First, it is much easier to protect copyrights on the mobile phone than on PCs because mobile phone carriers design handsets, the built-in operating system, and the network so that the copyright can be easily protected. Second, customers are more willing to pay for content on the mobile internet, as compared to content on the PC internet because mobile phone carriers handle billing of the content charges on behalf of content providers. It is more convenient and consumers feel more safe settling bills with the carriers than paying for content providers on their credit card, since many Japanese people feel uneasy about giving their credit card number over the internet (World Internet Project Japan, 2001).

Thirdly, and more importantly, the competition structure is quite different in the mobile internet market than in the PC internet market. The mobile phone carriers seek to attract more content providers to their network, since the carriers gain a commission from content distributors and a connection charge from users who consume content on the mobile phone. This is a win-win situation for content providers and the carriers. Thus, the mobile phone carriers have no incentive to become an integrator by acquiring a media company, while many PC ISPs are interested in acquiring a media company.

The mobile phone carriers have generally chosen an open policy to get more content providers to their network by providing a platform for content providers. The competition structure in the mobile internet market has facilitated the entry of many venture enterprises into the market. In the mobile internet, competitions occur at two different levels: carriers compete only with other carriers, while content providers compete only with other content providers. These situations give the carriers an advantage over the content providers. This advantage is reflected in that content providers on the mobile internet are much smaller than the carriers. Thus, some broadband companies are eager to expand into the mobile phone carrier business. For example, Softbank Co, the holding company of Yahoo!Japan, applied for licenses to test its 3G mobile phone systems ("Vodafone to apply for license," 2005).

Webcasters in the PC Market

In the PC internet, competitions can occur between ISPs and content providers. Thus, unlike mobile phone carriers, PC ISPs cannot directly earn profits from visitors on the PC internet, because visitors do not pay any connection fee on the portal sites. Hence, the PC ISPs are more interested in obtaining revenues from their own content business, although currently, few companies gain profit from the webcasting business on the PC internet.

Despite the diffusion of the most advanced broadband technologies in the world, Japan has not yet developed a full-fledged webcaster business. The number of paid subscribers to the webcasting service is still small, and the amount of webcasting content is limited. For example, three PC ISP portals listed in Table 17–3 offer 1,000–5,000 titles of video works, which is much less than the 18,000–23,000 titles that are offered at rental DVD shops on the internet[13]. ISP portals still regard the webcasting service as one of several goods to attract visitors to their sites. In this sense, the webcasters complement DVDs, but the webcasters do not compete with DVDs.

Three obstacles have prevented the growth of Japanese webcasters in the PC market. The first obstacle is the difficulty in rights clearance. Many persons and corporations, including actors, musicians, production companies, and others, hold a right regarding a TV program in Japan. It is especially difficult to clear all rights for a TV program to distribute through broadband networks. One of the reasons for the failure of Tresola was excessive personnel costs for rights handling (Harada, 2004). To merchandise a TV program for webcasters, the company needs permissions from a number of rights owners such as actors, music publisher, musicians, and singers. The government is also concerned about this problem because the rights clearance is one of keys to promoting broadband network. The government recently adopted "Intellectual property strategic program" which includes the development of a system for preparing a standard copyright contract (Intellectual Property Policy Headquarters, 2004). In March 2005, fifteen interested organizations of the broadcasting industry reached an interim agreement on royalty payments for broadcasting TV dramas via the internet (Institute for Information and Communications, 2005).

The second obstacle that impedes the growth of webcasters is the technological disadvantages. The webcasting service is still technologically disadvantaged as compared to DVDs. Viewing on a PC monitor is not as comfortable as viewing on TV. An informant from NTT Resonant regarded small PC monitors as the major obstacle to the webcasting business. Web streaming does not achieve the highest picture quality of DVD, even via high-speed broadband. In this sense, the webcasters cannot displace DVDs.

The third obstacle is the closed media market structure. Existing commercial TV broadcasting companies are not fully motivated to take on the webcasting business. As opposed to major countries in the world, the penetration rate of CATV is still low (33%) in Japan, thus these companies have maintained a satisfactory level of advertising revenues. As a result, the TV broadcasting companies are reluctant to take a risky step of proceeding with a webcasting service. However, technological developments in IP technology are changing the positions of the existing media companies in the status quo structure. The government also has a plan to allow TV companies to distribute terrestrial digital broadcast programs online using fi-

---

[13]As of 2004, 34,700 titles of DVDs are available for sale in Japan (DVD sofuto catarogu, 2005).

ber-optic networks and internet Protocol technology to promote the broadband industry ("Digital BROADCAST," 2005).

In the future, the authors anticipate increased vertical combinations between content holders and ISPs through acquisitions and mergers especially in the PC internet market. The recent spate of takeovers and alliances suggest the germination of a new order in the webcasting industry. In March 2005, Yahoo!Japan launched a music downloading service in alliance with LabelGate Co., the largest online music distribution company, funded by the major music production companies in Japan (Yahoo!Japan, 2005d). In March 2005, an internet service provider Livedoor Co. attempted to takeover the Fuji TV group. Fuji TV Network and Livedoor agreed to form their business alliance in April 2005 ("Fuji TV, Livedoor make peace," 2005). In April 2005, the Usen Co. acquired a majority stake in movie studio Nikkatsu Co. ("Usen to take over movie studio," 2005). Index Corp., a leading content distributor company on the mobile phone, put 22.2% of its funds into Takara Co., which is a major animation production company in Japan (Index Corp., 2005). In October 2005, a virtual mall operator Rakuten Co. proposed a management integration with TBS (Tokyo Broadcasting System) which is one of the major TV broadcasting companies ("Rakuten boosts TBS stake," 2005).

Content owned by clicks-and-bricks is attractive to PC ISPs because it can produce a huge profit through the integration of the broadband infrastructure and content. For PC ISPs, acquiring a media company means gaining access to a vast volume of content. It may take some years to complete the vertical combination in the market, but these movements suggest the emergence of a new order in the Japanese media market where the traditional media have maintained the status quo over the past 50 years.

ACKNOWLEDGMENTS

The authors are grateful to NTT Resonant Inc., NIFTY Corporation, and Video Research Interactive Inc. for providing useful information on the webcasting business. The first author also would like to thank two students for performing a content analysis of webs.

REFERENCES

Commerce and Information Policy Bureau, MITI. (2004). Dejitarukontentsuhakusyo 2004. (Digital content white paper, 2004), Tokyo: Digital Content Association Japan.

Dentsu Soken. (2003). 2004 Joho media hakusyo [Information media white paper, 2004]. Tokyo: Dentsu Soken.

Digital BROADCAST: Govt net distribution plan rattles TV industry. (July 22, 2005). *The Nihon Keizai Shimbun*. Retrieved July 29, 2005, from Nikkei Telecom 21 database.

DVD sofuto katarogu 2005 [DVD Content Catalogue in 2005]. (2005, January 1). Tokyo: Hinode Shuppan.

Frieden, R. (2005). Lessons from broadband development in Canada, Japan, Korea and the United States, *Telecommunications Policy*, 29(8). 595–613.

Fuji TV, Livedoor make peace, agree to share NBS. (April 19, 2005). *Nikkei English News*, Retrieved April 20, 2005, from Nikkei Telecom 21 database.

Ha, L. & Ganahl, R. (2004). Webcasting business models of clicks-and-bricks and pure-play media: A comparative study of leading webcasters in South Korea and the United States. *The International Journal on Media Management*, 6(1&2), 74–87.

Ha, L., Ganahl, R., Arampatzis, A., Allagui, I., Bakker, P., Chausse, M.et al. (2005). Emerging media business models worldwide: A study of leading webcasters in 13 countries. Paper submitted to the Communication Technology and Policy Division, Association for Education in Journalism and Mass Communication Annual Conference, San Antonio, Texas.

Harada,Y. (2004, November 18). Haigun no syou hei wo kataru [A defeated general talks about his lost battles]. *Nikkei Business*, pp. 169–172.

Ikkyoku marugoto daunrodo [downloading a full tune]. (2005, March 12). *Yomiuri Shimbun Evening Version*, p.7.

Index Corp. (2005). IR Report. Retrieved April 27, 2005. from http://www.indexweb.co.jp/index.html

Institute for Information and Communications (Soumusyo Joho Tsusin Seisaku Kankyusyo). (2005). Henbo suru contentu bizinesu [Changing content business]. Tokyo: Toyokeizai.

Institute of Socio-Information and Communication Studies. (2001). Nihonjin no joho kodo 2000 [Information behavior 2000 in Japan]. Tokyo: University of Tokyo Press.

Intellectual Property Policy Headquarters. (2004). Intellectual Property Strategic Program 2004, Retrieved July 27, 2005, from http://www.kantei.go.jp/foreign/policy/titeki/kettei/040527_e.html

Ishii, K. (2003). Diffusion, policy, and use of broadband in Japan. *Trends of Communication*, 11(1), 45–61.

Ishii, K. (2004). Internet use via mobile phone in Japan. *Telecommunications Policy*, 28(1), 43–58.

Ishii, K. & Wu,C. (2006). A comparative study of media cultures among Taiwanese and Japanese youth. *Telematics and Informatics*,23(2), 95–116.

Kuramoto, G. (2005, November 11). Usen reconfiguring webcast model—GyaO streaming service lets sponsors design advertising for specific consumer groups. *The Nikkei Weekly*, p.12.

Ministry of Public Management, Home Affairs, Posts and Telecommunications. (2004). Johotusin hakusyo [Telecommunications whitebook]. Tokyo: Gyosei.

Ministry of Internal Affairs and Communications. (2005). Burodobando keiyakusyasuu no suuii heisei 16 nendo [Broadband subscribers statistics as of March 2005], Retrieved July 27, 2005, from http://www.soumu.go.jp/s-news/2005/050708_3.html

Nielsen/Netratings. (2005). Top 10 web properties, month of November 2004. Retrieved April 5, 2005, from http://www.nielsen-netratings.com/news.jsp?section = dat_to&country = jp

NTT Holdings. (2005). IR Information. Retrieved April 10, 2005, from http://www.ntt.co.jp/ir/fin_e/subscriber.html

NTT DoCoMo. (2005a). Investor Report. Retrieved December 23, 2005, from http://www.nttdocomo.co.jp/english/corporate/investor_relations/business/list_e.html

NTT DoCoMo. (2005b). Press Release. Retrieved December 23, 2005, from http://www.nttdocomo.com/presscenter/pressreleases/press/pressrelease.html?param[no] = 590

Rakuten boosts TBS stake above 19% with ¥20bn-plus investment. (October 26, 2005) Nikkei English News. Retrieved October 27, 2005, from Nikkei Telecom 21 database.

Telecommunications Carriers Association. (2005). Number of subscribers. Retrieved March 20, 2005, from http://www.tca.or.jp/

Uranaka,T. (2004, December 11). Cell phones answer music players' call. *The Japan Times*. Retrieved April 28, 2005, from http://www.japantimes.co.jp/cgi-bin/getarticle.pl5?nb20041211a1.htm

Usen to take over movie studio Nikkatsu to beef up content ops. (2005, April 22). *Nekkei English News* Retrieved April 20, 2005, from Nikkei Telecom 21 database.

Video Research Interactive. (2003). Keitai denwa no riyou jittai [Current status of mobile phone usage]. Retrieved March 20, 2005, from http://www.videoi.co.jp/service/mobile/index.html#06

Vodafone to apply for license to test 3G cell phones in 1.7Ghz band. (2005, April 25). *Nikkei English News*. Retrieved April 20, 2005, from Nikkei Telecom 21 database.

World Internet Project Japan. (2001). Internet usage in Japan—Survey report 2000, Tokyo: Communications Research Laboratory.

World Internet Project Japan. (2004). Internet usage in Japan—Survey report 2003, Tokyo: Communications Research Laboratory.

World Internet Project Japan. (2005). Internet usage in Japan—Survey report 2005, Tokyo: Communications Research Laboratory .

Yahoo!Japan. (2005a). IR Information. Retrieved December 20, 2005, from http://ir.yahoo.co.jp/en/bizres/gaikyo/20050420/

Yahoo!Japan. (2005b). IR Information. Retrieved December 20, 2005, from http://ir.yahoo.co.jp/en/bizres/gaikyo/20051021/

Yahoo!Japan. (2005c) Yahoo!Japan Streaming. Retrieved March 20, 2005, from http://streaming.yahoo.co.jp/ranking/

Yahoo!Japan. (2005d) Press Release. Retrieved December 20, 2005, from http://pr.yahoo.co.jp/release/2005/0224a.html

CHAPTER 18

Australia: Webcasting:
"Pretty Dead, Really"—Or Is It?

Niranjala D. Weerakkody
Deakin University, Australia

Webcasting, sometimes labeled the "last frontier" or "the next stage of evolution" of the internet era, has been slow in its diffusion in Australia, due to technical constraints related to internet transmission speeds and bandwidth (Morrissey, 2003, cited in Lin, 2004, p. 446). According to Craig Preston, Operations Coordinator for New Media and Digital Services at the Australian Broadcasting Corporation (or ABC, a national broadcaster), webcasting in Australia is "pretty dead, really" (C. Preston, personal communication, August 23, 2005). This statement will be examined in this chapter, especially since the Australian Media Guide does not list "webcasting" or "streaming" as a category or include the terms among its long list of entries (Gee, 2005)

AUSTRALIA AND ITS PEOPLE

Australia officially became a British colony in 1788 and was used as a destination for the transportation of convicts until 1868. Descendants of those convicts and British migrants who settled in the country at various times make up the majority of the nation's population today. At the end of World War II, Australia began to accept non-British, European migrants in large numbers and since the official end to the "White Australia Policy" in 1972, has accepted migrants from Asia and elsewhere based on their job skills, family links, as well as humanitarian grounds (Jupp, 2002). Today, Australia is a highly multicultural society. The official language of Australia is English, but many of its more recent and post World War II

migrants and their descendants still speak languages other than English at home.[1]
The comparatively small size of the population dispersed across a large geographic
area makes Australian media and its policy making unique among other developed
nations.

AUSTRALIA'S MEDIA INDUSTRY STRUCTURE

An island continent with a population just over 20 million (Australian Bureau of
Statistics, 2005), Australia's media industry is described as "one of the most sophisticated in the world and one of the most competitive" ("Industries and issues,"
2005, p. 1). At the same time, one must also note that Australia had very much
lagged behind other developed nations in the adoption of color TV (introduced in
1975), subscription (Pay) TV (in 1995) and digital TV (in 2001) due to the competing interests of and lobbying by the various stakeholder groups influencing government policy (Weerakkody, 2003; Weerakkody & Tremblay, 2003).

Australian commercial media are also considered the most concentrated in
terms of ownership patterns among developed nations (Turner & Cunningham,
2002), because a handful of large media companies dominate the Australian media
landscape through direct and cross-ownership among various media outlets and industries. Still, calls are often made for the further deregulation of the Australian
media industry mainly to remove the remaining limits on foreign and cross-ownership. These limits currently enforce caps on an entity's maximum holdings, and
impose limits on ownership of a newspaper and a TV station in the same market.
They also require minimum levels of local content on broadcast (55%) and subscription (10%) TV for drama and for the higher rated 6 p.m. to 12 midnight time-
slot (Murray, 2005).

Broadcast TV

Approximately 99% of the 7.3 million Australian households in 2004 had at least
one working TV set and were able to receive free-to-air and subscription TV (Aus-

---

[1]In 1901, the Australian population born overseas was recorded as 23%. By 1947, this figure has
been reduced to 10%. At the 2001 census, the figure had increased to 24% (http://www.abs.gov.au). The
three most common languages other than English spoken at home by Australians, according to the 2001
census were Chinese languages (2.1%), Italian (1.9%), and Greek (1.4%). The United Kingdom and
Ireland were the countries of origin (birth) for the majority (6.1%) of Australians according to the 2001
census. Next were New Zealand (2.0%), Italy (1.2%), and Greece (0.68%). Germany, the Philippines,
India, Netherlands, Malaysia, South Africa, Lebanon, Hong Kong (SAR of China), Poland, Yugoslavia,
the U.S., and Sri Lanka (listed in descending order) each had numbers high enough to be included in the
summary data. The indigenous or Aboriginal population in Australia is 1.5% of total (Australian Bureau of Statistics, 2005).

tralian Broadcast Authority, 2005). The Australian broadcast television industry consists of two national broadcasters funded by the federal government, namely the Australian Broadcasting Corporation (the ABC) and the Special Broadcasting Service (the SBS, the multicultural broadcaster). Unlike the ABC, the SBS broadcasts in English as well as in other languages spoken by a third of the Australian population. It also accepts advertising.[2]

Most Australian schools teach a language other than English with German, French, Indonesian, Japanese, and Mandarin Chinese being the most popular, from primary school to Year 9 (in the State of Victoria). Many students in Years 10 to 12 opt to take their language studies further at the high school certificate level, to be counted towards their performance and standardized scores for university admissions. Interestingly, many students either born overseas or are of non-British migrant ancestry, often choose to study a language not related to their ethnic heritage or national origin. Australians are also well known for their love of travel to foreign countries, with "backpacking" overseas being a right of passage for many young people.

The SBS TV also produces its own comprehensive daily local and international news bulletins and produces many current affairs programs; airs documentaries; broadcasts soccer games from Europe and a daily World Sports bulletin—all in English (SBS, 2005). It also regularly broadcasts acclaimed foreign language films and entertainment programs (with English subtitles) from across the world and is the channel that aired the drama *Queer as Folk* in Australia.

The Australian Broadcasting Corporation (ABC)—nicknamed "Auntie"—generally airs entertainment and cultural TV programming produced in the United Kingdom, in English. It is well respected for its own local and international news and current affairs programming and documentaries and generally attracts a higher educated audience.

The commercial broadcasters serving the metropolitan areas of Sydney, Melbourne, Adelaide, Brisbane, and Perth are Channels 7, 9, and 10, which own their respective stations in those cities. Channel 7, which broadcast the Athens Olympics, is owned by Kerry Stokes, the owner of Pacific Magazines, a leader in magazine publishing (Seven Corporation, 2005). Channel 9 is owned by Australia's richest man, Kerry Packer, who passed away on Dec 26, 2005. His Publishing and

---

[2]The Special Broadcasting Corporation (SBS), broadcasts via satellite the daily TV news bulletins from the following countries in their original languages without English subtitles, for the benefit of those in Australia who speak them. They are: Japanese News (from NHK Tokyo), Cantonese News (ATV Hong Kong), Mandarin News (CCTV Beijing), Italian News (RAI Rome), DAS Journal (DW Berlin), Spanish News (RTVE Madrid), Le Journal (FR2 Paris), Russian News (NTV Moscow), Greek News (ERT Athens), Arabic News (DRTV Dubai), and Indonesian News (TVRI Jakarta). In addition, it also airs the Business Report (from PBS, Miami and New York), News Hour with Jim Lehrer (from PBS, Washington D.C., U.S.), and The Journal (DW Berlin) broadcast in English (SBS, 2005).

Broadcasting Limited or PBL, owns ACP Magazines, and also has interests in the Hoyts cinemas chain (PBL, 2005; "Industries and issues," 2005). Channel 10 is 57.5% owned by Canada's CanWest Global Communications (Network 10, 2005). All three networks air most of the popular TV programs from the U.S. and some locally produced entertainment, news and current affairs programs. Rupert Murdoch's News Corporation, which owns the Fox Network in the U.S., does not currently own a TV network in Australia via its subsidiary News Limited, even though News Limited is a leading media conglomerate operating in Australia.

Eight regional commercial TV companies serve regions outside metro areas and are affiliated to the three networks. They include WIN TV, NBN TV, Prime TV, Ten Network (Queensland, North and South New South Wales, and Victoria), Southern Cross TV in Tasmania, Seven (in Queensland), and TND and NTD in Northern Territory ("Industries and issues," 2005).

Imparja, serving the indigenous communities, uses two channels in rural and remote Australia. It is owned by aboriginal stakeholders in South Australia and Northern Territory and is a commercial operation affiliated with Channels 9 and 10. It also produces local content for its services (Imparja, 2005).

Subscription (Pay) TV

Subscription (Pay) TV, introduced on October 23, 1995, is currently operated by six companies serving different geographic areas or markets. The largest is Foxtel, which is jointly owned by the telecommunications giant Telstra (50%), News Limited (25%), and Publishing and Broadcasting Limited (PBL) (25%). In October 2005, 1.8 million households had subscription TV, which offers up to 150 channels (Day, 2005). The high cost of subscription TV which ranges between A$50.95 (US$36.50) for the basic service and A$98.85 (US$71) for the full package (Day, 2005), is considered the main reason for the low penetration (25%) of Pay TV in Australia. This contrasts with 89% in the U.S., 45% in Britain and 42% in New Zealand (Day, 2005). The high subscription charges are attributed to the high cost of obtaining rights to Hollywood movies, one of Pay TV's main attractions (Day, 2005). The median weekly income of all Australians over the age of 15 in the 2001 census was A$300–A$399 (US$214–US$285; ABS, 2005).

Digital TV, which launched in January 2001, only had 658,000 set top boxes or integrated digital TV sets (that convert the analog TV signal to digital) by the end of 2004 (Australian Broadcasting Authority, 2005), indicating a pattern of slow adoption of the technology by consumers (Weerakkody, 2003; Weerakkody & Tremblay, 2003). However, a 130 channel digital TV service was made available via subscription TV in 2004 with "Foxtel digital" (Foxtel, 2005). This appears to have invigorated its diffusion to new customers as well as to 75% of existing customers who upgraded their analog service to digital (Day, 2005), paying an additional subscription fee and installation costs.

The other subscription TV providers are Austar, Optus TV (owned by Singapore Telecommunications—SingTel), Neighbourhood Cable (a regional service in Victoria), TransACT (a regional provider for the Australian Capital Territory, Canberra), and UBI World TV (a niche foreign language program provider). Each of these providers offers similar services because of industry deals and agreements (Wikipedia, 2005).

Radio

Currently there are 37 million radio sets with an average of 5.1 sets per household, in Australia. Of the total 257 commercial radio stations, 40 are based in metro areas and 217 in regional areas. ABC radio operates 60 metro and regional stations and four national networks viz. ABC Classic FM, Radio National, ABC Newsradio, the youth network Triple J, and the internet based music service "dig" (Commercial Radio Australia, 2005). At the moment, 80% of Australia's commercial radio stations are owned by 12 radio networks, indicating a high concentration of ownership. Recently, the Australian government granted permission to existing radio broadcasters to adopt digital radio, leading to a further convergence of ownership (R. Monaghan, personal communication, October 26, 2005).

Additionally, there are 230 community radio stations and about 1500 low power narrowcasting and temporary community radio stations ("Industries and issues," 2005). Not surprisingly, Australia is considered to have one of the most long standing and vibrant community broadcasting services in the world (Community Broadcasting Foundation, 2004). Community radio serves much of Australia's multicultural population who speak languages other than English, and the indigenous populations dispersed across rural and remote areas, and speak a variety of Aboriginal languages.

The Movie Industry

The movie industry in Australia, while small, boasts of having developed the talents of actors Mel Gibson, Hugh Jackman, Oscar winners Nicole Kidman, Geoffrey Rush, Russell Crowe, Cate Blanchett, and Hollywood directors Baz Luhrmann (*Moulin Rouge*) and Peter Weir (*Witness, Master and Commander*), among many others. In 2004, director Cate Shortland's *Somersault* was screened at 10 international film festivals. However, in recent times, the production of local films has been reduced to 19 features in 2004–2005 and 16 in 2003–2004 from a 10 year average of 24, signaling a crisis situation. Local feature film and TV drama production expenditures only amounted to A$536 million (US$382.9 million) in 2004–2005. The gross box office earnings for local films were only A$11.9 million (US$8.5 million) or 1.3% of total film revenue. The total number of films (both local and overseas productions) screened in Australia in 2004 was 318 of which only 5% were Australian productions while 63% were from the U.S. The number of cinema screens in Australia in 2004 was 1,909 (Australian Film Commission, 2005).

Fox Studios in Sydney has produced many popular Hollywood movies, providing local employment and experience to Australia's talented film technicians and other professionals. Recent productions include the *Matrix* trilogy, *Mission Impossible 2*, *Charlotte's Web*, and *Ghost Rider* (Australian Film Commission, 2005). Unfortunately, such productions force the local movie industry to compete in terms of pay scales, making production costs too high for an industry already struggling with low returns on investments and competition from Hollywood blockbusters.

Nevertheless, as evident from the above discussions, the Australian media industry offers a wide variety of content to its audiences. Advertising revenues for broadcast and other media organizations are healthy, as detailed in Appendix C included in the accompanying CD.

INTERNET AND BROADBAND USAGE

In March 2005, the total number of Australian internet subscribers was 5.98 million, using 689 Internet Service Providers (ISPs). Of these, 180 had less than 100 subscribers, indicating a highly fragmented market. Just over 50% of Australian households have internet access with less in regional and rural areas. Access to a computer is enjoyed by two thirds of households, depending on age, geographic location, and other demographic factors across the nation (James, 2005).

The Australian Bureau of Statistics defines broadband as "always on" (i.e. having a continuous internet connection, instead of dialing-up each time a connection is needed) with more than 256 kbps speed. In March 2005, 1.8 million Australian households had broadband connections, a 39% increase since September 2004 ("Census on internet access," 2005). However, in 2003, the broadband service was only available to 75% of the population. The reduction in March 2003 of the installation fee from A$300 to A$29 (A$129 with a A$100 cash back offer) created 23,000 new subscribers in March 2003 for Telstra's Big Pond service—Australia's dominant provider of broadband. Connections had more than doubled between July 2002 and July 2003. Still, only 5% of homes in Australia had broadband access in 2003. Increased competition between service providers and falling prices are expected to increase the number of connections in the future (Hallaby, 2003).

However, the provision of broadband services to all regional, rural and remote areas in Australia (referred to as "the bush") is a contentious issue as not many commercial telecommunications providers are willing to make the investment required to serve these sparsely populated areas, because of the low returns that can be expected.

Telstra holds the monopoly on the Asymmetric Digital Subscriber Line (ADSL) and Unbundled Local Loop (ULL) markets in Australia. However, competition among resellers of these services such as OzEmail and Primus, and carriers such as Request and XYZed, is expected to bring retail prices down for broadband services. ADSL uses the copper wire telephone infrastructure accounts for three fourths of the market, even with a data download speed that is 10% that of cable. Cable uses the fiber optic infrastructure, available either through the subscription TV companies Foxtel and Optus or through independent broadband providers operating in major metropolitan areas (Hallaby, 2003). This means the regional and rural areas (which use satellite dishes or antennas for receiving subscription TV signals instead of via cables), will most probably be denied broadband connections altogether, unless some other funding arrangements for the necessary infrastructure are made.

ADSL has more opportunities for providing internet connections to households due to its geographically wider coverage and ease of installation. At the same time, the current broadband rollout is mostly focused on business customers even though household users provide a larger subscriber base (Hallaby, 2003).

Broadband issues in Australian telecommunications were examined by two Senate inquiries that supported the upgrading of the necessary infrastructure to improve broadband connectivity, and suggested more proactive regulation (James, 2005). The inquiry on "Competition in Broadband Services" suggested the need for structural changes to the telecommunications industry to remove Telstra's media interests (e.g., 50% interest in Foxtel subscription TV) and to set a ten year national target for broadband service provision (James, 2005).

HELPING THE BUSH TO GET BROADBAND

In response to the report of the "Regional Telecommunications Inquiry," the Australian government has set aside A$142.8 million (US$102 million) over a four-year period to address the provision of broadband services to regional, rural and remote areas. It also proposes the development of an "Australian National Broadband Strategy." Such steps are needed to address the issues related to bandwidth for consumers outside the major metropolitan areas (James, 2005). Australia's population distribution is unique as the majority of the people live in and around the five major cities and the rest of the continent is sparsely populated. Even though development costs for the infrastructure are high, providing a profitable commercial service that is affordable and equitable to the regional, rural and remote area customers is necessary. The Australian government acknowledges the market is the primary determinant of broadband delivery and services, and its own role and responsibility to promote market driven outcomes. It envisages taking action if the market fails to provide services at a fair and reasonable price within an acceptable time frame, and intends to work with the commercial and private sectors (DCITA, 2004).

BROADBAND AND WEBCASTING

The success of webcasting depends on the provision of broadband connections to customers and the goal of a webcasting organization is to optimize its usage by customers. The high bandwidth requirements for webcasters involve costs to provide server upgrades, new routers, upgrades to the network infrastructure, and for the provision of maintenance services. Thereafter, regular maintenance to meet the market and technological advances is needed. Content creation will add to these costs with staff time and resources to develop new programming, convert existing content (e.g., radio/ TV to audio/video streaming) and maintaining the content. Consumers too will need to upgrade their end user software (e.g., Windows Media Player, Real Player, etc.) if they are to receive the full benefits of the webcasts. The content provided by a webcast must also be useful or appealing to the consumer, if the webcast is to be successful (Bing, 1997; Rothman, 2005).

AUDIENCE RESEARCH ON WEBCASTING

At present, no ratings company in Australia appears to be officially collecting data on audiences for the webcasting industry. The Department of Communication, Information Technology and the Arts (DCITA) or the Australian Bureau of Statistics (ABS) do not provide any figures or include any information on or make any references to webcasting. In September 2001, an Australian Chapter of the International Webcasting Association (IWA) is reported to have been established, with the aim of "offering its members exclusive research on the webcasting market, promotional space on the website and priority access to industry conferences, publications and products" ("International Webcasting Association launches in Australia," 2001). However, in 2005, none of the contact details or the website of this organization listed in the original news article existed. The IWA website also does not make any references to a Chapter in Australia. The website of the Internet Industry Association of Australia (http://www.iia.net.au), which is the National Internet Industry Association for Australia, also makes no references to webcasting.

COLLECTING DATA ON WEBCASTING IN AUSTRALIA

As the Australian Media Guide (Gee, 2005) makes no references to webcasting, the author interviewed Ross Monaghan, an Australian academic in Public Relations at Deakin University for his views on the webcasting industry in Australia. He is a former journalist and PR practitioner, who has served as an executive in the Australian telecommunications industry. He named the Australian Broadcasting Corporation (ABC) and the commercial news media as the most likely current leaders in webcasting and suggested the Commonwealth Parliament of Australia and activist groups as other noteworthy webcasters. Accordingly, the author examined the available websites of all major commercial, public and community broadcasters, major national and regional newspapers, and subscription TV providers in Australia, as well as websites of organizations such as Yahoo!7 (now Yahoo7) for Australia and New Zealand and those with an Australian URL (i.e. ".au") for suitable webcasters to be included in the 20-strong sample for a content analysis.

Only websites that included audio and/or video content in addition to text and still images were included in the sample. Thus, some of the news media websites did not qualify as webcasters. The sample was a "purposive" one, involving aspects of "snowballing," as some webcasters and organizational websites provided "leads" to other suitable ones. Given the current early stage in diffusion of webcasting in Australia, this sample may well be very close to a census (Wimmer & Dominick, 2006, p. 125) of leading webcasters in Australia.

The author also searched the Mass Media Complete (formerly the Matlon Index) database for scholarly literature on the subject and the Factiva database (similar to LexisNexis) for newspaper articles on webcasting in Australia, in addition to Google searchers, all carried out on several occasions during 2004 and 2005. A good portion of the citations however, proved to be websites of, and publicity material from, vendors of webcasting related products and services, mainly aimed at the corporate market to serve corporate and organizational communication functions, and were not aligned with media or broadcasting industries. The databases of the Australian Bureau of Statistics (ABS) and the Department of Communication, Information Technology and the Arts (DCITA) were also searched for related information.

As the content analysis indicated the Australian Broadcasting Corporation (ABC) as the most involved in webcasting in Australia, the author also interviewed Craig Preston, the Operations Coordinator of ABC's New Media and Digital Services for his insights about the state of webcasting in Australia.

Webcaster Profiles

Table 18–1 summarizes the profiles of the 20 selected webcasters (see Appendixes A and B in the accompanying CD) as to their parent companies, ownership, types, and the business models used. However, statistics related to streams, unique users, and revenue figures are not included, as official figures are not currently available for the Australian webcasting industry.

TABLE 18–1
Webcaster Profiles in the Australian Sample (in alphabetical order)

Webcaster	Parent Company	Type	Ownership	Business Model
ABC dig	ABC	CB	Government	BC
ABC Online	ABC	CB	Government	BC
ABC Radio 1222 Newcastle	ABC	CB	Government	BC
ABC Rural	ABC	CB	Government	BC
AFL	Australian Football League	PP	Non-profit Foundation	BC
The Australian (newspaper) website	News Limited	PP	Public	BC
FoxSports Audio	Foxtel	CB	Public	BC
Melbourne Indymedia	Oceania Indymedia	PP	Independent	BC
NRL	National Rugby League	PP	Public	BC
NINEMSN–Channel 9 TV	PBL and Microsoft	CB	Public	CA
Parliament of Australia	Parliament of Australia	CB	Government	BC
PBS106.7FM Melbourne	Progressive Broadcasting Service	CB	Independent	BC
Radio Australia	ABC	CB	Government	BC
Radio National Saturday Night Country	ABC	CB	Government	BC
Real Radio 2Ser 107.3FM	Sydney Educational Radio (2SER)	CB	Privately owned*	CA
SBS Online	SBS	CB	Government	CA
Sydney Morning Herald	Farifax Ltd.	CB	Public	CA
Triple J Radio	ABC	CB	Goverment	BC
Triple M Radio	Austereo Pty Ltd.	CB	Public	CA
Yahoo!7 Australia and New Zealand	Yahoo	PP	Public	CA

Key: ABC: Australian Broadcasting Corporation; BC: Branded Content; CA: Content Aggregator; CB: Clicks and Bricks; Goverment: Australian Government Owned National Broadcaster; ISP: Internet Service Provider; PBL: Publishing and Broadcasting Ltd.; PP: Pure-Play; SBS: Special Broadcasting Service.

*Owned by Macquarie University and University of Technology (UTS), Sydney

Ownership Patterns

Nine of the 20 webcasting sites or 45% of the sample are from organizations that belong to the Commonwealth Government of Australia. They are: The Parliament of Australia (one site); seven sites belonging to the Australian Broadcasting Corporation's (ABC) various channels and services, and one site belonging to the Special Broadcasting Service (SBS)—also a national broadcaster.

Of the remaining 11, 8 are owned by domestic companies and the remaining three (3) by joint commercial ventures between a domestic and a foreign company. The domestically owned public companies included the two (newspaper) webcasters, namely the *Sydney Morning Herald* (owned by Fairfax Ltd., which is a dominant print media conglomerate) as well as *The Australian* (the national newspaper) and Fox Sports (owned by the subscription TV company Foxtel), both owned by News Limited with the global media conglomerate News Corp. as its parent company.

The other domestically owned webcasters are the Australian (Rules) Football League[3] (AFL; owned by the non-profit AFL Foundation) and the National Rugby League (NRL; owned by News Limited) representing the two most popular football codes in Australia. Triple M Radio (Melbourne, Sydney, and Brisbane) is a commercial radio station publicly owned by Austereo Pty Ltd., a radio network. PBS 106.7 FM Melbourne (called 3 PBS or the Progressive Broadcasting Service) is an independent organization, and Real Radio Sydney (2Ser107.3 FM) is privately owned by Sydney Educational Radio, with Macquarie University and the University of Technology Sydney (UTS) serving as partners. Both 3PBS and 2Ser107.3 FM are community radio broadcasters.

The three webcasters jointly owned by a domestic and a foreign company are NINEMSN (of Channel 9 TV), owned by Publishing and Broadcasting Ltd. (PBL) and Microsoft; Melbourne Indymedia (which is jointly owned by Indymedia and Oceania Indymedia and is an independent activist station); and Yahoo!7 Australia and New Zealand, (owned by Yahoo! and Channel 7 TV).

Channel 10 TV (owned by CanWest) offers a live streaming webcast during its *Big Brother* reality TV broadcasts, which was not on during the content analysis

---

[3]The game of Australian Rules Football, known as Australia's only indigenous (home-grown) sport, is administered by the Australian Football League (AFL; http://www.afl.com.au). It is played on an oval shaped field by teams of 22 players (with 18 on the field), using a ball similar to that of Rugby Football. The game is fast moving, often high scoring, and exciting, and dates back to 1858. Players are allowed to run with the ball as long as they bounce it every 15 meters. Passing the ball in all directions is permitted, but in such situations, it must either be kicked or "handballed" (punched) and cannot be thrown. Four goal posts are positioned on each end of the field. A goal scored between the two inner posts carries six points while one scored between an inner and outer post carries one point. The players wear football shorts, football boots, and a fitted shirt called a Guernsey, which can be either long sleeved or sleeveless.

for this study in January 2005. This webcast is considered the most popular one in Australia (O'Neill, 2005a) among the under 30-year-old age group that attracted three million visitors for *Big Brother 3* webcasts in 2005. While the reality TV show is on, the webcast is on live streaming, 24 hours a day, seven days a week, providing a wide range of views and angles of the *Big Brother* house (C. Preston, personal communication, August 23, 2005), whereas the Channel 10 TV broadcasts only provided two hours a day of edited content. The reality TV program also enjoyed high ratings during its free-to-air broadcasts. However, even if Channel 10 has watched the progress of these webcasts (or "Net TV") with interest, it has no plans to licence the content for the medium (O'Neill, 2005a).

Type and Business Models

Among the sample of 20 webcasters, 5 or 25% of the webcasters were pure-plays while 15 or 75% were clicks and bricks. As for the business models used, 14 or 70% used branded content on their webcasts while 6 or 30% used the content aggregate model. Overall, the existing smaller radio stations and networks and national broadcasters were more active (by including audio or video streaming in their websites in addition to text and still images) than non-broadcast organizations or other commercial media. The higher percentage of clicks and bricks indicates that these existing broadcast media have taken the lead in adopting the new medium of webcasting and that branded content leads over content aggregation.

O'Neill (2005a) argues that it is premature to expect business models in Australia to take form as webcasters first need to find out what customers need and how much they are willing to pay for the content. Customers also need to be provided with something different to what's available on free-to-air broadcasts. He cites Shande Wood, the Head of Cross Platform Development at Channel 7, that broadcasters' protective attitude towards their content is natural (when they do not want to webcast their content), but are gradually becoming open to alternative distribution models as the online experience increases and becomes more real.

The issue of Australian commercial broadcasters' lack of enthusiasm for webcasting may also relate to the need for a "critical mass" of consumers (O'Neill, 2005a), the lack of which, for a nation with only 20 million inhabitants and a low penetration of broadband connections, is quite understandable. The lack of competition from subscription TV is another factor responsible for webcasting in Australia to be less developed than in the U.S. (O'Neill, 2005a). However, it is important to note that subscription (or Pay) TV in Australia experienced low penetration rates until recently and therefore may take time to embrace webcasting, as they too need a critical mass for Pay TV before adopting webcasting. However, Fox Sports, a popular channel on pay TV, has already adopted webcasting.

Analyst Brigid Wilson of Ovum Telecommunications (cited in O'Neill, 2005a) thinks that subscription TV (such as Foxtel) is expensive in Australia in compari-

TABLE 18–2
Media Content Categories of Webcasters in Australian Sample

Type of Content	Number of Webcasters	Percentage of Webcasters
Original	3	15%
Repurposed	2	10%
Simulcast	5	25%
Unknown	10	50%

son with world standards, thus webcasting or Net TV should target consumers currently not subscribed to Pay TV. However, it is quite possible that many customers who cannot afford subscription or Pay TV could also be those who cannot afford broadband connections, internet services, and computers necessary to receive webcasts.

Media Content Sources Used by Webcasters

Table 18–2 indicates the breakdown of original, repurposed, simulcast, and unknown content used by the 20 webcasters in the sample analyzed.

Even though the coding instrument of the content analysis for this research project was designed to examine the percentages of original, repurposed, simulcast, and unknown sources of media content separately for each webcast analyzed, in the Australian sample, it was not possible to gauge the break down of each source of media content. In the case of 50% or 10 of the webcasters, it was not possible even to identify which category the content belonged to, and therefore had to be coded as "unknown."

However, it appeared that 3 webcasters or 15% of the sample (viz., *The Australian* newspaper, Indymedia, and ABC-Newcastle radio) were including original content in their webcasts. Repurposed content was the source for 2 or 10% of the webcasters (viz., ABC Radio National's *Saturday Night Country* and *ABC Online*). Simulcasts were the content sources for 5 or 25% of webcasters that included 3PBS Community Radio, 2SER Radio, Triple M Radio, Radio Australia, and The Parliament House. The remaining 10 or 50% of webcasters used content of "unknown" sources.

Bing (1997) sees content of a webcast as its most important component. The main areas for consideration will be if the content is of vital importance to the customer, what will be its use to the end user, and what will they accomplish by receiving the content. Other considerations include the questions: Will the content improve products and services for the webcaster?; Does delivery have to be guaranteed?; What type of content forms will be used such as audio, video, text, animation etc.?; and How often should the content be delivered? The content must also be tailored to the needs of the consumer, and the consumers must value the content if it is to be successful.

Webcasting gives large as well as small media organizations and individuals an opportunity to establish a webcast presence. However, to create audience appeal, each webcaster needs to provide unique and compelling content or provide alternative content (Breamser, 1998) not already available on free-to-air broadcasts. This was clearly seen with the *Big Brother* webcasts in Australia—considered too risqué to be broadcast unedited on free-to-air TV. As the webcast industry in Australia is not currently bound by the Film and Literature Censorship Board regulations, providing specific or alternative content to certain niche markets may be an avenue Australian webcasters should explore (C. Preston, personal communication, August 23, 2005).

Revenue and Funding Sources of Webcasters

The content analysis examined the various sources of revenue and funding received by the webcasters. The revenue sources were coded as advertising/sponsorships, e-commerce, subscription, pay per view or use, content syndication, tip jar/voluntary contributions, and "other." All sources used by each webcaster were coded.

Table 18–3 indicates that 5 webcasters or 25% used advertising or sponsorships, 9 or 45% used e-commerce (making it the most commonly used form of revenue source), 3 or 15% used subscriptions, and 2 used tip jar or voluntary contributions. Under the "other" category, 9 or 45% of webcasters were coded as receiving funding from the Australian government in the form of government grants (7 of the webcasts are from the national broadcasters ABC and SBS and the other 2 are from the Parliament House and the community radio station 2SER).

These findings indicate that the webcasters most active in Australia appear to be the ones funded by the government and that pay per use and content syndication have not yet been used by any of the webcasters, indicating the immaturity of the webcasting market.

DISCUSSION

In answering the question "why is the ABC (and not the commercial broadcasters) the most active in the webcasting industry in Australia?" Ross Monaghan commented that webcasting is not commercially viable for commercial broadcasting organizations and that the issue of possible "cannibalization of the audience" (Ha & Ganahl, 2004, p. 83) is an obvious concern for commercial media. Non-webcast media also provide a better viewing experience where one can view it in the lounge

TABLE 18-3
Sources of Business Revenue or Funding for Webcasters in the Australian Sample

Types of Revenue or Funding	Number of Webcasters	Percentage of Webcasters
Advertising / Sponsorship	6	30%
E-Commerce	9	45%
Subscription	3	15%
Pay per Use or View	—	—
Content Syndication	—	—
Tip Jar or Voluntary Contribution	2	10%
None	1	5%
Other	—	—
Government Funding	9	45%

Note. More than one type of revenue/funding source used by most webcasters.

room more comfortably than at a computer terminal (R. Monaghan, personal communication, April 13, 2005), even though the new iMac G5 computer comes with a flat screen monitor and a remote control that would circumvent this shortcoming (R. Monaghan, personal communication, October 26, 2005). Increasingly, many Australian households also appear to be opting for larger plasma screens more suited for viewing sports on broadcast or Pay TV. This raises the question whether subscription TV may be the future of webcasting because it can provide a more enjoyable viewing experience with larger screens.

This proposal fits in with the Australian experiences with digital TV, which was facing low consumer and broadcaster interest while only free-to-air broadcasters were allowed to adopt the technology, due to Australian government regulations (Weerakkody, 2003; Weerakkody & Tremblay, 2003). Since subscription TV was allowed to adopt digital TV on March 14, 2004—a move recommended in Weerakkody (2003), the adoption of digital TV has very much improved with 1.1 million homes currently receiving Foxtel or other related Pay TV services (Foxtel, 2005).

According to Craig Preston, commercial broadcasters have no incentive to develop their webcasting services, as no rating measurements are currently taken for webcasts, which would have justified an investment as ratings can be linked to advertising revenue for the webcaster. Due to low levels of broadband penetration, webcasts would not attract large audiences in order to make an investment in webcasting profitable for commercial media organizations. As the national broadcaster however, ABC is not concerned about large audiences but is dedicated and expected to serve the nation and its information and entertainment needs (C. Preston, personal communication, August 23, 2005). The ABC radio is also sometimes a main source of broadcast information for consumers located in rural areas.

ABC Online and The Australian Newspaper

The content analysis indicated *ABC Online* as the most comprehensive in terms of its content among the 20 webcasters examined. It had obtained information from a variety of sources-both local and international, in developing their content. It also carried out e-commerce where DVDs and videos of ABC programs can be purchased online. It contained audio, video and text including transcripts, and had received awards for its services and performance.

In contrast, the webcast of *The Australian* newspaper was a web version of the newspaper, except for one video clip, which qualified it for inclusion in the sample for this study. This video, which was available for on demand streaming, was actually promotional material from the U.S. National Aeronautics and Space Administration (NASA). However, when the author accessed this website on at a later date for verification purposes, this video clip was no longer available. But two sets of still photos related to outer space were included in its large photo gallery.

Indymedia

Indymedia provides a very good quality webcasting service. This organization is a grassroots advocacy group dealing with worldwide issues related to humanitarian and environmental concerns. It carries viewpoints not often covered in the mainstream media. The content of the site was very comprehensive as it included issues related to and represented voices from, a very large number of countries including those in the developing world, providing diverse viewpoints and a cross-cultural overview of issues addressed by the site.

Indymedia's webcast can be described as a good example of an alternative media organization making use of a new medium. However, the downside of this site was the slow downloads, even for printed text, which would be a disadvantage in attracting visitors to the site. It depends on voluntary contributions from visitors to the site as a source of revenue.

Sports and News

In terms of webcasting genres, sports and news appeared to be the areas most often included in webcasts. In addition, the Australian (Rules) Football League (AFL) and the National Rugby League (NRL) have their own webcasting sites, also indicating that sports may be a more viable area for commercial media to explore for potential webcasting services in the future. The AFL and NRL sites were also highly organized for e-commerce especially for selling their sports related merchandise.

ABC Radio–Newcastle

The ABC Radio's Newcastle webcast was an interesting case. It provided on demand downloading of videos and included several videos such as a movie about the radio station and its region. This regional radio station is expected to produce local news only and its provision of several videos including those from past years as an archive is commendable. Newcastle is also a regional city much smaller than Melbourne or Sydney. When presented with this unusual case, Craig Preston explained that at the ABC, how much or how far webcasting services are to be provided and developed depends on how the individual stations and their staff are willing to contribute in resources and their time. Overall, the ABC network also has set aside large amounts of funding from capital works and special projects to develop webcasting (C. Preston, personal communication, August 23, 2005), which may have helped ABC-Radio–Newcastle to embrace the technology.

Success not Always "Good"

Successful webcasting can create adverse effects when unexpectedly high numbers of visitors are attracted to a webcast. In other broadcast media, having a larger audience is always welcome as their popularity translates into higher ratings and prestige. Larger audiences do not involve additional costs or efforts for broadcasters. In contrast, increased numbers of visitors to a webcast create problems of overloading the servers and crashing them or drastically slowing them down (Saleh, 2004; C. Preston, personal communication, August 23, 2005). This situation results in many visitors being unable to log onto the site and increasing the time taken to download materials, which can actually discourage current as well as future visitors. After all, customer satisfaction is a powerful determinant of a customer's intention to return (Jeong, 2004).

Forming Partnerships

O'Neill (2005b) sees Australian media or telecommunications companies as unable to launch webcasting services on their own. Therefore, partnerships between the two sectors would help build and pay for the infrastructure, the purchase or creation of content and its dissemination. He refers to a deal signed by NINEMSN (owned by PBL which provides content and Microsoft which provides the necessary software and is the country's software leader) with Optus (a subscription TV and telecommunications company using broadband cable and owned by SingTel of Singapore) for broadband and mobile phone content provision. Webcasting is also defined as a "team sport." Therefore, such partnerships could be the future of webcasting in Australia. The telecommunications companies will be well established in the areas of customer relationships and billing (O'Neill, 2005b) for which content providers are not generally set up, but which helps maintain the viability of the business once in operation. After all, Australian subscription TV's biggest player Foxtel is such a partnership between content providers PBL and News Limited and the telecommunications giant Telstra contributing the necessary infrastructure. However, such partnerships will lead to further convergence and concentration of media ownership-domestically as well as globally.

Future Directions

While the Australian telecommunications companies and the government are looking at providing broadband services to the bush and larger media companies are slow to take up webcasting, other technologies appear to be developing that can do the job of webcasting and are showing promise for the future. The highly popular mobile phones and the iPod media players could well be the next step in webcasting for Australia.

Mobile Phones

Ross Monaghan sees mobile phones today as "almost a form of webcasting" because they have converged audio, video, and multimedia content, the world wide web and internet (functions)." He also sees video calls as "personal webcasting" and that audiocasting, podcasting, and webcasting are the same with different names. He also thinks that the reason webcasts are difficult to locate when someone wants to view them is because they can not be searched via Google etc. (R. Monaghan, personal communication, April 13, 2005).

In view of the rapid growth of mobile phone adoption in Australia, which at the end of the 2003–2004 fiscal year was 16.5 million subscribers or an 82% market penetration rate (IBIS World Pty Ltd., 2005), one can wonder if this medium could be used for webcasting instead of waiting for broadband to be provided to the wider population in Australia. The heaviest users of mobile phones in Australia are in the 18–34 age-group (Australian Mobile Telecommunications Association, 2005). This techno-savvy generation may be catered to by webcasting via mobile phones, if the suitable content and functions can be found for them, as the telecommunications industry has done with ring tones, games, photo/text messaging etc. In November 2005, the 3G mobile telephones were offered live video broadcasts of the Australia vs. The West Indies cricket games.

Podcasting

Podcasting could be an alternative to webcasting due to the high proliferation of iPods and MP3 players that can store audio, etc. A local Geelong (Victoria) radio station is now podcasting and produces an hour-long segment that can be downloaded with MP3 and listened to immediately afterwards. With the growing youth iPod population, Ross Monaghan thinks podcasting can be a powerful tool radio stations can use to reach that audience (R. Monaghan, personal communication, April 13, 2005). In October 2005, Apple announced a new video iPod that combines i-tunes with video. However, Craig Preston sees podcasting as a phase, just as personal webcams linked to the internet for broadcasting used to be during the early stages of their adoption, and points out that the audience has limited capacity to absorb podcasting. Podcasting allows access to lesser media similar to a radio experience and therefore is most suitable for the reproduction of radio programming (C. Preston, personal communication, August 23, 2005).

A world's first experiment involving podcasting was conducted in New Zealand in August 2005, during New Zealand's general election campaign (O'Neill, 2005b). It used MP3 players and computers allowing voters to access their party leaders' policies as a half hour unmediated recording, which was available online a few hours afterwards. The cost of production for the recording was low and the podcast interviews were considered more intimate as they were one-to-one in style. The Voice Booth, the company in Christchurch that carried out the experiment, expects podcasting to become a mainstream tool of communication in the near future, but is not sure if and how the service can be commercialized (O'Neill, 2005b).

The "i-mode" Mobile Phones

The "i-mode" mobile phone was introduced to the Australian market by Telstra on November 1, 2004. It provides games, sends and receives emails, serves as a portable music player, provides access to 165 content sites, and receives news alerts and headlines (i-mode Magazine, 2005). Since the next development or the 4G (fourth generation) mobile phones are capable of receiving TV broadcasts (Richtel, 2005; Day, 2005), as its next step i-mode is promising a 24-hour news channel that can be "watched" (i-mode Magazine, 2005; p. 11). This indicates that webcasting may develop in a variety of ways. However, currently many rural and remote areas in Australia also lack reliable mobile phone reception facilities at all or at an affordable cost when available. In other words, be it broadband internet or i-mode mobile, the problem of servicing the bush adequately in an equitable and affordable manner, is not expected to be solved any time soon, simply by changing the mode of delivery or the technology used.

Globalization and Local Content

One could also argue that in an era of globalization and advanced synchronous telecommunications, Australia need not worry about its own webcasting industry as Australian audiences as English speakers can always access the more established webcasts produced elsewhere in the world, provided they have access to the technology required, and that one should not worry too much about developing our own webcasting industry. However, this gives rise to the argument that providing local content via webcasting to the Australian population is similar to the content requirements for free to air and subscription TV in Australia. These local content requirements are currently facing the threat of deregulation, in the wake of Australia's Free Trade Agreement (FTA) with the U.S., which is being extended to cultural content, amid protests from local artists, technicians, and content producers (Murray, 2005), who fear the deregulation would further reduce investment in local TV content production.

This raises the issue that Australia may need to develop its local webcasting industry with local content after all, in order to avoid the situation currently faced by the once vibrant Australian film industry, which has been overpowered by Hollywood productions both in terms of the decreased number of movies produced in recent times and exhibited locally and the very low levels of revenue earned by them during 2003–2005 (Australian Film Commission, 2005). This was mainly due to the local film industry's inability to fund local productions adequately and thereafter compete with the high gloss, highly funded, highly cross promoted, and highly advertised Hollywood fare, released in Australian cinemas and as DVDs or videos.

CONCLUSION

The customers in metropolitan areas already have access to a range of information, entertainment sources and options, even without webcasting or podcasting being added to them. It is the regional, rural, and remote customers who are already experiencing a "digital divide" with existing media and other communication technologies and services (Hindman, 2000, p. 558) and who can most benefit from this new technology of webcasting, provided they can access it efficiently and at an affordable cost in a timely manner. Therefore, webcasting has the potential to widen the "digital divide" between metropolitan and non-metropolitan populations in Australia, due to the issues related to providing broadband connections and other telecommunications services to the bush.

Craig Preston saw the webcasting industry in Australia as "dead" in terms of its adoption by established broadcasters as it was not yet a lucrative source of revenue for them. However, the content analysis suggests that as far as the national broadcaster—the ABC—is concerned, webcasting is in its infancy and exists mainly due to its access to government funding and the efforts and desires of its individual stations and their staff. Webcasting by the larger commercial media on the other hand, is yet to be embraced, which is unlikely unless it proves itself as a significant source of revenue.

At the time subscription (Pay) TV adoption was debated in Australia, its opponents described the technology as "the fifth wheel" (of a car), as it was not meant to make much of a difference due to the country's well functioning free-to-air broadcast system and a thriving video market. It has taken ten years since implementation for Pay TV to show a significant growth in its adoption and diffusion, with sports and movies proving to be the most popular. So at the moment, one could consider webcasting in Australia in the same light, as "a fifth wheel." Hopefully, it would gradually be adopted by the bigger players such as commercial broadcasters in a similar way as Pay TV, with some help from the Australian government to develop broadband or other necessary infrastructure.

Note: The CD accompanying this book includes a brief discussion of the program genres and details of the content offered by the 20 webcasters in the Australian sample with Table 18–4 and Appendixes A and B. Appendix C and Table 18–5 provide a summary of advertising shares of Australia's various media sectors.

REFERENCES

Australian Broadcasting Authority. (2005). Licenced commercial broadcasters. Retrieved September 7, 2006, from http://www.aba.gov.au

Australian Bureau of Statistics. (2005). Population of Australia. Retrieved August 29, 2005, from http://www.abs.gov.au

Australian Film Commission. (2005). The Australian Cinema Industry. Retrieved August 29, 2005, from http://www.afc.gov.au

Australian Mobile Telecommunications Association (2005, July 26). Mobile carriers are distinct in demographic make up and content consumption. Retrieved September 2, 2005, from http://www.amta.org.au

Bing, M. (1997). Implementing webcasting. Database, December, 42–44. Retrieved June 25, 2005, from http://www.outlineinc.com

Breamser, W. (1998). Pump up the volume. Computer Life, 4(1), 90–96.

Census on internet access services provided by ISPs in Australia. (2005, March 31). Internet Activity Survey. Retrieved August 28, 2005, from http://www.abs.gov.au/Ausstats

Commercial Radio Australia. (2005). Radio in Australia. Retrieved August 29, 2005, from http://www.commercialradio.com.au

Community Broadcasting Foundation (2004, September 15). Press release. Retrieved August 30, 2005, from http://www.cbonline.org.au

Day, M. (2005, October 13). Foxtel about to hit paydirt. The Australian. Retrieved October 14, 2005, from http://www.theaustralian.news.com.au

DCITA (2004, February). Australia's national broadband strategy. Canberra: The Government of Australia, Department of Communication, Information Technology and the Arts.

Foxtel. (2005). Foxtel history. Retrieved September 7, 2006, from http://www.foxtel.com.au

Gee, M. (2005, July). *Margaret Gee's Australian media guide, No. 79*, Melbourne, VIC: Information Australia–Margaret Gee Media.

Ha, L. & Ganahl, R. (2004). Webcasting business models of clicks and bricks and pure-play media: A comparative study of leading Webcasters in South Korea and the U.S. *International Journal of Media Management, 6*(1&2), 75–88.

Hallaby, D. (2003, July 2). Need for speed. *IDG News Service*. Retrieved August 29, 2005, from http://www.arnnet.com.au

Hindman, D. B. (2000). The rural urban digital divide. *Journalism and Mass Communication Quarterly, 77*(3), 549–560.

IBIS World Pty Ltd. (2005). Mobile telecommunications carriers in Australia J 7122, *IBIS World Industry Report*, April 28, 1–20.

i-mode Magazine (2005). *1*(June). West Melbourne, VIC: Pepper Publishing Pty Ltd.

Imparja. (2005). Retrieved August 30, 2005, from http://www.imparja.com.au

Industries and issues. (2005). *Nielsen Media Research*. Retrieved September 2, 2005, from http://www .nielsenmedia.com.au

International Webcasting Association launches in Australia. (2001, September 19). International Webcasting Association launches in Australia. *QuickStream*. Retrieved May 23, 2005, from http://www.quickstream.com.au

James, M. (2005, February 8). *The internet telephone: Voiceover Internet Protocol (VoIP) Research Note 29, 2004–2005*. Canberra: The Parliament of Australia Library.

Jeong, M. (2004). An exploratory study of perceived importance of website characteristics: The case of the bed and breakfast industry. *Journal of Hospitality and Leisure Marketing, 11*(4), 29–44.

Jupp, J. (2002). *From White Australia to Woomera: The story of Australian migration*. Cambridge, UK: Cambridge University Press.

Lin, C. A. (2004). Webcasting adoption: Technology fluidity, user innovativeness and media substitution. *Journal of Broadcasting and Electronic Media, 48*(3), 446–465.

Morrissey, B. (2003, February 26). Study: Over 100 million have used internet audio, video. *Internetnews.com*. Retrieved March 3, 2003, from http://www.internetnews.com

Murray, S. (2005). Think global, act global: Corporate content streaming and Australian media policy. *Media International Australia—Incorporating Culture and Policy, No. 116*, 100–116.

Network 10. (2005). About Ten. Retrieved September 7, 2006, from http://www.ten.com.au

O'Neill, R. (2005a, July 12). TV set to cast a wider net. *The Age*. Retrieved July 12, 2005, from http://theage.com.au

O'Neill, R. (2005b, August 12). Kiwi firm claims podcasting first. *The Age*. Retrieved August 18, 2005, from http://theage.com.au

PBL. (2005). About PBL. Retrieved September 7, 2006, from http://www.pbl.com.au

Richtel, M. (2005, August 30). An iPod cell phone said to be imminent. *The New York Times*. Retrieved September 2, 2005, from http://www.nytimes.com

Rothman, B. (2005, August 16). Onstream media corporation reports Fiscal 2005 third quarter results. *PR Newswire*. Retrieved August 17, 2005, from http://www.onstreammedia.com.

Saleh, A. (2004, June 9). Venus transit bogs down servers. *ABC Science Online*. Retrieved June 25, 2005, from http://www.abc.net.au

SBS. (2005. SBS corporation: An overview. Retrieved September 7, 2006, from http://www.sps.com.au

Seven Corporate. (2005). Company profile. Retrieved September 7, 2006, from http://www.sevencorporate.com.au

Turner, G., & Cunningham, S. (Eds.). (2002). *The media and communications in Australia today*. Sydney: Allen & Unwin.

Weerakkody, N. D. (2003). More dominant in their inactivity: Consumer response and the adoption of digital TV in Australia. *Online and CD ROM proceedings of the Informing Science and IT Education 2003 Conference (InSITE"03)*, June 23–27, Pori, Finland. Http://2003InSITE.nu or at http://ecommece.lebow.drexel.edu.eli/2003Proceedings.doc\129Weera.pdf

Weerakkody, N. D., & Tremblay, W. (2003). A cross-impact analysis of the adoption and diffusion of digital TV in Australia and the U.S.. *Proceedings of the Annual Conference of the Australian and New Zealand Communication Association (ANZCA 2003)*, July 9–11, Brisbane, QLD, Australia. Retrieved August 8, 2003, from http://www.bgsb.qut.edu.au/conferences/ANZCA03/Proceedings/papers/weerakkody_full.pdf

Wikipedia. (2005). TV in Australia. Retrieved September 7, 2006, from http://en.wikipedia.org

Wimmer, R. D., & Dominick, J. R. (2006). *Mass media research: An introduction* (8th ed.). Belmont, CA: Wadsworth-Thomson Learning.

PART V

Webcasting Business Practices and Dynamics in the Arab Region

CHAPTER 19

The Arab World: The Broadband Market Is Taking Off—How Far Away Is Webcasting?

Ilhem Allagui and Claude Martin
University of Montréal

The Arab Telecommunication market has been witnessing an important change over the last decade. Transformations have occurred in the broadcasting industry as satellite television has disrupted the traditional stability of the broadcasting market. Transformations have also occurred in the internet industry as connectivity rates have grown tremendously in free oriented markets in many Arab countries. Although webcasting is at an early stage, it has a great potential for development within the region since the internet is becoming more popular and broadband access is increasingly being introduced in many countries.

AN OVERVIEW OF THE ARAB REGION

The Arab region occupies a large geographical area, about 10% of the earth's surface. It straddles two continents, Africa and Asia, on a surface estimated at 14 million square kilometers, or 8,699,000 square miles. Arab countries are stretched from the Atlantic Ocean in the west to the Arab Gulf in the east and from the Mediterranean Sea in the north to Central Africa in the south. The Arab world is usually associated with two geographical regions: North African countries which generally include Morocco, Algeria, Tunisia, Libya, Egypt, and Sudan, and the Middle East which includes Jordan, Lebanon, Syria, Palestine, Bahrein, Kuwait, Oman, Qatar, Saudi Arabia, United Arab Emirates, Yemen, and Iraq. Egypt is also usually considered part of the Middle East. In most definitions the Middle East refers to more than the Arab area, and includes Iran and Turkey, each of which have some Arab minorities (respectively 1.3% and 1% of population) but are not Arab countries.

TABLE 19–1
Pan-Arab Advertising Revenues by Media (January–December, 2004)

Media	Amount	Percentage
TV	1,641,055,955	90
Magazines	92,865,419	5
Newspapers	86,266,969	5
Totals	1,820,188,343	100

Source: M. Elie Aoun, IPSOS-STAT Middle East and North Africa.

The term MENA region refers to the Middle East and North Africa countries. While these countries are mainly Arab countries, the designation MENA could include countries such Iran, Israel, Malta, and Djibouti.

In 2005, the population of Arab countries is estimated at 260 million. It's a youthful one since more than half of the population is under age of 18. Egypt has the most inhabitants with 77 million people (based on 2005 estimates) followed by Algeria and Saudi Arabia. Algeria is the largest area of the Arab countries, followed by Saudi Arabia which covers more than two-thirds of the Arab peninsula, known as the Gulf peninsula. The Gulf peninsula countries are Saudi Arabia, Oman, Bahrain, Kuwait, Qatar, and the United Arab Emirates (although Yemen is located at the peninsula, it is not part of the Gulf Countries Council). It is the most flourishing part of Arab countries due to its oil and gas reserves. Reserves in oil were discovered in this region relatively recently (in 1938), which gave it a strategic recognition. While the gap between the super-rich Gulf countries and other Arab countries becomes more and more important, the major benefits derived from a U.S. strategic alliance is protection and the associated western "way of life" for business projects, multinational companies, entertainment products, etc.

ARAB MEDIA MARKET: GOING TRANSNATIONAL

Media markets in the Arab region benefit from cultural similarities. Arabic is the official and dominant language for all Arab countries although dialects vary between countries and regions. Second languages vary as well, and are primarily determined by the history of each country. In North Africa, French colonialism has made French the most common foreign language. In the Middle East, English is more popular. But above all, Arab history is tightly tied to the history of Islam as 95% of Arabs are Muslims. Thus, religion is also an important common cultural aspect throughout the region. Furthermore, there exists among Arabs shared beliefs, traditions, and values which are particularly articulated in the concept of "transnational" (Alterman, 1998) cultural industries. While Rugh (2004) recognizes diversity between countries, he states that they share coherent cultural and psychological characteristics:

> The people of the eighteen Arab states feel bound together by strong cultural and psychological ties. The vast majority of them regard Arabic as their mother tongue; most of them share a single culture, language and religion, and their sense of a common destiny is very strong. Nationalism, both in the pan-Arab sense and as felt toward the newer individual nation-states, separate and distinct from Western or any other identity, is a powerful force (p. 1)

In general, the film industry, television productions, and cultural industries have been dominated by Egypt because of its historical and political importance. Egypt's film industry, for example, while state-subsidized in the early 1930s, was already a leading market in the 1920s. It reached its heyday in the 1960s. This gave it an advantage in distributing cultural products over other nations with developed film industries such as Lebanon, Tunisia, or Syria. To resist Egyptian hegemony, other local markets such as the Gulf or the Maghreb work upon "niches" and try to protect their own markets while looking for foreign and Arab joint-ventures and public or private investments.

Currently entertainment productions are most often produced in Lebanon, however, the United Arab Emirates, and more particularly the city of Dubai, are recognized for their advancements in media production. Dubai is a "state-city," one of the seven members of the United Arab Emirates Federation (Abu Dhabi, Dubai, Sharjah, Fujairah, Ajman, Ras al Khaïmah, and Oumm al Qaïwaïn) which have showed development and success in the last decade or so. A number of factors have contributed to this success including the local reinvestments of gas revenues, a commercially oriented government, and an open and less conservative environment than other Gulf regions. Dubai Media City (along with Dubai Internet City) are members of Dubai Technology, Electronic Commerce and Media, and Free Zone Authority, which facilitate the establishment and attraction of global IT and media companies as well as qualified workers within an area with almost no business taxes. MBC, CNN, Reuters, and the Associated Press have Dubai-based companies.

On the other hand, the success of some satellite news channels such Al-Jazeera and Al-Arabiya which offer an alternative to local and public news coverage or general-interest channels such as MBC, have provoked a serious reconsideration of the media's role, which had previously been dominated by the state. The popularity of these media created a new challenge for other satellite channels by generating more vigorous competition for audiences and advertisers.

TABLE 19–2   Daily Newspaper Circulation in Some Arab Countries

Countries	Total Daily Newspaper Circulation (000s)	Daily Newspaper Circulation per 1000 Inhabitants	Number of Daily Newspapers
Egypt (1999)	2,080	31.19	16
Saudi Arabia (1996)	1,105	57.00	13
Lebanon (1996)	435	107.00	15
UAE (1996)	384	156.00	7
Jordan (1998)	352	75.45	5*

*In 2000.
Source: United Nations Development Program (2002).

This reflects the commercial success of Satellite TV in the Arab world. In 2004, Satellite TV channel's advertising revenues were about 90% of total pan-Arab media revenues; they also represented almost half of the total Arab advertising revenues (domestic and transnational media markets). According to IPSOS-STAT Middle East and North Africa, 41% of the advertising revenues go to Pan-Arab media. One should also note that television (domestic and satellite channels) account for a third (37%) of the total advertising revenues (based on the Pan-Arab market and nine major markets: UAE, Saudi Arabia, Lebanon, Kuwait, Bahrain, Jordan, Qatar, Oman, and Syria). As shown in Table 19–1, Pan-Arab ad revenues are estimated at $1,820,188,343, with satellite TV accounting for 90%. Regarding advertising revenues, the three major countries United Arab Emirates, Kingdom of Saudi Arabia and Lebanon account for 41% (respectively, 16%, 14%, and 11%). As for online advertising revenues, precise data are not yet available, except an estimate of $8 to $10 million in 2003 by the Arab Advisors Group (Usage Watch, 2004).

The transnational Arab media market is flourishing, especially in the music and satellite TV industries. Satellite TV has contributed to transformations and developments in the music industry under new standards and has contributed to new music formats. The proliferation of satellite music channels, such as Rotana, ART music, and Dandana among others, and their involvement in music-video production in particular, have shown a new dynamism in the music industry and Arab cultural industries in general, including the internet. A significant number of music and celebrity websites have appeared alongside websites offering free songs and music-video downloads. The lack of regulation and intellectual property rights in the Arab states has contributed to the proliferation of free cultural products on the internet, although some states, such as United Arab Emirates, are moving towards developing appropriate regulation.

The publishing industry has a century-old history. In 1816, *Jurnal al-Iraq* in Baghdad was apparently the first Arab newspaper carrying news written by and for Arabs (Rugh, 2004). Soon thereafter, many other Arab publications appeared in Cairo (1820), Algeria (1847), Beirut (1858), and Tunis (1861). "Professional writers" appeared along with the development of house publishing, contributing to the modern thinking and literature that lead a cultural revolution that splits mainly from the ancient religious heritage. The intelligencia gave a fresh start to an Arab public opinion facilitated by the establishment of the publishing industry. Discourse on the Arab world, nationalism, authenticity, modernity, cultural invasion, and intrusion emerged, highlighting the question of identity. But the roots of traditional literature, poetry, and philosophy were also carried by a number of daily newspapers. Economic factors and political pressures have influenced Arab journalism, accused of being the state's voice in numerous cases. As newspapers are generally considered the property of the states, there are instances of interferences in the editorial content.

Censorship and the free expression of issues are the main reasons for the development of an Arab "off-shore" publication industry. Either by choice (to get closer to the Arab Diaspora and have a larger pan-Arab audience) or necessity (because of wars, laws governing freedom of expression, etc.), important newspapers have appeared in the West and contributed to the development of transnational Arab media reaching nearly thirty million readers in the Arab world and elsewhere (Rugh, 2004), but generating low advertising revenues of $86,266,969 (IPSOS-STAT, 2004). Most Pan-Arab publications are Saudi property, established during the 1980s to 1990s in the United Kingdom:

> They were motivated by opportunities they saw to invest in media that would add to their prestige and might be commercially beneficial, and they were encouraged to base their operations in Europe where press freedom prevailed rather than in Saudi Arabia which maintained formal and informal restrictions on publishing. (Rugh, 2004, p. 168)

After the Saudi investments other publications appeared in Europe, most of them based in the United Kingdom such as *Asharq Al-awsat* (a Saudi property), *Al-Hayat* (originally a Lebanese property later sold to Saudi prince), *Al-Arab* (a Libyan property), and *Al Quds Al Arabi* (a Palestinian property), totaling an estimated circulation of 125,000 in 2003 (Rugh, 2004). Newspapers in Egypt and Saudi Arabia enjoy much higher circulation than pan-Arab offshore publications as shown in Table 19–2.

Most newspapers have adopted a web version of their publications which includes free access for all. According to Al-Shehri cited in Gunter (2003), daily

TABLE 19–3
Internet Connectivity in the Arab Countries (2005)

Countries	Population (2005 estimates)	Internet Usage in September 2005	Connectivity Rate (% Population)
Algeria	32,557,738	845,000	2.60%
Bahrein	707,357	152,700	21.60%
Egypt	69,954,717	4,200,000	6.00%
Iraq	26,095,283	25,000	0.10%
Jordan	5,788,340	600,000	10.40%
Kuwait	2,530,012	600,000	23.70%
Lebanon	4,461,995	600,000	13.40%
Libya	5,980,693	205,000	3.40%
Morocco	29,828,879	3,500,000	11.70%
Oman	2,396,545	245,000	10.20%
Palestine	3,997,861	160,000	4.00%
Qatar	768,464	165,000	21.50%
Saudi Arabia	23,130,024	2,540,000	11.00%
Syria	18,586,743	800,000	4.30%
Tunisia	10,116,314	835,000	8.30%
United Arab Emirates	3,750,054	1,384,800	36.90%
Yemen	19,600,009	180,000	0.90%
Total	230,422,149	15,654,084,800	6.79%

Source: Extracted and adapted from InternetWorldStats.com

electronic newspapers grew from 0 to 65 between 1994 and 2000. Taye (2000) says that news and information are the main usage among Egyptian and Arab youth (91.5%), followed by entertainment and time-wasting (88.8%), communication (45.5%) and shopping (1.9%).

The arrival of the internet in the Arab world was greeted with varying expectations. Its economic, social, and political potential has been discussed continuously. Two apparent opposing perspectives have flourished. The optimistic perspective asserts that the integration of new technologies will give Arab citizens the ability to better participate and integrate into the development process. The internet favors group participation, open dialogue, and undermines gender barriers. The internet provides access to rich and important information and enables users to be more conscious, and thus, more critical. Governments are facing a new reality that they may consider "threatening." On the economic level, the Arab world could take advantage of the employment opportunities offered by the West. Socially, many possibilities exist (such as E-education), however these opportunities are dependent on governmental financing and international aids.

The pessimistic perspective argues that the internet will disrupt and eventually change media traditions in the Arab world, well known for restrictive policies and information control. So the Arab world is facing local rather than global pressures, generated by the development of information technologies:

> The arrival of the internet has caused a great deal of concern. Governments and religious authorities were concerned lest the internet be used "inappropriately"; academics were concerned lest they miss an opportunity to become more closely integrated with the major seats of learning and invention; and businessmen were concerned that they would at least miss out on the benefits of being wired to broader markets and possibly get left out of the "new economy" altogether. Security services were universally opposed even as the state-owned telecommunications companies viewed the internet as a potentially bottomless well of new income. (Burkhart & Older, 2003)

These conflicting perspectives lead to a tension between two positions: Adopting the internet will accelerate modernization or the internet could constitute a threat to security, and therefore governments will censor and control the content of the internet.

INTERNET CONNECTIVITY AND BROADBAND SITUATION

The United Nations Developing Program's report (2003) states that the average telephone density in Arab countries is 7.6% of the population. It also shows that 1.6% of the Arab population benefit from internet access and reports a ratio of 18 computers for every 1000 inhabitants. This ratio is dramatically different if one considers the Gulf countries alone, which represent 11% of the Arab population. According to Madar, a pan-Arab research group, the PC penetration rate in the Gulf countries stood at 7.64% by the end of 2002. It is expected to reach 12.15% by the end of 2005. Madar also projects a ratio of 121 internet users for every 100 PC's in the Arab region. This compares with the U.S. rate of 109 PC's for every 100 internet users (Madar Research Journal, 2002).

By September 2004, 6.7% of the Middle East population benefitted from internet usage compared to 13% of the rest of the world (Internet Worldstats, 2004). Publicly accessible internet is a popular alternative for Arab users who can't afford computer equipment. Community-based approaches offer alternatives which increase access in these countries. For example, many Moroccans, Jordanians, and Tunisians access the internet from cyber cafés, while many Egyptians may go to Multipurpose Community Telecenters, just as many Emiratis visit Internet Surfing Centers. Such popular initiatives have their disadvantages, however, since navigation is supervised and slow in general.

Nonetheless, there's a great disparity among various Arab countries with regards to internet usage and computer equipment, as noted earlier. Indeed, whereas certain countries, such as the Gulf countries, the Emirats, Kuwait, and Bahrain, have an internet connectivity rate bordering that of developed countries which allows them to multiply electronic initiatives such as E-government and to encourage IT investments in the industry, other nations such as Yemen and Syria still lag far behind with extremely low connection rates. The Arab market counts for less than 10 Gbps of internet capacity. The UAE leads the market in terms of international voice circuit capacity and internet bandwidth capacity followed by Saudi Arabia and Egypt (The Information and Technology Publishing, 2005a). The number of DSL subscribers grew from 174,400 in 2002 to 482,330 in 2003, which makes it a fairly available technology in the region but with less than 1% of world capacity. Incentives for broadening bandwidth are increasing in other countries however, such as Bahrain, and Jordan, expected to take off rapidly due to government initiatives and tariff reductions. See Table 19–3.

The development of internet in this region relies not only on economic issues, but on political issues as well. Some countries benefit from the free media market which gives them an advantage over others. UAE and Lebanon, for example, enjoy free media zones, allowing them to attract global information and communication technology companies in zones very lightly taxed or not taxed at all.

The telecommunication industry in Arab countries varies, from state monopolies to private ownership, or public–private partnerships. In general, most of the Arab states hold a monopoly on local services, international services, and long distance services except for Morocco, Algeria, and Tunisia (International Telecommunication Union, 2005a).

For example, the UAE, which enjoys one of the most important internet markets in the region with the highest internet connection rates, the telecommunication market is owned, protected and controlled by the state. The public Emirates Telecommunications Corporation named Etisalat has been the sole ISP in the country since 1995, and possesses the biggest internet bandwith capacity in the Arab world. However, in April 2004, a presidential decree was issued canceling Etisalat's monopoly.

The Emirates are internationally connected with satellites ArabSat, Intelsat, and InmartSat, cable via FOG (Fiber Optic Gulf), and optical fiber cable SEA-ME-WE3 which starts in South East Asia, runs across the Middle East, and into Western Europe. The number of Emiratis ADSL subscribers was 3,260 by 2002, and it is expected to grow to 10,700 by 2005 (Escwa, UN, 2003). However, according to ITP (2005a), Etisalat had over 50,000 residential digital subscriber lines (DSL) operational by September 2005 in the UAE equating a penetration rate of 1.95%. Etisalat provides high speed internet via DSL (Digital Subscriber Line) and HFC (Hybrid Fiber Coaxial) infrastructure, which is also used for digital television. Significant price reductions, up to 46%, were announced in September 2005, in order to benefit Emiratis users with broadband internet. The 1MB customers pay about $65 monthly (based on Etisalat rates for October 2005).

Jordan announced for 2005 the complete liberalization of the telecom industry, initially dominated by national operator Jordan Telecom (40% of which belongs to France Telecom). The internet is delivered through fiber optic submarine cables from the operator FLAG (Fiber Link Around the Globe) and through ArabSat satellite. High communication levels and hardware costs undermine internet connectivity in Jordan and could in part explain the popularity of internet cafés. Other options to Jordanians are education centers such as universities or JITCC (Jordonian Information Technology Community Centers) which provide knowledge (education) and computer equipment. This is part of the national initiative REACH (Regulatory framework, Enabling environment, Advancement programs, Capital, Human resources development) which aims to transform Jordan into a knowledge-based economy, and to get Jordanians online in spite of financial difficulties and budgetary limits. High operation costs could explain why broadband is taking off slowly.

Egypt is headed towards a free fixed market by 2006 after the monopoly held by Egyptian Society of Telecommunication Telecom Egypt is terminated. In 2002, Egypt adopted free internet access, where users pay only local communication costs. However, voice communications on the internet are forbidden. International communication is possible via cable, satellite (ArabSat and IntelSat), and fiber FLAG. Egyptians are connected to ISDN (Internet Service Digital Network), DSL (Digital Subscribers Line), and ADSL offered by ISP (via negotiation with Telecom Company) which allow them competitive rates. According to the Arab Advisors Group, Egypt offers the lowest ADSL cost in the region (about $24 per month). This could be explained by a number of factors:

> The major Internet Service Providers in the country are allowed to negotiate their own international bandwidth agreements and not be tied to getting the bandwidth from the incumbent fixed operator (Telecom Egypt). Moreover, these ISPs are allowed to collocate at Telecom Egypt's exchanges and use Telecom Egypt unbundled copper wires at reasonable rates. They, therefore, own their infrastructure for the most part. Freed from monopoly pricing, and with government encouragement to

TABLE 19–4

Major Webcasters in the Arab Region (listed by webcaster's nature and reach)

Webcaster	URL	Country	Reach per Million Users*
Portals (ISPs)			
Arabia MSN	www.arabia.msn.com	Egypt	279,800.0
Menara	www.menara.ma	Morocco	283.5
Commercial Websites			
Maktoob	www.maktoob.com	Jordan	2,380.0
6arab	www.6arab.com/	Saudi Arabia	1,940.0
6rb	www.6rb.com	Kuwait	1,405.0
Masrawy	www.masrawy.com/	Egypt	1,220.0
Amr Khaled	www.amrkhaled.net	Egypt	1,215.0
Islam on line	www.islamonline.net	Qatar	1,110.0
6rbTop	www.6rbtop.com	Saudi Arabia	664.0
Mazika	www.mazika.com	Egypt	287.5
Naharnet	www.naharnet.com	Lebanon	96.0
The Emirates Network	Http://www.Theemiratesnetwork.com	UAE	85.0
Broadcasters' Websites			
Al-Jazeera	www.aljazeera.net	Qatar	2,920.0
Arab Radio and Television Network	www.art-tv.net	UAE, Jordan	109.0
Rotana	www.rotana.net	Kuwait*	85.0
2M TV	www.2M.tv	Morocco	82.5
LBC Group (Lebanese Broadcasting Corp.)	http://www.lbcgroup.tv/lbc/en/main/	Lebanon	71.0
Melodyhits TV	http://www.melodyhits.tv	Egypt	70.0
MBC (Middle East Broadcasting Centre)	http://www.mbcfm.fm/	UAE	40.5
EMI	http://www.emi.co.ae/home.asp	UAE	27.5

Note. Statistics based on reach by three months average. The three-month changes are determined by comparing a site's current reach and reach rank with its values from three month ago.

*Although Alexa shows Kuwait, Rotana is also based in Saudi Arabia, Lebanon, Egypt, and UAE.

Source: www.alexa.com

spread ADSL service in the country, Egyptian operators are giving the best ADSL value in the region. (AMEinfo, 2004)

In Lebanon, which also enjoys one of the highest internet penetration rates, the ADSL service is not yet available, likewise in Iraq, Libya, and Palestine. As for internet access, six ISPs officially share the internet market, in addition to black market internet providers. Lebanon connects via ArabSat and submarine cable with Cyprus and Syria.

Qatar's telecom market is monopolized by Qatar Telecom, and the internet industry is dominated by two ISP's, Qatar Telecom and Arab Web Networks. Internet connections are established primarily through telephone lines. By 2002, broadband internet service was introduced to almost 80% of internet users. Oman also has a state monopoly on communication services, and the Access Service Provider operates under the monopoly OmanTel.

The Saudi Telecommunication Company, STC, is the unique fixed telecom operator in Saudi Arabia, and Awalnet is the largest ISP. Connections are established via telephone, ADSL, DDN (Defense Data Networks), or Frame Relay networks. Saudi Arabia is connected internationally to ArabSat, IntelSat, and InmarSat, and is also a member of FLAG, SEA-ME-WE3, and SEA-ME-WE2 cable conventions. Mainly for control purposes, all internet communications pass through King Abdulaziz City for Science and Technology (KACST), the internet gateway for the kingdom that filters web content material.

Bahrain's market is also protected since Batelco is the sole telecom operator for the state, although it announced and started a liberalization for the Telecom market by 2004. Bahrein possesses three ISPs but Batelco is the largest. Beyond satellite connections, Bahrain also connects with local cable, FOG.

Kuwait enjoys a liberalized telecommunication industry that provides a competitive market and better prices for customers. Internet users can subscribe to dial-up service at $28 monthly or ADSL services at $85 monthly (for 128Kbps; based on QualityNet rates in October 2005), and choose from more than 15 ISPs. In addition to satellite connections, submarine cable and fiber facilities are available. Kuwait is also part of the FOG convention.

In Tunisia, broadband service is only available in institutions, with restricted access, and is not yet offered to residential internet users at large, although it is expected to be available by 2006. The Tunisian Telecom market is on its way to privatization as Tunisian Telecom is seeking to privatize 35% of its shares, and ISPs operate within a competitive market. Tunisia is connected to the SEA-ME-WE–2 submarine fiber optic cable, and is a member of Arabsat, Inmarsat, Eutelsat, and Intelsat.

In contrast, Morocco benefits from a liberalized market and residential broadband connections. Nonetheless low PC penetration rate, low monthly income and low literacy rate (under 50%) are still major impediments to a growing number of internet subscribers. Vivendi Universal, the main ISP serving more than 70% of the internet market share, now owns Maroc Telecom, previously the public Internet Service Provider.

In general, broadband internet access in the Arab region is recognized as a must for the near future. It is provided in most countries primarily via DSL, then via cable projects SEA-ME-WE and Flag. Wireless internet is also emerging mostly through indoor use of Wi-Fi for private LANs and public hot spots in cafés, hotels, etc. But it looks like broadband is not yet competing with dial-up service since cost is higher and domestic users are not heavy users. The regular dial-up offered for free in Egypt for example is not expected to disappear in the near future, at least until broadband costs are reduced effectively and content advantages or new applications are available.

Arab internet usage patterns are difficult to obtain, though some researchers have pointed out that the popularity of email indicates that they vary little from the rest of the world. An Egyptian survey indicates entertainment, communication, software downloading, and news are the most commonly visited webpages, followed by shopping and education (El-Nawawy, 2000). Four in five, or 43% of users declared they frequently use entertainment features (music, video and games) of the internet. It may be premature to talk about webcasting habits since it is difficult to collect information on the webcasting industry, which is not yet recognized as such.

Traffic rates on websites and other related statistics are not yet popular in the Arab world. Access to tracking devices is limited, and often not available for many websites. This may be explained by the near absence of online advertising. To discover traffic rates on some Arab websites, it is necessary to refer to sources such as Alexa.com, a division of Amazon, which provides websites' traffic rates in Arabic, among other languages.

Our list of the leading webcasters (See Table 19–4) aims to highlight two sorts of webcasting models in the Arab region: Commercial websites and portals on the one hand, and broadcasters' websites on the other. All have either audio or video content. The broadcasters shown in Table 19–4 are considered the most important broadcasters in the Arab region and are recognized as such by a vast community of academics (from the scientific journal Transnational Broadcasting Satellite, www.tbsjournal.com, among others) and professionals (such as the specialized press, AMEinfo, www.ameinfo.com). If some popular broadcaster is not shown, it's because its website had no audio or video content at the time of the study.

The list is determined by Alexa results, sorted by Arabic language and interviews with two subject experts. M. Mohamed Ali Elloumi is an expert on Arabic web content. He runs Access to E-Business and is the manager and content creator of the directory Hahooa.com, a subsidiary of Wanadoo (France Telecom) and imaghreb.com portal. M. Elie Aoun is the IPSOS-STAT Regional Director for the Middle East and North Africa. He confirmed that there is no accurate information on leading webcasters in the Arab region. However, both respondents have provided information based on their experience and expertise. Thus, it's important to note that the list may not include all major webcasters in the region, but it characterizes the webcasting industry through the most frequently visited Arab websites and leading Arab broadcasters websites. These websites are mainly concentrated in the Gulf region. This is no surprise because of the greater internet connectivity rates in the region, and because of the greater availability of broadband.

LOOKING AT MAJOR WEBCASTERS

Upon inspection of the list of webcasters, a connection between webcasting and Satellite TV is apparent. In fact, this list includes satellite broadcasters, individual/commercial websites, and very few Internet Service Providers. Arab ISPs in general are not webcasters. The well-known Etisalat or Batelco among others did not have any audio or video content by the time of this research. QualityNet does have some audio and video, but the portal is not as popular as Arabia MSN or Menara, despite its greater traffic rates compared to other ISPs.

Arabia MSN is the Middle East version of the global portal MSN.com and looks very similar. With 4.5 million subscribers by 2004, the website has the highest traffic in the Arab region, and as elsewhere in the world, this traffic is primarily driven by the Hotmail service as nearly 70% of users visit Hotmail. The bilingual portal (English and Arabic), www.arabia.msn.com, was launched in 2001 under the partnership of Microsoft and LINKdotNET, a private Egyptian Internet Service Provider and major shareholder of a number of Egyptian website networks such as Mazika and Masrawy (discussed below). This joint-venture with foreign companies brought with it more U.S. content, while other partnerships with local websites also sought to provide richer and various content; Egyfilm.com and yallacinema.com supply some of the Arabic video content. The portal is one of the few that has utilized video online streaming and video advertising, however only one banner ad has been observed on the home page.

This is not the case for Menara, which has more banner ads. Menara is a Moroccan portal owned by Maroc Télécom, initially a public operator and ISP, privatized in 2001 and now half-owned by Vivendi Universal. Menara is also a trademark of the internet service itself and is the dominant ADSL service provider in Morrocco for residential and business customers. The monthly subscription fees vary upon the speed of the service from 128 Kbps (DH149 or US$16.3) to 1024 Kbps (DH499 or US$54.6). Menara.ma receives 15,000 page hits daily, and similar to arabia.msn.com, the partnership with Vivendi Universal allows for more foreign content, such as American and French film previews. This French portal (ranked the 53rd most popular French website worldwide by Alexa), apart from being an ISP platform, offers practical information, news and entertainment. Advertising is prevalent in many forms, such as banner ads or affiliation links with Al-Jazeera for example and other local broadcasters. Webcasting is available for free, as are the SMS messages. The shopping channel, however, is limited to merchant's business addresses.

Apart from being an ISP and a Microsoft partner for arabia.msn.com, in 2002 LINKdotNET has acquired nine significant Egyptian websites and internet companies, among them Masrawy (meaning Egyptian) and Mazika (meaning music). Masrawy is a locally oriented Arabic language portal, as some services, such as translation, are exclusively available for Egyptian users. Free streaming is available for religious, sport and entertainment content. Ring tones and SMS for mobile phones are the only services that require subscription. When looking at advertising banners, it is apparent that LINKdotNET owns promoters. Banner ad links rotate through the company's websites. Similar patterns can be noticed on the bilingual English and Arabic Mazika website, which specializes in Arabic music content and free downloads (such as MP3, WMA, and RAM files). Its business model includes no other advertising except cross-promotional advertisements. Music ring tones are available for free. It's worth noting here that subscription is required, however, for all streaming audio or music video, and some of the content is exclusively limited to Egyptian users.

Online music is one of the best ways to reach the Arab youth audience (entertainment-based communities are also popular amongst this demographic). Thus it's not surprising that some of the major webcasters are music oriented. The following three websites not only feature Arab celebrities, classical and modern music, and downloads, but their names are also synonymous. 6rb, 6arab and 6rbtop all mean Tarab (a mix of pleasure and nostalgia). 6arab.com is a bilingual Saudi website (English and Arabic) launched in 1999 with Arabic music content and updated daily. 6rbtop, also based in Saudi Arabia, offers Arabic music and audio poetry. The Kuwaiti 6rb.com was launched in 2002, and provides Arabic music content, foreign music and video clips, in Spanish, Irani, or Turkish. The video section contains comedy clips taken from theater productions, and some of the original webcast production is shown exclusively on the website. Like many other portals and music websites, downloads are available for free and no subscription is required (except for chat sections). The difference with music websites, however, is the abundance of banner ads and pop ups, which slow navigation. None of these websites, such as Rotana, generate revenues from selling music products or related products. Rotana.com is also a Saudi-based company, that is part of the media group Al Walid Ibn Talal (a major shareholder of EuroDisney and ART-TV) which offers streaming audio and video of Arabic music on demand. Its web catalogue includes more than 600 audio and video-clips. Rotana is also a music production and distribution company and an entertainment network with six free on-air satellite channels. In contrast to other music websites, Rotana contains no advertising banners except an affiliated link to Amazon.com.

Maktoob is the largest portal in the Middle East, developed in Jordan in 1998, and undoubtedly the most successful portal. The bilingual Maktoob.com is also an email service provider and the leading online community with more than 4 million registered users. The English–Arabic portal offers a variety of content: Audio (Arabic and foreign music, and ring tones), video (sport and entertainment), interactive games, chat, auctions, etc. It is one of the few portals that offer e-commerce in partnership with cashU.com, a pre-paid payment system in the Arab world. In addition to banner ads, the portal has sponsored sections such as M&M's Movies, Nescafe Chat, or Snickers football. Maktoob also has a partnership with the broadcaster Arab Radio and Television to support lifestyle and cultural programs with online websites, containing forum, show-related downloads, etc. Maktoob's integration strategy is acquiring content websites such as SportUp, AdabwaFan and Strategiy, a marketing and advertising portal. Recently Abraaj Buyout Fund, a Dubai-based private equity house acquired 40% of Maktoob shares (Strategiy, 2005).

Based in Qatar and launched in 1999, Islamonline, a "moderate" (Anderson, 2004) religious website is a property of Al-Balagh foundation and has one of the largest online communities. It's well known as a bilingual (English and Arabic) portal in the Middle East, and provides news, information, Islamic values and live discussions about community questions with Islamic scholars and thinkers. Audio and video files contain musical or religious content such as lectures, Koran readings, prayers, and Friday speeches. The website offers advertising spaces, although no advertisements were present at the time of data collection. The portal requests donations from members as a source of revenue.

Amrkhaled.net is an individual Islamic website. Amr Khaled is an Egyptian Islamic thinker and preacher, who became a celebrity as the presenter of religious programs on satellite television at ART-TV and on the Iqraa channel. This led to the phenomenon "Amr Khaled" and his project Sunaa al hayat (Life makers). The website offers live dialogue, e-books, cartoons, recordings of his sermons, and conferences. Four million streaming hours of lectures per month (ZadSolutions, 2005) are mainly taken from his religious shows at ART-TV and Iqraa TV, and are published through web broadcasts and multi-language translations. Furthermore, the portal has video content and a radio series produced by the website, all of which are available on RealAudio files. Some advertising banners are also on the website.

Al-Jazeera.net, launched in 1998, is the web version of the Qatari-based satellite TV channel Al-Jazeera. In 1996, the Qatari government welcomed former Arabic journalists of the British Broadcasting Channel (mostly subsidized by the Saudi Orbit channel), to launch a 24 hours news channel with a budget of $100 million and promises of non-censorship and total independence. The Al-Jazeera team was offered the opportunity to challenge Arab media, which are state voices in most cases, and to broadcast a new, more free, alternative to Arab television. It proved disturbing and provocative to many Arab governments and the U.S. The Al-Jazeera network gained international popularity first in the Afghanistan's conflict, and then in the U.S.–Iraqi war as it showed what were perceived as a more realistic side of the war. The Al-Jazeera website grew more popular and was subject to many attacks by hackers. In 2003, the Al-Jazeera website was chosen one of the 25 websites that was changing the world of the internet and politics by the American website PoliticsOnline (PoliticsOnline, 2003). The portal provides news, in-depth analysis, special reports, etc., in both English and Arabic, and received more than one million hits in 2004 (Al-Jazeera, 2005). However, only the Arabic version of the website offers webcast service. Audio and video programs (news, sports, economic bulletins, etc.) are available for free through a large database, all previously broadcast by the channel. The live webcast is no longer available. Diverse marketing tools are used on the website: Paid mobile service, syndication links, and advertising.

MBC-FM is the unique commercial radio station in Saudi Arabia and is a member of the Dubai based MBC network (Middle East Broadcasting Center). It is a property of Aranet, the Saudi communications group. MBC-FM was launched in 1994 for youth and female audiences in Saudi Arabia, the Gulf countries, and Jordan. The website www.mbcfm.fm streams the MBC-FM radio broadcast. Neither advertising nor e-commerce is used on the website. The networks MBC, MBC1-TV (entertainment), MBC2 (movies), MBC3 (Kids content), and MBC4 (non-movie entertainment programs) have no streaming content on their websites.

Three networks represent Pay-TV in the region: ART-TV, OrbitTV and Showtime. While this last network provides no webcasting, both ART-TV and Orbit have some streaming content, although Orbit contains a much lower amount. ART-TV is a leading broadcaster in the region with a much different business model. ART-TV is a member of the Arab Media Corporation conglomerate, owned in part by Saudi El Walid Ibn Talal. The company was established in 1993 in Saudi Arabia, Jordan, and Italy but has since moved to Dubai. The network has 16 channels broadcasting in the Middle East and North Africa, Europe, North and South America, and Australia. Art-tv.net mainly provides scheduled programs. The Tarab channel website includes audio clips for Arab singers, mainly classics, and the sports channels' websites include video content.

2M TV is a Moroccan channel that was initially privately owned (1989–1996), before it was sold to the Moroccan government (68% of shares). It is the most watched network in the country with a market share of 45.7%, according to Sigma Council (Babnet, 2005). The 2M-TV website is a bilingual (French and Arabic) portal. It broadcasts live 2M radio, which is also an offline radio channel. No video content is available on the website but it contains Flash archives of photos to download. The website www.2m.tv contains no advertising or e-commerce.

The website www.lbcgroup.tv is the Lebanon-based portal of the LBC broadcaster, the private general channel owned by Lebanese and Saudi shareholders. Its

TABLE 19–5
Distribution of Music Content: Arabic and Foreign

Origin of Music Content	Number of Webcasters
All or primarily Arabic music	16
Half Arabic music, half foreign music	2
All or primarily foreign music	2

webcasts offer audio, and more recently, live video streaming for some TV series, movies, news and TV programs. While some audio and video content can be accessed without registration (for example, entertainment video-clips), the live webcast is exclusively limited to registered members using an account system. For $10 a month, payable by credit card, members can watch unlimited number of current news programs, but each movie or news archive watched deducts a unit from the account. Each program is assigned a specific cost that is deducted from the account, but members can recharge their accounts any time.

MelodyhitsTV is another Egyptian music channel and producer. This English website, www.melodyhits.tv, contains a huge database of music, videos-clips, songs, and cell ring tones. It also offers a radio station for users. Free registration is required to access its audio and video content, though mobile features (ring tones, images, videos) are paid through an ISP in the region who collects the fees.

TEN (The Emirates Network) is a popular English multi-service portal, famous primarily for its movie section. TEN movies is a bilingual movie portal distin-

TABLE 19–6
Type of Video Content Transmitted by Webcasters

Type of Content	Number of Webcasters
Trailers, entertainment video clips	7
Music video	7
Cartoons and animation	4
Religious	3
Sports	2
Talk shows	2
News clips and nonbusiness interviews	2
Variety shows	1
Comedy	1

guished for its movie trailers' variety and quality, as well as other services such as box office reports by region, reviews, synopsis, etc. The webcast content consists mainly of American previews. Synopses are also available for domestic Arabic cinema content whereas trailers are not. Advertising is present on the movie page, but not on the home portal page. For music content, the site relocates users to the vh1.com music website (Video Hits 1, part of the MTV network), where the TEN music banner is still displayed. All of its foreign music is primarily American.

Naharnet.com, launched in 2000, is a leading Lebanese provider of mobile content in partnership with local mobile operators of the region. Naharnet is also a member of the Lebanese private An-Nahar Media group active in the publishing industry and well known for the *An-Nahar* newspaper. The portal webcasts six live radio stations, and offers important mobile services to its registered members, which, in addition to advertising, is part of its business model.

The Emirates media corporation is a multimedia conglomerate. It consists of three satellite TV channels, seven radio channels, three magazines, one newspaper, and five websites. The bilingual portal (Arabic and English) www.emi.ae, offers live audio content (namely radio), and webcasts music, and religious files for free.

WEBCASTERS' TECHNICAL AND COMMERCIAL PRACTICES

The webcasters considered in this study are divided into two categories: Pure-players and the clicks and bricks. While 10 of them exclusively operate in the internet industry, eight are online versions of offline broadcasting counterparts. MSN Arabia and Menara are the sole Internet Service Providers and also the sole joint ventures with foreign companies, in this case Microsoft and Vivendi Universal. Among the 18 Arabic webcasters, five are Egyptian, four Saudi Arabian, and three Emirati. There are also two Lebanese, Moroccan, and Qatari, and one Jordanian and Kuwaiti.

Most are commercial websites and even if they lack advertising on some home pages, all webcasters have a link "How to advertise." It was impossible, however, to know financial results revenues, or profits for these commercial webcasters. There's a tendency in the Arab media environment that favors commercialization in media sector. Youth audiences combined with increasing advertising expenditures and a weakness of dynamism in civil society (Sreberny, 2001) could explain the role of commercial media as providers of news, entertainment, and opportunity for public expression.

It is not common to have a search engine on the websites. While 12 webcasters have a search engine or internal directory, eight do not. Furthermore, more than half (13 of 20) have their own branded content, and seven are content aggregators, primarily as portals.

Utilizing the Ha and Ganhal's (2004) online media business model framework, this data is analyzed based on three principal aspects: Accessibility, content strategy and sources of revenues.

Accessibility

Of the 20 webcasters, 16 adopt a multi-transmission method of audio and video content. Push technology is the least popular technology used (10%), and the most popular technology is on-demand streaming (90%), followed by on-demand downloading (55%), and live streaming (35%), mostly for radio broadcast. Again, technology trends indicate that Windows Media Player is most popular. While 85% use it, 70% use RealPlayer and only 20% use Quicktime Media Player. Regarding file formats, MP3s are not yet popular since the adoption rate is only around 15%. In general, the quality of transmission is good, but some broken transmission emerged in seven cases, as well as three other problems involving "page can not be found."

Connection speed is another aspect of technology that is informative about the facilities. Indeed, only five webcasters offer two choices of internet connection speed, three of which are Egyptian. However, most offer no choice.

Content

The webcasters offer a wide choice of content. Only two websites lack audio content entirely, while 90% include audio. Music is undoubtedly the most common content (75%). Furthermore, Arabic music is the most popular and provided by 80% of the webcasters' (See Table 19–5). When foreign music exists, it's primarily American music. But we have noted one website, www.6rb.com, offering Indian, Irani, Turkish, and Spanish music.

After music content, music ring-tones is most popular and offered by seven of the 20. 70% of the webcasters have video content and 60% have both audio and video content. Video content consists mainly of movie trailers and entertaining video-clips or music videos. Fewer cases involve cartoons and animation (See Table 19–6). Local Arabic characterizes most of the webcasters. In fact, 80% of webcasters transmit exclusively or primarily Arabic content. Only TEN (The Emirates Network) distributes foreign content, especially western movie trailers. Only synopses are offered; Arabic trailers are not available. TEN is not alone in repurposing webcast content, as at least 80% of the webcasters do the same. Simulcast transmission is the preferred choice for six of the webcasters. Original content is much less popular and has been adopted by two webcasters: Amr Khaled and Al-Jazeera.

Interactive games and animation are not very popular among webcasters, as they are offered only by 20% and 30% of the sites, respectively. The use of chat and message boards is much more common though, as 75% of webcasters offer them. In thinking about the political restrictions and the lack of expression that confront the media and public, these interactive technologies offer an alternative to bypass these restrictions. Marc Lynch (2003) comments:

> New media, including satellite television stations such as al-Jazeera, Arabists and Islamist newspapers distributed free of charge on the internet, and rapid distribution of news via-email, listservs, and instant messaging, have given citizens in states such as Jordan, Egypt, Lebanon, and throughout North Africa and the Gulf the means to undermine state censorship and control. (p. 000)

Revenue Sources

The analysis shows the difficulty of revenue structures of webcasters in the Middle East. Although most popular, the advertising model is used by just over half of the webcasters (only 55%). Among these, nearly 55% use it exclusively as their business model, while the remaining 45% use it in conjunction with other revenue sources. E-commerce is not yet popular as only four use e-commerce, most often for mobile services in Egypt, Lebanon, and Qatar (except the Jordanian Maktoob). Pay-per-use (2 of 20), content syndication (2 of 20), and subscription (1 of 20) are used by few webcasters. In almost all cases, except for LBC Group website, no fees are collected from users and no personal information is required. Maktoob, which has e-commerce facilities uses CashU, a prepaid card system available worldwide and within 16 Arab countries. ISPs, on behalf of Naharnet, are responsible for mobile charges collected from users, and vary from one country to another. Otherwise, webcasting content is transmitted free without any registration in 17 of the cases. The three remaining cases, LBC group, Melodyhits, and Mazika, require users open an account to access the webcast content. Thus, members must provide personal information as well as demographic or interest information.

CONCLUSION: MOVING TOWARD A PROMISING INDUSTRY

Rich content beyond texts and images is necessary to offer users a technological environment where they can experience audio and video features in a webcasting context. The study of these major webcasters demonstrates their capacity to offer various types of content despite market constraints. Economic and technical obstacles, including infrastructure, are major barriers to progress. Site navigation can be very frustrating and expensive for users with no wide bandwidth connection, or for those who usually pay for access per-minute. Therefore, widening broadband facilities in the Arab region is the first step to offering better webcasting experiences.

As noted earlier, some states are pursuing this goal by offering higher speeds at lower costs, reassuring online companies who are investing in the internet and e-commerce channels.

The Arab e-commerce market value was estimated at three billion dollars in 2000–2001 and is expected to grow to five billion dollars by 2005, with Saudi Arabia and Egypt emerging as the major pioneers (United Nations Conference on Trade Development, 2002). Although e-commerce is far from flourishing in the region, this dream is realized for some, such as Maktoob. By offering a variety of services to its users, Maktoob, claims the only positive cash flow in the region, combines diverse sources of revenue including advertising, auction, and e-commerce. It's worth observing that e-commerce faces many challenges since basic infrastructures are lacking in many countries. Small initiatives have been taken in electronic certification, electronic payment platforms and e-banking facilities. Furthermore, few people hold credit cards in Arab countries. Besides, if available, these credit cards are mostly national. Security has been identified as a major problem in expanding e-commerce since its early development, in addition to a lack of product availability and discomfort with making purchases on-line (NUA, 1999).

It is evident that there is a lack of product variety offered by the webcasters we visited. Cultural products like CDs or DVDs are rarely available for purchase. In addition to the problem of product variety, it appears that regulation is also a problem for the future. Of course, e-commerce is not the only alternative source of revenue. Advertising is also a revenue resource that has not yet been fully utilized. Higher internet connection levels will increase the internet market, whether users are men or women. Online advertising is particularly attractive because of its ability to target consumers based on their content interests rather than their gender. This is true for pop-ups, rich-media, banners, etc. Subscriptions or pay-per-use are less popular revenue sources, but LBC is considered because of its subscription and pay-per-use models. Possibly, Lebanon's expatriate community may become an important source of subscription revenue. Also, we've seen that a number of webcasters derive benefit from cellular use. This is especially important since the cellular market flourishes in the Arab region. There were more than 30 million cellular subscribers by 2004. In 2002, total mobile subscribers surpassed the number of fixed line subscribers (International Telecommunication Union, 2005b). This study suggests that current revenue is insufficient to maintain the websites' attractiveness. Hopefully, some webcasters may receive government aid, NGO, personal support, or sponsorship to help them.

What becomes evident while navigating through Arab webcasters and cyberspace is the variety of interests: Business, entertainment, sports, religious, etc. What is also evident is the great potential for a transnational webcasting industry built on a common language, a common culture, and religion. Some say the great success of transnational TV lies in its female audience that attracts advertisers. And data shows that more Arab female use the internet such as in Saudi Arabia where female users outnumber males. But we believe ad revenues do not necessarily follow gender, as men may be as interested as women to purchase online. It's also important not to forget that the pillars of broadband progress are not only content or infrastructure, but also legislation and national planning. It's promising for webcasters to see such alliances between business organizations such as the Arab Broadband Internet Forum and the Arab Business Forum for Information and Communication Technology (ABFICT) promoting and improving the broadband situation in the Arab region. But most importantly, Arab countries need an effective public policy that includes more state incentives help it develop.

REFERENCES

Al-Jazeera. (2005). 1.138 milliard page vues by 2004. Retrieved August 27, 2005, from http://www.aljazeera.net/NR/exeres/E93162D5-83DE-4AE2-B467-AF814E334EE0.htm

Alterman, Jon B. (1998). *New media, new politics: From satellite television to the internet in the Arab world.* Policy paper N.48, p. ix. Washington D.C: The Washington Institute for Near East Policy.

AMEinfo (2004). *Egypt emerges as the Arab world's ADSL star.* Retrieved August 25, 2005, from http://www.ameinfo.com/56440.html.

Anderson, J. W. (2004). *Des communautés virtuelles? Vers une théorie "technico-pratique" d'Internet dans le monde arabe* [Toward a "technico practique" on internet in the Arab world]. Maghreb-Machrek. N 178. Winter 2003–2004, 45–58.

Babnet. (2005). *Au Maghreb, suprématie des télés locales* [Supremacy of local TV in Maghreb countries]. Retrieved September 4, 2005, from www.babnet.net/rttdetail-2569

Burkhart, G., & Older, S. (2003). *The information revolution in the Middle East and North Africa.* Retrieved September 25, 2005, from http://www.rand.org/publications/MR/MR1653/MR1653.pdf

El-Nawawy, M. (2000). *Profiling internet users in Egypt: Understanding the primary deterrent against their growth in number.* Retrieved August 26, 2005, from http://www.isoc.org/inet2000/cdproceedings/8d/8d_3.htm#s14

Escwa, United Nations (2003). *Regional profile of information society in western Asia.* New York: United Nations.

Gunter, B. (2003). *News and the Net.* Mahwah, NJ: Erlbaum.

Ha, L., & Ganahl, R. (2004). Webcasting business models of click-and-bricks and pure-play media: A comparative study of leading webcasters in South Korea and the United States. *The International Journal on Media Management, 6*(1&2), 75–88.

Information and Technology Publishing. (2005a). *The UAE leads in regional growth.* Retrieved September 30, 2005, from http://www.itp.net/news/details.php?id = 15122&category =

Information and Technology Publishing. (2005b). *UAE broadband price cuts official.* Retrieved October 18, 2005, from http://www.itp.net/news/details.php?id = 17704&category =

International Telecommunication Union. (2005a). Tendances des réformes dans les télécom munications 2004/2005 [Tendencies in telecommunication reforms 2004/2005]. Retrieved August 16, 2005, from www.itu.int/ITU-D

International Telecommunication Union. (2005b). *ITU world telecommunication indicators: Data collection and dissemination.* Retrieved October 15, 2005, from http://www.escwa.org.lb/wsis/meetings/7–10june/14ITU_telecom_inds%20ITU_VGrayE.ppt#7

Internet Worldstats. (2005). *Middle East internet usage and marketing report.* Retrieved October 10, 2005, from http://www.internetworldstats.com/me/Reports.htm

Lynch, M. (2003). Beyond the Arab Street: Iraq and the Arab Public Sphere. *Politics & Society, 31*(1), 55–91.

Madar Research Journa. (2002). *PC penetration vs. internet user penetration in GCC countries*. Retrieved October 31, 2005, from http://topoics.developmentgateway.org/ict/rc/filedownload. do~itemID-267801

NUA. (1999). *Arab ecommerce market worth USD95 million.* Retrieved September 10, 2005, from http://www.nua.ie/surveys/index.cgi?f = VS&art_id = 905355005&rel = true

PoliticsOnline. (2003). *Special reports.* Retrieved April 2004, from http://www.politicsonline.com/ pol2000/specialreports/25Changing_2003/

Rugh, W. (2004). *Arab mass media: Newspapers, radio and television.* Westport, CT: Praeger.

Sreberny, A. (2001). Mediated Culture in the Middle East: Diffusion, Democracy, Difficulties. *Gazette, 63*(2–3). 101–119

Strategiy. (2005). *Abraaj capital acquires stakes in Maktoob.* Retrieved Spetember 5, 2005, from http://www.strategiy.com/mnews.asp?id = 20050614145950

Taye, S. (2000). Estekhdam al-Internet fy al-alam al-arabi [Internet usage in the Arab world]. *The Egyptian Journal of Public Opinion Research, 4*, 33–68.

Usage Watch. (2004). *Communication technologies in the Arab world.* Retrieved August 12, 2005, from http://www.usagewatch.org/usage_of_the_web/

United Nations Conference on Trade Development. (2002). *E-commerce and development report 2002, UNCTAD/SDTE/ECB/2.* Retrieved October 20, 2005, from http://r0.unctad.org/ecommerce/ ecommerce_en/edr02_en.htm

United Nations Development Program. (2003). Rapport Arabe sur le développment humain [Arab human development report]. Retrieved August 20, 2004, from http://www.undp.org/rbas/ahdr

ZadSolutions. (2005). *Major clients.* Retrieved September 8, 2005, from http://www.zadsolutions.com/ inner/inner.php?id = 23

CHAPTER 20

Lessons From the Leading Webcasters Around the World and the Outlook of Webcasting as an Emerging Global Medium

Louisa Ha
Bowling Green State University

Richard Ganahl
Bloomsburg University

The practices of leading webcasters in the 17 markets or regions we present in this book illustrate how webcasting as an emerging medium is shaped by the media's market environment. The accessibility-content-revenue (ACR) framework serves as a productive analytical tool to examine the business models of webcasters.

In this concluding chapter, we offer our insights about the patterns and trends in the development of webcasting. We suggest that five factors influence the development of the webcasting industry in a market: (1) geography, (2) political structure, (3) media market tradition and environment, (4) technology infrastructure, and (5) cultural background. Next, we discuss the dynamics of webcasting's revenues sources and then explore the possible paths of the webcasting industry's future. We conclude the chapter with some suggested directions for future research by those interested in joining our exploration of this brave new world of webcasting.

GEOGRAPHICAL FACTORS

The size and population density of the market can be a facilitator or an obstacle to the development of webcasting adoption and broadband penetration. In markets with small geographic size but high population density, it is much more cost-efficient to provide broadband services via either coaxial cables or digital phone lines. Hence when broadband is being promoted in markets with small land and dense population such as South Korea, Hong Kong, and the Netherlands, the cost to provide broadband service per person is much lower than large land markets with low population density. High market penetration can be achieved quite easily in these densely populated markets. In large land markets such as the United States and China, the digital divide can be high within the country. Large cities generally enjoy a low-cost broadband service and the broadband penetration are high. But small towns have little or no broadband access at all. If broadband service is available, the cost is often prohibitive for the average consumer. This problem is most acute in Australia and the government now has to intervene in the development of a national broadband service. Interestingly the digital divide in broadband and internet service is quite low in Canada, a country where the land is large and the population is dispersed. But, the Canadian government and its people envisioned the internet as a means to create unity among its geographically dispersed citizens. They funded and promoted broadband internet as a cost-efficient means of cultural cohesion through communication across the vast country.

POLITICAL STRUCTURE

The political structure of a market can foster or hinder the growth of the webcast market and broadband services. In constitutional monarchies such as Denmark and Norway, or in the relatively authoritarian democracies in many Asia countries, the government takes an active role in promoting the internet or broadband services as a nation-building tool or economic growth trigger. Consequently, webcasting in these countries benefits from supportive government policies. In a sense it is an extension of the public service model of broadcasting.

But in markets with a political structure that discourages opinions of opposition such as China, regulations are implemented to control the access to broadband services and webcast content. But, because the Chinese government believes the development of broadband services will benefit international trade and economic growth, it supports the webcast industry within narrow boundaries that do not violate the government's policies. Government-owned media rush to the web for additional audiences and revenues.

On the other hand, political structures that are capitalistic democracies such as the U.S. powerful lobby groups from large media corporations and existing telecommunications services can stifle the growth of broadband or webcast as a competitive service by enforcing digital copyright laws and discouraging government intervention in the pricing and provisions of broadband services.

MEDIA MARKET ENVIRONMENT AND TRADITION

Old Media: Friend or Foe of Webcasting?

Different markets are at different points along the learning curve of the emerging medium of webcasting. In highly developed webcast markets such as the U.S. and Japan, native internet media brands or portals (pure-plays) are most likely to play a dominant role in the webcasting market. In markets where broadband penetration is not very high and webcasting is not commonly used, traditional media can extend their market domination in webcasting as the clicks-and-bricks with well-known media brands to support their webcasts. The supply of professional quality webcast content for general consumption is largely dependent on the support of traditional media such as television networks, movie studios, record labels, etc.

In markets where traditional media see webcasting as a threat or a market rival, such as the U.S., the development of webcasting faces obstacles from major media companies that hold copyrights to popular media content. Their resistance to webcasting and their refusal to supply full length content to webcasters parallels the rivalries between American radio stations and the record labels in the 1920s and 1930s, and the conflict between the U.S. movie studios and television networks in the 1950s, and cable and broadcast television in the 1960s through the 1980s. Only when traditional media embrace webcasting as an inevitable medium that they must work with will they be more willing to invest in the medium as a sister medium they can peacefully coexist with. At present, many clicks-and-bricks webcasters see webcasting as a supplementary medium or an alternative platform to their on-air content. To achieve the status as a stand-alone medium in its own right, the medium must demonstrate significant profit potentials to commercial media, or social and political benefit to non-profit media.

Copyright as the Barrier to Webcast Industry Development

Webcasters who take their services as businesses seriously seek a mix of mainstream copyrighted materials and original materials. The Webcaster Alliance, a U.S. association that represents small commercial webcasters, refused to comply with the U.S. Small Webcasters Settlement Act of 2002, which mandates a minimal charge of $2,000 in addition to fees per performance. At the moment, its members pay no copyright fees (personal communication with Webcaster Alliance President, A. Gabriel, October 28, 2005).

As of October 28, 2005, the Recording Industry Association of America has not taken any action against any Alliance members, and the webcasters continue to refuse to pay the copyright fee until lower rates are established for the 2006–2010 royalty period. The Webcaster Alliance is in the process of submitting information to the Copyright Royalty Board in an effort to establish reasonable royalty rates for their members. It wants to adopt the terrestrial radio model. The larger webcasters were accused of using the royalty rates to increase the cost of operation for smaller webcasters and thereby reduce the number of rival webcasters. While the copyright issue remains unsettled in the U.S. and many other countries, the supply of full-length established copyrighted materials in webcasting will be very limited. In countries where copyright is well-protected, commercial webcasting takes off less readily than public media webcasting, because public media webcasters own more of their programs than commercial webcasters.

More copyright protection forces are under way across the world, affecting the use of materials in webcasting. Recently, the World Intellectual Property Organization (WIPO) introduces a proposal called the Broadcaster Treaty that will grant the distributor of content in both broadcast, cable, and on the internet a 50-year exclusive right to authorize or prohibit the copying or redistribution of its distributed content. The proposed new right will empower webcasters, especially leading portals who aggregate content, to prohibit further retransmission of content on the web (Love, 2005). The initiative is led by the United States government and the European Commission with the support of the Digital Media Association (DiMA), an association of leading transnational content aggregators such as Yahoo!, Microsoft, AOL, and RealNetworks (Digital Media Association, 2005). A special diplomatic conference is expected to be held in December 2006 or early 2007 to confirm the provisions (Consumer Project on Technology, 2005). If the treaty is passed, small webcasters will have a hard time finding materials to webcast because materials shown in other webcasts require copyright clearance (retransmission permission). It will foster the use of original materials that have never been shown in other webcasts and also relinquish the right of creative owners to control the licence of their own work and subject to the control of the intermediaries, the webcasters.

Public Media vs. Commercial Media

The world market can be divided into two camps based on their broadcast media tradition: The public media (non-profit) tradition as exemplified by European markets such as Denmark, Spain, and Norway; and the commercial media tradition such as the U.S. and Japan. Although China's media is government-owned and controlled, it is very similar to the public media in many ways except in the restriction of dissident views. In recent years, more and more commercial broadcasters have introduced their services in Europe and some have become potent competitors to the traditional public broadcasters as discussed in the European chapters. Nevertheless with the support of the public funding through licence fees (or de facto the government), these public webcasters have extended their dominance to the web with rich resources. Hence we see webcasting inherits the broadcast media tradition of its home market.

For example, non-profit or public webcasters usually prosper in markets with strong public broadcasting traditions, such as Norway, Denmark, and the Netherlands. Commercial webcasters lead in markets with strong, commercial media traditions such as the United States and Japan. The only exception to this pattern is Hong Kong where the media market is highly commercialized, but the webcasting industry is led by non-profit government funded organizations or units such as the Trade Development Council and the Department of Education. Perhaps the small domestic media market in Hong Kong can explain easier success in public services and the lack of commercial interest in substantial development of the medium for the Hong Kong market.

Technology Infrastructure

Adoption of webcasting is largely a function of a market's technological infrastructure. Needless to say, a healthy and strong broadband market with high market penetration is essential to nurture the growth of webcasting. The broadband services in the U.S., where the internet was invented, are limited by an existing infrastructure that primarily relies on wired services such as cable and telephone lines. Thus, U.S. web use is closely tied to computers.

But in the Scandinavian countries and Asia, many new means of internet access are being utilized such as wireless technology and 3G mobile phone services. As the chapter on Japan demonstrates, the potential to provide webcast services on the mobile phone is much greater than computer delivery because of the service's portability. In Asian countries such as China and South Korea, the development of IPTV is also growing at a faster pace than other parts of the world. Possibly, the return of webcasting on a television-based platform may not be too distant.

Cultural Factors

There is no clear evidence of cultural domination by a particular country in our study of leading webcasters except the few U.S. transnational webcasters that have established local versions in several countries. Very little of the leading webcasters' content is foreign produced. Yet the domination of the software essential to display the webcast content by Microsoft is a phenomenon that should be red-flagged. By a very large margin, Microsoft's Windows Media Player leads as the world's most commonly used media player. In the extreme case of Denmark, Microsoft Windows Media Player is the only player allowed to display webcast content originated from Danish public broadcast web sites on computers. Windows Media Player's default web link is the MSN's Windows Media Page. Such integration of software to content services creates a formidable advantage for the

MSN webcast and poses a serious threat to other non-Microsoft users because the non-use of Microsoft deprives them of access to much of the webcast content.

Global Sites as Local Sites

As shown in our 13-country comparison in Chapter 2 and in our individual chapters, while the internet has a global reach, much of the mainstream consumption is local, at least within the nation state. Hence while we examine webcasting as a global medium, we must remember the power of the home market's economics, cultural proximity and cultural discount of foreign webcast content. Many webcasters focus only on audiences of their own language and culture. Foreign webcasters who want to capture the host country's audiences have localized their content to appeal to the host country's audiences. Only a few leading webcasters offer more than one language on their sites. Quite possibly, English-language speaking countries have the potential to dominate the web because of English's popularity as the second language. The globalness of the webcast audience is primarily realized only among those who can read and listen English.

Despite the hype about the globalization of media giants, there are only a few webcasting brands that can extend their leadership on a global basis. As identified in Chapter 2, leading transnational webcasters are all content aggregators such as Yahoo!, MSN and RealNetworks. The localized content of these content aggregators show that U.S. webcast content is not as popular as commonly believed. But the U.S. supremacy in aggregating content, marketing, and technological expertise on the web enables them to lead the world in the provision of aggregating content services. The web merely offers an easier means for consumers to obtain more media content variety, but it cannot alter the consumer's preference for local content.

Cultural and Geographic Proximity and Regionalization Possibilities

Although the appeal of global content may be hard to achieve, content that appeals to a culturally similar region is a viable possibility. In this book, we find only two regions that are likely candidates for successful regional media content: The Arab region and the Scandinavian countries. The Arab region countries share the same Arabic language, the same Muslim religion, and similar political systems. Al-Jazeera successfully positions itself as the pan-Arab regional newscaster both on satellite and the web. The Scandinavian countries share a similar Nordic culture, the same religion, and a high fluency in English as a common language. All Scandinavian countries are constitutional monarchies. The cross-country ownership of media companies within the region continues on the web. Pan-Scandinavian webcasters have been successful in capturing the leading spots.

Nevertheless, a common language is not necessarily supportive of regional content acceptance. A strong counter example is the Greater China region (including Hong Kong, Taiwan, and China). Even though the three markets share the same Chinese written language, their webcast development is vastly different from one another. There are no Chinese language webcasters that lead in all three markets. None of the leading Chinese webcasters in the three Greater Chinese markets spent any effort to expand their services to their neighboring Chinese market. They are all content with staying in their own market and build as much traffic as possible. One possible reason is the difference between the simplified Chinese text used in mainland China and the traditional Chinese text used in Taiwan and Hong Kong. The large difference in program taste and preference of consumers in the three markets also make it difficult for any Chinese language webcaster to appeal to all three markets. Finally the lack of a large transnational Chinese media conglomerate in the region may explain the lack of ambition to conquer the three markets.

Participatory Culture

In discussing the future of webcasting, one should recognize the participatory culture of the internet. Through the presence of interactive features such as voting, ratings, self-submission, message boards and chat rooms, the webcast differs significantly from its radio and television predecessors. It encourages participation from the audience and empowers them to influence other users of the webcast. The rating of programs is no longer the privilege of professional media critics. All users willing to provide their opinion have a place to post their comments. If they want to consult peer comments and reviews, they are easily available on the web site. We cannot underestimate the impact of the democratization and liberalization of consumer reviews and rating systems on new and upcoming music bands, actors, or shows. But the continued assessment of their impact on the media industry and audience's experience of the show is essential to the full understanding of media consumption dynamics.

CONTENT STRATEGIES: USER-GENERATED
CONTENT VS. PROFESSIONAL MEDIA CONTENT

Content strategies and the nature of webcast content is notably different from traditional media, especially in light of the cultivation of the participatory culture of the internet as discussed above. In addition to the originality and the cost of the content, the source of media content as amateur versus professional made will have a far-reaching impact on the development of media in this century. As digital media recording devices are now easily available to home users such as digital cameras, a breed of amateur producers who may or may not be interested in developing a career in media can contribute their works to various webcasters that encourage submissions or display their work via personal blogs, to the public or their friends. Stupidvideos is one of the commercially successful examples in the use of such participatory content. Amateur media content provides different values to consumers from professional media content. Yet their increasing presence will create a new virtual social network experience that can supplement or even replace some of the offline social experience. The use of videos increases the vividness of such social experience. Hence webcasters can choose between a traditional professional media service provider role or a party house role for amateurs to share their work or a hybrid of both if sufficient supply of both professional and amateur work on the topic is available.

From Mass Media to Customized Media Consumption

The interactive technology of the internet facilitates the customization of media content to the individual user's taste and preference. Many leading webcasters featured in our book offer customized playlists and other personalized features that are not available through traditional media. When consumers get accustomed to these features, then they will only be exposed to content they have selected on the webcasts. Such customization will further encourage selective exposure to media content. The vast range of content available on a webcast will be consumed differently by different individuals with different customized settings. Common content consumed by every user may be less and less. Niche content may be consumed much more when it is part of the user's selected playlist.

Direct Payment and Indirect Payment

We discovered a variety of revenue sources for the leading webcasters through this book. Most of them opt for indirect payment such as advertising and e-commerce. When the medium is new and needs to minimize the cost to the consumers, providing free content is an easy way to build audience size and traffic. Many of the traditional electronic media counterparts such as radio and television have chosen the same non-direct payment route in their early days. Content genres that more easily command direct payment for consumption are genres that consumers have previously paid for offline such as adult content, movies, recorded popular music, sports, and games. Thus it is no surprise that webcasters who charge for their content either as pay per view or by subscriptions focus on these content genres.

OPTIMISM VS. PESSIMISM OVER THE FUTURE OF WEBCASTING

Our authors express different views regarding the future of the webcasting industry ranging from pessimism such as Australia and Spain to optimism such as China and the United Kingdom. Such varying views can be largely attributed to the future of broadband adoption and the development of communication infrastructure within the particular country. Those countries that are slow in broadband adoption because of monopolies or the high cost of broadband services are unlikely to envision a bright future in webcasting. The business models employed by the webcasters and current quality of content offering also affect our contributors' view on the future.

Markets that are developing a variety of communication devices that use internet Protocol such as 3G cellular phone mobile content services and Internet Protocol Television (IPTV) will see much potential in webcasting because the webcast audience can include television, cellular phones, and other portable devices such as iPods and hand-helds. The video display capacity of the iPod video player generates great consumer interest and shows much promise. In just three weeks since Apple offer video download service, more than one million videos were downloaded from the iTunes web site for $1.99 per video (Business Report, 2005). There are more than 2,000 titles collection of television series, animations, and music videos on iTunes.

We believe webcasting has enormous potential because of its versatility and freedom from a single display device. Unlike its broadcast cousins that are confined by the television set or radio receiver, webcast can be consumed through any device that can display video or audio content through the Internet Protocol. Despite the occasional control of the medium by a few governments, the web is relatively free compared to all other media because of its decentralized nature. For example, in China, although there is regulation on webcast ownership, there are many illegal webcasters that consumers can access. There is no middleman, such as cable system operators or satellite TV service. Government interference is minimal in most countries. Best of all, the webcast channels are immediately available as long as the broadband connection is there and one knows where to find it. The broadband service providers cannot prohibit users from selecting specific webcasts.

Changing Scope of the Audience

Another important theoretical implication of webcasting is the change in the scope of audience consumption of electronic media content. In the past, electronic media were limited by the electro-magnetic spectrum and geographic coverage. Now audience consumption of audio and video content can be categorized into local-local, local-foreign, foreign-foreign, and expatriate-home country. Local-to-local webcast consumption refers to the consumption of locally made webcast content by the local audience such as a U.S. consumer watching ESPN. Local-foreign consumption refers to the local audience consuming webcast content originated from a foreign country such as a Japanese consumer watching CNN or ESPN on the web in Japan. There is also a foreign-foreign consumption such as a Japanese visiting Germany watching ESPN on the web. Finally, the homesick expatriates definitely value the opportunities to have the expatriate-home country consumption such as U.S. expatriates in Japan watching their ESPN shows on the web.

Webcasting is also changing the nature of the web as the information hub to also the entertainment hub of web savvy consumers. The success and dominance of television and video games as the main entertainment source of consumers illustrate the importance of video content to consumers for relaxation and enjoyment. The ubiquity of the web in an individual's life in the future cannot be underestimated. From workplace to home and from transit to travel, the web becomes a convenient source to pull information, get entertainment, and communicate to others. The additional video and audio content on the web delivered via a variety of devices such as cellular phones and television sets, further enhances the media and communication experience. This represents media convergence. Although the display of video and audio content on the web still have many rooms for improvement, once the technological bottleneck problem is solved and infrastructure is in place, it can unleash its potential as the next primary medium for consumers.

DIRECTIONS FOR FUTURE RESEARCH

The application of the ACR framework in this book demonstrates it is possible to develop analytical tools that can be applied across markets and national state borders. All emerging media owners, including both for profit or non-profit webcasters, must face the realities of sustaining their media services in their business models through different accessibility features, content strategies and revenue sources. By emphasizing the relationship between number of display methods, usability, with revenue sources, and the impact of webcaster type on content strategies, the ACR framework shows that one must relate the business model of an emerging medium with its technological characteristics that affects its accessibility to the audience, and the different combination of these factors in shaping its business model.

This is only the first step. One important area we encourage our readers and other fellow researchers to study is the use of webcasting by non-profit organizations. Non-profit organizations can become media producers and distributors through webcasting. They act as an alternative source of information and entertainment services to web users that television and radio stations are unable or unwilling to provide. On the web, it is possible to build a global audience with a common interest for charity organizations, religious organizations, and other activist organizations such as Green Peace International. These non-profit organizations do not need to have the highest audience traffic. But they can utilize the web to unite people around the world with common interest through vivid videos and audios. Many successes have been reported on the non-profit use of webcasting such as the state of Washington's government webcasting of training sessions for foster parents either live or on-demand (Fritz, 2005). The success of Edcity is another example of the tremendous value of webcasting for education purposes.

On the commercial front, the growth in online advertising definitely can fuel the growth of webcasting because online rich media ads are considered much more eye-catching and effective than regular banner ads. Indeed, the Interactive Advertising Bureau of the United States reported the first half of 2005's internet advertising revenue reached a record high of $5.8 billion (Interactive Advertising Bureau, 2005). The provision of more video content in media sites to attract rich media ads is now advocated by the National Association of Television Programming Executives in the United States. The association organized a webinar how online video ads support video's rapid growth jointly with iHollywood Forum and the research consulting firm, Forrester Research in December 2005.

The competition of print and broadcast media is converged online where consumers can choose between text, graphics, audios, and videos. Webcasters that commit to a non-direct payment revenue source will definitely rely on online advertising and work to insure its effectiveness for advertisers. And, e-commerce is another non-direct payment revenue source that webcasters can choose. A full embracement of the e-commerce model will involve the transformation of the webcaster from a media content provider to an online retailer. How the webcaster acquires the expertise to perform this new dual role as both a media content provider and an online retailer is a great challenge.

Direct payment for webcast content must provide additional value to the consumer that is not available elsewhere. Acquisitions and protection of valuable content becomes the top priorities of webcasters that charge consumers by subscription or pay per view. The most viable candidate for direct payment is the downloading service so that media consumption is not an intangible service or experience, but a tangible property that consumers can own, store and retrieve later. How to manage the consumer's perception of risk in paying for the service through previews and other recommendation methods such as consumer reviews or expert rating systems is another avenue to develop.

The prevalence of short clips and webisodes (original short programs for internet use) on most leading webcasters' sites is a result of bandwidth saving. Nevertheless, it also creates a new platform of short audio and video content. Webcast users who consume this short form of content may have different perceptions of the traditional 30 minutes program. Whether such short media form is a transitional or permanent feature in webcast is debatable. But more and more full-length programs and other classical titles that would not jeopardize the sales or current releases will be available on the web. For example, Time Warner announced that America Online will offer an ad-supported, free broadband channels for more than 300 full-length episodes of classical Time Warner TV shows such as "Wonder Woman" in January 2006 (Donohue, 2005). The broader question is, will the short form, fast-paced media consumption style further shorten the attention span of consumers?

Lastly, broadband technology is increasing in penetration in other parts of the world this book is unable to cover. We encourage our readers to test the ACR framework and analyze business models and the social impact of leading webcasters in other countries with growing broadband penetration.

REFERENCES

Business Report. (2005). *Apple racks up 1 million iTune video sales.* Retrieved November 18, 2005, from http://www.busrep.co.za/index.php?fArticleId = 2975213

Consumer Project on Technology. (2005). *The proposed WIPO treaty for the protection of the rights of broadcasting, cablecasting and webcasting organizations.* Retrieved December 29, 2005, from http://www.cptech.org/ip/wipo/bt/

Digital Media Association. (2005). *Getting to know us.* Retrieved December 29, 2005, from http://www.digmedia.org/aboutus/faq.cfm

Donohue, S. (2005). *AOL is getting "In2TV."* Retrieved November 14, 2005, from http://www.multi-channel.com/article/CA6283355.html?display = Breaking+News&referral = SUPP.

Fritz, M. (2005). Case study: Webcasting fosters better parents in Washington. Retrieved October 28, 2005, from http://www.streamingmedia.com/r/printerfriedly.asp?id = 9141.

Interactive Advertising Bureau. (2005). *IAB/PwC release first half 2005 internet ad revenue figures.* Retreived December 15, 2005, from http://www.iab.net/news/pr_2005_9_26.asp

Love, J. (2005, November 30). *A UN/WIPO plan to regulate distribution of information on the internet.* Retrieved December 29, 2005 from http://www.huffingtonpost.com/james-love/a-unwipo-plan-to-regulat_b_11480.html

Glossary

Asymmetric Digital Subscriber Line (ADSL): A technology that allows more data to be sent over existing copper telephone lines (POTS). ADSL supports data rates of from 1.5 to 9 Mbps when receiving data (known as the *downstream* rate) and from 16 to 640 Kbps when sending data (known as the *upstream* rate). ADSL requires a special ADSL modem.

Broadband: Data transmission of greater than 56 Kbps (kilo-bytes per second) that can carry multiple signals at once.

Digital Subscriber Line (DSL): A service that offers a faster Internet connection than a standard dial-up connection. DSL technology uses existing 2-wire copper telephone wiring to deliver high-speed data services to homes and businesses. DSL offers users a choice of speeds ranging from 144 Kbps to 1.5Mbps. This is 2.5 to 25 times faster than a standard 56Kbps dial-up modem. This digital service can be used to deliver bandwidth-intensive applications like streaming audio/video, online games, application programs, telephone calling, video conferencing and other high-bandwidth services.

European Economic Area (EEA): The Agreement creating the European Economic Area (EEA Agreement) was negotiated between the Community, the then Member States, and seven member countries of the EFTA and was signed in May 1992. Subsequently, Switzerland decided not to participate following a referendum, and three others joined the EU. The EEA was maintained because of the wish of the three remaining countries—Norway, Iceland, and Liechtenstein—to participate in the Internal Market, while not assuming the full responsibilities of EU membership. The EEA Agreement entered into force on January 1, 2004.

European Union, The (EU): The first step in European integration was taken when six countries (Belgium, the Federal Republic of Germany, France, Italy, Luxembourg, and the Netherlands) set up a common market in coal and steel. The aim, in the aftermath of the Second World War, was to secure peace be-

419

tween Europe's victorious and vanquished nations. It brought them together as equals, cooperating within shared institutions. The Union now has 25 member states, and will continue growing as more countries join in the years ahead.

Fiber to the Home (FTTH): The scheme to provide broadband ISDN services to homes using fiber connections. Japan is the country most supportive of this scheme with its NTT plan to have the whole of Japan wired for broadband ISDN by the year 2015.

Fixed Network: A full service telephone company which provides local phone service, long distance call service, international call service, and other related telephone services.

Information and Communication Technologies (ICT): According to OECD, the ICT sector comprises computing equipment, radio, television, and communication equipment, telecommunication services, computer services, and other technologies such as wire and cable.

Integrated Services Digital Network (ISDN): An ISDN is comprised of digital telephony and data-transport services offered by regional telephone carriers. ISDN involves the digitization of the telephone network, which permits voice, data, text, graphics, music, video, and other source material to be transmitted over existing telephone wires. The emergence of ISDN represents an effort to standardize subscriber services, user/network interfaces, and network and internetwork capabilities. ISDN applications include high-speed image applications (such as Group IV facsimile), additional telephone lines in homes to serve the telecommuting industry, high-speed file transfer, and videoconferencing. Voice service is also an application for ISDN.

Internet Protocol Television (IPTV). A system where video signals are distributed to subscribers' or viewers' television sets using a broadband connection over Internet Protocol.

Internet Service Providers (ISPs): Companies that provide subscribers' connection to the internet either via cable, regular or digital phone lines or cellular phone services. When the companies provide content services in addition to the internet connection service, then they are called online service providers.

iPOD: A brand of portable digital audio and video player designed and marketed by Apple Computer. Devices in the iPod family offer a simple user interface designed around a central scroll wheel.

Local Area Network (LAN): A computer network that spans a relatively small area. Most LANs are confined to a single building or group of buildings. However, one LAN can be connected to other LANs over any distance via telephone lines and radio waves. A system of LANs connected in this way is called a wide-area network (WAN). Most LANs connect workstations and personal computers.

Media Player: The software on the client computer that decompresses the streaming video or audio using a codec and plays it back on the computer screen. The media player can be used as a stand alone application or embedded in a web page to create a video application interacting with HTML content.

Middle East and North Africa countries (MENA): The region includes countries that are mainly Arab countries and also non-Arab countries such as Iran, Israel, Malta, and Djibouti.

Movie Pictures Experts Group 2 Layer 3 (MPEG3 or MP3): A   compressed digital format using an algorithm that achieves a compression of factor of about twelve while preserving sound quality. The standard is set by the Movies Pictures Experts Group of the International Organization for Standardization (ISO).

Multiple System Operators (MSO): MSO refers to cable system operators owning multiple systems in a country. Web MSO means multiple platforms for webcasters.

Nordic countries (members of the Nordic Council): Denmark,   Finland,   Iceland, Norway, and Sweden.

Official site: This term is used In Japan only, a website directly linked to the ISP's menu page on the Japanese mobile phone. Official sites can charge an information fee with its connection fee charged by ISPs.

Organization for Economic Co-operation and Development (OECD): An international organization of 30 member countries sharing a commitment to democratic government and the market economy. With active relationships with some 70 other countries, non-government organizations, it has a global reach. Best known for its publications and its statistics, its work covers economic and social issues from macroeconomics, to trade, education, development and science and innovation.

Personal Digital Assistant (PDA): A handheld device that combines computing, telephone/fax, internet, and networking features.

Repurpose: The media content management strategy of using the same text, audio, or graphics content again in other media channels by the copyright owner of the content. It is called repurpose because content created for one purpose (a

TV newscast) can be used for another purpose (a webcast). The media content repurposed can be longer or shorter than the original content or exactly identical as the original content. The media content is still considered the same and under the protection of copyright law even though the distribution media have changed.

Scandinavia: Denmark, Norway, and Sweden.

Streaming: The technology of sending a continuous data signal through the internet with special software. Streaming enables the user's computer to decode a signal as soon as it is received and play it almost immediately in the correct order. Unlike downloading that requires the storage of the data in the user's local hard drive before playback, streaming data are not cached (stored) in the user's local computer drive and play back the data at almost the same time as they are transmitted.

Third Generation (3G) Mobile Phone: The mobile telephone protocols that support much higher data rates, measured in Mbps, intended for applications other than voice. 3G networks trials started in Japan in 2001. 3G supports bandwidth-hungry applications such as full-motion video, video-conferencing, and full internet access.

United Nations, The (UN): The United Nations was established on October 24, 1945 by 51 countries committed to preserving peace through international cooperation and collective security. Today, nearly every nation in the world belongs to the UN: Membership totals 191 countries.

Video On Demand (VOD): A set of technologies or services that enable individuals to select videos from a centralized computer server for viewing on a television or computer screen.

Wireless Fidelity (WI-FI): A term for certain types of wireless local area networks (WLAN) that use specifications conforming to IEEE 802.11b standard. WiFi has gained acceptance in many environments as an alternative to a wired LAN. Many airports, hotels, and other services offer public access to WiFi networks so people can log onto the Internet and receive emails on the move. These locations are known as hotspots.

Worldwide Interoperability for Microwave Access (WiMax): A certification mark for products that pass conformity and interoperability tests for the IEEE 802.16 standards. These products are capable of forming wireless connections carrying internet packet data. It is similar to WiFi in concept, but has certain improvements that are aimed at improving performance and permit usage over much greater distances.

Author Index

423

Subject Index

427